OSCAR CHARLESTON

OSCAR CHARLESTON

The Life and Legend of Baseball's
Greatest Forgotten Player

JEREMY BEER

University of Nebraska Press | LINCOLN

Portions of chapter 2 previously appeared, in a somewhat
different form, in "Hothead: How the Oscar Charleston Myth
Began," *Baseball Research Journal* 46, no. 1 (Spring 2017).

Library of Congress Cataloging-in-Publication Data
Names: Beer, Jeremy.
Title: Oscar Charleston: the life and legend of baseball's
greatest forgotten player / Jeremy Beer.
Description: Lincoln: University of Nebraska Press, [2019] |
Includes bibliographical references and index.
Identifiers: LCCN 2019006779
ISBN 9781496217110 (cloth: alk. paper)
ISBN 9781496217820 (epub)
ISBN 9781496217837 (mobi)
ISBN 9781496217844 (pdf)
Subjects: LCSH: Charleston, Oscar, 1896–1954. | Baseball
players—United States—Biography. | African American
baseball players—Biography. | Negro leagues—History.
Classification: LCC GV865.C433 B44 2019 |
DDC 796.357092 [B]—dc23 LC record available
at https://lccn.loc.gov/2019006779

Set in Minion Pro by E. Cuddy.

For my wife, with immeasurable gratitude.

In his terms, and in the terms of his culture,
the Negro league player was a great success.
The Negro leaguer had more money, more
attention, more lasting fame, and a richer life
than almost all the rest of his contemporaries. The
result was that Negro leaguers, in general, were
not bitter men. Even in the face of racism and the
certain knowledge that, had they been white, they
would have been major leaguers, these players
achieved more than enough to be satisfied.

—DONN ROGOSIN

The greatest player I have ever seen in eight-and-
a-third decades, and one of the greatest men.

—BUCK O'NEIL

If there is any excellence, if there is anything
worthy of praise, think about these things.

—ST. PAUL

CONTENTS

PREFACE

Sometime in the spring of 1992 Larry Lester was watching a documentary with his friend and fellow Negro Leagues historian Dick Clark, at the home of another Negro Leagues historian named Jerry Malloy, when a woman named Anna Charleston Bradley appeared on screen. She was identified as Oscar Charleston's niece. That got Lester's attention.

Lester, Clark, and Malloy were pioneers in the small but growing community of Negro Leagues researchers. They made it their business to collect as much information and material about former Negro Leagues players as they could, and Oscar Charleston was no marginal figure. He was a Hall of Famer—"the first shrink-wrapped player," as Lester liked to say, who excelled in every facet of the game. But having died in 1954 with no descendants, Oscar was, in his afterlife, elusive. Virtually everything known about him was buried in old newspaper pieces or came from the fragmented, piecemeal accounts of those who had played with him.

So Lester, working on behalf of the Negro Leagues Museum and Hall of Fame in his hometown of Kansas City, wasted no time getting in touch with Anna. He flew to Indianapolis to meet her, won her trust, and acquired treasures never seen by any historian, writer, or researcher: Oscar Charleston's personal scrapbook and photo album, which together contained hundreds of photos, American and Cuban newspaper clippings, annotations, personal letters, and Cuban cartoons. (Lester also acquired Oscar's set of 1923–24 Cuban League baseball cards.)

The materials dated from 1914, when Charleston was serving in the army as a seventeen-year-old, until his death in 1954. Anna Bradley had obtained these personal effects from her aunt Katherine, Oscar's sister, who had buried him in Indianapolis and represented him when he was enshrined in Cooperstown in 1976. Katherine had herself received the items from Oscar's estranged widow, Janie.

These Charleston artifacts are still at the Negro Leagues Museum today. Unpublicized and unindexed, and previously perused by very few researchers, they offer mute testimony to the accomplishments, personality, interests, and interior life of baseball's greatest forgotten player.

Such items are gold for any historian, but they are especially valuable to the Charleston biographer. My heart thrilled as I leafed through the scrapbook and album in April 2016, taking pictures of every priceless page. I had already come to realize that Oscar was a difficult man to know. Given enough time and a little luck, the diligent researcher can uncover pretty much everything ever written about Oscar by others. But these external sources tell us little about Oscar's own mind. Neither Oscar nor his close relatives were ever interviewed at any length, and neither Oscar nor his family ever wrote anything about his private life. The sediment of legend that has come to settle on the Oscar Charleston story in the secondary sources is often more misleading than revealing. In short, the public sources shed rather faint light on Oscar's priorities, his worldview, his beliefs, his loves.

The scrapbook and photo album help fill in the gaps. They don't tell us everything about the private world of Oscar Charleston, and probably because Janie helped compile much of the contents, some years (1923–34 especially) are better covered than others. But even what these items leave out speaks volumes.

The pages that follow narrate the story of Charleston's life— his career as a Negro Leagues and Cuban superstar, pioneering scout, and successful manager. We will cross paths with Rube

Foster, Cool Papa Bell, Bob Meusel, Lefty Grove, Satchel Paige, Josh Gibson, Dizzy Dean, Jesse Owens, Rogers Hornsby, Roy Campanella, and Branch Rickey. But without the scrapbook and photo album, there's so much we wouldn't have known.

We wouldn't have known how proud Oscar was of his accomplishments, including some of his fights on the diamond. We wouldn't have known which of his fellow players he most admired and envied. We wouldn't have known how much he loved boxing and true crime. We wouldn't have known how intellectually curious and socially ambitious he was, or that he took a lively interest in certain political questions, or that he successfully befriended prominent journalists and musicians. We wouldn't have known that he took an increasing interest in civil rights and race relations as he aged, or that he was strongly committed to advancing the well-being of African Americans. We couldn't have suspected how emotionally devoted he remained to the pretty, petite, and intelligent Janie, despite his own marital failings and their eventual separation.

Oscar Charleston, it turns out, isn't just one of the greatest athletes in American history. He is also one of the most fascinating. Nearly seventy years after his death, it's time finally to get to know him.

OSCAR CHARLESTON

Introduction

Craftsman

BLACK BASEBALL WASN'T WHAT it used to be.

The Negro Leagues had been dying for more than seven years by the time the Indianapolis Clowns bus, jammed with players, entertainers, and gear, rolled into Joplin, Missouri, in mid-September 1954. That was how long it had been since Dodgers star Jackie Robinson had first stepped out of the Brooklyn dugout. It had been six years since a catcher named Roy Campanella, thanks in no small part to the recommendation of Clowns manager Oscar Charleston, had joined Jackie in Brooklyn. Robinson, Campy, and pitcher Don Newcombe had quickly made the Dodgers the black community's favorite team. Just as quickly, the Negro Leagues' fans had disappeared.

It had all happened so fast. Just two seasons after Jackie's April 15, 1947, debut with the Dodgers, the Negro National League had collapsed. Every year since, it seemed, another club had folded. As more black players were given opportunities to prove themselves in the previously white Minors and Majors, the level of play in the Negro Leagues had declined too—not as fast as attendance, but just as certainly. The few remaining teams, like the Clowns, now had to work harder than ever to stay afloat. Official league games didn't draw ten thousand or even five thousand fans anymore. Attendance was now more often measured in the hundreds, and contests were more frequently staged in small, out-of-the-way burgs like Joplin.

No, black baseball wasn't what it used to be, and proud veterans of the game like Oscar Charleston had been forced to adapt—for example, by accepting the fusion of their craft with entertainment. Here is where the Indianapolis Clowns shined. The Clowns played good baseball—a nineteen-year-old Hank Aaron had made his professional debut with the team in 1952, playing for a little over a month before owner Syd Pollock sold his contract to the Boston Braves—but their games also included comedy acts. Before the game the team would play shadow-ball; the Clowns were so practiced, so precise, that it was hard to believe there wasn't really a ball being tossed around. Once the contest was under way, the team's primary routines featured the between-innings, vaudeville-esque stylings of the tall and lanky King Tut and his partner Spec Bebop, a dwarf. Some Clowns players would also pepper their play with circus catches, hidden-ball tricks, and whatever else they could do to make fans laugh, gasp, and applaud—without placing the outcome of the game at much risk. In 1953 the Clowns had even added to their roster a woman, Toni Stone. The next year the team had replaced Stone with two other women: Mamie "Peanut" Johnson, who pitched occasionally, and Connie Morgan, who played second base.

The Negro Leagues had definitely declined, but in 1954 the Clowns were still something to see.[1] Their fifty-seven-year-old manager—quite overweight now and often looking a little tired—was a draw in his own right. A generation earlier the fiery Oscar Charleston had dominated the Negro Leagues as a center fielder and first baseman. By 1954 he no longer took the field except to stand in the third base coach's box, and he no longer got in the fights for which he had once been famous. But he was still an attraction. The black press frequently referred to him as the greatest all-around player in Negro Leagues history. His name and likeness were prominent in the Clowns' publicity efforts. He was feted in pregame newspaper articles and in the Clowns' promotional materials for the stellar record he had assembled playing, coaching, and managing in the Negro Leagues since 1915. There could hardly have been a black sports fan in America over the age of thirty who hadn't heard of him. Probably most non-sports fans among America's black community knew his name too.

Syd Pollock was white, but as a veteran Negro Leagues team builder and promoter he was well aware of his manager's historic status. Proud to have Charleston piloting his team, he inserted a lengthy bio of Charleston into the Clowns' 1954 program. "Oscar Charleston," he wrote, "has compiled one of the greatest records in baseball, and is well known to old-timers as one of the game's greatest natural athletes." Indeed, history would one day record that Oscar had been "one of the most renowned . . . athletes in all baseball history, rating with the greatest sluggers the game has ever known."[2] Public relations rhetoric—right in Pollock's line. But also, as it turned out, the truth.

The buildup to the Joplin game of September 10, 1954, typified how the Clowns went about their business. Pollock fed publicity notes to the local paper, which dutifully printed his talking points a few days prior to the game: "Big crowd expected." "Between-innings comedy show which all baseball men agree is the best in baseball." It would "cost at least $500 to stage a similar show ahead of a Joplin game." Pollock added that this game was an important league matchup. Buck O'Neil's Kansas City Monarchs and Oscar Charleston's Indianapolis Clowns— without any star players left, Pollock was sure to highlight the names of both widely respected managers—were engaged in a "bitter struggle for the Negro American League pennant." That was a fib. The Clowns were the league's best team and the Monarchs its worst. And after Joplin only a few league games would remain.[3]

Not that it mattered. We can be reasonably sure that the Negro American League pennant race meant little to the *Joplin Globe*'s readers. But comedy routines or no comedy routines, the men (and women) in uniform wanted to win, none more than the legendarily competitive Oscar Charleston. Unfortunately, the Clowns committed seven errors that day on their way to a 6–4 loss. The fans on hand, reported the *Globe*, "agreed the players afield did more funny tricks than the clowns, which were not very funny." The game was also delayed by at least thirty minutes because the umpires did not show up.[4] It was a bad night all around.

The next day things got worse. No one seems to have known he was suffering, but Charleston hadn't felt well all season.[5] Finally, things got bad enough that he checked himself in to Joplin's St. John's Hospital. His name was included without comment among several dozen "hospital notes" in the next day's edition of the *Globe*: "Oscar Charleston, Philadelphia, Pa., was admitted yesterday as a medical patient, and later dismissed."[6] Fourteen hundred Joplin citizens had been present at the Clowns–Monarchs contest, but the reporter charged with the tedious task of writing up the *Globe*'s hospital notes made no mention of Charleston's baseball connection. As was the case for the vast majority of white people alive at the time—and today—the name Oscar Charleston meant nothing to him.

Shortly after the Joplin debacle the Clowns clinched the Negro American League championship. Charleston was optimistic enough about his health to accept Pollock's offer to manage the Clowns again in 1955. But the hospital stay in Joplin proved portentous. On September 23, 1954, Oscar fell down a flight of stairs at his Philadelphia row home and was taken to Philadelphia General Hospital. Multiple myeloma, said the doctors. Cancer of the plasma cells. Oscar's sister Katherine made plans to come from Indianapolis to help care for him. Friends and former players visited his hospital room, finding him in good spirits. It seemed to some of them that he might recover, that no one as tough and strong as Charleston could ever truly be defeated. But at 3:45 p.m. on October 5, 1954, Oscar Charleston died.[7]

Charleston's friend and managerial opponent in Joplin, Buck O'Neil, later described him as "Ty Cobb, Babe Ruth, and Tris Speaker rolled into one." He was "the greatest player I have ever seen in eight-and-a-third decades," said O'Neil, "and one of the greatest men."[8] Yet when Charleston died, few outside the rapidly shrinking world of the Negro Leagues noticed.

The occupation given on his death certificate was baggage handler.

• • •

By October 1954 the old, pre-integration world in which Oscar Charleston had once enjoyed widespread fame was separated from the new, post-Jackie era by a thick imaginative boundary. Three days before Charleston's death the New York Giants had completed a four-game World Series sweep of the Cleveland Indians. The Giants' star player—and the National League MVP that year—was a twenty-three-year-old former Birmingham Black Baron named Willie Mays. Mays was joined in the Giants' starting lineup by two other former Negro Leaguers, Monte Irvin and Hank Thompson. Former Newark Eagle Larry Doby, meanwhile, starred in center field for the Indians. All he did in 1954 was lead the American League in home runs and RBIS and finish second in the MVP race to the Yankees' Yogi Berra.

Baseball's integration wasn't complete—the Yankees, Phillies, Tigers, and Red Sox had yet to field a black player—but with Mays, Irvin, Doby, Robinson, Newcombe, Campanella, Aaron, Minnie Minoso, and Ernie Banks the Major Leagues now had a cadre of established and rising black stars. What reason was there, in October 1954, to dwell on the old days? To revisit the era in which men like Charleston had excelled? To do so was embarrassing and painful. The wound of baseball's segregated history was still fresh, progress stupefyingly slow. Black civil rights activists' eyes were focused on the needs of the present, including implementation of the desegregation order handed down by the U.S. Supreme Court just a few months earlier in a case called *Brown v. Board of Education*. The erstwhile defenders of baseball's and society's racial status quo had no interest in being reminded of the talented players they and their predecessors had ignored. Everyone seemed to agree: let the dead bury the dead.

When news of Charleston's passing came, then, it did not spark curiosity among those outside the diminishing Negro Leagues community about this man known as an—if not *the*—all-time Negro Leagues great. It amounted to little more than the fact that another old black ballplayer had died. He was said to have been incredible, but who could tell? Even if you were curious to learn more, there were no reliable statistics, no audio or video evidence, no books, no reference materials, nothing with which to substantiate virtually any claim made about Oscar Charleston or any other player whom you hadn't seen with your own eyes.

Charleston's death gained only the briefest mention in non-black sources. *The Sporting News* ran a one-paragraph notice. Charleston's hometown *Indianapolis Star* ran a short obituary. The *Philadelphia Inquirer* ignored his death completely, even though he had lived in the city for nearly fifteen years. Thus did Oscar Charleston enter an afterlife of persistent, and entirely unmerited, obscurity.

For the rest of the 1950s and 1960s Charleston's name was rarely mentioned outside the black press. That was true, of course, of virtually every Negro Leaguer who never played in the Majors. But even those black players who became big league stars during the postwar period generally refrained from name-checking Oscar. Jackie Robinson, the African American with the biggest public platform in the 1950s and '60s, never mentioned Charleston in his various autobiographies and articles, even though Charleston was closely involved with Branch Rickey's plan to break baseball's color line. For Jackie as for most others—including Hank Aaron—who made their names in the post–1947 world, the Negro Leagues were something about which to be embarrassed. Jackie's teammate Roy Campanella attempted to credit Charleston for helping to scout him, but in his 1959 autobiography either he or his ghostwriter mistakenly devoted a paragraph to "Oscar Robertson" rather than Charleston. Suffice to say that the Cincinnati Bearcats basketball star, although he grew up in the same Indianapolis neighborhood as Charleston, had nothing to do with Campanella's entry into the National League.[9]

It took the opinionated and iconoclastic Ted Williams to puncture the imaginative barrier segregating pre-integration black players from their white contemporaries and the black stars who came later. "The other day Willie Mays hit his 522nd home run," said Williams from the podium during his 1966 Hall of Fame induction speech at Cooperstown, New York. "He has gone past me," Williams continued, "and he's pushing, and I say to him, 'Go get 'em, Willie.' Baseball gives every American boy a chance to excel. Not just to be as good as someone else, but to be better. This is the nature of man and the name of the game. I hope that one day Satchel Paige and Josh Gibson will be voted into the Hall of Fame as symbols of the great Negro players who are not here only because they weren't given the chance."[10]

It was the first time any inductee had such a thing. Williams's speech spurred the Hall of Fame to begin seriously considering pre-integration black players for induction. But note that Williams only called for *Paige's* and *Gibson's* election specifically. Earlier stars like Charleston remained absent from his, and everyone else's, radar.

That began to change in 1970, when Robert Peterson published *Only the Ball Was White*, the first comprehensive history of Negro League baseball. Based on numerous interviews and extensive archival research, Peterson's work brought the attention of the post–civil rights generation to dozens of long-neglected black players, games, and incidents, not to mention the texture of day-to-day life in the Negro Leagues. With Peterson, Charleston began to get his due. "If an old Negro ballplayer is asked to name an all-time team, the odds are good that the discussion will start with Oscar Charleston," reported Peterson. Former player Jimmie Crutchfield told Peterson that he'd have a hard time choosing between Charleston and Gibson as the best player he had ever seen—and Crutchfield's career didn't begin until Oscar was thirty-three years old. Charleston hadn't just been great. He had been popular, too—"at his peak, . . . perhaps the most popular player in the game," claimed Peterson. He cited a *Pittsburgh Courier* report that, in Philadelphia, "Scores of school kids turned out regularly just to see Oscar perform. He was to them what Babe Ruth is to kids of a lighter hue."[11]

Around the same time, duly shamed by Williams and others, the Hall of Fame began to stir. Jackie Robinson had been inducted in 1962, but he was deserving for his on-field accomplishments in the Majors alone, let alone his social significance. It was Satchel Paige who in 1971 became the first figure to go into the Hall on the basis of his achievements in the Negro Leagues. Paige's entrance inaugurated a process whereby one or two Negro Leaguers were voted in by special election each year through 1977.

Charleston's turn came in 1976. He was the seventh Negro Leagues star to be elected to the Hall via the special Negro Leagues Committee. More newspapers ran more articles about Charleston in 1976 than in any year since. But his induction also, and predictably, received only a fraction of the media coverage given that year's best-known inductees, pitchers Robin Roberts and Bob Lemon. For contemporary journalists, besides the fact that very few non-black Americans had ever heard of Charleston, there was the further inconvenience that no one was publicly tending his flame. Although he was twice married, Oscar left no descendants. And neither his estranged wife in Harrisburg nor his relatives back in Indianapolis were loquacious sorts. (Only at the last second did the Hall of Fame manage to locate Oscar's sister Katherine so that he had a representative at the induction ceremony.) With no obvious person for sportswriters and historians to approach for the Oscar Charleston Story, that story remained basically untold.

Fragments of the tale did come into sharper focus as a result of the Hall of Fame induction, as the growing rank of Negro

Leagues historians began to document the history of black baseball and as former players began to be formally interviewed. Charleston, many of their informants routinely told historians, stood a cut above his peers, whether in his range in center field ("Mays can't go back the way Charleston did," said Cool Papa Bell), in his ability as a left-hander to hit left-handers ("I was awful surprised when left-handers hit me. But Charlie could do that," said Willie Foster), or in his general greatness ("I say that the ballplayers I'm telling you about are of the caliber in baseball of Jack Johnson and Joe Louis . . . in the world of athletics," explained Dave Malarcher).[12]

Yet most of the Negro Leagues veterans whom researchers interviewed had encountered Charleston only at the end of his playing and managerial career. He stood larger than life in their reflections, many of them secondhand, but also shrouded in the mist of a fast-receding and quasi-legendary oral history. He had once ripped the hood off a Klansman, reported Cool Papa Bell (unsubstantiated and unlikely). John McGraw said he was the greatest player he ever saw (not impossible, but no one has ever found such a quote). He threatened to throw a professional wrestler through a train window (probably true). He had fought a bevy of soldiers on the field in Havana (well, one soldier at least). He could rip the cover off a baseball with his bare hands (well attested).[13]

For the most part the older Charleston wasn't central to the interviewees' own baseball biographies. Nor was he central to the stories that the historians were telling, which tended to focus on the exploits and achievements of the last generation of Negro Leagues stars. As a result, few people bothered to subject the scattered tales and memories about Charleston that emerged to the test of sober historical analysis. Even fewer bothered to integrate them into a larger narrative of his life. The facts began to be buried under layers of legend, myth, and half-truths.

Telling Charleston's story would have been difficult in any case. Charleston left behind little in the way of a paper trail.

He was literate and highly intelligent, but there is no Charleston memoir—unlike, say, those of Satchel Paige, Monte Irvin, Quincy Troupe, and Buck Leonard. There are no Charleston diaries and only a few known extant letters. He was quoted in the papers from time to time and he gave a few radio interviews, but the audio recordings seem to be lost to history, and he wasn't quotable like Paige.[14] Charleston's scrapbook and photo album were not discovered until 1992 and are still not officially indexed or listed online. Consequently Charleston remained relatively unknown and underappreciated even after the Hall of Fame came calling and even as book after book, article after article, began to be published on the history of the Negro Leagues.

• • •

Bill James tried his best to change that. Today, James is known as the pioneer of Sabermetrics, the older word for what is now more often called analytics—the intellectually rigorous use of data to increase our knowledge about baseball or any other sport. But James has always been as much a writer and historian as math nerd (he majored in both English and economics at the University of Kansas, and his writing extends well beyond baseball to encompass, for example, true crime).[15] James's genius lies in his ability to bring these skills together to productively interrogate the stories we tell—for example, about what makes a hitter valuable, or about the relative value of pitching and hitting, or about the repeatability of clutch performances—in order to revise those stories so that they more faithfully reflect the truth. The classic James volume is the *Bill James Historical Baseball Abstract*, in which he, among other things, ranks the top one hundred players of all time.

In the first edition of the *Historical Baseball Abstract*, published in 1985, James apologetically declined to consider Negro Leagues players. This project was about how good so-and-so was compared to so-and-so, he explained, and the evidence needed to do that kind of comparison with Negro Leaguers simply wasn't available. But by 2001, when James published a revised edition of the *Historical Baseball Abstract*, things had changed, thanks in large part to the work of a small battalion of indefatigable Negro Leagues researchers. This time James decided that he had enough information to consider Negro Leagues players for his all-time top-one-hundred list.[16]

Of the six other such lists James consulted before completing his own, five excluded Negro Leaguers entirely. The sixth, produced by *The Sporting News* in 1998, included only five Negro Leaguers. Among these five—Josh Gibson, Satchel Paige, Buck Leonard, Cool Papa Bell, and Oscar Charleston—Charleston was ranked last, sixty-seventh on the entire list. When James finished his own rankings, however, twelve former Negro Leaguers had made the cut. And he had rated Charleston as the greatest Negro Leagues player of them all—indeed, as the *fourth-greatest baseball player of all time.*

Only Babe Ruth, Honus Wagner, and Willie Mays were greater than Charleston, wrote James, who slotted Charleston just above Ty Cobb, the player to whom he was often compared by the press during the early part of his career. Gibson, James's second most highly rated Negro Leaguer, ranked ninth (and as the greatest catcher of all time). James's ranking of Charleston represented a bold reassessment of a player about whom many of his readers didn't know a thing. It was met, James later recalled, with little but "stunned silence."[17]

That surprised James. He had expected his aggressive rankings of Charleston and other Negro Leaguers to be controversial. In the *Historical Baseball Abstract* he immediately cross-examined himself. Was he wrong to include more than twice as many Negro Leaguers on his list as had *The Sporting News*? Had he succumbed to sentimental muddleheadedness or, God forbid, political correctness? Not at all, he concluded. After all, thirty-four of James's ranked white players were born during the same time frame (1867–1918) as his twelve Negro Leaguers. If anything, he reasoned, he was being too *hard* on the Negro Leagues veterans. Consider: over the course of five years (1947–51), the Negro Leagues had produced Jackie Robinson (thirty-second on James's list), Roy Campanella (fifty-third), Willie Mays (third), Hank Aaron (twelfth), and Ernie Banks (seventy-seventh). "If those leagues could produce five players like that in seven years, what about the previous forty?" asked James.[18] We might add that it's not as if the Negro Leagues had to compete against other sports for America's best black athletic talent. Other than boxing and possibly track and field, which didn't employ many athletes to begin with, baseball was often literally the only game in town for the aspiring black athlete of the 1900s through the 1940s.

But what about Charleston specifically? *The Sporting News* had ranked him sixty-seventh, behind Gibson, Paige, Leonard, and Bell. James chalked this up to ignorance: Charleston simply hadn't gotten any ink. There were no biographies of Charleston when James made his list, and there still weren't until the publication of the book now in your hands—versus a dozen or so of Paige and a handful of Gibson. Charleston, to James's knowledge, had never appeared on a single magazine cover.[19] His anonymity, rather than a considered, informed process whereby the other list makers had come to a different opinion of Charleston's accomplishments and abilities, accounted for why he was rated lower or not at all by other sources.

Besides, wrote James, "It's not like one person saw Oscar Charleston play and said that he was the greatest player ever. Lots of people said he was the greatest player they ever saw. . . . His statistical record, such as it is, would not discourage you from believing that this was true. I don't think I'm a soft touch or easily persuaded; I believe I'm fairly skeptical. I just don't see any reason not to believe that this man was as good as anybody who ever played the game."[20] In fact, James contended, "I believe that if there were a poll of experts about the Negro Leagues, Oscar Charleston would be selected as the greatest player."[21] A few years later such a poll was taken—and James was proved right.[22] Furthermore, James concluded, "I believe that if skeptical, intelligent readers would take the time and trouble to learn about Charleston, this is about where he would be commonly rated."[23] For the truth was that Charleston is "regarded by many knowledgeable people as the greatest baseball player who ever lived."[24]

One of those people was a former star basketball player, Minor League baseball player, and longtime Cardinals scout named Bennie Borgmann, a white man who could not reasonably be supposed to have harbored a pro-Charleston or pro–Negro Leagues agenda. Soon after former Negro Leagues catcher Quincy Trouppe started scouting for the Cardinals in 1953, Borgmann, who had probably played against Oscar in exhibition games during the late 1920s and 1930s, told him, "Quincy, in my opinion, the greatest ball player I've ever seen was Oscar Charleston. When I say this, I'm not overlooking Ruth, Cobb, Gehrig, and all of them."[25]

Buck O'Neil claimed that Charleston was even better than Willie Mays, whom O'Neil regarded as the greatest Major Leaguer he had ever seen. "Charlie was a tremendous left-handed hitter who could also bunt, steal a hundred bases a year, and cover center field as well as anyone before him or since," said O'Neil, using a common late-life nickname for Charleston.[26] It was in Game One of the 1954 World Series, just a few days before Charleston's death, that Mays made his famous overhead catch. Major League fans had never seen such a play, but Negro Leagues veterans swore that it had been part of Charleston's repertoire. "You couldn't hit a ball over his head," said Judy Johnson. "He was like Tris Speaker, you know. He could go back on a ball and it looked like the ball would wait until he would catch up with it."[27] As a manager, Charleston taught the turn-and-sprint-backward move to players like Gene Benson. "In the Negro League you had to turn your back on the ball and take your eye off it. [Charleston would] hit the ball over my head and tell me to go get it."[28]

In a section of the *Historical Baseball Abstract* devoted to the Negro Leagues, Bill James got more specific. He rated Charleston as the best Negro Leagues player in 1921, 1922, 1923, and 1925 and as one of the two best players (along with Cuban outfielder Cristóbal Torriente) from 1917 through 1919. Charleston, in other words, was James's retrospective Negro Leagues MVP for up to seven years. Josh Gibson was James's Negro Leagues MVP choice for five years, Buck Leonard for four, John Henry Lloyd for four, and Torriente for up to four (if we give *him* credit for 1917–19).[29] Charleston was named by James as having had the "best power/speed combination" of any player in the Negro Leagues. He was one of six players who could lay claim to the title of "most aggressive base runner." (We shall learn about some of Charleston's spikes-up base running exploits in the following chapters.) Charleston also made James's Negro League Gold Glove team.[30]

MVP-level hitting, power, speed, base running, and fielding—not a bad combination. Good enough to make Charleston, in James's estimation, the best center fielder in Negro Leagues history. And with respect to two more highly celebrated center fielders, "Charleston, in a sense, put Mays and Mantle together. He combined the grace, athleticism, and all-around skills of Mays with the upper body strength of Mantle, plus he was a left-handed hitter."[31] In sum, along with Josh Gibson at the plate and Satchel Paige on the mound, Oscar Charleston was for James one of three Negro Leaguers who could stake a credible claim to being the best ever at their positions.[32]

Paige, Gibson, and Charleston played together for the 1932–34 and 1936 Pittsburgh Crawfords. Not only did Charleston man first base for that team; he was also its manager.

• • •

The Hall of Fame induction and the Bill James ranking have been the high points in Charleston's reputational afterlife. Black-baseball historians like John Holway, James Riley, Ted Knorr, and Geri Strecker and journalists such as John Schulian have tried to make Charleston better known. But it has not been enough to overcome the factors perpetuating his obscurity. When I encountered James's Charleston discussion in the *New Bill James*

Historical Baseball Abstract, I had no idea who Charleston was—even though he was, like me, from Indiana, and even though I took pride in knowing something about my home state's famous personages, especially its athletes. How had Charleston escaped not only my notice, but also the notice of each of my sports-loving friends? Aside from the factors described above, part of the answer lies in the neglect of his hometown.

Indianapolis has done little to claim Oscar Charleston, even though, along with Oscar Robertson, who grew up a generation later in the same neighborhood, he is one of the two greatest athletes ever to emerge from the city. There are no statues or public monuments honoring Charleston anywhere in Indianapolis, aside from a park named after him in 1998 and a mention in a plaque marking where his first team, the Indianapolis ABCs, used to play. From time to time the *Indianapolis Star* or a local magazine will run a Charleston retrospective, but momentum has never built toward a more permanent recognition of Charleston's achievements.

There are several reasons for Charleston's forgotten-son status. First is Charleston's race. As we shall see in the next chapter, Indianapolis has not exactly won fame for the enlightened nature of its race relations over the years. Second, Indianapolis has simply not evinced much interest in, or knowledge of, its own history.[33] Last, there is the erasure of the physical fabric of Charleston's childhood; each of the ten homes in which Charleston is known to have lived before he began his professional baseball career is gone. So are the stadiums in which his ABCs played. There is left almost no physical reminder of Charleston's Indianapolis life. Nothing, that is, except a grave.

A few years ago my wife and I went to pay our respects to Charleston. Arriving at Indianapolis's Floral Park Cemetery office, we asked where we might find him. The name "Oscar Charleston" didn't ring a bell for the cemetery attendant. She took out a thick directory, found his name, and directed us to the proper section and row.

Floral Park isn't where Indianapolis's most famous are buried. The prime final-resting-place real estate is in Crown Hill, a sparklingly manicured, gently rolling landscape with thick green grass and beautiful stands of old-forest sycamores, maples, and oaks. There you find the substantial, literally monumental tombs of President Benjamin Harrison, poet James Whitcomb Riley, novelist Booth Tarkington, and former Indianapolis Colts owner Robert Irsay, among others. The grave of John Dillinger, a hero to some, is usually scattered with coins and other mementos. Twenty-two former Major League players lie peacefully in Crown Hill, from true cup-of-coffee-ers like Rex Dawson, a pitcher who pitched one inning in one game for the Washington Senators in 1913, to Deadball Era stalwarts like John Grim, a catcher and infielder who appeared in 708 games in the late 1800s for several teams.

In comparison to Crown Hill, flat and scruffy Floral Park has a distinctly working-class flavor. No one truly famous in the wider world is buried here unless one regards bluesman Leroy Carr or murderer Steven Judy as celebrities. Following the cemetery attendant's directions as best we could, we eventually located Charleston's gravesite and found ourselves looking down on a simple, flat, military headstone.

Oscar M. Charleston
Indiana
Cpl Cen, Inf Off Tng School
World War I
Oct 14 1896 Oct 5 1954

There were no flowers, or coins, or any other sign of regular visitors. Nor was there any mention of baseball.

· · ·

Enough about Charleston's neglect. Why should he be remembered—even celebrated? I will give you five reasons. First, Oscar Charleston is one of the greatest athletes in American history. The evidence suggests that James was right: outside, perhaps, of Babe Ruth, Charleston is in the conversation for best baseball player ever. One could plausibly rank him as highly as second, and one could plausibly rank him in the twenties—but no lower. At the plate he was a threat to go long, drive a liner into the gap, or lay down a bunt. Built like a linebacker, he was a terror (I use the word advisedly) on the base paths, frequently stealing, taking extra bases, and taking *out* infielders. His speed and instincts gave him fantastic range, which allowed him to play a shockingly shallow center field. His weakest tool was his arm, but even that rated as at least average. As Bill James predicted, in a poll of twenty-four Negro Leagues historians conducted around the turn of the millennium Charleston received more votes for greatest player in Negro Leagues history than anyone (Gibson was second, Buck Leonard third).[34] And while the statistical record is still incomplete, according to one Sabermetric source he accumulated more Wins above Replacement (WAR) than any other player in Negro Leagues history.[35] Comparisons? Willie Mays is a good one. Tris Speaker, but with more home run power. Ken Griffey Jr., but with more speed. In terms of today's game, think of a left-handed, considerably more cantankerous Mike Trout.

Second, Charleston starred for some of the greatest teams in baseball history, white or black. The strongest clubs on which Charleston played were probably the Homestead Grays and Pittsburgh Crawfords of the first half of the 1930s, clubs that collectively included seven other future Hall of Famers in Cool Papa Bell, Willie Foster, Josh Gibson, Judy Johnson, Satchel Paige, Smokey Joe Williams, and Jud "Boojum" Wilson. At age thirty-eight Charleston was the hero of the dramatic 1935 Negro League World Series, arguably the greatest in black baseball history. Other notable Charleston-led teams to claim championships include the 1916 Indianapolis ABCs, the 1923–24 Santa Clara Leopardos of the Cuban League, the 1930 and 1931 Homestead Grays, and the 1933 Crawfords.

Third, Charleston was a pioneering and discerning scout, a role in which he served as an un-self-conscious—and unrecognized—trailblazer for African Americans. Charleston seems to have become the first black man to work as a scout for a Major League Baseball team when Branch Rickey used him to evaluate Negro Leagues players for the Brooklyn Dodgers. The Dodgers may not have signed future Hall of Fame catcher Roy Campanella were it not for Charleston's advice.[36]

Fourth, beginning with the Harrisburg Giants at the age of twenty-seven, Charleston built a reputation as a talented manager. One poll of Negro Leagues veterans ranked him as the best in the leagues' history.[37] Charleston-managed teams won several black-baseball championships, and on his last team, those league-champion 1954 Indianapolis Clowns, Charleston mentored two of the three women ever to play in the Negro Leagues. He took this responsibility so seriously that he put Connie Morgan through drills in wintertime Philadelphia to prepare her for the season. As a manager, Charleston also partnered with Olympic track star Jesse Owens. After winning gold in Berlin, Owens traveled with Charleston's Toledo-Indianapolis Crawfords for two seasons, racing men, motorcycles, and horses before, during, and after games. Add Charleston's sterling playing and scouting record to the evaluative mix, and it is not insane to think he might have the best overall résumé of baseball accomplishment ever compiled.

The fifth and most important reason is what Charleston meant to the larger African American community. During his long career he was perhaps the most respected man in the Negro Leagues because of his fierce commitment to his craft. He played hard, and he was not, shall we say, disinclined to take part in physical altercations. There were nights in jail cells. There were fights with teammates, rivals, umpires, and soldiers. There was plenty of trash talk (to the likes of Walter Johnson and Sammy Baugh, allegedly, among many others). And there was an attractive personality marked by keen intelligence and a passionate desire to win. Fans, owners, and sportswriters didn't always condone his actions, but Charleston illustrated for the black community the toughness necessary to make it in an unjust world, and they revered him for that.

Charleston filled a critical imaginative need within the black community: he was more *representative* than either the theatrical Satchel Paige or the California-bred, college-educated Jackie Robinson. To other Negro Leaguers and to black America at large, the temperamentally flawed but hard-working, reliable, blue-collar Charleston was an everyman who nevertheless served as an exemplar of what excellence looked like. His mastery of the quintessentially American sport revealed what was possible for the black baseball player to achieve and, by extension, what was possible for black flourishing more generally.

• • •

For some writers Charleston's temper has tended to overshadow his abilities. Charleston could explode in rage, especially as a young man, and he was sometimes accused of dirty play. But he was not a hooligan, as he has sometimes been portrayed. There were bad men in both black and white baseball, men whom no one liked or trusted. Charleston was not one of them.

Mark Ribowsky, among others, chose to portray Charleston as a barely human berserker. "With his scowl and brawling tendencies, Charleston was a baleful man, and he enjoyed watching people gulp when he got mad," wrote Ribowsky in his not entirely reliable history of the Negro Leagues.[38] Charleston was an "autocrat," he claimed, a man with a "thuggish reputation" who was "barbaric on the basepaths."[39] He was "a great big snarling bear of a man with glaring eyes and a temper that periodically drove him beyond the edge of sanity." Oscar may have "compiled a long record of achievement on the field," but he also had "a police record almost as long."[40]

Such a portrait is wildly distorted. No contemporary sportswriter or anyone who knew Charleston personally ever called him a thug, and Charleston emphatically did not have a substantial police record. While he was happy to join fights in progress, he did not usually start them. And although at times he had a quick temper, he was not, to use Ribowsky's adjective, "barbaric."

Context is important here. In both the Negro Leagues and the white Majors violence was vastly more common during the first decades of the twentieth century than it is today. Ballplayers routinely got into fights with opposing ballplayers, with their own teammates, with coaches and managers, with umpires, and with fans. As Charles Leerhsen demonstrates at length in his judicious biography of Ty Cobb, it was a time in which fighting and violence were integral to the game—and, arguably, to American society as a whole. Leerhsen notes that one fan, drama critic George Jean Nathan, "counted 355 physical assaults on umpires by players and fans during the 1909 season alone."[41] The Texas League's rules specifically allowed players who engaged in an on-field fight to finish it; the only ones to be penalized were teammates who interfered.[42]

Oscar Charleston, in fact, was usually self-disciplined and reasonably good humored, not to mention significantly more intellectual than most of his ball-playing peers, black or white. Many extant photos show him smiling. Everyone agrees that Charleston was exceptionally tough, and we know he had a passion (and talent) for boxing.[43] But John Schulian, who spoke to a number of ex-teammates and relations for a splendid *Sports Illustrated* essay on Charleston, said that "you get the feeling . . . that here is this rough ballplayer who would fight anybody, crash into anything, take out fielders, but was a real puppy dog."[44] Rodney Redman, whose father knew Charleston well and who himself was close to Charleston's brother Shedrick, said that he never heard anything negative about Oscar: "My father only said good things about him." Mamie Johnson, who played for Oscar on the 1954 Indianapolis Clowns, said, "What I would say is that he was a beautiful person." Did she enjoy playing for him? "Oh, yes; he was great." James Robinson, who played for Oscar on the 1952 Philadelphia Stars, remembered him as "mild" and "friendly." Clifford Layton, another member of the 1954 Clowns, recalled Charleston as "a very intelligent man" whose "personality was beautiful."[45]

In short, Charleston was certainly not a dark-souled, frightful psychopath. He was universally respected and widely perceived to personify the black pursuit of excellence under the conditions of segregation. Before we turn to Charleston's early life and baseball career, it is worth considering just what that meant.

The pursuit of excellence, the sense of meaning and accomplishment that comes with fidelity to a well-articulated tradition, the sense of identity and connection that attaches one to compatriots in one's own time and across time—these are what make sport compelling, to both those who play and those who play vicariously through an act of the imagination. Winning is the stated point of any game, but it is circumscribed within not just written but also unwritten rules because the import of a game for its participants goes far beyond wins and losses. "Winning is not everything," George Will writes, *pace* Vince Lombardi and countless others. "Baseball—its beauty, its craftsmanship, its exactingness—is an activity to be loved, as much as ballet or fishing or politics, and loving it is a form of participation."[46]

Given the peculiar historical and social circumstances in which they played, this point about winning was especially true for Negro Leagues players. For them winning was important, but it couldn't be and never was *everything*. First, the circumstances of the leagues often made it difficult to crown a universally acknowledged champion. Second and more deeply, black baseball was socially significant because it provided a locus for the formation, expression, and maintenance of a positive collective identity in the face of prejudice, fear, and hatred. In this sense it played a role similar to that of black religion. Finally, black baseball provided a public arena for the display of excellence. There were few such arenas for blacks in the first half of the twentieth century—music, for example, being one of those few others.

Black men in America played in all-black baseball leagues because they had no choice. Once they were given the choice, those leagues and their teams died remarkably quick deaths. But black baseball was nevertheless a *good* thing. The talent that flourished in the Negro Leagues was not "wasted," as is sometimes said by unintentionally condescending writers.[47] As the embodiment of a living tradition that demanded the achievement of excellence with respect to specific practices, the Negro Leagues provided an institutional venue for the creation of meaning and the achievement of virtue. To portray the players in those leagues as the mere victims of history is certainly not to portray them as they saw themselves.[48]

It may not be strictly true, as the classical Greek tradition has it, that to have one virtue is to have them all, but if later reports of the general character of former Negro Leaguers are to be believed, there may be *some* truth to that doctrine. The unanimous verdict of the writers who interviewed and got to know Negro Leagues veterans in the 1970s and later was that they were notable, as a group, for their depth of character and strength of personality. Perhaps this is not just the typical white sentimentalization of the archetypal Old Black Man at work. Perhaps it says something about what excellence requires—especially under adverse circumstances.

Something like this framework constitutes the unarticulated context for what black baseball meant to both fans and players in the prewar era. For them, a transcendent star like Oscar Charleston revealed what virtue and excellence looked like with respect to the practices of baseball. Charleston's mastery of those practices represented the apex of their tradition's development. To powerfully influence the black imagination, Charleston didn't have to talk. He didn't even have to play in the white Major Leagues. He simply had to symbolize black equality, if not superiority, through his achievements on the diamond. And that is precisely what he did.[49]

No wonder the story later circulated widely among black

baseball veterans that Oscar was the man who had discovered Jackie Robinson for Branch Rickey. As it turns out, this is yet another Charleston story that isn't true, but it was believed because it is *fitting*.[50] Had that happened, it would have been just. It would have served as a concrete link between those who constituted the living tradition of black baseball and the man who would carry that tradition so well into the Majors. In any case, Jackie's success simply proved beyond doubt what black stars like Charleston had personally demonstrated during the previous three or four decades: the best black players not only could be but already *had been* as good at the craft of baseball as the best white players. Maybe better. To honest observers of any color, that this might be true in every other arena could hardly be denied.

•••

Thinking of baseball as a craft and its leading players as master craftsmen offers a helpful frame for reflecting on the Negro Leagues in particular because baseball's earliest black players lived in close proximity to the legacy of slavery. Even the last cohort of Negro Leagues players, the players of the 1940s, were generally just three generations removed from ancestors who had been born into involuntary servitude. Middle-era players like Charleston had grandparents or even parents who had toiled as slaves, and some first-generation black players had at one point been legally regarded as someone else's property. Slavery existed within living memory. The world the slaves made was in some respects still the world inhabited by African Americans.

What did that mean? As the historian Eugene Genovese put it, African American slaves had waged an unending "struggle to make a livable world for themselves and their children within the narrowest living space and harshest adversity."[51] For many slaves, one part of that struggle consisted in taking fierce pride in the quality of their work—that is, it consisted in appropriating the craftsman tradition for themselves. This independent attitude surprised, and sometimes flummoxed, slave owners; such slaves were not always easy to manage.[52] The same attitude, in the post-slavery world, led to frustration and disorientation when black men who had migrated northward found themselves barred from doing skilled work.[53] In response, blacks created alternative institutions in which the spirit of the independent craftsman could find release.

A second part of American blacks' "struggle to make a livable world" consisted in the realist vision the slaves appropriated from Christianity. Their faith promised ultimate deliverance and full freedom in the next world, not this one. Utopian and revolutionary dreams were discouraged. "The slave communities," Genovese notes, "counseled a strategy of patience, of acceptance of what could not be helped, of a dogged effort to keep the black community alive and healthy—a strategy of survival that, like its African prototype, above all said yes to life in this world."[54]

Both the craftsman tradition and this realist, self-help tradition were important parts of the early-twentieth-century black cultural landscape. The institutions of black baseball and the attitudes of its participants become much more intelligible if we keep these legacies in mind. Music and sport were, for example, two areas in which alternative institutions allowed black craftsmen to thrive, at least comparatively. "You could say Negro league ball was one of the black arts, like jazz and the blues," wrote Buck O'Neil, who, like his peers, was offended when his art was represented as an unorganized joke. "We had a *tradition* of professional men," he maintained, "going back to the 1800s."[55] O'Neil believed, not without reason, that the Negro Leagues included a higher proportion of college-educated men than did the white leagues.

Not only were the Negro Leagues characterized by a cult of professionalism that, in historian Donn Rogosin's words, "stressed discipline, hard work, competency, sacrifice, and the pursuit of on-the-field excellence,"[56] but they also represented one practical way in which the realist strategy of accepting that which could not be changed played out. It was a strategy with a limited shelf life, one that made sense only as long as change was impossible. When, later, proud players like Henry Aaron and Jackie Robinson sensed that change was in the air, they had an instinctively negative reaction against the Negro Leagues and other institutions that implicitly accepted segregation. But for the first few decades of the twentieth century such institutions made intuitive sense to most blacks. They represented pride and independence—precisely the opposite of what they represented to Robinson and many others in the postwar era.

Pride and independence. These were two of the most salient features of Oscar Charleston's character. He didn't give a damn what anybody else thought. For forty years he played and managed the game of baseball with an intense fervor that was punctuated by occasional brawls and a few run-ins with authority—but no self-pity. Charleston allowed nothing and no one to get in the way of the pursuit of his craft, which he brought as close to perfection as anyone ever has. The perfection was its own reward. It had to be.

CHAPTER 1

Batboy, 1896–1912

IT IS NOT EASY to reconstruct Oscar Charleston's life, especially his childhood and adolescence. The trail is cold. Nearly all of the firsthand witnesses are dead, and the record is often spotty or contradictory. Assorted half-truths and legends further cloud the picture, as does the fact that the public officials charged with documenting the mundane facts of blacks' lives a century or more ago were not always sticklers for accuracy.

What we know for certain is that Oscar Charleston's childhood was shaped decisively by the legacy of slavery, by the challenges presented by a fast-growing industrializing society, and by poverty. The Charlestons, like virtually every other large black family at the fin de siècle, lived on the margins. Their lot was never easy, and their passionate natures sometimes made things worse.

• • •

Oscar McKinley Charleston was born in Indianapolis on October 14, 1896. His family had arrived earlier that year, migrating to Indiana by way of Tennessee, the home state of Oscar's mother, Mary Jenny Thomas. Mary was born on March 6, 1872, seven years after Appomattox, to Jeff Thomas and Martha McGavock. This information is gleaned from Mary's death certificate, and it is the most definite evidence we have concerning Mary Charleston's family background.[1] We have even fewer definite facts about the family background of Oscar's father, Tom Charleston. According to the 1900 census, he was born in South Carolina in October 1867. According to that same census, Tom's mother was a native South Carolinian, but his father had been born in France. That, to put it mildly, is surprising.

As they pertain to the Charleston family, the facts given in that 1900 census are not always accurate. Several birthdays are wrong, and one Charleston child is completely unreported.[2] But let's consider for a moment the possibility that Tom Charleston's father—Oscar's paternal grandfather—really *was* born in France. That would presumably mean that Tom's father was white. In the social context of Civil War–era South Carolina, how plausible is it that a white Frenchman would have married a black South Carolinian? (Tom himself is recorded in the census as being black, and he is described in newspapers of the time as "colored," so we can be reasonably sure his mother was black.) Not very. Yet it seems just as unlikely that Tom's father was a *black* Frenchman.

Is there any way we can make sense of this datum? Possibly. According to a letter written much later by Oscar Charleston's niece Anna Charleston Bradley, Tom Charleston "came from the Sioux tribe."[3] Oscar himself never seems to have publicly claimed to be part Native American—no one, in fact, other than his niece ever made such a claim even privately, as far as we know. Rodney Redman, whose family was very close to two of Oscar's siblings, told me that a Native American heritage for the Charlestons was never mentioned. But he also said that such an ancestry is not implausible, based on the Charleston family's physical characteristics. The Charlestons "were a little fairer-complected than most." They also had unusually straight hair. Redman recalled that Oscar's brother Shedrick "used to brush his hair straight back." And "Miss Katherine," Oscar's sister, "had beautiful hair" that was also rather straight. The same—a lighter complexion, straight hair—can be said of Oscar's letter-writing niece Anna.[4]

Did Oscar Charleston himself have American Indian features? One black journalist did refer to Oscar as "Indian-colored," and another recalled his "creamed-coffee complexion," for whatever those observations are worth.[5] The reader can examine the photographs reproduced in this book, as well those found online, and decide. In any case, perhaps the idea that Tom Charleston was part Sioux can help make sense of the notion that his father was born in France. For example, Tom Charleston's father may have been a French trader or trapper who married a Sioux woman he encountered in the tribe's homeland west of the Mississippi; it would not have been an unusual place for a Frenchman to be in the 1850s or 1860s. Perhaps Tom's father then moved with this Sioux woman to South Carolina, where a substantial French community flourished, especially in the city of Charleston, in the mid-1800s. And perhaps this explains the family surname of Charleston, which could have been taken by Tom's French father or by Tom himself in the hope of better assimilating into American society.

As the offspring of a Native American mother and white father, Tom could have been considered non-white in the post–Civil War south. His unconventional ethnic ancestry would have placed him on the social margins, and his marrying a black woman would therefore not have been scandalous or even particularly surprising. As for Tom being referred to as "Black" and "colored" in public documents, this could reflect little more than the fact that he wasn't lily white and had a black family. On the one hand, this is an extremely speculative hypothesis. On the other hand, it would seem odd for Anna Bradley simply to invent a claim of Sioux ancestry.[6] However it came about, it is quite possible—and that is as strongly as I would be comfortable putting it—that Oscar Charleston was ethnically part Native American on his paternal side.

Negro Leagues historian Larry Lester, to whom Anna's letter was written, was the first to report—in *The Negro Leagues Book*, published in 1994—that Tom Charleston was a Sioux Indian.[7] A few other writers have since repeated the claim, and as a result Oscar Charleston gained an entry in the reference work *Native*

Americans in Sports in 2004. It is surprising that Charleston's status as part Sioux was so readily accepted by such a reference book without qualification.[8] In any case, if Oscar *was* really part Sioux, his competition as greatest American Indian athlete in history consists primarily of Jim Thorpe and Tiger Woods. He has a stronger claim to greatness than any other Native American baseball player, including Charles "Chief" Bender, Zack Wheat, Johnny Bench, Willie Stargell, Cool Papa Bell, and Smokey Joe Williams (a Negro Leagues legend whose American Indian heritage is even more speculative than Charleston's)— all Hall of Famers.[9] And he has a significantly better claim to overall athletic accomplishment than any part–Native American star in other sports, such as NFL quarterback Jim Plunkett. In short, if Oscar Charleston was part American Indian, it makes his story all the more noteworthy. But as with his life as a whole, the assertion that Oscar had a multiethnic heritage has not attracted much notice.

• • •

At some point Tom Charleston made his way from South Carolina to Tennessee, where he met young Mary Thomas. Mary's father was allegedly employed in construction at Fisk University. This is believable enough in that Fisk, a black college founded in 1866, went through a major construction phase in the 1880s. Given that Tom is said to have worked as a construction worker for most of his life, this could explain how he came into contact with Mary's family.[10]

Fisk's most famous alumnus, W. E. B. DuBois, arrived in 1885. DuBois studied Greek and Latin, but as Tom Charleston was illiterate, there is little chance that he swapped Juvenalian bon mots with DuBois as the latter strolled by his worksite. His illiteracy did not prevent Tom from marrying Mary, who *could* read and write, sometime in the latter half of 1886 or the first half of 1887, when he was between eighteen and twenty and she either fourteen or fifteen.[11] Tom and Mary made their home in

Nashville, and soon children began to arrive: Roy Stanley in January 1888; Berdie (later known as Berl) in March 1890; and Shedrick in February 1892.

Whatever else it may have offered, late-1800s life in Nashville was filled with frustrating economic and social realities for poor black families like the Charlestons. There were more opportunities in the North, at least in the larger cities. Industrial growth there meant jobs were plentiful. And while there was certainly no racial equality north of the Mason-Dixon Line, there *was* more social freedom, fewer occasions in which men and women of color were forced to swallow their pride, and fewer occasions on which they had stoically to endure humiliation. That aspect of northern life may have been particularly attractive to the Charlestons. They were not a clan naturally inclined to meekly accept the insults of others.

So in 1896 Tom and Mary picked up and moved, taking their three sons and joining the wave of black migrants from the South that was already washing over the industrial Midwest.[12] The Indianapolis to which they came was a bustling, smoke-filled, rapidly growing place brimming with the spirit of boosterism and proud to be "the 100 Percent American City!"[13] The town had witnessed a sixfold increase in its population between 1860 and 1890, when it reached 105,436. With migrants like the Charlestons arriving at a brisk pace, Indianapolis would again triple in size, to 314,000, by 1920.

Most of the Hoosier capital's new residents in these decades came from the countryside and nearby states, especially the upper South.[14] A large number of those from the South were black. Although it was not exactly a point of pride for its boosters, Indianapolis was becoming an unusually black city; by 1910 it would contain a higher proportion of African American residents than any other urban center north of the Ohio River.[15] The black population reached 15,931 in 1900—nearly 10 percent of the city's total population. A decade later the number of black residents would increase to 21,816 (9.3 percent of the total population); by 1920 it would rise to 34,678, and by 1930 it would reach 43,967 (12 percent of the total population).[16] By contrast, in 1910 blacks constituted just 1.9 percent of New York's population, 2 percent of Chicago's, and 1.2 percent of Detroit's.[17]

Indianapolis's African American community was served by a handful of black newspapers, including the *Indianapolis Colored World*, the *Indianapolis Recorder*, and the *Indianapolis Freeman*.[18] Many subscribers lived in the city's two principal black neighborhoods. The first was concentrated on the near west side, north and south of Indiana Avenue, a thoroughfare that runs northwest from downtown and was the black community's main shopping and business district. Later, in the late 1910s and into the 1920s and '30s, Indiana Avenue would become a major venue for blues and jazz performers, its clubs helping to establish the city's strong musical reputation.[19]

The second principal black neighborhood was clustered along Martindale Avenue (now known as Dr. Andrew J. Brown Avenue), a few miles northeast of downtown. This area was both an industrial and a residential center that in the decade or two before the turn of the century became increasingly populated by African Americans, their churches famously lining Martindale Avenue (then called Beeler Avenue; the road's name has a confusingly shifting history). The neighborhood's major employers included the Monon Railroad yards, the National Motor Vehicle Company, Eggles Field Lumberyard, the Indianapolis Gas Works, and Hoosier Sweat Collier Factory. In most years, most of the time, there was work here for black laborers.

Martindale was where the Charlestons rented their first home when they arrived from Tennessee in 1896. Their presence in Indiana was first mentioned in the newspapers after Oscar was born that October. The front page of the October 21 issue of the *Indianapolis News* was devoted to coverage of that November's presidential contenders, Democrat William Jennings Bryan and Republican William McKinley. A few pages later, under "Birth Returns," it was reported that to Thomas and Mary Charleston, living at 287 Yandes, a boy had been born.[20] No name was reported, but Thomas and Mary let it be known where their electoral sympathies lay when they made the Republican candidate's surname the middle name of their newborn child.[21]

• • •

The Charleston family home on Yandes Street was a small frame dwelling. Across the street to the west was the Talge Mahogany Company Veneer and Sawmill. The Indianapolis Stove Company's large plant was just a few hundred feet to the east. The tracks of both the Monon Railroad and the Cleveland, Cincinnati, Chicago, and St. Louis Railway were fewer than two blocks away. It was not a quiet neighborhood.

The Charlestons didn't stay on Yandes long. They didn't stay *anywhere* long. The year 1898 found them a few blocks away on Martindale Avenue, just north of Twentieth Street, in a little one-story house hard by the massive, smoky Atlas Engine Works. The following year found them in another home, in the adjacent southern lot, on Twentieth Street itself, and in 1900 they were living in a rented two-story dwelling on tiny Guffin Street between Sixteenth and Seventeenth Streets. All of these homes were in the Martindale neighborhood, but whether because of their need for ever more space, better living conditions, cheaper rent, or more understanding landlords, the Charlestons drifted constantly from one place to another.[22]

As more children were born—a fifth boy, Casper, in 1898, followed finally by a girl, Clarissa, in 1901—Tom Charleston supported the family as best he could by working in construction.[23] There was plenty to be built. In 1888 *Harper's Weekly* had praised Indianapolis as a "solid, pushing city."[24] The new State House and Union Station were both dedicated that year. High-rises like the ten-story Majestic Building (1896), the ten-story *Indianapolis News* Building (1897), and the eight-story L. S. Ayres Department Store (1905) shot up downtown. The iconic obelisk of the 248-foot State Soldiers and Sailors Monument was dedicated in 1902.[25] Construction workers like Tom worked long days for low pay on worksites where their safety was not necessarily a priority, but at least they worked.

Industry was flourishing, too, at the turn of the century, as Indianapolis experienced a natural gas boom followed by the advent of the automobile industry. The city's manufacturing output doubled between 1900 and the advent of World War I, when Indianapolis ranked twentieth in the nation in the value of its manufactured goods.[26] The good times meant not only jobs for blue-collar workers, but also pollution in increasingly prodigious amounts. Soot was beginning to fill the Indianapolis air. In the early 1900s dirty smoke would become so integral to the city's landscape that it served as a literary device in the novels written by Indianapolis native Booth Tarkington. Black soot streaks the city's statues and residents' curtains in *The Magnificent Ambersons*. At times it is so thick that it can be shoveled.

In Indianapolis, as elsewhere, smoke was regarded as a tangible symbol of progress—and Indianapolis had progress in spades. As one resident recalled, smoke fell from the sky so thickly that "if you rocked on the back porch all morning and then went in for lunch, when you went out again after lunch you had to clean the chair thoroughly again."[27] The anti-smoke ordinances passed in the late 1890s and early 1900s provided little if any abatement of the nuisance.

The city's ubiquitous smoke signified an obsession with growth. In Tarkington's portrayal, turn-of-the-century Indianapolis was fairly frenzied by a "profound longing for size." "Year by year the longing increased until it became an accumulated force: We must Grow! We must be Big! We must be Bigger! Bigness means Money! And the thing began to happen."[28] The factories and, just a bit later, the automobile were the primary instruments by which the "thing began to happen," argued Tarkington. Together they brought "Death [to] the God of Things as They Are."[29] It was a period of profound optimism—and profound social dislocation.

. . .

The Charlestons' travails illustrate both the problems endemic to such upheaval and the spirit necessary to confront it. The years 1899–1903 were especially full of trouble. First, Tom was injured in a bicycle accident bad enough to make the papers. On May 14, 1899, he was cruising across the railroad tracks near the family home when the bike's front fork snapped in two, launching him headfirst onto the unforgiving ground. Onlookers called for help, and soon a doctor arrived. Tom suffered severe cuts all over his body, including his face, but thanks to the doctor's aid he was able to avoid the hospital.[30]

Then Tom experienced trouble finding, or keeping, a job. By June 1900 he had been unemployed for at least the last six months. One wonders if his bicycle accident had anything to do with it. In an age that had only the skimpiest of social safety nets, the family must have found it difficult to survive.

Money problems were accompanied by desperate measures. In August 1901 a deputy constable of the court showed up on the Charlestons' doorstep to serve a writ of replevin, a common-law remedy used to repossess property whose ownership is claimed by someone else. We do not know what the property in question was (it could have been the house itself), but we do know that Mary Charleston aimed to keep it. She greeted the deputy constable with an ax. Fortunately for her, before she could do damage, he overcame her and dragged her to the court that had issued the writ. She was released on a fifty-dollar bond paid by Tom.[31]

Mary was tried on August 26. The court was lenient, fining her sixteen dollars for "drawing a deadly weapon," but sixteen dollars was still an unpayable amount for the penurious Charlestons. After the sentence had been rendered, Tom returned to court with Mary and six of the Charleston children to plead for some other solution. It must have been a moving scene, but the *Indianapolis News*, allegedly quoting Tom, played it for laughs:

"Jedge, I'se a poo' man, I is, an' I kain't pay dat fine. Hyer is ma ol' 'oman an' kids. Jes' take 'em an' do wot youse please wid 'em, kos I kain't pay dat money nohow."

He was told to go home and do the best he could, and the court would deal leniently with him, and, followed by his family, he left, rejoicing.[32]

Despite their roles as witnesses to this legal drama, the Charleston boys were not scared straight. All of them inherited Mary's fire, some more than others. The oldest pair, Roy and Berl, found trouble at early ages. When he was eleven, Roy broke into the neighborhood's corner drugstore—apparently without much thought as to what would come next. The July 24, 1900, *Indianapolis News* ran the story:

> Early this morning, the plate-glass window of C. M. Hatfield's drug store, at Bellefontaine and Seventeenth streets, was broken in, and the crash was heard by Frank Eroth, a grocer on the opposite corner. Eroth ran to the place and found a colored boy in the drug store, helping himself to anything that struck his fancy. Eroth captured the boy and held him until bicycle patrolmen . . . arrived. At the police station the boy gave his name as Roy Stanley Charleston. He was barefooted, and in stepping over the broken glass in the drug store his feet were badly cut. A baseball [taken from the store] and a pocketbook containing 43 cents were found in his pockets.

Roy was booked for burglary and petit larceny.[33] In November, after a grand jury returned an indictment, Judge Fremont Alford committed him to the Indiana Reform School for Boys.[34]

Berl fared little better in corraling his animal spirits. In the same week Judge Alford sent Roy to reform school, he also found a ten-year-old Berl "incorrigible" and remanded him to his mother Mary after she filed an affidavit.[35] A year and a half later, in May 1902, Berl was in trouble again. Two months past his twelfth birthday, the state hauled him into criminal court on another charge of being "incorrigible." Whatever this meant exactly, Berl pleaded not guilty. Judge Alford heard the evidence and ruled in favor of the state. Berl was given a suspended sentence dependent on good behavior.

Berl didn't keep his nose clean for long. Just eight months later, in early January 1903, he found himself in the Marion County jail, awaiting the report of a grand jury on a charge of petit larceny. He stood accused of having stolen a pair of fifty-cent glasses from a dry goods store. The jury's report came back on January 9; it recommended indictment. This time Berl, or whoever was defending him, pleaded guilty. He was immediately sentenced to the Indiana Reform School for Boys until he was twenty-one years old.[36] How much of this sentence Berl actually served is not clear, but fortunately for him it was not the entire term, as by 1909 he was once again living with his family.

The Charlestons' fifth son, Casper, also must have had significant run-ins with public authorities. In 1910, when he was eleven, the U.S. census listed him as a ward of the Julia E. Work Training School in the small town of Plymouth, Indiana, more than one hundred miles north of Indianapolis. The facility, colloquially known as Brightside, served as a home and training center for physically and mentally disabled boys and girls, as well as juvenile delinquents and "incorrigible" children sent there by the courts.[37]

Yes, there really was a Mrs. Work. Brightside was located on her 270-acre farm, was superintended by her, and would have had about two hundred resident children when Casper was there. He and his fellow male wards were trained in agricultural work and gardening and fed by the farm's own vegetable, dairy, and meat products. A 1911 article claimed that Brightside was "as happy a home, in the literal sense of the term, as such a home could be. There is nothing about it to suggest the tragic, nor yet is there any signs [sic] amid its environment other than brightness without and within."[38] Maybe, but Casper's residence there was likely not a source of happiness for him or the

Charlestons—except that it meant a fuller stomach for him and one less mouth to feed for them.

Not all Charleston news during these years was bad. On Labor Day, September 1, 1902, several months before he was sentenced to reform school, the twelve-year-old Berl acquitted himself well in a pie-eating contest. The "contest took place on a long table," reported the *Indianapolis Journal*. "The experts presented themselves and said they were pie-eaters and willing to give an exhibition. Seven were colored boys and three were white. Their hands were tied behind them and they were made to kneel. At the word 'Go,' they began to eat pie. Albert Mulkey, a white boy, . . . was the first to eat the last bite. [Berl] Charleston, colored, . . . finished second. Mulkey ate more scientifically than Charleston, eating as if it were his professional business."[39]

Later, Roy found a more constructive outlet for his *thumos* by taking up boxing. He was no slouch in the ring. Roy made his public debut against Cincinnati's Kid Ash on December 15, 1911, as a middleweight and "put up a great battle against his more experienced opponent," gaining a no-decision.[40] By July 1912, having bulked up, he was being referred to as the "colored champion heavyweight of Indianapolis" and was the featured fighter at a series of bouts held at Northwestern Park on Independence Day.[41] Within the black community he was famous enough that summer to be a character in a local musical.[42] In November 1912 the *Indianapolis Freeman* ran a photo of a shirtless Roy in boxing shorts and shoes, left fist raised toward the camera. Roy had by then reportedly fought twenty times, winning eighteen by knockout. His backers, "a good class of men who believe in him," were willing to put five hundred dollars on Roy against anyone in his weight class.[43] The next week, fighting at the Indiana Theater on Indiana Avenue, Roy beat an opponent "back to stupidity."[44] He was not the last Charleston to do so.

• • •

By the time of Mary's ax incident in 1901, when Oscar was four, the Charlestons had relocated from the Martindale neighborhood a couple miles west to the area north of Indiana Avenue, Indianapolis's other black ghetto. Another boy, Thomas, was born in 1904, followed by a second girl, Katherine, in 1905; Benjamin, in 1907; and James (who died before his first birthday), in 1909. The family continued its practice of moving from rented house to rented house on a nearly annual basis. From 1902 through 1910 they lived in at least seven different homes in an area bounded by Indiana Avenue on the southwest, Fall Creek Parkway to the northwest, Seventeenth Street to the north, and Capitol Avenue to the east.

None of these homes remain. Slum clearance, housing projects, commercial development, and the construction of Interstate 65 have rendered a very different urban landscape, especially north of Tenth Street. (The construction of Interstate 70 had a similar effect on Martindale; Indianapolis's two freeways were both routed to run through the city's historically black communities.) Built in 1927 in order to pacify whites who wished to segregate black children into their own high school, the old Crispus Attucks High School (now Crispus Attucks Medical Magnet School) is situated roughly in the middle of this neighborhood. The school's most famous athletic alumnus is basketball great Oscar Robertson, who rose to stardom there in 1954, the year Oscar Charleston died. Today, the road that runs to the south of the school is named after the Big O; there are no neighborhood monuments to Charleston.

But this is to peek ahead. By 1954 Indiana Avenue was near the end of its golden period as one of America's most vibrant black communities. For the previous five-plus decades the Indiana Avenue neighborhood was for many of its African American residents "a heavenly place."[45] Nearly everyone agreed that it was a dynamic neighborhood where a decent, hopeful, entertaining life could be lived.[46]

The houses, most of which were rentals, were, although nicely kept, nothing special. In fact, they could be quite uncomfortable. The Charlestons' homes were like most of the others: wood-frame shacks consisting of four to six rooms. A centrally located potbelly stove was typically the only source of heat, and the thin, flimsy tar-paper roofs made cold winter nights that much worse. On hot summer days residents sat on their front porches and hoped for a cooling breeze. There was no running water in the early years of the 1900s and no indoor toilets until decades later. Nor were there bathtubs; tin washtubs had to suffice.[47]

Of course, these were the typical living conditions for blacks—and many whites—everywhere. Unlike most places, in the Indiana Avenue neighborhood there were the compensatory pleasures of a thick community life. On the eight-block stretch of Indiana Avenue that ran through the community could be found dozens of black-owned, or at least black-friendly, businesses. In 1916 there were "33 restaurants, 33 saloons, 26 grocery stores, 17 hairstylists, 16 tailors, 14 shoemakers, and 13 dry goods stores" on the avenue.[48] Naturally the street acted as a neighborhood gathering spot—a place not only to do errands, but also to exchange gossip, watch parades, and do some courting. If you were so inclined, you could also drink and do a little gambling. "If you hadn't been on the avenue, . . . you hadn't lived that day," recalled one resident. "Indiana Avenue was a part of your everyday life."[49]

Life on the avenue made for a "rich, lush, *interesting* world," recalled former resident Thomas Howard Ridley Jr.[50] Its self-contained nature lifted spirits by limiting the necessity of experiencing the deflating acts of racial discrimination that made up daily life outside the community. Then, too, compared to the South, race relations in Indianapolis didn't seem so bad. "There was definitely segregation in my home city," wrote Ridley, "but nothing like what I experienced in Georgia and Mississippi [during the early 1940s]. At home in Indianapolis, we could not go to downtown theaters or restaurants, but we were allowed to go into department stores. . . . On the buses and streetcars we sat in any vacant seat, and it was not normal to be insulted or called 'n——' to our faces in public. When walking down the street, we were not expected to step off of the curb to enable a white person to pass by, as was common practice in the South."[51] If one had experienced life in Dixie, as so many neighborhood residents and their ancestors had, such differences stood out.

Moreover, Indiana Avenue offered evidence that prospects for blacks were genuinely improving. Black professionals—doctors, lawyers, teachers—were highly visible members of the community. In 1909 a black woman, Madame C. J. Walker, began manufacturing her hair product for black women in the community; before long she had become one of the nation's first millionaire businesswomen. Other flourishing enterprises on the avenue further demonstrated that blacks could succeed in the world of commerce. The way people dressed and carried themselves generally indicated a high level of pride and self-esteem.

This was the optimistic feeling that many neighborhood kids, including Oscar Charleston, imbibed and that some of them would later articulate. They also remembered having a great deal of freedom. Roaming in packs, in the early years of the avenue's heyday, they might play by the river or stop and watch a blacksmith work or head to the nickelodeon. Or peek in at a baseball game.

• • •

Oscar spent his formative years in the Indiana Avenue neighborhood, moving from one rented house to another during his grade-school years but always within the same community. As we have seen, the Charleston boys were more exuberant than most. No doubt they learned to handle themselves physically by getting into the usual kinds of juvenile altercations with other neighborhood boys. At Indianapolis Public School No. 23, Oscar also learned to read and write.

The nature of Oscar's schooling was shaped by Indianapolis's attitudes toward African Americans. Although the Ku Klux

Klan did not gain power in Indianapolis until the 1920s, when an astonishing 27–40 percent of native-born white men in the city were official members of the group,[52] and although it was not as bad as the South, there was still plenty of racism in the city during Oscar's youth. Not only did Indianapolis have a higher proportion of black citizens than other northern industrial cities in the late nineteenth and early twentieth centuries, but it also had fewer foreign-born citizens. Its comparative lack of ethnic diversity seems to have led to an even greater focus on race than was the norm for northern cities at the time.[53] One result was the segregation of the city's elementary schools.

Oscar likely entered Public School No. 23 in 1903. There he was doubtless taught by a black teacher according to a curriculum more vocational than academic.[54] Whatever else school taught him besides reading and writing, his penmanship and spelling would become quite good. Oscar finished the eighth grade, probably in 1910, but did not attend high school.[55] Most likely his family needed him to work. Even had he wished to go to high school, he could not have played on school teams. While, unlike its elementary schools, Indianapolis's high schools were integrated during Oscar's youth, their athletic teams did not become open to blacks until 1942.

By summer 1910 Roy (twenty-two) and Berl (twenty) were working, although they still lived at home. Shedrick (eighteen) was probably working and living at home too. The Charlestons' address was 1514 Mill, near the northern edge of the Indiana Avenue community. Now out of school, Oscar could contribute to the family finances while nurturing his passion for baseball.

Along with boxing, in the early 1900s baseball was Indianapolis's most popular spectator sport. There had been black baseball teams in Indianapolis since the end of the Civil War. Often these club teams were organized around vocational lines—in the late 1860s the city's black barbers had a team called the Mohawks, for example. As more and more African Americans arrived from the South, more and more teams were formed. In addition, black traveling teams from other cities—such as the Cuban Giants—would sometimes come through Indianapolis on tours. The Cuban Giants would play against white teams such as the Indianapolis Hoosiers, who were part of the National League from 1887 through 1889. In 1884 Indianapolis also had a team in the American Association. These two teams' four combined years in the American Association and National League constituted the whole of Indianapolis's Major League era, but residents could watch numerous semipro and club teams play at diamonds throughout the city.

After the turn of the century, denizens of the Indiana Avenue neighborhood didn't have to go far at all to see at least one of the local black nines: the Indianapolis ABCS. The ABCS were connected to the American Brewing Company, founded in 1897 by Indianapolis resident Joseph C. Schaf. Former player William "Dizzy" Dismukes later claimed that the ABCS were organized by the brewery as a way of advertising the company's product. The obituary of former ABCS manager Randolph Butler, however, stated that the team was named for its three co-managers, whose surnames were Adams, Butler, and Conoyer.[56] In this account, only after the team started to play as the ABCS did the brewery with the same initials come on board as a sponsor.

In any case, by 1902, when they were first mentioned in extant newspaper accounts, the ABCS were one of several black teams in Indianapolis, along with the Unions, Vendomes, Herculeans, Crescents, and others. At the time the Unions were considered the city's top black team, but by 1906 the *Indianapolis Freeman* was referring to the ABCS as the "champion baseball club of Indiana." They were now owned and managed solely by the popular and debonair Ran Butler. The ABCS were a side hustle for the wide-bodied, squirrel-cheeked, bowler-sporting, cigar-puffing Butler, who otherwise occupied his time with the saloon he owned and the local politics in which he was influential.

As early as 1905 the ABCS were playing games at Northwestern Baseball Park; by 1907 they were playing major out-of-state teams and held a lease at the park, giving them a decided advantage over most other local clubs, who had to scramble to find places to play. Northwestern Park was located at the corner of Eighteenth and Canal Streets—the very northern tip of the Indiana Avenue black community. From 1903 through at least 1910 the Charleston family lived no more than six blocks away from the diamond. Ran Butler was one of the Charlestons' neighbors. His tavern and his home were both located just a couple of short blocks south of the park.

For the Charlestons and other Indiana Avenue baseball fans there was just one problem: on the one day a week they had off, Sunday, baseball was illegal. Booth Tarkington, of all people, tried to change that. In 1903, when he served in the Indiana state legislature, he promoted—and later wrote a short story about—a bill to legalize Sunday baseball. It was a hugely controversial issue. (White-hot opposition to the move among Indianapolis's higher social echelon—*his* people—was one of the incidents that ultimately made Tarkington suspicious of his class's tendency to engage in obnoxiously intrusive paternalism.) The 1903 bill failed, but continued pressure from Tarkington's allies on the issue finally led to the legalization of Sunday baseball in 1909. Oscar, not to mention the ABCs, would be one of the many beneficiaries of this effort.

Since at least the time Roy had broken into the corner drugstore to steal a baseball, the Charleston boys seem to have had a special affinity for the game. The proximity of the ABCs' home park must only have fanned the flames of their enthusiasm. Oscar was later said to have been one of the ABCs' batboys. His exposure to Ran Butler's increasingly professional team was the beginning of his induction into the black baseball tradition.

• • •

Alas, one can't be a batboy forever, and the work then available to a black teenager in the Indiana Avenue community could not have been particularly rewarding. A century ago no less than today, the U.S. military offered an attractive alternative to a poor young man wishing to escape, or at least delay, a life of occupational drudgery. So in early 1912, fewer than two years after he had completed his eighth-grade year, Oscar Charleston, acting with characteristic familial aggressiveness, decided to join the army. Being only fifteen years old was no reason to wait.

Giving his birthday as October 14, 1893 (rather than 1896), Oscar enlisted on the bone-chillingly damp day of March 7, 1912, either with parental permission or by forging Tom or Mary's signature (the army required parental consent for enlistees under twenty-one). Later it would typically be said that Oscar had run away from home to join the military. Since Oscar probably spread this story himself, it is likely true.

Physically, Oscar was still a boy. Fully grown he would be between 5 feet 8 inches and 5 feet 9 inches.[57] At the time of his enlistment he was just 5 feet 5½ inches. Fortunately, the army didn't ask many questions of willing recruits. Oscar was accepted and assigned to the Twenty-Fourth Infantry, Company B. For a young man who had likely never been outside the state of Indiana—never, perhaps, outside of Marion County—a very different life was about to begin.

CHAPTER 2

Hothead, 1912–1915

OSCAR BEGAN LIFE IN the army at California's Fort McDowell. From an aesthetic perspective, there were worse places to start a stint in the service. Fort McDowell encompassed the entirety of Angel Island, which peeks out of San Francisco Bay a couple of miles north of Alcatraz and commands beautiful views of the Marin peninsula, the Golden Gate, and the city of San Francisco. Its strategic location led President Millard Fillmore to declare the island a military preserve in 1850. The army got around to setting up camp there in 1863, and during the Spanish-American War the fort served as a jumping-off point for troops headed to the Philippines. Having been made a major center for processing overseas-bound recruits in 1910, Fort McDowell was still serving the same purpose when Oscar arrived in March 1912.[1]

Private Charleston wasn't on the island for long. On April 5, less than a month after he enlisted, he shipped out for the Philippines, a seven-thousand-mile voyage from the northern California coast. Charleston and his fellow recruits arrived on May 4. Oscar joined Company B at Camp McGrath, about seventy-five miles south of Manila on the island of Luzon.

Even in early May it was hot. Oppressive tropical heat is a year-round reality in the Philippines; average daytime highs hover between 85 and 90 degrees no matter the month, and average nighttime lows never dip below 75. Other features of life in the Philippines in 1912 included malaria, cholera, disease-carrying rats, mosquitoes, and the occasional plague of locusts.

In just about every conceivable way Camp McGrath was

not Indianapolis. Except for the matter of segregation. The all-black Twenty-Fourth Infantry, organized in 1869, was one of the army's original Buffalo Soldier regiments. In the years prior to Charleston's enlistment, the Twenty-Fourth had seen action in the Comanche Wars and in the war with Spain prosecuted by Oscar's presidential namesake. By 1912 the regiment had been to the Philippines several times, arriving most recently in 1911. During previous deployments it had helped squelch insurrections in San Isidro and on Luzon, but things had quieted down considerably by the time Oscar arrived. Legend has it that Charleston and his unit helped "to quell a guerilla uprising that turned savage on both sides," but according to the record the Twenty-Fourth was not involved in any formal military campaigns during Oscar's three-year enlistment.[2] That left time for baseball.

The sport had taken root quickly in the Philippines. The first game was staged a few weeks after American troops took Manila in 1898, and, as in Latin America, it was an immediate hit with the locals.[3] (Unlike in Latin America, some natives played nearly naked; a team formed by Ingorot tribesmen was known as the "G-String Baseball Team.")[4] In light of baseball's popularity with Filipinos and its increasingly predominant place in Americans' self-mythologizing, it didn't take long for the sport's promotion to become central to U.S. colonial policy. During his term as the Philippines' governor general from 1901 to 1903, William Howard Taft encouraged baseball's spread as a way of giving "the natives some means to occupy their time that would tend to elevate."[5] The result of this policy, along with the continued presence of U.S. servicemen, was the establishment of the Philippines' first professional circuit, the Manila League, in 1909.[6]

Playing from November through June in order to avoid the rainy season, by the time Charleston arrived, the Manila League consisted of four teams: a native All-Filipino team (known as the "Brownies"), a white civilian Manila club, the All-Army team, and a Marines team. Beginning in the 1913–14 season, games were played at the three-thousand-plus-seat Nozaleda Park, which had been built just in time to host the star-studded, world-touring New York Giants and Chicago White Sox in December 1913. Manila League crowds were typically energetic and appreciative—especially the Filipino rooters seated in the bleachers. Players shared in the profits generated by games, usually earning forty-five to sixty dollars per month.[7]

Oscar must have had considerable experience playing baseball before his enlistment. He had likely been a batboy for the ABCs, and sandlot games were common during the baseball-crazy early 1900s. Pitcher Elvis William "Bill" Holland, who was four years younger than Charleston and went on to have a long Negro Leagues career himself, grew up on Indianapolis's east side and knew the Charleston family well. He recalled intense pickup games during his boyhood between his "Eastern Stars" sandlot team and a comparable team from the west. "All the girls would be there. If the west boys came over on the east side and beat us, they'd try and get some of our girls, and we'd run 'em back."[8] Surely Oscar was involved in these or similar contests.

In all likelihood Charleston started playing for the Twenty-Fourth Infantry's regimental team in 1912, the year he arrived on the islands.[9] Although it did not play professionally, during the 1912–13 season the Twenty-Fourth built a reputation as a "fast" unit. And no wonder: the team featured two future Hall of Famers in Charleston and Charles Wilber Rogan, later to gain the nickname of "Bullet" or "Bullet Joe." As the 1913–14 season approached, it was thought that the Twenty-Fourth might replace the Marines in the Manila League. But the logistics were not favorable, as the Twenty-Fourth's companies were not all located in the same place, and at the last moment the Marines decided to again enter a team.

League play began on Thanksgiving Day, November 27, 1913. It was briefly interrupted by the visit of Charles Comiskey and his White Sox (which for the purposes of the tour included

Red Sox center fielder Tris Speaker and Tigers right fielder Sam Crawford) and John McGraw and his Giants (featuring Jim Thorpe). The Giants and White Sox played two exhibition contests in Manila. Attendance for the second game was held down because of rain, but the first, played on December 17, was held in front of a joyous overflow crowd full of Filipinos and homesick Americans. Numerous soldiers were in attendance. Oscar could well have been among them, and one wonders whether his signature style of playing a shallow center field was inspired by Speaker's similar strategy. None of the big leaguers got a chance to see Charleston play on this trip—as later, in the States, many of them would.

The first half of Manila League play came to an end on February 1, 1914, with the army club in first place at 16–5 and the dreadful Marines in last at 4–16. A several-week hiatus followed so that the clubs could put on special games as part of the national carnival celebration. The Twenty-Fourth, which had been playing so well in 1913–14 that it was now "considered one of the best soldier nines in the Islands," replaced the Marines for these games, Charleston manning center field.[10] The Twenty-Fourth lost more than it won, but it held its own and was invited to replace the Marines for the league's second half.[11] Two spectacular professional baseball careers were about to begin.

• • •

The quality of play in the Manila League wasn't all that high. Only a few players from this era went on to get cups of coffee in the Majors, and the league's most celebrated pitcher, Joseph Coffindaffer, never made it to the big leagues. The All-Filipino team had toured the United States in the summer of 1913 and had frequently gotten spanked by college squads. Overall, the Manila League was probably roughly equivalent to the low Minors. Charleston and Rogan were by far the most talented players in the circuit. Only the fact that they were young and raw kept them from making a mockery of the competition.

The Oklahoma City–born Rogan was three years older than Oscar and had entered the army in 1911. He had a catcher's build. At 5 feet 7 inches, even when fully grown he was still, in Satchel Paige's words, a "chunky little guy."[12] But catching was about the only thing that Rogan wouldn't go on to gain a reputation for doing fantastically well. Newt Allen, who played with both Rogan and Paige on the Kansas City Monarchs, claimed that Rogan was a better pitcher than Satchel. That probably isn't true, but he was certainly one of the best pitchers in Negro Leagues history, and he also posted an elite career slash line of .341/.403/.526.[13] His two-way abilities made Rogan incredibly valuable, possibly the most valuable player in the entire Negro Leagues in the 1920s. Larry Lester has made the credible argument that Rogan was the greatest player the game has ever seen.[14]

Charleston and Rogan not only had a similar level of ability, but they also had similar miens. Both were extraordinarily competitive. Both had no-nonsense personalities on the diamond. And on both the military would leave its mark. Oscar's later difficulties in controlling his temper aside, Charleston and Rogan were disciplined men who expected discipline from others. Charleston's self-discipline manifested itself in a close study of the game, a rejection of alcohol and tobacco, and a commitment to punctuality.[15] Rogan was more of a martinet. When he later served as manager of the Kansas City Monarchs, he sometimes practiced drill-sergeant severity with his players, especially rookies. George Giles recalled that during his first season with the team, Rogan wouldn't let him drink water during practices or games.[16] Rogan also had a talent for obscenity that, even among military men, stood out.[17]

When the second half of the 1913–14 Manila League opened on February 28, the Twenty-Fourth's two young stars quickly made names for themselves on the mound, in the field, and at the plate. In the first game of his professional baseball career Oscar, slotted in the cleanup spot, went 0 for 3. But Rogan pitched a one-hitter and added a triple to lead the Twenty-Fourth to a 3–2 victory over Manila.

On March 15, in a muddy 4–2 loss, Oscar—"the big colored man"—started on the mound and struck out eleven army batters, including four in the first inning (one of the batters reached based on a dropped third strike).[18] On March 22 he took another loss, 5–2, but he began to show what he could do with the bat by going 2 for 3; he also stole two bases. Rogan, meanwhile, was impressing as a catcher. In another 5–2 loss, "The colored men at the earnest behests of Mr. Rogan fought hard and fast, but somehow or other they could not gather. Therefore Mr. Rogan contented himself by playing the game alone. He caught dead half a dozen army men trying to commit grand larceny on second; stabbed severely in the ribs when they tried to come home, and generally conducted himself around home plate like the whole show," reported the *Manila Times'* impressed correspondent.[19]

After ten games the Twenty-Fourth was 2-8 and hadn't fared any better than the Marines team it had replaced. But it found its stride as Oscar began more regularly to take the mound and Rogan settled in as the team's unquestioned leader and trash-talking entertainer.[20] On April 18, against the All-Army squad, Charleston hurled a two-hit, eleven-strikeout shutout. The rest of the team began to get hot. After twenty games and another Charleston victory the Twenty-Fourth was 9-11. The press was composing poems to Rogan, and Charleston was being hailed as "one of the brightest boys on the diamond." Not only could he pitch, but he also "conducts himself on the diamond like a thorough sportsman. And he can hit."[21] Oscar proved that he could patrol center field well too, the press taking note of one astounding catch that stole away a sure triple.

Rogan, Charleston, and their mates weren't always treated with dignity. For some reason Charleston's first name was continually given as "Charles." On one occasion he was referred to as a "little darkey."[22] But generally the Twenty-Fourth was shown a good deal of respect. As the season came to a close, with the team tied for second place, the *Manila Times* noted that given more time, the Twenty-Fourth looked like it could win the pennant. Charleston, it noted, was "a main-stay. An enthusiast, cool and resourceful, but a poor up-hill fighter," the latter criticism referring, one assumes, to a perceived inability to pitch well when behind.[23] Oscar responded by finishing the season with two more shutout victories. On June 28 the Twenty-Fourth wrapped up the 1913–14 season alone in second place at 17-15. The Philippines' black community feted the team with a "smoker" featuring "music, dancing, singing, and refreshments" at a private club in Manila.[24]

Baseball wasn't yet over for Charleston or Rogan. After the *Manila Times* announced its year-end all-star team, which included Rogan at catcher, the rival *Manila Cablenews–American* selected its own squad, including Charleston at pitcher, and it challenged the *Times* to a game. When, after numerous delays, this integrated all-star game finally came off, Charleston hurled a one-hit shutout, striking out ten and walking two. He also hit a triple.[25] In the space of five months, the seventeen-year-old Oscar had become, in the Philippines at least, a star.

Charleston and the Twenty-Fourth would not get another chance to compete in the Manila League. The fans, and apparently the league itself, wanted the squad back for the 1914–15 season, but their commanding officers decided not to field a team. In January 1915 the manager of the Manila team, Carl Clifford, made an effort to sign Charleston for his otherwise all-white team. Charleston's commanding officer, however, would not allow it. (Press accounts do not indicate that the objection was a racial one.) Manila's fans held out hope that Oscar would join the team after he was discharged from the service, but Oscar had had enough of the South Pacific.[26] On February 13, 1915, he boarded the U.S. transport ship *Sherman*. Several weeks later, after stops in Nagasaki and Honolulu, he arrived again in San Francisco. From there, having received his honorable discharge, he caught a train home.

Besides reports from Manila newspapers, our only glimpses into Charleston's life in the Philippines come from two letters he saved in his scrapbook. The first is dated August 1, 1914, and was written by an acquaintance stationed at the headquarters of the Philippine Constabulary in Manila. The newspaper all-star game in Manila had apparently prevented Charleston from keeping an appointment. "My dear Charleston," writes the correspondent:

> Your good letter explaining why you did not come out to the house as promised, came to me some days ago. We knew something of more than passing interest prevented you from keeping the promise. Your explanation has been accepted and you are forgiven.
>
> The baseball game in which you twirled such classy ball for the Cablenews-American team, was interesting to us all—more so because you are Oscar Charleston, and a member of the 24th U.S. Infantry. All of us and 90% of the fans around Manila, believe that in addition to being the best pitcher in the Philippine Islands, you are also all around, the best ball player in this neck of the woods. Mr. Springer, of Springer & Co., was so well pleased that he said he had ₱10—or it may have been ₱20, for you. I suppose you received it.
>
> Just now, Manila is dry—no baseball nor anything of interest but rain and that of course, is nothing out of the ordinary.
>
> I hope you may win the regimental cup for your Company and we know you will do it if you get any kind of support.
>
> Captain Loving and Mr. Waller join me in wishing you success in all your undertakings. Let us hear from you again. Dont [sic] fail to drop in on us at any time you are in Manila. We shall only be too glad to have you come out.

The gift of money was not unusual. It was common practice in the baseball world at this point—and actually until well into the second half of the twentieth century, especially at baseball's lower levels—for fans to reward players by giving them money, clothes, and other goods. More important, the letter indicates that at a young age Oscar was already taking delight in, and had a talent for attracting, thoughtful companions. His scrapbook and photo album make clear that throughout his life Charleston maintained an interest in music and ideas. He tended to seek relationships with those who shared these interests and who were striving to rise socially, a category that included his two wives and their families. Charleston aspired to membership in, or at least to be on terms of social familiarity with, the African American elite—that self-conscious world of culture, high standards, and accomplishment that Margo Jefferson has called Negroland.[27]

The "Captain Loving" mentioned in this letter fits the pattern. Walter Howard Loving, son of a slave, was the well-known head of the constabulary band, which he had led at Taft's inaugural presidential parade in Washington DC. In 1914 he was in the midst of a long and distinguished military career that would include serving as an undercover agent for the U.S. government during World War I. Few black Americans in the Philippines would have been more prominent than Loving. To have established a friendly acquaintance with him as a seventeen-year-old private must have been, for Oscar, quite a thrill. One suspects that Charleston was already able to comport himself with dignity and to hold his own in conversation.[28]

The second letter is dated April 27, 1915, more than a month after Charleston had been discharged, and is a piece of official correspondence sent to him in Indianapolis by his former commanding officer. The captain reports that he has sent by registered mail "the watch fobs which you won as first and second prizes at the Department field meet." One of these prizes was likely for Charleston's performance in the 100-yard hurdles, which he allegedly ran in 15.1 seconds. The other was probably for his finish in the 220-yard dash, which he reportedly completed in 23 seconds. (The world 200-meter record as of 1912 was 21.3 seconds, so while 23 seconds would have been fast, it wasn't *Olympics* fast. Of course, the conditions under which Charleston recorded this time are unknown and could well have been relatively unfavorable.)[29]

Both letters confirm that Oscar compiled an impressive record of athletic achievement while in the army and that he made a sizeable impression on baseball fans throughout the Philippines. Updating readers on the "famous" Charleston's exploits in the states, the *Manila Times* claimed in late 1915 that there had been "few more popular baseball players in the islands than Charleston" and that "everybody knows that he is the boy to make good in any position."[30] Everybody was absolutely right. But the path to making good would soon become a rocky one.

• • •

If Charleston hadn't known what he wanted to do with his life prior to joining the army and establishing himself as a baseball prodigy, he certainly did now. Shortly after he returned to Indianapolis, he presented himself to Indianapolis ABCs manager C. I. Taylor for a tryout.[31] Taylor knew immediately that he had something special. By April 9, 1915, he was telling the local papers that he had signed a "crack southpaw."[32] Two days later, on a cool spring day at Northwestern Park, a couple of blocks from where his family now lived, Oscar's career in the Negro Leagues would begin.[33]

Black baseball and its luminaries were mostly (but not entirely) unknown to the white fans of 1915. In the Major League game the twenty-eight-year-old Ty Cobb was unquestionably the biggest star. The Red Sox had their own elite center fielder in Tris Speaker, the Indians featured Shoeless Joe Jackson, and the White Sox had just acquired the great Eddie Collins from the Athletics. George Herman Ruth had begun his career with the Red Sox in 1914 but was a few years away from overtaking Cobb as the game's most famous player. In St. Louis two more Hall of Fame careers would be launched in 1915 with the debuts of George Sisler (Browns) and Rogers Hornsby (Cardinals). The Senators' Walter Johnson was indisputably the best pitcher in the game, and Pete Alexander, hurling for the Phillies, was about to have his finest season. In 1915 and for the rest of the decade these would be the best players in the white game, and it was to them and other stars that the best black players would be ceaselessly compared by members of both races.

There was as yet no organized league for non-white players in 1915. That would not come until 1920, when the indefatigable and imperious Andrew "Rube" Foster (who had earned his nickname after besting white pitcher Rube Waddell in a 1903 exhibition) successfully organized the Negro National League.[34] Instead, there were dozens of independent black clubs of varying abilities scattered across the country from the Atlantic to the Mississippi, playing unpredictable (and, as we would say now, heavily unbalanced) schedules against white, black, and Latino clubs alike. These teams inflated their records in the press and competed for mythical city, regional, and national championships. Because there was no reserve clause and no powerful league to penalize rule-breaking teams or players, rosters were fluid—as they would remain, to some extent, for virtually the entirety of the Negro Leagues' existence. In this world C. I. Taylor's Indianapolis ABCs were just coming to be considered, rightly, to be one of the nation's top black clubs. Rube Foster's Chicago American Giants, the Cuban Stars (yes, most of the players were Cuban, barnstorming in the States during their off-season), the New York Lincoln Giants, and the New York Lincoln Stars were the nation's other top black teams.

Among these clubs, no less than in the white Majors, fabulous careers were in progress. New statistical analyses made possible by volunteer researchers' painstaking gathering and reconstruction of the era's box scores show that the top black position players during 1915–20 included the Cuban outfielder Cristóbal Torriente, shortstop John Henry "Pop" Lloyd, mammoth slugger Pete Hill, catcher Louis Santop, and Candy Jim Taylor, brother of CI. The top mound aces included the ABCs' William "Dizzy" Dismukes, Dick "Cannonball" Redding, John Donaldson, and "Cyclone" or "Smokey" Joe Williams.[35] All told, in 1915 nine future Cooperstown inductees would play on black teams: Charleston, Foster, Hill, Lloyd, Santop, Torriente, Williams, Ben Taylor (another brother of CI), and José Méndez.[36] Another handful of men could stake strong claims for induction.

Once Taylor had announced Charleston's signing, it didn't take long for Oscar to start putting his own stamp on this world. On April 11, 1915, in his first game for the ABCs, he shut out the white semipro Indianapolis Reserves, giving up two hits in the first inning but only one more for the rest of the game. He also struck out nine, walked none, and pitched six perfect innings.[37] It was an auspicious beginning. No one could have anticipated that by the end of the year Oscar would ignite one of the most chaotic brawls the black game had ever seen or ever *would* see, get jailed, lead city authorities to threaten an end to games between black and white teams, and be kicked off his club by an exasperated manager. All of that lay six or more months ahead.

• • •

In April, C. I. Taylor was simply trying to put together the best team he could. Taylor had purchased a half interest in the ABCs in 1914 from Thomas Bowser, a white bail bondsman who had himself bought the team from Ran Butler in 1912. In the last years of Butler's ownership the ABCs' talent and fan support had declined. The late Butler years saw the team playing mainly at home, presumably to save money, and using gimmicks like a 793-pound umpire known as Baby Jim to lure folks to games.[38] It took just one year for Taylor to change the ABCs' fortunes dramatically.

Rube Foster is more commonly named one of black baseball's most important institutional pioneers, but C. I. Taylor was nearly as formidable as Rube—and significantly less given to chest-thumping egotism. (The "C. I." stood for Charles Isham, but Taylor was universally known by his initials.) Like the rotund Foster, the thin CI was a southern minister's son. Born in 1875, he was also an army veteran and a graduate of Clark College in Atlanta. Aside from his consuming commitment to baseball, this background played out in predictable ways: CI believed in self-help, discipline, practice, conditioning, and strategy— "scientific" baseball, as it was called at the time. He detested rowdiness, drunkenness, and gambling. Once, when he believed an umpire had been wronging the ABCs, he strode up to the man and said, "Mr. Umpire, I've been watching you for the last twelve innings and you've been robbing my men continuously. If I was a cursing man, I'd curse you." He then calmly returned to the bench.[39]

CI preferred to surround himself with intelligent, well-mannered men like himself. At least two of his players later published poetry, many were recruited from black colleges, and a number went on to successful managerial careers. CI was civically active too, the sort of man who served on YMCA fundraising committees and as the vice president of the Boosters' Club.[40] His managerial efforts led to increased community support for the ABCs, more stadium improvements, and—gradually, haltingly—a more female- and family-friendly game environment.

Winning was also high on the list of things in which CI believed. There he had an advantage, for three of his brothers—Ben, Candy Jim, and "Steel Arm" Johnny, all of them college men like CI—were exceptional ballplayers themselves. They didn't always play for CI's teams, but when they did, they were a tremendous help. When CI came to Indianapolis from West Baden, Indiana, where he had been leading a team called the Sprudels, he brought Ben, a first baseman, with him. From the Sprudels he also brought pitcher Dizzy Dismukes, swift outfielder George Shively, and light-hitting shortstop Morty "Specs" Clark.

Thanks to CI, by early in the 1915 season the ABCs had accumulated a good deal of talent. Taylor, Shively, Clark, third baseman Todd Allen, and catcher Russell Powell formed the position-player core. The rookie Charleston was joined in the three-man starting pitching rotation by Dismukes and Louis "Dicta" Johnson, an accomplished spitballer (a perfectly legal, if unhygienic, pitch). Former Sprudel second baseman Elwood "Bingo" DeMoss—perhaps the best bunter in Negro League history—came on board in early May.[41]

Oscar's first start for the ABCs, along with his record in the Philippines, seemed to augur a future as a dominant starting pitcher, but the second game he pitched in 1915 for this talented ABCs team complicated things. Against a team of white Minor League players calling themselves the All-Leaguers, he gave up six runs in an ABCs' loss. He also homered to right and was robbed of another hit when the left fielder snared a line drive. The eighteen-year-old Oscar's home run was "one of the longest drives seen at the local park" and the longest ever to right field, claimed the *Indianapolis Freeman*. Within days, although he had not been back in the States for a month, Oscar was being hailed as "one of the most promising" young players on the scene. "He pitches like a veteran, besides fielding his position and batting in great fashion. The fans should watch this youngster, he will be one of the best."[42]

The following Sunday, Taylor put Oscar in center field for a rematch with the All-Leaguers. The ABCs had been left with a hole in their defense when Jimmie Lyons—then known, like numbers of good outfielders in the Negro Leagues, as the "black Ty Cobb"—jumped to the St. Louis Giants, so to the outfield Oscar went.[43] He homered yet again in the ABCs' 14–3 victory.[44] It was now becoming clear to Taylor that Charleston's bat was far too valuable not to be in the lineup every day and his glove and legs too valuable not to be in center field. Oscar would start on the mound four days later, but for the rest of the season he would serve only very occasionally as a starting pitcher. No one complained. Oscar's fielding, base running, and power, in that order, stood out much more than did his hurling, even though he had acquitted himself reasonably well on the mound.

About halfway through the 1915 season the *Indianapolis Freeman* ran photos of the speedy ABCs outfield of George Shively, Charleston, and midseason addition Jim Jeffries. The caption claimed that "this trio of outer gardeners looks to be the best in the game."[45] In the black game, at least, that was probably not an exaggeration. Even when Charleston screwed up—as he did on June 24, when he misplayed an easy fly to center against the Chicago American Giants, allowing the winning run to score in the five-game series' rubber game—he was liable to redeem himself in short order. A few days after that costly error against the Giants, when the ABCs took on the Cuban Stars before a record crowd at Northwestern Park, he made two fantastic one-handed catches, one of which led to a double play.[46]

In June, against the Indianapolis Merits, reputedly the best white team in the city,[47] "Charleston made a circus catch in deep center, pulling the ball down with one hand," helping to win the game, 14–1, and the city championship for the ABCs.[48] Given the short, thin mitts then in use, the one-handed catch was rare, and Charleston was one of its first virtuosos. Wilmer Harris, who later played for Charleston on the Philadelphia Stars, remembered how impressed he had been, as a boy, with Charleston's unique method of catching fly balls. "Back in that time, you didn't see players catch one-handed," said Harris. Charleston "was an oddity. He slapped at the ball. From the stands it looked like he was slapping the ball down."[49]

The press frequently reported that Charleston's fielding "featured," the era's term of choice. Sometimes it was "sensational," and once it was so good that fans were "startled." In August the *Freeman* praised Charleston for playing center field "for all there is in it."[50] Given how shallowly he played his position, Oscar's range was what most impressed observers. Oscar's teammate Dizzy Dismukes thought at first that the cocky rookie was lucky in being able to track down flies to deep center, but after

Oscar had let nothing land over his head for several weeks, Dizzy admitted to CI, "That guy's not lucky. He knows what he's doing out there."[51] Oscar's arm was good too. In games against top-tier opponents he finished second on the ABCs to George Shively with nine outfield assists. By the end of the 1915 season Dismukes was convinced that Oscar was the best defensive outfielder he had ever seen. C. I. Taylor felt the same way.[52]

The 1915 ABCs liked to run—that was part of "scientific baseball," as taught by Taylor and practiced in the big leagues with such flair by Cobb. Against the Fort Wayne Shamrocks, for example, the team stole nine bags.[53] Charleston was not the team's most prolific base stealer, but he held his own with speedy teammates like Shively and DeMoss. In fifty-seven games he stole fourteen bases and legged out five triples, tied for tops on the team, and he gained a reputation for audacity. For a while, later in the year, Taylor batted him leadoff.

Oscar's power came and went in this rookie season, fading down the stretch as the ABCs faced better pitching and as pitchers seeing Oscar for the second and third time made adjustments. But by homering in three of his first six games, Charleston had left a lasting impression; each homer had been a no-doubter, and this was still the Deadball Era. (Against top competition the mammoth Pete Hill's six home runs was highest in the Negro Leagues in 1915.) Oscar was the "slugging soldier," the "heavy-hitting outfielder," even though he only hit one more homer the rest of the year.[54] At this point he was only an average hitter; he hit .258 against top opponents in 1915, while his teammates Shively and Ben Taylor hit significantly better. Oscar's best series came against the talented Cuban Stars in June, when he went 7 for 19 with a home run, a double, and three stolen bases to help the ABCs win four out of five.

Charleston may not have been the ABCs' best player—not yet—but the well-rounded quality of his game led the *Freeman* to dub him, on one occasion, the "Benny Kauf [*sic*] of the semi-profs." Kauff manned center field for the Brooklyn Tip-tops of the upstart Federal League. Brash and flashy, he was well known to locals, first because he had played center field for the Federal League's pennant-winning Indianapolis Hoosiers in 1914, and second because prior to Dizzy Dean he was probably the greatest trash-talker in baseball history. Kauff had no problem saying things like, "I'll make them all forget that a guy named Ty Cobb ever pulled on a baseball shoe," and, "I'll hit so many balls into the grandstand that the management will have to put screens up in front to protect the fans and save the money that lost balls would cost." To top it off, he dressed, in the words of Damon Runyon, like "Diamond Jim Brady reduced to a baseball salary size." With respect to their games the comparison of Charleston to Kauff was not totally inapt. But unlike Benny, Oscar did not boast in the press—and he didn't have the funds to indulge in diamond tiepins and silk underwear.[55]

On the whole, in 1915 Charleston performed as well as anyone might have hoped for an eighteen-year-old rookie. But there is one indication that there may have been trouble behind the scenes. For a period of at least three games in July, Oscar did not play for the ABCs. No reason for his absence was given in the *Star* or in the *Freeman*, but when he returned to the team Elwood Knox of the *Freeman* remarked on his being "back in the fold again."[56] Perhaps he had been injured. Or perhaps Oscar was having trouble controlling that troublesome family temper and he and CI had butted heads.

• • •

On September 9, 1915, the ABCs played their last game of the year against a top-tier non-white team, winning 4–2 against the Cuban Stars. They had gone 37-25-1 against the premier clubs, and they had absolutely rolled through lesser competition,[57] including contests with white teams like the Chicago Gunthers, the Indianapolis Merits, and the Terre Haute Champagne Velvets.[58]

One should not assume that just because these teams were semipro or independent they were not sometimes formidable. The athletic meritocracy did not function as thoroughly one hundred years ago as it does today. Talent was far from efficiently distributed. Racism, which kept non-white ballplayers from competing in "organized" Minor League and Major League baseball, was one reason for this inefficiency. But it was not the only one. Pay, and pay disparities, were much smaller than they would later become; professional scouting was virtually nonexistent; and there was no radio, television, or internet to make those in purportedly "higher" leagues rapidly and acutely aware of the talent present in "lower" ones. For all of these reasons many players who could have performed well in the Majors toiled in the Minors; players who could have excelled in the high Minors played in the low Minors; players who could have dominated the low Minors played semipro ball; and so on. Moreover, the spread of talent on any given team could be remarkably wide, with the best and worst players being equivalent, perhaps, to a Major League starter and a Class A backup, respectively, today. (It will be good to keep this in mind as we learn about the ABCs and other black teams playing teams composed of white Major Leaguers, Minor Leaguers, and semipros.)

At any rate, no matter whom they had faced in 1915, Dizzy Dismukes and Dicta Johnson had been fantastic at the top of the ABCs rotation, with Dismukes throwing a no-hitter against the Chicago American Giants on May 9 and matching the Lincoln Stars' Dick "Cannonball" Redding pitch-for-pitch in a 1–1, fifteen-inning tie in which both pitchers went the distance. (To be relieved, in those days of smaller rosters but perfectly healthy egos, was both an inconvenience to the team and mildly humiliating to the player.) First baseman Ben Taylor had shown himself one of the best hitters not playing in so-called "organized baseball," and Shively and DeMoss had also had fine seasons. The ABCs had gone 9-3 against the Chicago American Giants, 13-9 against the Cuban Stars, and 4-4-1 against the Lincoln Stars, the three teams that were their top competition—in the argot of the time the "fastest" teams out there.[59] No one doubted that the ABCS were a very good team.

This is how things stood in late September 1915 as the ABCS prepared to undertake what was becoming an annual tradition of postseason games against white all-star teams at Indianapolis's Federal Park. Since the middle of the season the ABCS had been playing their Sunday home games at this new stadium, thanks to growing crowds that their usual home field of Northwestern Park simply could not accommodate. These all-star teams—the term was used loosely—consisted largely but not exclusively of Indianapolis natives returning home after their seasons in organized ball had ended, as well as players for the high Minors Indianapolis Indians and other city teams.

The papers loved these games. The *Indianapolis Star* promoted them heavily, breathlessly reporting who would and who would not play for the all-star teams, inserting editorial asides about the relative strengths and hopes of the teams, printing taunts and jibes, playing up the racial rivalry angle, and fairly openly taking the side of the white teams as the games went on. For the brawl that occurred on October 24 the white press shoulders at least a little of the blame.

The first games between the ABCS and the all-stars came in a doubleheader scheduled for Sunday, September 26. "The colored champs"—the ABCS, that is—"had fairly easy sailing on their trip over the state" recently, admitted the *Star*; the ABCS had beat up on teams from Kokomo, Rochester, Columbus, and other Indiana towns. But "Sunday it is thought they will meet with stronger opposition."[60] The white all-stars would include players from various leagues in and levels of the Minors. The ABCS would be tested, predicted the *Star*. "The ABCS always take delight in polishing off any league teams, but they probably will be forced to step at their best today to turn the trick."[61] Not really.

The team of mostly low Minors "all-stars" that showed up on September 26 was no match for C. I. Taylor's club, which won the first game, 12–1, and the second, mercifully shortened after five innings by darkness, 7–0. Collectively, Dicta Johnson and Dismukes gave up but seven hits on the day. Charleston went 2 for 8 with two stolen bases. The ABCs stole eleven bags in the first game alone. "Manager Taylor of the ABCs has drilled so much base running knowledge into his colored champs that it is going to take an all-powerful outfit to grab a game from them," conceded the *Star*.[62]

The white players set out to put together such a club. Frank Metz, who played first base for the American Association's Indianapolis Indians, organized a new squad to take on the ABCs the following Sunday. The Indians' Smiling Joe Willis, who had had a brief Major League career with the Cardinals, would pitch, and several other Indians and players from the Louisville Colonels would join in. "It looks like the ABCs are due for a trouncing Sunday when they battle Frank Metz's All-Stars at Federal Park," chortled the *Star*.[63] The all-star outfield was "expected to show something in the way of distance slugging," and Smiling Joe Willis's left-handed pitching would "prove quite puzzling to the colored champs." Willis even called his shot: "The big fellow says he'll win if given a few runs."[64]

Metz's all-star team proved much better than the previous Sunday's, but still it could not beat the ABCs, the game ending in a 3–3 tie after twelve innings. Dismukes pitched seven innings of no-hit ball in relief of Dicta Johnson, and Charleston went 3 for 5 with a stolen base. Three thousand fans saw a "spicy game" full of "swell stops and neat catches" but no winner.[65]

By now the big league season was over, and there was no more messing around. Detroit Tigers shortstop and Indianapolis native son Donie "Ownie" Bush was coming back to town, and he would lead the all-stars the following Sunday against the ABCs, just as he had the previous year, when his all-stars went 2–2 against Taylor's club.[66] Bush, twenty-eight, couldn't hit his way out of a paper bag, but he was fast, exceptionally disciplined at the plate (he had led the Majors in walks five times already), and a slick fielder at short. That combination of talents was good enough to place him third in the MVP voting of 1914. With him would be three of his Tigers teammates: outfielder Bobby Veach, who had led the Majors in both doubles and RBIs that year; George "Hooks" Dauss, who had won twenty-four games with a 2.50 ERA and was also an Indianapolis native; and George Boehler, a reliever from nearby Lawrenceburg, Indiana. Also scheduled to play was the Yankees' Pat Bauman, yet another Indianapolis man who as a utility player had just hit .292.

This new all-star team was a different beast. Bush's club beat the ABCs, 5–2, on October 10. Dauss and Boehler frustrated the ABC batters with curves, striking out twelve. Oscar went 0 for 4.

The ABCs were a "disappointed lot."[67] Two games remained in the series, and these were the only contests all year in which they could show to others, and to themselves, how well they stacked up against Major League, or at least *near* Major League, competition. Then, too, the racially tinged needling of the white papers had to be annoying; as the *Star* wrote the next week, "The All-Stars expect, next Sunday, to teach Tom Bowser's men their ABCs."[68]

Taylor had his club practicing all week. On Thursday, Bush announced that the Brooklyn Robins' Dutch Miller would be added as the all-stars' catcher. CI responded by welcoming back Jimmie Lyons as his right fielder. Unfortunately, Dismukes had decided to head to Honolulu with Rube Foster's American Giants, so Dicta Johnson would start this time for the ABCs, while for the all-stars the White Sox's Reb Russell would fill in for Hooks Dauss, whose wife had taken ill. Russell had just posted a 2.59 ERA for the Sox, so this was not necessarily a downgrade.

At Federal Park on the afternoon of Sunday, October 17, 4,500 fans showed up. They watched Dicta Johnson throw a masterful game, giving up only four hits over eleven innings. The ABCs, sporting new uniforms for the occasion, finally won, 3–2, on Ben Taylor's walk-off (the term wasn't used then) base hit, scoring Shively from second. It was far from a boring game. In fact, "until the deciding run was registered in the eleventh the fans were kept in an uproar by sensational plays on both sides."[69] Oscar, who had turned nineteen three days earlier, went 2 for 4 with a double off the Mississippian Reb Russell, who "would no doubt draw the color line in the future," chuckled the black *Freeman*.[70]

The rubber game was set for the next Sunday, October 24. Excitement was high, and it built even more when it was reported first that Benny Kauff himself was headed to town to play for the all-stars and next that Cannonball Redding, "the best colored hurler in the business," would pitch for the ABCs.[71] Redding wasn't coming to Indianapolis from New York for just one game. In early October CI had announced that his club would undertake a Cuban tour immediately after the season's end. They were scheduled to leave right after this final game of the season, and Redding would accompany them. Reb Russell, allegedly angry over his defeat, would take the mound again for Bush's club.

The day finally arrived. The all-star team wasn't at its best. Kauff had not made it, and neither Veach (who had played only the first game) nor Miller would play. Bush, Bauman, and Russell were the white team's only true big leaguers. Perhaps that only put the ABCs more on edge. Not only were they tired from the long season, but with the all-stars not at full strength the ABCs felt like they *had* to win this game—especially with five thousand screaming fans in the stands.

The all-stars scored first, plating one in the top of the second. In the meantime, the ABCs were having trouble solving Russell. When the fifth inning began, it was 1–0 all-stars. Donie Bush made it safely to first (it is not clear how). Then he took off on Redding. ABCs catcher Russell Powell threw to second, where Bingo DeMoss was covering. The throw beat Bush, but umpire Jimmy Scanlon, who was white, signaled safe.[72] That's when all hell broke loose.

When Bush started for second, Charleston, playing his usual shallow center field, sprinted in to back up the play. Thus, after Scanlon's safe signal, he was already close to the action when he saw DeMoss lose it. DeMoss pushed Scanlon, then swung at him. Scanlon put up his fists, and the men began to grapple. A moment later Oscar, running at top speed, arrived and clocked Scanlon. His punch to the umpire's cheek left Scanlon gashed, bloodied, and lying on the ground.[73]

Violence on the field was far more common in those days, including violence involving umpires. Earlier that season, at Northwestern Park, an umpire had allegedly hit Chicago American Giants outfielder Pete Hill over the head with a pistol—the mere fact of pistol-packing umpires giving one some idea of the era's temper.[74] (Donie Bush himself, some years later, slugged an umpire in the stomach and jaw and wasn't even ejected—not until he punctuated his outburst by throwing a ball at the same ump after the inning ended.)[75] Nevertheless, for a black man playing in a mixed-race game to punch a white umpire who was already engaged with another black player was to cross any number of lines, and Charleston must have known that immediately.

If Oscar didn't know, the enraged fans that began to stream onto the field probably clued him in. Players from both teams began to converge on the action at second base. The police—twelve patrolmen and six detectives—were close behind. The scene was chaotic. Just who fought whom is uncertain, but it seems that most of the combat at this point took place among fans; it was very nearly, said the next day's Star, a full-fledged "race riot."[76] The police used their billy clubs freely to break up the fighting. Several drew revolvers but fortunately did not use them. The players themselves—from both teams—tried to restore order. Finally, the police gained control of the situation, and the fans returned to the stands.

Oscar, however, had slipped away. The Star claimed that "he kept on running" after decking Scanlon, and if that was true, it was the last time he ever ran away from a fight.[77] He may have been genuinely scared for his life. The Indianapolis of 1915 wasn't all that friendly to blacks in the first place, and blacks who assaulted white representatives of authority were not assured of dispassionate justice. It took a few hours for the police to find Oscar, reported the *Star*, but eventually they located him. He and Bingo DeMoss were placed under arrest and carted off to jail. The game, meanwhile, continued, Scanlon still umpiring. The ABCs, perhaps pondering whether and how they would get out of the park unscathed, managed just one hit and were defeated, 5–1.

C. I. Taylor was embarrassed and angry. It was his fervent wish to make baseball a more reputable activity, and his entire identity was centered on being a respected member of the Indianapolis community. He also knew that this ugly incident would be held against the African American residents of the city as proof of their ineradicable savagery, especially at a time when a fresh wave of black migrants from the South was contributing to heightened racial tensions. But he had made arrangements to take this team to Cuba, and probably realizing that the best thing to do was to get the club out of town as quickly as possible, he went forward with his plans. His co-owner, Tom Bowser, bailed Oscar and Bingo out of jail, and by evening the ABCs were embarked on their journey.

When the team's train stopped in Cincinnati, Taylor wired the *Star* with a statement. He made it clear where his sympathies lay: not with his young players—and especially not with Oscar.

> That was a very unwarranted and cowardly act on the part of our center fielder. There can be no reason given that will justify it. Umpires Geisel and Scanlon are gentlemen. I am grateful to Bush and Bauman and all the players of the All-Stars for their earnest efforts to ward off trouble and their kind words to me after the incident.
>
> The colored people of Indianapolis deplore the incident as much as I do. I want to ask that the people do not condemn the

ABC baseball club nor my people for the ugly and unsports-manlike conduct of two thoughtless hotheads. I can prove by the good colored people of Indianapolis that I stand for right living and clean sport.

I have worked earnestly and untiringly for the past two years in an effort to build a monument for clean manly sport there and am sorely grieved at the untimely and uncalled for occurrence at Federal Park today. Again I ask that the people do not pass unjust judgment on my club or me.[78]

It must have been an awkward trip to Florida. Bingo DeMoss had started the fight, but it was Oscar who took all the heat. His actions had escalated things terribly, but from his point of view he had come to a teammate's aid.[79] Was that entirely wrong? It would remain true throughout his career: Oscar didn't often start fights, but he loved to join them. And when he came to someone's aid, it was with fists flying. The man was simply not a natural peacemaker.

The next day, Oscar and Bingo were formally charged (in absentia) with assault and battery, and their case was continued until November 30. A couple of days later they and the rest of the ABCs disembarked in Havana.

• • •

By the time he reached Cuba, Oscar had cooled off. On November 1 he sent a statement to the *Freeman*. It is the first time we hear his voice in the historical record:

> Realizing my unclean act of October 24, 1915, I wish to express my opinion. The fact is that I could not overcome my temper as oftentimes ball players can not. Therefore I must say that I can not find words in my vocabulary that will express my regret pertaining to the incident committed by me, Oscar Charleston, on October 24th.
>
> Taking into consideration the circumstances of the incident I consider it highly unwise and that is a poor

benevolence. I am aware of the fact that some one has said that they presume I am actuated by mania, but my mind teaches me to judge not, for fear you may be judged.

Yours respectfully,
Oscar Charleston[80]

Was the "some one" who had accused him of "mania" CI? It isn't clear. In any case, the apology was good enough for the *Freeman*, which encouraged readers to accept it. The paper emphasized that Oscar had "become exceedingly sorry. . . . An apology was due from Mr. Charleston, a fact which finally dawned on him. He has done the very graceful thing in acknowledging his error, and which leaves him no less a man. The bravest are the tenderest. Considerable harm has been done because of the happening, and which a string of apologies from here to Cuba could never altogether righten. However, he has helped some, and he has set himself right individually and with his team and race."[81]

CI, on the other hand, remained angry, even after a few days in the Caribbean. He remained eager to deflect any blame from landing on his own head. Four days after Oscar wrote his apology Taylor sent from Cuba another statement about the whole affair in which he partially excused DeMoss but continued to take Charleston to task. While Bingo, wrote CI, was certainly in the wrong, "his conduct was worse than his heart." Oscar, on the other hand, "really doesn't know. He is a hot-headed youth . . . and is irresponsible." Taylor thought Charleston ought "to be pitied rather than censured."[82]

It all added up to a bad time for Oscar in sunny Cuba, to which black teams had been coming in the late autumn almost every year since 1900. Following the established tradition of the "American Series," the ABCs were installed at Havana's Almendares Park, where they played twenty games against three Cuban teams—Habana, Almendares, and San Francisco—between October 30 and December 2.

In subsequent years Oscar would perform so well in Cuba that he would become a national idol. But with the brawl still fresh and his manager criticizing him in the press, in 1915 he just could not get going. He batted .188, showing no power (he had only two extra-base hits in seventy-three plate appearances) and was caught stealing on half of his attempts. Taylor started him on the mound once, and he was hammered, giving up ten runs, seven earned.

Certainly the competitive and proud Oscar must have been in a sour mood, which couldn't have helped advance the cause of reconciliation with CI. On November 25, midway through the ABCs' Cuban tour, Taylor announced that he had kicked Oscar off the team. He had "persisted in disobeying club rules."[83] For whatever reason, the expulsion didn't last long. Oscar missed exactly one game. After the ABCs played their last game on the island on December 2, finishing their tour with a record of 8-12, Charleston returned to Indianapolis with the rest of the club.[84]

Oscar and Bingo missed their November 30 trial date of course, costing Bowser his $1,000 bond, and they were promptly rearrested upon their return to the city. Their trial took place on December 7, Scanlon testifying for the prosecution. To their relief, Judge Deery dealt with them leniently. Neither would have to serve any time. Oscar was fined ten dollars plus court costs, and Bingo, five dollars plus costs.[85]

The legal drama was at an end, but the ramifications of the brawl were still playing out. Several days before the trial, the police used the fight as an excuse to declare that no games between black and white teams would henceforth be allowed in the city. "It occurs to me that it is time to call a halt in baseball playing between whites and blacks when two teams of mixed colors can not play a game without trouble," announced a police captain. It was a good time to make such an announcement, since blacks could be blamed for the decision. "I have talked to several witnesses, and there is no doubt but what the two colored players incited trouble."[86]

Such a ban would have been a major blow to the ABCs, who had played a couple of dozen games against white teams in Indianapolis in 1915. Thankfully, perhaps because it would have hurt white clubs as well, the ban never materialized. Still, C. I. Taylor was left with the problem of what to do with his extraordinarily talented but hot-tempered center fielder. And that problem soon became entwined with another: a bitter feud with his business partner, Tom Bowser.

CHAPTER 3

Riser, 1916–1918

AS THE CALENDAR TURNED to 1916, Oscar Charleston, only recently turned nineteen, had seen the ports of San Francisco, Manila, Honolulu, Key West, and Havana. That was improbable for a young, poor black man from Indianapolis. Less improbably, for a Charleston, he had also had his first run-in with the law. Now, with the advent of spring, through no fault of his own he became entangled in yet another controversy as C. I. Taylor and Tom Bowser struggled for control of the ABCs. The cause of the co-owners' rift is unknown, but the confusing result was the formation of *two* ABCs teams in 1916: Taylor's ABCs and Bowser's ABCs. Oscar, along with Bingo DeMoss, George Shively, Dicta Johnson, and several other members of the 1915 ABCs went with Bowser. Perhaps Taylor was not terribly sad to see Charleston and DeMoss go.

Oscar wasn't with Bowser's club for very long. The team began play in mid-April, taking Northwestern Park as its home grounds, and Oscar played in a handful of games, including a 16–1 victory against the overmatched white Indianapolis Reserves on April 30. But soon after that, Oscar jumped ship. Somehow the Harlem-based Lincoln Stars had recruited him, and in early May he lit out for New York.

The Lincoln Stars were one of the top black teams in the nation. In 1915—the second year of the mere three in which the club operated—the Stars had swung through Indiana in late July for a five-game series with the ABCs. Billed by the press as a battle for the "colored championship of America," the series had ended in a tie when the rubber game was called after fifteen innings with the score 1–1. That was the game in which the Stars' Cannonball Redding and the ABCs' Dizzy Dismukes both went the distance, Redding striking out eleven. Two weeks later the teams hooked up for five more games in Indiana. This time the Lincoln Stars took three out of five. The Indianapolis papers declined to mention anything about a championship having been won.[1]

In the ten games he played against the Lincoln Stars in 1915, Oscar went just 10 for 42 at the plate, but he was hailed for his fielding, and his promise must have been evident enough for the Stars to recruit him. Plus, the 1916 Stars had a lot of holes to fill. The talented 1915 squad had featured elite players in Redding, outfielder Spottswood Poles, shortstop John Henry Lloyd, and catcher Louis Santop. Now, only Santop remained, and he was surrounded by journeymen. Charleston would be replacing Poles in center field. In Bill James's opinion, Spot Poles was black baseball's best player from 1914 through 1916, so replacing him was no small task.[2] (Poles was the first man to be widely referred to as the "black Ty Cobb.")[3] Oscar's job was made all the more difficult by the fact that he was the youngest player on the 1916 Stars by a couple of years, just as he had been by far the youngest regular on the 1915 ABCs, when he was four years the junior of the next youngest.

Two white brothers, Edward and Jess McMahon, owned the Lincoln Stars. (Jess also promoted boxing and other sports; his grandson, Vince, is familiar to anyone who has ever watched pro wrestling.)[4] The team's home ground was the Lenox Oval, located in Harlem at 145th Street and Lenox Avenue—a good place for a black baseball team to be based and not a bad place for a black ballplayer to live. As hopping as Indianapolis's Indiana Avenue was, for Charleston the dynamism of Harlem must have been a revelation.

It was during the 1910s that Harlem began to become heavily African American, going from 10 percent black in 1910 to more than 30 percent black in 1920.[5] By 1916 the Harlem chapter of the NAACP, founded in 1910, was on its way to becoming the largest in the nation. Marcus Garvey started his Universal Negro Improvement Association in Harlem the same year Oscar arrived. The associational life of Harlem's African American community was strong and growing stronger, and within a couple of years the artistic renaissance that would make Harlem a byword for the flowering of African American culture would be well under way. Some of the Lincoln Stars may have been keyed into these developments. The roster included a college man in starting pitcher Franklin "Doc" Sykes, a graduate of Howard University, and the previous year former Fisk football star Bill Kindle had manned second base. Oscar, too, probably found Harlem's intellectual energy attractive.

As he had with the ABCs, Oscar immediately made a positive impression. In mid-May, in what may have been his first game with the team, he "made a big hit with the fans" at Lenox Oval by going 4 for 4 at the plate. In another early contest he stole second on the first pitch on each of the two occasions he reached first.[6] And in a later game he saved four runs when he ran back to the wall and, on a dead sprint, leapt and robbed the hitter of what would have been a grand slam, a feat "which brought forth thunderous applause."[7] Keep an eye on Charleston, said the press. He "is there with the 'hello stuff.'"[8]

Charleston was one of the reasons that the *Indianapolis Freeman* could claim, in early June, that the Lincoln Stars looked "like the best team in the east."[9] Yet in truth, even with two future Hall of Famers on the team in Oscar and catcher Louis Santop, the 1916 Lincoln Stars were not one of the top teams in the East or anywhere else. Against top Negro League clubs they went just 8-21.[10] Of course, it took a while for the Stars' relative mediocrity to become clear. The team usually played in front of impressive crowds at the Oval and not infrequently on the road, as when it took on the Baltimore Black Sox in Baltimore in early July. During that series the national Elks convention was in town, and as a result an unusually high number of white fans turned out to see Oscar and the Stars sweep the Black Sox—reportedly the winners of twenty-eight straight contests—at International League Park.[11] Clearly, the Stars had enough firepower to defeat good teams. But mostly they spent the first half of the 1916 season beating up on semipro squads like General Electric, the Paterson (New Jersey) All-Patersons, and the Elmhurst (New York) Grays.

On July 22 the Lincoln Stars embarked on a midwestern tour. They were coming west, reported the *Chicago Defender*, to play Rube Foster's Chicago American Giants "for the championship of the world"—as usual, a highly contestable proposition.[12] First, though, the Stars would stop in Indianapolis for a five-game set with C. I. Taylor's ABCs. Oscar was coming home.

• • •

In hyping the series, the press presented the usual misinformation: "The Stars have a lineup much stronger than the team of last year." They had "played sixty games, winning fifty-two." Cannonball Redding, "the speediest colored hurler in the business, is . . . performing with the Stars." None of these statements was true. (Redding was pitching for the Lincoln *Giants*; it was hard to keep the teams straight when their names were so similar.) The one fact the Indianapolis press didn't much emphasize was the return to the city of the player who had left under such an ignominious cloud. The *Indianapolis Star* merely stated that "Charleston, a former ABC player, is covering an outfield position for the Lincolns," as if no one had likely ever heard of him.[13]

Taylor's ABCs had been doing just fine without Charleston, a fact they readily proved over the course of their series with the Stars, winning the first four games by a combined score of 41–24 before dropping the fifth and final game, 10–8. Charleston managed only five hits in twenty at bats during the series, but he took his walks (four), stole a base, and threw two men out from center. He seems, in fact, to have become a notably better hitter with the Stars. Prior to the ABCS series we have complete at-bat and hit data for fifteen games. In those contests Oscar batted .344. He also stole five bags and gunned down four base runners. Whatever C. I. Taylor saw on the field in Indy, he likely had heard about Oscar's improvement in the East. He knew the ABCS could use Oscar again.

For his part Oscar was probably happy to reconnect with his family. As we shall see, he may have been even happier to see a certain girl. And he was certainly *unhappy* about the trouble the Lincoln Stars were having making payroll. These factors all added up to a reconciliation with CI while the Stars were in town. On August 5, just over a week after the Lincoln Stars left Indianapolis for St. Louis, it was reported that Charleston, along with his old brawling mate Bingo DeMoss, was jumping back to the ABCS.[14] Bingo was in Taylor's lineup the next day, but for some reason it took more than two weeks for Charleston to take the field for the ABCS. He finally returned on Sunday, August 20, against a white team from McHenry, Illinois, called the Henry Greys. Oscar didn't get off to a good start. He dropped an easy fly ball in center that allowed the Greys to tie the game in the top of the ninth, and the ABCS went on to lose in ten.

At least Charleston was on hand in time to play in the games that mattered most to the ABCS and their fans: those against their hated and talented adversaries, Rube Foster's Chicago American Giants. With Oscar and Bingo in tow, the ABCS headed to Chicago in late August for a five-game series. "As the feeling is so bitter between the rival clubs the fans will witness the most bitterly contested games seen in Chicago between two clubs bent on victory," predicted the *Chicago Defender*.[15]

The *Defender* was right. With two outs in the top of the ninth inning of the very first game, DeMoss was called out on a close play at the plate, ending the game and giving the American Giants a 3–1 victory. Enraged, Bingo popped up and punched the umpire in the face. Somehow, and quite fortunately, order was quickly restored. (Few commentators seem to have noticed that in these years, at least, umpires had as much to fear from Bingo as they had from Oscar.) DeMoss was back in the lineup the very next game.[16] In that second contest C. I. Taylor was ejected in the second inning, and DeMoss was again thrown out, this time at second, to end the game, which was won by the American Giants, 4–2. With a large and vocal crowd on hand, including many ABCs supporters, these were electric affairs.

Charleston's rocky start with the 1916 ABCs proved auspicious. Perhaps it was the tougher competition offered in the west, but for whatever reason his batting, base running, and fielding numbers with the ABCs dipped considerably from those he had compiled with the Lincoln Stars. In the twenty-two games for which we have complete data, he hit .231 with just four extra-base hits and had one stolen base and two outfield assists.[17] He made another critical error in the final game of the American Giants series, muffing a fly ball that allowed Foster's club to tie the game in the ninth. Thanks to darkness, the game ended in a tie after ten. The ABCs had gone 1-3-1.

Oscar and the ABCs spent a few weeks clobbering semipro white clubs, losing a series versus J. L. Wilkinson's All-Nations team (a model of diamond diversity that featured black baseball's best pitcher in John Donaldson, as well as two elite Cubans in pitcher José Méndez and center fielder Cristóbal Torriente), sweeping the Chinese University team of Hawaii, and grinding out a win in their traditional October matchup against a white all-star team. At last their season came to a close with a final seven-game tilt against the American Giants in Indianapolis. Predictably, but this time more or less correctly, the series was billed by various newspapers as being for the "colored championship of the world."

Everyone who followed black baseball knew it would be an intense and emotional set of games. Serious money was being laid down, reported the *Chicago Defender*, with the American Giants getting 2–1 or 5–3 odds.[18] That Foster's club was favored wasn't surprising. Rube's team was the most celebrated black squad in the country, and its powerful lineup featured three legends in center fielder Pete Hill, catcher Bruce Petway, and shortstop John Henry Lloyd. In 1916 each of these men was in his prime.

It was stingingly cold for the opening Sunday doubleheader at Federal Park, former home of the defunct Federal League's Indianapolis Hoosiers. Only 2,300 fans saw the American Giants win 5–3. The second game was called on account of darkness after three and a half innings, with the American Giants up 3–0. It therefore didn't count. The next day the ABCS won, 1–0. It was in the third official game, on October 24, when the fun started.

Five hundred enthusiastic fans showed up and saw another pitching battle take shape. The ABCS were up 1–0 in the seventh inning when American Giants manager Rube Foster and ABCS first baseman Ben Taylor got into a strange argument over the fact that Taylor was wearing a mitt while standing in the first base coach's box. Why this mattered, even to the habitually argumentative Rube, is anyone's guess, but the contretemps led to an extended dispute between Foster and the umpires, and when they finally ordered him off the field, Rube refused to leave. The police were called down from the stands, Foster pulled his club off the diamond, and the umps forfeited the game to the ABCS.[19] The ABCS now led the series 2-1, but, frustratingly for Foster, three of four contests had ended with his team on top!

The fourth official game was won 8–2 by the ABCS. Charleston led the charge, going 4 for 4 at the plate. The series now stood at 3-1 in favor of the ABCS. A doubleheader scheduled for Sunday, October 29, would decide things unless the American Giants extended the series by winning both ends. ABCS fans looked forward to Sunday's games with great anticipation. "Colored fans of the city are singing the praises of the ABCS," reported the *Indianapolis Star*. There was history at stake: "If the local team wins the title it will be the first time any western club other than Foster's has annexed the championship."[20]

That is just what happened. The American Giants jumped

off to a quick 3–1 edge against Dizzy Dismukes, but powered by a Charleston triple the ABCs roared back with three runs in the third. Indianapolis added seven more runs in the sixth, ultimately winning 12–8. With the series decided and the game taking what for the time was an eternity at two hours and twelve minutes, the umpires decided not to play another. Charleston had gone 2 for 5; with hits in his first two plate appearances, he had had six straight hits in the series, and he had gone 7 for 18 in total. He and the rest of the ABCs were the 1916 champions of black baseball.

Actually, neither Foster nor the black Chicago press conceded the title. Foster was never accused of being a gracious loser, and now he claimed that the forfeited game didn't count. He also claimed that it wasn't enough to win a majority of the series' games anyway. Prior to the season twelve games had been planned, so regardless of how many were really played, to be the champ one team had to win seven.[21] It was all ridiculous yet rather typical for this rivalry.

Foster's sour grapes didn't stop the ABCs or their fans from basking in the sunlight of their victory. "Let us take our hats off to C. I. Taylor," wrote the *Indianapolis Freeman*'s Elwood Knox. "He has put Indianapolis on the base ball map. Monday morning, the news was all over the country that the ABCs had beaten the American Giants," the big, bad bullies of the black baseball world.[22] What Taylor had accomplished with the ABCs in just a few short years was indeed impressive. And it had depended quite a lot on the defense, speed, and hitting of his young, rising center fielder.

• • •

In mid-December 1916 the *Freeman* reported on what the champion ABCs were doing in the off-season. CI and his brothers were operating a billiard room and cigar store on Indiana Avenue, where CI also kept his office. In keeping with the Taylor personality, it was "the finest and most orderly pocket billiard parlor in the Middle West." Several ABCs were working there. Dicta Johnson was working at a restaurant, "making a splendid boss on the dining-room floor." Russell Powell was working in the coal mines of northern Ohio. Dizzy Dismukes was working in a freight house in East St. Louis. Jim Jeffries was learning to be a barber. Dave Malarcher had returned to his studies at New Orleans University. And George Shively was hunting the hills and hollers of Monroe County ("He sends Manager Taylor a few rabbits and quail occasionally"). These athletes were worthy of citizens' adulation. "Thus it is shown that the players representing the State of Indiana and the great city of Indianapolis are an industrious set and are citizens of the highest mark. They are scarcely ever seen on the streets."[23]

Charleston was as industrious as the rest. He had found work as a grocery clerk on Indianapolis's north side, where his boss was "a baseball fan and an admirer of the whole ABC outfit."[24] He had another admirer on the north side. Her name was Hazel M. Grubbs, a name that sounds unpromising enough, but in fact she was an accomplished young woman. At the time the *Freeman* gave its rundown on the ABCs' offseason activities, she and Oscar were less than a month away from tying the knot.

Hazel Grubbs came from a good family—one of black Indianapolis's best. William E. Grubbs, her father, was the highly respected principal of Public School No. 42, where he began working in 1904. Called "professor" by those who knew him, he had taken his bachelor's degree from Butler University and taught mathematics for a while at Tuskegee Institute, where he attracted the notice of Booker T. Washington. Grubbs's outlook was in fact very Washingtonian. He believed in self-help, education, and civil society, and he was interested "in all problems bearing on the uplift of the community as a whole." A musician who played the viola, among other instruments, he occupied an "enviable position in the community" and was known for his "congeniality, cooperation and respectability." Director of the Boys Club Orchestra of North Indianapolis, leader of YMCA membership and war-bond drives, active member of the First Baptist Church, Grubbs was not only a civic leader, but a good-humored man too, possessing "the ready capacity to shunt aside for a time the cares of work in favor of a good laugh."[25]

William and his wife, Alberta, seem to have been a wonderful match. She was just as energetic and highly respected as he was. Even more than William's, her life centered around music. Alberta taught piano out of the Grubbs's home on Twenty-Fifth Street, often directed musical performances around the city, and served as the organist at her church. Blessed with a "superb voice," she also sang and acted.[26] The papers made frequent mention of her advanced musical abilities. "She is a fine musician," reported the *Indianapolis Recorder* in 1914, "and is doing much to develop the talent of our city to a higher plane in high class music."[27] In August 1918 she played before a Chautauqua audience of five thousand in Rush County. This was a very refined woman.[28]

Hazel had followed in her parents' footsteps. By her early teens she was playing piano for her father's boys' orchestra and taking part in other performances as both a pianist and vocalist—at banquets given by the Ethical Culture Society, for example, and for the Shiloh Baptist Church's Booker T. Washington Musicale.[29] So how did such an accomplished and cultured young woman meet, and fall for, the ball-playing Oscar? The Grubbs's home was a mile or so north of the Charlestons' immediate neighborhood. William and Alberta, both listed as "mulatto" in the 1910 census, were of a higher social class than Thomas and Mary Charleston. At a time when baseball was still considered rather disreputable, it would be somewhat surprising to learn that the Grubbses were big fans. Then again, the Indianapolis black community wasn't all that big. Oscar could have run into Hazel or her parents in any number of ways, including church. C. I. Taylor and Mary Charleston probably knew the Grubbs family through their civic activities (Mary would in the 1920s serve as the national grand queen mother of the

Ancient Knights and Daughters of Africa, a fraternal organization). And everyone would have known that Hazel and her family had what the socially ambitious Oscar valued so highly: respectability, honor, class.

Oscar and Hazel were married on January 9, 1917. The *Indianapolis News* of January 10 listed "Oscar McCharleston [*sic*] and Hazel M. Grubbs" under its "Marriage Licenses" section, but the black press didn't mention the marriage at all.[30] Hazel was seventeen or eighteen at most—a young age for a bride even at that time and especially young for an upwardly mobile, socially prominent family like the Grubbses. One suspects that there may have been extenuating circumstances, yet there is no evidence that this was a shotgun wedding. And one would think that William and Alberta would have had serious misgivings about the eighth-grade-educated, ball-playing, brawl-inciting, grocery-clerking Oscar marrying their daughter, yet they apparently gave the union their approval. The wedding presider was the respected Rev. B. F. Farrell, founder and pastor of the neighborhood's Mt. Paran Baptist Church, where Alberta now directed the choir. One ultimately suspects, therefore, that Oscar charmed the Grubbses just as he had charmed his prominent friends in the Philippines. It would be the story of Oscar's life: whatever troubles his passions might temporarily cause, his personality was such that people always forgave him.

• • •

Oscar and Hazel had been wed for only a couple of weeks when Oscar left to play winter ball.[31] That year, with no ABCS trip to Cuba, he headed to Palm Beach to play in the Florida Hotel League.

The Hotel League wasn't much of a league. There were just two teams, one representing Palm Beach's Royal Poinciana Hotel and the other, Palm Beach's Breakers Hotel. The hotels were separated by a golf course, and the players didn't simply "represent" them: they worked for them—as busboys, waiters, and the like.

The whole setup was the brainchild of Henry Flagler, who had built the hotels in the 1890s and soon thereafter had the brilliant idea of hiring the "best black players he could find" as part of the help. The players could then stage games for the entertainment of Flagler's well-heeled guests, there not being a whole lot to do in Palm Beach at the turn of the century. (Among the Poinciana's guests the previous winter had been Ring Lardner, whose short story "Gullible's Travels" is set at the hotel. An avid baseball fan who at the time covered the sport for the *Chicago Tribune*, Lardner surely took in some ballgames during his stay.)[32]

The plan worked well. Because the money was good and the living comparatively easy, Flagler was able to recruit top black talent to his league, which consisted of two games per week from late January to mid-March—about fourteen games in all. Rube Foster, Charlie Grant, Pete Hill, Grant "Homerun" Johnson, John Henry Lloyd, and other first-generation black stars played in the Hotel League during the first two decades of the twentieth century. Imagine Bryce Harper, Manny Machado, Buster Posey, and Clayton Kershaw playing for the Ritz against Andrew McCutchen, Paul Goldschmidt, Carlos Correa, and Chris Sale for the Four Seasons, and you get some idea of the quality of play. The guests enjoyed these games greatly, and by the mid-1910s fans were affording the players a large measure of respect. The local press began to cover league games in detail. The contests increasingly drew fans not just from the hotels, but also from the surrounding area, even Florida's gulf coast. Buck O'Neil recalled traveling from his childhood home in the state's Panhandle to see some Hotel League games in the winter of 1923 with his father and uncle.[33]

Oscar, along with his ABCs teammates Bingo DeMoss and Dan Kennard, latched on to the Royal Poinciana team for the league's winter 1917 season. The squad consisted primarily of players from the Chicago American Giants; it's possible that the ABCs players were invited to join the Royal Poinciana team during the 1916 season-ending series between the two clubs. With

John Henry Lloyd, Pete Hill, Bruce Petway, Frank Duncan, and Jessie Barber on the team, the Poinciana lineup was extremely strong. The Breakers club featured better pitching—Smokey Joe Williams and Cannonball Redding were its starters—and it had Spot Poles, Louis Santop, and Jimmie Lyons in the lineup. Williams managed the Breakers, while Rube Foster came down from Chicago to take the reins of Poinciana.[34]

Charleston made a strong impression in the league's first week. One correspondent wrote that "Charleston . . . is pulling them down at a distance never before seen here. He is fast, covers a world of territory, and is a good thrower and hitter."[35] Once again we see that in these earliest years it was Charleston's defense—especially his range—that so impressed those who saw him. But Charleston never got it going at the plate in Florida. He batted just .158 with zero extra-base hits in the eleven games he played. He also committed two outfield errors. Happily, the Cuban Juan Padrón pitched brilliantly for Poinciana, starting eight of the fifteen games played, finishing each and every one of them, and compiling a 0.83 ERA. Thanks largely to Padrón, Poinciana captured the title for the first time since 1913 by going 7-6-2. Oscar was again a champion, but in terms of his performance at bat, this winter-league season was, like the Cuban tour of late 1915, a dud.[36]

Perhaps Oscar wasn't yet up to the task of facing elite pitchers like Williams and Redding; he was still only twenty years old, after all. Perhaps his poor hitting simply reflects the small sample size. He seems to have enjoyed himself in Palm Beach nonetheless, if the one photo from this period in his photo album is any indication. In it a baby-faced Oscar stands, with arms crossed and a soft smile, between his teammates Tom Johnson, Padrón, and Leroy Grant. The men are dressed casually, Oscar wearing a driving cap. He looks confident and relaxed. Perhaps he and his buddies had just finished tweaking American Giants pitcher Frank Wickware back in Chicago, to whom they liked to send packages of photos including images of "surf bathing, menu cards of the big hotels, and a picture of a multi-millionaire woman pitching the first ball over the plate in the opening game."[37] Of course, Oscar had also just gotten married. Maybe *that* is why his hitting in Florida was so bad.

• • •

After the Hotel League finished, Oscar returned to Indianapolis to rejoin the ABCs. C. I. Taylor had initially wanted to hold 1917 spring training in New Orleans or Birmingham, but that plan had not come to fruition. Instead, on March 26 he took his team to his old stomping grounds of West Baden, one hundred miles south of Indianapolis. There, over the course of ten days, he put his men through two-a-days and sent them jogging in the surrounding hills. No coach ever believed in practice and conditioning more than C. I. Taylor.

Back in December, Taylor had looked forward to fielding an outfield of Shively, Charleston, and Jeffries. He had predicted that in 1917 they would form "an outer defense without a weakness. It will be the nearest perfect outfield in captivity. They would easily rank with an outfield composed of Ty Cobb, Tris Speaker, and Hooper."[38] Personnel changes complicated that plan. Owing to various defections, injuries, and additions, Taylor moved the promising young Dave Malarcher to right field, where Malarcher soon learned that he wouldn't have to range very far to his right. As he joked later in life, "Some people asked me, 'Why are you playing so close to the right-field foul line?' What they didn't know was that Charleston covered all three fields, and my responsibility was to make sure of balls down the line and those in foul territory."[39]

There was a much bigger complication—at least a potential one. On April 6, a couple of days after the ABCs returned to Indianapolis, the United States declared war on Germany. The draft would be instituted a month later. For the rest of the year Taylor could not be sure which of his players would remain available. Oscar dutifully registered on June 5, 1917, giving his birth year as 1893 rather than 1896 in order to be consistent with his previous lie to the military. He gave his address as 367 West Fourteenth Street. Since his family was living a few blocks away at 608 West Seventeenth, it seems that he and Hazel had set up independent shop.

Play began on Saturday, April 21, amid a springtime- and war-fueled atmosphere of buoyant patriotism. Taylor had secured the use of the Indianapolis Indians' home field, Washington Park, for most ABCs home games, and it was from Indiana Avenue south to that ballpark across the White River that an opening-day parade marched at one o'clock. Following behind the "colored YMCA band" were the ABCs, the opposing Chicago Union Giants, approximately one hundred newfangled auto-mobiles, and various civic leaders.[40] The defending champion ABCs sported new white uniforms with "INDIANAPOLIS" arc-ing across the jersey front. Their socks, featuring a broad white stripe above the ankle, were worn high, in the style of the time, and their low white caps had short, dark bills. Alas, the ABCs were defeated, 5–4, but Dismukes defeated the Union Giants the next day, 4–0. The 1917 season was under way.

For the team, it wasn't a particularly successful season. The ABCs played sub-.500 ball against elite opponents, and they struggled against Foster's American Giants, who reestablished themselves behind Hill, Lloyd, and Redding as the best black ball club in the world. It was the year, however, in which Charleston really began to establish himself as one of the Negro Leagues' best hitters, as well as a fan favorite. ("I think Charleston is the dearest thing—is he married, Louise?" asks a woman in a car-toon that appeared in the *Freeman*.)[41] In mid-August the *Freeman* gave Oscar's batting average as .369, highest on the team. Modern calculations also show that against top opponents he was the ABCs' best hitter, producing at a rate about 50 percent above league average. In all black baseball, among players with at least two hundred plate appearances, only the great Lloyd seems to have fared better.[42]

In a five-game series against the Cuban Stars, which again featured the talented Juan Padrón on the mound, Oscar went 6 for 19. In a five-game set against the American Giants he also went 6 for 19. In a later doubleheader against Foster's team he went 2 for 7 with a triple and an inside-the-park homer. (Perhaps this was the game for which American Giants batboy and future Negro Leagues star Alec Radcliff was present. Late in life he recalled an American Giants–ABCs contest in which Foster told the pitcher to walk Charleston. The pitcher disobeyed, and Oscar homered. When the pitcher returned to the dugout, Foster spit in his face and roared, "That'll cost you $150, you son of a bitch; when I tell you to walk a man, *walk* him!")[43] In late September the ABCs met the Indianapolis Indians, who had just won the American Association championship, for two games. At this point the ABCs had been crippled by injuries—Oscar himself had been out for several weeks with an ailment described by C. I. Taylor as a charley horse—and the Indians won both games rather easily. But in the first game Charleston impressed at the plate, going 2 for 4 and rocking a screaming triple to center field that looked, according to the *Indianapolis Star*'s white reporter, "like it was shot out of a cannon."[44]

Oscar had become one of black baseball's best all-around players, but it was still his defense that was most remarked upon. In a game against the Cuban Stars in Evansville on June 22 he amazed spectators by making "a miraculous one-hand snare of a fly ball," then doubling off a shocked runner. The play helped the ABCs hang on to win, 4–2. Later in that series he made a play on which the press was compelled to report at length:

> A miraculous catch by Charleston of a long fly[,] which left the plate as a sure home run, snuffed out a Cuban rally in the sixth. There was one out at the time and a runner on first. Pedrosa, the Cubans' heavy hitter, took a healthy swipe at the ball and away it sailed toward the hardware sign in left-center.

Charleston got away with the crack of the bat, raced like a shot to the fence, turned like a flash and when a few feet away from the barrier, bent his body sidewise, straightened out again, and took the ball with one hand with his back to the diamond and traveling faster at the time than scared small boys out of a melon patch.

Not content with this, Charleston made a perfect heave to first from deep left center and doubled up Gonzales, who had turned second base, thinking the catch a certain home run. He was not to be blamed for his mistake, for there was not a fan at the game who would have bet a nickel against a hundred dollars that Charleston would get anywhere near the ball. Charleston was cheered to the echo when he came back to the bench and he deserved every bit of the applause he received.[45]

The ABCs may not have been as good in 1917 as they had been in Charleston's first two seasons, but (to use an anachronism) their brand was bigger. They drew large crowds at home and on the road: ten thousand for opening day, twelve thousand for a game in Chicago, seven thousand for another contest in Indianapolis. They also broadened their geographic range, playing a number of games in Kansas City against the All-Nations and taking their rivalry with the American Giants on the road to cities like Cincinnati and Detroit. In fact, they staged two sets of games in Detroit against their Chicago rivals. The first two contests were played at Navin Field, the Tigers' home grounds, on August 3 and 4. The opening game was a fifteen-inning classic. The ABCs scored two in the third, and the American Giants got one back in the bottom of the fourth and another in the bottom of the ninth. Neither team would score again. Both Cannonball Redding, for the American Giants, and Andrew "String Bean" Williams, for the ABCs, pitched all fifteen frames. It was "brilliant baseball," reported the *Indianapolis Star*, with "sharp and snappy" fielding on both teams. Charleston, Malarcher, and Ben Taylor were singled out for their defensive work.[46] The second game in Detroit was won by the American Giants, 3–2. It was an affair at which, the *Chicago Defender* proudly noted, "the richest people of both races mingled together" among the crowd of nine thousand.[47]

The quality of the Negro Leaguers' play made an impression on the white Detroit media: "If the American league could consistently dish up as good a brand of the nation's pastime as the dusky warriors put forth the magnates would have to build seating extensions," wrote the *Detroit Free Press*'s correspondent, adding that both Redding and Williams "would surely be stars in big ring baseball" were it not for their "unbleached exterior."[48] The white umpires were similarly impressed; according to Dave Malarcher, they told the players that they had "never seen this kind of baseball before."[49] After the second game the ABCs and American Giants were honored at a banquet given by the Young Negroes Progressive Association, the president of which expressed his hope that the Great War would result, finally, in "real democracy" for American blacks. All the Negro needs is "half a chance," responded Foster.[50]

A couple of months later, in their traditional season-ending game against Donie Bush's all-stars, the ABCs did all they could to prove Foster's opinion correct. They won, 6–1, on Sunday, October 14, Dicta Johnson beating Tigers star Hooks Dauss. There was still no mention at all of the 1915 riot. To C. I. Taylor's relief, when people talked about Oscar now, they talked about his glove and his bat, not his fists. For two years, in an era when brawls were common, Oscar had not been involved in any controversies or fights—none that were reported, anyway.

• • •

The same could not be said of his former regiment. On December 11, 1917, thirteen members of the Twenty-Fourth Infantry were hanged for their role in the bloody Houston race riot that had erupted in August. Forty-one other men were given a life sentence and sent to Leavenworth. The riot had begun when members of the regiment tried to come to the aid of a black woman being abused by Houston police officers. When the police, already hated by the soldiers for their aggressive enforcement of Houston's Jim Crow laws, beat up a couple of soldiers, things escalated until at last 150 or so members of the Twenty-Fourth marched on the city and killed several people. It was a horrifying affair.

It is quite possible that Oscar knew some of those involved in the riot. What does it say about the military culture he imbibed in the South Pacific? At the very least, that it was not one which formed men afraid to oppose authority. Or who were inclined to retreat from fights.

Oscar's own fights may have been taking place at home. By the first part of 1918 he and Hazel had separated. In that year's city directory Oscar is listed as living at 518½ Sixteenth Place, where his parents and younger siblings then lived. It's possible that Hazel lived there as well, but it's more likely she had gone back to live with her parents, for one of the Charlestons filed for divorce on June 26, 1918. Surely they were separated before then. The divorce case was dismissed on October 8—we do not know why—but by the next year Hazel was again living with her parents on Twenty-Fifth Street. She was working as a waitress.

Although no divorce went through in 1918, Oscar and Hazel almost certainly never lived with one another again.[51] They were finally divorced on September 15, 1921. Oscar was the filer, and Hazel did not contest it. She would later marry a man named Murphy and move to Detroit. There are no photos of Hazel, nor any documents mentioning her, in Oscar's personal photo album or scrapbook.

• • •

After the close of the 1917 season Oscar took up work as a porter and waited for spring training to arrive—or for his draft number to come up, whichever came first. His plan had been to go to Cuba again with the ABCs in February 1918. But the trip never materialized; as draft registrants, he and most of his fellow ABCs were not allowed to leave the country.

C. I. Taylor nevertheless had a productive off-season. To the delight of the team's fans he recruited John Donaldson—"the sensational crooked arm flinger"—from the All-Nations, and he brought fine outfielder Jimmie Lyons back into the fold. The underrated George Shively would be back too. Lyons, Shively, and Charleston promised to form a speedy, aggressive outfield for the 1918 edition of the ABCs—one fan later remembered that the three men "always kept the spikes sharpened, and would not hesitate to cut infielders down"—and Ben and Candy Jim Taylor, Dave Malarcher, and Specs Clark, with Frank Warfield in reserve, would constitute an excellent infield.[52] Dizzy Dismukes was planning to pitch for—and manage—the Dayton Marcos, and Dicta Johnson was in the army and stationed at Indianapolis's Camp Grant. But with Jim Jeffries back in the rotation along with curveball specialist Donaldson, this was still a fine squad—if everyone didn't get sent off to France.

On this team full of good players Oscar was now regarded as the man with the most star potential. "Oscar Charleston, who is only 21 years old," reported the *Indianapolis Star*, "has been proclaimed by experts as one of the greatest colored ball players in the game. He is the type of outfielder that gets almost everything that comes his way. He also has an uncanny ability to judge the [batter's] driving power and where he is going to hit it."[53]

Charleston and his teammates gathered at Northwestern Park on March 25, 1918, for their first workout of the year. Taylor announced with patriotic pride that the players "were sent through exercises with the medicine ball and went through other exercises used by the United States in conditioning its soldiers."[54] CI had a good feeling about this team. He let it be known that he thought it his best yet, maybe the finest ever to represent Indianapolis, black or white. Perhaps it was because of the high expectations he formed during the spring that as the 1918 season went on, CI acted more and more erratically.

He seemed to lose his equilibrium as his obsession with besting Rube Foster's American Giants reached Ahabian proportions.

Dismukes's Marcos would be the ABCS' first opponents of the year. It doesn't seem to have surprised anyone that Dismukes, twenty-eight, had been given the reins of a club. Despite the implications of his nickname, Dizzy was a highly reliable, college-educated man who would later write a column for the *Pittsburgh Courier* and ultimately become the secretary for J. L. Wilkinson's Kansas City Monarchs. He had the intelligence and leadership abilities to be a successful manager, and Oscar, among others, seems to have looked up to him.

The *Indianapolis Star* predicted that the Marcos, though young, would give the ABCS "a hard run."[55] Nothing could have been further from the truth. On Sunday, April 7, 1918, at Washington Park, Dismukes—tight, overamped, or simply ineffective—laid a colossal egg. The ABCS ambushed him for twenty-one runs (Dismukes nevertheless pitched all nine innings), Malarcher and Ben Taylor gathering five hits each. Oscar had two hits off his old friend, including a long home run. A week later, in Dayton, the ABCS destroyed the Marcos again, 13–0, all of those runs again coming against Dismukes. The next day they shut out the Marcos, 5–0; Dismukes, mercifully, did not pitch. That game featured a splendid shoestring catch by Shively in left and "a running catch by Charleston in deep center field."[56]

Charleston started off the 1918 season fast and never looked back. In the first couple of months of the season Taylor placed him third in the lineup, and Oscar usually justified the position. In May, when the Cuban Stars came to town for five games, he went 9 for 22. (It is worth noting that the opening doubleheader took place in front of four thousand fans, which apparently was a *low* number. The *Chicago Defender* noted that a "big parade uptown" had depressed turnout. Moreover, it had "kept many of the whites from coming out," a comment that indicates that even in these early, non-league years, matchups between teams of color drew a significant number of white fans. Indeed, the *Freeman* noted on at least one occasion during this period that nearly as many whites as blacks attended ABCs games.)[57] In two games against a strong white semipro team from Anderson, Indiana, Charleston led the ABCs to wins by going 4 for 8. He hit two doubles, including one down the right field line just as Shively dashed home in a steal attempt, knocked in another run on a long sacrifice fly to center, and made a "running catch [that] was one of the best plays ever seen" in Anderson.[58]

Military mobilization made for new opponents. Camp Grant had a team, for example, and so did the aviation repair department stationed at the Indianapolis Motor Speedway. Taylor, ever ready to be generous in support of the American cause, scheduled two games against the latter club for Saturday, June 1, and Sunday, June 2, at Washington Park. The proceeds would allow soldiers stationed at the speedway to buy athletic equipment.

The ABCs won the Saturday game, 4–1. Sunday's game, as was the custom, would feature more pomp and circumstance. Prior to the game an airplane repaired by the boys at the speedway would fly over the park and drop baseballs trailing long streamers onto the field. Captain Edwin P. Webb, who like virtually every other person on earth in 1918 had never before flown in an airplane, would do the ball dropping, and Major Guy L. Gearhart, ranking officer at the speedway, would take care of the flying. "The fans will be given a first-hand example [of] how American aviators are dropping bombs onto German lines at the present time in France," promised the *Star*.[59] But things went terribly wrong.

The game was scheduled to begin at 3:30. At 3:15, as Oscar and the other players warmed up on the field and fans found their seats, Major Gearhart's airplane came into sight at an altitude of about one thousand feet. All eyes looked up to watch for the promised baseballs. The first one thrown by Webb missed the stadium completely. He tried again, but this time the streamer attached to the ball got wound around part of the plane. Webb was now 0 for 2. Gearhart, the pilot, decided to give it a try.

Not wanting to get the streamer tied up with the plane again, he heaved a ball as hard as he could. It cleared the plane, but the force of his throw knocked the small machine off balance. It turned into the wind, went sideways, and started to go into a spin. Gearhart tried with all his might to regain control.

The first thing the two thousand spectators in the stadium noticed was the strange sound of the motor. Then they realized the plane was headed toward the ground. At first no one thought much of this; Major Gearhart was probably pulling some kind of flying stunt, they thought. But when they saw the plane go into a spinning nose dive, they knew this was no show. When he first lost control, Gearhart's immediate fear was that the plane would crash into the crowded grandstand. So as he realized he wasn't going to be able to keep the machine in the air, he did everything he could to steer it away from the stands and onto the diamond. In this, at least, he had success. The players, temporarily frozen in mute horror by the unfolding scene above them, finally grasped that they were standing very much in harm's way. As the plane came spinning toward them, they furiously scrambled for shelter. Moments later, before the horrified eyes of the thousands on hand, the airplane smashed into the field just behind second base.[60]

Players from both teams rushed to the wreckage. They extricated Major Gearhart, who, miraculously, was alive. Nothing could be done for Captain Webb. He was dead.[61]

• • •

Not long after this incident C. I. Taylor began acting strangely. Following the tragedy at Washington Park, the ABCs traveled to Chicago for their first game of the year with the American Giants. Donaldson started, and the ABCs were defeated, 5–2. The game meant comparatively little; there would be many more games against Foster's club as the season progressed. But Taylor was furious with his newly acquired southpaw, despite the fact that he had pitched very well to that point. Taylor slashed

Donaldson's salary from $250 per month—reportedly the highest salary in black baseball—to just $100 per month. It was a rash decision that would soon have consequences.[62]

Then things got weirder. After a brawl in Peoria, Illinois—sparked when the home team's mouthy catcher heckled Charleston from his spot behind the plate, a decision that swiftly resulted in Oscar's punching him in the head—the ABCs headed to Cincinnati for a series with the Cuban Stars. But CI didn't go with them. He had abruptly decided to quit as manager, saying that his business interests had become too pressing and important for him also to manage the team. Just like that, Candy Jim, his brother, was handed the managerial reins. Jim managed a few games, and then CI announced he was back—indeed, he claimed (even more oddly) that he had never really quit.

In the last of a long June series of games against the Cuban Stars, Charleston committed an error in the second inning that led to an unearned run. He misplayed another ball later in the game for his second error. Oscar had been brilliant in the field and at the plate all season long, but after the second error CI decided to humiliate him by taking him off the field in the middle of the game and putting shortstop Specs Clark in center. As far as we can tell, these were only Oscar's second and third errors of the year. CI also started batting Charleston lower in the batting order, usually fifth or even seventh, even though for the seven games against the Cuban Stars in June for which we have box scores Oscar went 11 for 28.

The great John Donaldson didn't need this kind of drama. By the end of June he had jumped to the Brooklyn Royal Giants. String Bean Williams, who had played for CI on the West Baden Sprudels and on the ABCs prior to Oscar's debut in 1915, arrived to replace him. Dismukes, too, was lured away from the Marcos after CI saw the American Giants needed eleven innings to beat him. The obsessive and suddenly mercurial CI must have been getting on everyone's nerves. But Oscar didn't let it affect his play. When in July the ABCs played the Cuban Stars in Anderson, Indiana, Charleston hit two home runs in one inning. At that point only three Major League players had ever accomplished the feat. Everyone was amazed.

Around this time it looked like the federal government would soon put a stop to weekday baseball by requiring all able-bodied men to either work or fight. Taylor didn't want that, of course; he and Rube Foster had made big plans to go barnstorming together in the East, hitting cities usually never reached, like Pittsburgh and Washington. But if weekday baseball *was* ruled out, Taylor had a plan: the whole ABCs team would go, en masse, "to the farm" and play ball only on the weekends. "This announcement was made by Manager Taylor last night," reported the *Indianapolis Star*. "Taylor said that any farmer wishing the services of fourteen able-bodied men may apply at the ABC baseball headquarters."[63] Who was this loopy man, and what had he done with the level-headed and clear-eyed C. I. Taylor?

Thanks in part to Washington Senators owner Clark Griffith's influence with President Woodrow Wilson, baseball was allowed to go on. The ABCs and the American Giants made their trip east, and it proved to be a smashing success. On July 27 at Pittsburgh's Forbes Field, home of the Pirates, the ABCs beat the American Giants, 16–11, in ten innings; Oscar had two doubles and a stolen base. They then played Foster's men to a 7–7, eleven-inning tie at Forbes. In that contest "Clark, at short, and Charleston, in center, turned in some circus fielding stunts," and Oscar complemented his play in center with two hits and two steals.[64] He also tried to score from second on a ground ball that had bounced off the third baseman's glove and caromed toward the middle of the diamond. On a wild dash that only he or Ty Cobb would have attempted, wrote Ira Lewis of the *Pittsburgh Courier*, Oscar was nipped at the plate by a perfect throw from shortstop José Méndez, despite his headfirst "fadeaway" slide.[65] In a third game, won by the ABCs, 8–7, Charleston's swinging bunt in the top of the ninth drove in the winning run. He had several other infield hits in that game, stole a base, and even managed to score from second on a bunt.[66] Oscar's speed was as remarkable as his defensive instincts and his power. One local white reporter was impressed: "A colored youngster with winged heels was behind the slickest swinging bunt we have seen this season in the game between the fast colored teams at Forbes Field yesterday. The boy, whose name is Charleston, bats from the left side of the plate, but he engineered his dexterous play on a left-hand pitcher and fairly flew across first steps ahead of the ball."[67] Oscar clipped that notice for his scrapbook.

The two teams then moved on to Washington DC, where despite increasingly widespread feeling that ballplayers ought to be doing more for the war effort, eight thousand fans turned out to the Senators' home park for a Sunday matchup and saw the American Giants prevail, 6–1. It was a gala affair for the city's African American community. Various dignitaries were present, including officials from the Treasury Department, the War Department, and Howard University. "Many ladies in bright costumes lent color and beauty to the picture," observed the *Chicago Defender*'s reporter, and prior to the game both Foster and Taylor paid their formal respects to the fans and received hearty ovations.[68]

Then, in early August, it was back to Chicago for a doubleheader against the Cuban Stars. In the first game Charleston knocked in all three ABCs runs by hitting a bases-loaded triple. In the second game he again hit a triple, this time with two men on base. The man was on fire.

In all, the ABCs played sixteen games on their big road trip of July and early August 1918, going 8-5-3. One man had impressed above all others, said the *Star*: Oscar Charleston, "the fleet-footed centerfielder" who not only "made several wonderful catches," but also "hit the ball hard in every contest."[69] Back at home Charleston maintained his stellar play. In an August 18 doubleheader versus the Red Caps, not only did Oscar, now batting cleanup, go 4 for 7 with a double, but he also stole two bases (including third) and again made a jaw-dropping play in center: "Probably one of the greatest catches ever made in Washington Park was made in the third inning, when Charleston stabbed a drive in right-center that was labeled three bases," reported the *Star*. "Charleston was away with the crack of the bat and by wonderful speed reached the ball with his gloved hand and held on. . . . He was given a huge round of cheers."[70]

And with that, Oscar Charleston's superb 1918 baseball season came to a sudden end. After the games against the Red Caps the Great War finally caught up with him. Word came down that six ABCs players had been drafted: Lyons, Malarcher, Dismukes, Jeffries, Clark, and Charleston. The black press reported that the men were happy to serve, which may or may not have been true, but their manager, despite his patriotism, was probably less than thrilled. C. I. Taylor's ABCs were decimated, and he seemed to be losing his grip. The ABCs finished out the season, but neither the quality of play nor the crowds were the same.

• • •

On August 22 Oscar was welcomed back to the army. He was given the rank of corporal, assigned to the 163rd Depot Brigade, and sent along with his ABCs mates to Camp Dodge in Johnston, Iowa, site of the famous aerial photograph showing eighteen thousand men in uniform forming a human Statue of Liberty (the photo was taken in July, so it does not include Oscar). Two months later, on October 23, he was selected to attend the Colored Students Infantry Officers Training School at Camp Pike in Arkansas.

The school at Camp Pike had been created as the result of black protests—from inside and outside the military—against various rules and practices viewed, correctly, as intended to limit the number of black soldiers being trained as officers or promoted to officer ranks once trained. Many whites, particularly at installations located in the South, resented the idea of blacks becoming officers, and they found repugnant the notion of saluting them. Some flat-out refused to do so. This attitude was reflected in that of local authorities, who would sometimes arrest black officers traveling with white parties for breaking Jim Crow laws, even when the officers were in uniform.⁷¹

A man of Charleston's temper and pride must have confronted any number of challenging and insulting situations while at Camp Pike. A few years later, after Charles Young, the army's highest-ranking black officer, died, Oscar placed in his scrapbook an article discussing the racial insults and discrimination Young had faced at West Point. Perhaps Young's experiences in the military reminded Oscar of his own. In any case, Oscar seems to have successfully navigated the fraught situation at Camp Pike. No doubt he relished knowing that being selected for the training school meant his superiors held a high opinion of his intelligence and leadership abilities.

Charleston never became an officer. The armistice, signed on November 11, came too soon for that. He was honorably discharged on December 3, fortunate to have avoided the bombs and bullets that killed, among so many millions of others, former Negro Leaguers like Captain James Smith, whose letter sending his best wishes to Foster, Taylor, and their teams was published in the *Chicago Defender* on August 17, 1918, shortly after Smith's death.⁷² But by being sent to Camp Pike, Oscar had at least proved one thing: that outside of baseball, as well as inside, he was on the rise.

• • •

In his third year of ball in the States, 1917, Oscar had tantalized with his abilities. Everyone had agreed he was a comer. In 1918, as a twenty-one-year-old, he began truly to fulfill his potential. The high praise given his play in game accounts is only reinforced by the statistics reconstructed by contemporary researchers. Their work reveals that in forty games and 171 plate appearances against top competition, Oscar hit .390, with a .437 on-base percentage and a .604 slugging percentage. He had three home runs, eight triples, and eight doubles—keep in mind that we are still in the Deadball Era—along with thirteen stolen bases. If we extrapolate those statistics to a 162-game season, we get twelve home runs, thirty-two triples, thirty-two doubles, and fifty-three stolen bases. That same year Babe Ruth led the American League with a .555 slugging percentage. Charleston's fellow Hoosier Edd Roush led the National League by slugging a mere .455. The Majors' on-base-percentage leaders were Ty Cobb at .440 and Heinie Groh at .395. Cobb led the AL with a .382 batting average. Zack Wheat led the NL by hitting .335.

To make direct comparisons between Negro League and Major League statistics would be somewhat silly. Ruth, Cobb, and their Major League brethren faced better pitching and defense, on the whole, than did Oscar and his fellow Negro Leaguers. But not *that* much better. Remember that the Charleston numbers cited here already screen out games against lower levels of competition—games played against semipro and Minor League teams.

Just how good the best black baseball teams were in 1918, relative to those in the white Majors, is difficult to say. In the next chapter we shall see that from 1920 through 1922 a middling St. Louis Negro League team that included Oscar held its own in postseason series against barnstorming Major Leaguers. A bigger sample size tells a similar story. Researcher Scott Simkus found the results of 250 games played between 1901 and 1950 in which Major League players competed against Negro Leagues squads. The black teams won 128, lost 115, and tied 7.[73]

These figures are a bit misleading, as the rest of Simkus's data show. Against all other levels of competition—military, AAA, AA, high Class A, low Class A, semipro, and college— the Major League teams posted higher winning percentages than did Negro Leagues teams, usually by more than one hundred percentage points. That sample includes 7,402 games. The conclusion to which Simkus's research points is that the average Major League team was noticeably better than the average Negro Leagues team during this period, but not by a huge margin, and that clearly the Negro Leagues offered the next highest level of competition after the Majors.[74] This was also the subjective judgment of numerous former players, both black and white (although, if anything, both black and white players tended to underestimate the quality of black baseball).[75]

To get a sense of how good Oscar Charleston had already become by 1918, compared with his Major League peers, we should probably discount his offensive statistics by no more than 10–15 percent; his numbers then would still be elite. His defense needn't be discounted at all; those skills would have been elite no matter where he played. It is not unreasonable, then, to believe that by 1918 the youthful Charleston would have been one of the top five or ten players in the white Major Leagues.

In the Negro Leagues Oscar's 1918 season made him one of two or three men who could claim to be the best position player. Probably his top competition for that title was Cristóbal Torriente, who was twenty-five and in the early prime of his career as the 1919 season approached.[76] For the previous few years Torriente had played with one of the touring teams featuring Cuban and other foreign players. Now both he and Oscar were headed for Chicago, where they would join forces with the indomitable Rube Foster.

CHAPTER 4

Star, 1919–1922

THE ARMISTICE SIGNED AT Compiègne between the Allies and Germany on November 11, 1918, brought the horrific slaughter of the Great War to an end, but the Treaty of Versailles still lay six months in the future. Many Negro League players lingered in Europe. As the 1919 calendar advanced, it wasn't clear when, or where, they would return. Race riots like those in Houston in December 1917, the rising popularity of the reorganized Ku Klux Klan, the acceleration of the Great Migration of southern blacks to the North—the cessation of hostilities in the filthy trenches of the old world meant no end to hatred and tumult in the new. Everything was up in the air.

C. I. Taylor wasn't immediately equal to the situation. He had acted erratically during the 1918 season, and when the war ended, he hadn't yet recovered his balance. In the winter of 1918–19 Dave Malarcher—Taylor's young, promising, college-educated infielder—showed up at his door. Malarcher had been discharged from the army with sixty dollars and the clothes on his back. CI, he figured, could help. "Well here I am back home," said Malarcher to his old boss. "I want to go and see my mother and my girlfriend. I've been away a long time from the folks down South and I need seventy-five dollars." CI responded by offering him an ABCS contract for 1919 at $120 per month, but he hesitated to lend Malarcher any cash. Funds were probably low; many ABCS games and many paying customers had been lost the previous summer. "Naturally when you put out money like that in the winter time, you just don't know what will be the result," CI said, in the manner of a man who was a bit tight, worried about his bank account, or both.[1] "Let me think about it."[2]

Rube Foster had been thinking about it since the previous autumn. He had even sent a letter to Malarcher—along with who knows how many others—while the young player was in France, telling him he'd like him to join his club when Malarcher returned stateside. So the morning after CI put him off in his quest for a loan, Malarcher hopped on a train to Chicago, where Foster, sitting behind a rolltop desk at his Vernon Avenue home, warmly welcomed him. Foster and Malarcher exchanged small talk before Malarcher came out with it. "Well, the thing I came to tell you is I'm just out of the Army and I don't have any money, and I want to go to see my mother and my sweetheart in New Orleans. I would like to borrow seventy-five dollars."[3] Foster reached in his desk, counted out the money, and handed it to Malarcher, no questions asked. "That is when I became a Giant," Malarcher later recalled.[4]

Actually, Malarcher didn't become a Giant—not right away. For Foster had hatched a scheme whereby he would essentially field two teams in 1919: the Chicago American Giants and the Detroit Stars. Foster had taken note of the crowds his club had drawn in Detroit when it had played there in recent years. The dynamic city was growing rapidly, especially its black population. Establishing an outpost in Detroit could only benefit him financially. And if he ever got his dream of a formal black baseball league off the ground, Detroit would surely have to be part of it. As usual, Foster was ahead of the curve.

C. I. Taylor responded by sitting out the 1919 season entirely. One imagines that as he realized the shrewd way in which Foster had used the wartime caesura to strengthen his forces and expand his empire, the despondency to which CI began to succumb in 1918 became even deeper. Thus, whether they had been drafted or not, all the old ABCs now had to find a new team. Many of them migrated to Chicago. Soon, Foster had more players than he knew what to do with. At ten o'clock on the cold

Monday morning of March 31, 1919, he gathered forty of them—including Charleston, Malarcher (to whom Foster had offered $150 per month), and Frank Warfield, all members of the 1918 ABCS—at Schorling Park, located on the corner of Thirty-Ninth and Shields on the city's South Side, to work out and discover for whom they would be playing that season: Foster's American Giants or Pete Hill's Detroit Stars.

A contemporaneous *Chicago Defender* report implies that the question of who went where was determined like a sandlot game: Foster and Hill stood there and picked their men, turn by turn. On the one hand, it's hard to believe that a controlling personality like Foster would have left such a matter to chance, so perhaps the teams' compositions had been determined earlier. On the other hand, Foster was wise enough to know it was in his interest to have a strong rival—especially when he had a business stake in that rival's success—and he had played with and managed his old friend Pete Hill, then thirty-six, since 1904, when the two had been members of the Philadelphia Giants.

However it came about, by the end of the day both managers had excellent teams. Hill's Stars featured Bruce Petway, Warfield, and Malarcher. The core of Foster's club consisted of Jessie Barber in right, Bill Francis at third, captain Bingo DeMoss at second, Leroy Grant at first, and Charleston and Torriente in the outfield.[5] After choosing sides, the two teams spent the next two weeks being drilled by Foster in the details of their craft: precisely how to field, how to slide, how to tag. Opening day was less than two weeks away.[6]

The press expected Torriente to man center for the American Giants when the season opened, with Oscar patrolling left.[7] Cristóbal, a playboy who loved the night life, had a big arm and an even bigger thirst—alcoholism shortened his career and probably contributed to his death in 1938, when he was just forty-four years old.[8] He had been a regular center fielder for his traveling Cuban clubs since 1914, and no less than Charleston he had a reputation as perhaps the black game's finest outfielder. But contrary to expectation (and to the claims of some later historians), it took Rube Foster less than two weeks of practice to determine his best outfield combination consisted of the fast, rangy Charleston in center and the strong-armed Torriente in left.[9]

Those were their positions on opening day, Sunday, April 13, when the American Giants met a white club called Rogers Park at the American Giants' home grounds. Foster's guess that the end of the war, the North's swelling African American population (the population of predominantly black Bronzeville, just to the east of Schorling Park, went from thirty thousand to sixty thousand in the 1910s), and fatter paychecks for working-class Americans would mean big business for black baseball proved correct. An estimated crowd of eight thousand turned out for the game, which meant that about three thousand people had to be accommodated on the field. Hundreds of white fans were present to cheer on the Rogers Park team. Tom Johnson led the American Giants to victory, 3–0, and Charleston had two hits in his Giants debut, including a double.[10]

In a May game against a team from Kenosha, Wisconsin, Charleston and DeMoss demonstrated the way a Foster club—or a Taylor club, for that matter—ran the bases. After Charleston lined a single to center with Bingo on first and a man on second, both men took an extra base when the throw went home. When the next batter grounded to the mound, Bingo and Oscar took off as soon as the ball was hit. The surprised pitcher lost his composure and overthrew the catcher, allowing both aggressive base runners to score.[11]

Twenty thousand fans reportedly turned out on June 1, 1919—Decoration Day weekend—to see the American Giants take on the Cuban Stars. The latter won, 5–4, in eleven innings (Torriente, amazingly, managed to be thrown out on the base paths five times).[12] Monstrous crowds kept showing up for Sunday games all season, no matter where the American Giants played: fifteen thousand for a home game against the Detroit Stars in June;[13] ten thousand in Darby, Pennsylvania, in August for a game against Hilldale;[14] twenty-five thousand in New York that same month for a doubleheader against the Treat 'Em Roughs at Dyckman Oval in Harlem.[15]

In front of all those fans Oscar Charleston continued to establish himself as a star. As had become the norm, it was his defense that was most remarked upon in the press. Against the Cuban Stars in July his running one-handed catch of a liner was singled out for mention.[16] In the first game against the Treat 'Em Roughs he made what one reporter described as a "hair-raising catch . . . that set the fans talking. I'll say it was some catch."[17] Against the Dayton Marcos—once again featuring Oscar's friend Dizzy Dismukes—Charleston "as usual came through with the fielding feature of the game when he stabbed a hard hit line drive with one hand that was ticketed for the score board."[18]

Foster also made sure to push Oscar on the base paths. One such instance, in a game versus white semipros, was described in detail by a local sportswriter:

Oscar banged out a slashing single through second base territory in the fourth inning; urged on by "Rube," he stole second, and on the throw down to catch him, the lad was forced to make a long hook slide, landing on his back; the ball rolled out to center field and before Charleston had cleared the ground, the fielder had the ball up; urged on by "Rube," Charleston sprang to his feet and made a break for third; he gained that base after one of the speediest exhibitions of running and injury-defying hook slides ever executed upon a diamond. If that boy is not pushed into a severe injury, we predict that he will shatter all things ever attempted on the base paths. After acquiring third, Oscar romped home on a throw down to second, and beat the return of the ball so far that the former big leaguers who compose the Fairbanks-Morse team were made to look like common back-lotters.[19]

The bat was no less spectacular. No one calculated such numbers at the time, but in forty-six games versus top competition in 1919 Oscar compiled a .400/.460/.650 slash line in 206 plate appearances. Only the truly remarkable Pete Hill (.396/.488/.892) fared better. In the Majors Babe Ruth was heralding the death of the Deadball Era with a mind-blowing twenty-nine home runs. The Babe hit one homer in every nineteen plate appearances in 1919. Charleston hit eight homers, or one in every twenty-six times at the plate, and threw in sixteen stolen bases and fantastic center field defense to boot. (Hill, defying age, hit sixteen home runs in just 165 plate appearances.) By the offensive WAR metric, which takes into account base running as well as hitting, Oscar's 1919 season rates as the best compiled to that point in black baseball history. His teammate Torriente compiled the fourth-best season ever.[20]

The *Chicago Defender* was far from unbiased, but in its judgment Foster had in 1919 succeeded in molding Charleston into the "greatest player in the world; he has no superior, even outclassing the great Cobb." Foster had "patiently developed Charleston's natural abilities" and, more important, had "cooled his temper, so much so that the fans idolize him. . . . Fans, take the *Defender* dope—when you see Charleston with the American Giants you will see the greatest player in the world, barring nobody."[21]

Despite Charleston's efforts, Pete Hill's Detroit Stars put up a slightly better record than Foster's American Giants in 1919. Hill won the season series against Foster as well. The Stars and the American Giants were the top two clubs in the West by a fair margin, but since Foster effectively controlled both teams, their competition lacked the heat that used to characterize Foster's rivalry with C. I. Taylor's ABCs. At least twice Foster even loaned Charleston to Hill's club.

Perhaps Charleston didn't mind getting out of Chicago for those games. The city's racial environment was less than hospitable. A week-long riot had broken out on July 27, 1919, when an African American boy named Eugene Williams drifted on a railroad tie into the waters of an informally segregated beach. A white man began to chuck stones at Williams and other black swimmers. One throw struck Williams in the forehead, causing him to fall off and drown. In the confused rage and violence that followed, much of it instigated by ethnic Irish gangs, thirty-eight people were killed, including twenty-three blacks. Chicago's South Side, where most of the city's African Americans lived, took the brunt of the hostility. The American Giants were in Detroit, luckily, when the riot started. Some of their later home games were canceled or moved to Detroit, but otherwise Foster's team and Schorling Park escaped the damage.[22]

After the American Giants' regular season ended and the team's neighbors from Comiskey Park got to work throwing the World Series, Oscar headed back to Indianapolis.[23] Although his marriage had foundered, Oscar was glad to be home. He hadn't been happy in Chicago. His discontent may have had something to do with the loss of his father, for at some point in 1919 Thomas Charleston died. He was fifty-one or fifty-two years old. No death certificate has been found, nor any newspaper announcement of his death.

• • •

With the baseball season over, Oscar took a job as a chauffeur. (The previous offseason, after his discharge from the army, he had worked briefly as a porter.) He lived with his mother and five of his siblings at 732 West Twelfth Avenue, the same north-of-Indiana-Avenue neighborhood the Charlestons had called home since 1901. With Thomas dead, and Roy, Berl, and Casper all out of the house, surely Oscar did what he could to contribute to the family's income. So did everyone else. Oscar's mother, Mary, took in laundry. Shedrick worked at the Indiana School for the Blind. Clarissa did housework. Thomas Jr. labored as a porter. Only Katherine and Bennie, thirteen and twelve years old, respectively, when 1920 arrived—were still in school.

Oscar worked and waited for what the next season would bring. Did he sense that his craft had reached an inflection point? Baseball was fast becoming more professionalized, more lucrative, more middle class, more oriented around power, and even more popular. Ruth, not Cobb, was becoming the face of the game for white America. Charleston would fill the same role for the nation's African Americans.

· · ·

Today, baseball is stereotyped as a sleepier sport suited for more discriminating palates. One hundred years ago it was universally considered an exciting, fast-paced affair perfectly accessible to working-class sensibilities and pocketbooks. In the late 1910s, a ticket to see a game between two top black teams cost about twenty-five cents in the bleachers or thirty-five cents in the grandstand. Most fans were be-hatted males, though not exclusively, and black, also not exclusively. Spectators were neither passive nor quiet; they were active participants in the action. During the game—which rarely lasted more than two hours—they stood and cheered frequently, and just as frequently they jeered umpires and players. At least part of their passion could be traced to the fact that many had bets on the game. Then, too, many took in the game while drinking beer or, more often, something stronger they had brought themselves or acquired under the stands. Fist fights and gunplay were not unknown.[24] And sometimes, if their passions overran their better judgment, fans pelted players and umpires with bottles, food, and even seat cushions and chairs. When that happened, players were not reluctant to climb into the stands and pummel their detractors—if those detractors hadn't already jumped onto the field themselves.[25]

The biggest game day was Sunday, which usually featured a doubleheader. This was the most respectable day on which to take in a game, and therefore there were usually more women and families in the stands. Until 1919, when crowds began to grow dramatically, a few thousand folks typically showed up for a Sunday doubleheader in cities like Chicago, New York, or

Indianapolis. Games usually started at 3:00 or 3:30 on week-days, a time that allowed many working men to see the first pitch and still get home in time for dinner. Sunday doubleheaders started an hour or two earlier. Many a contest was called on account of darkness.

Black teams' uniforms and equipment were not appreciably different from those of white teams. Negro Leagues clubs wore the same kinds of tiny gloves, donned the same heavy flannel uniforms and leather shoes, and used the same bats. The game itself was fast and rough, even violent. Fights between players, and between players and umpires, were not at all uncommon. Runners slid into bases high and hard. Fielders made sure base runners knew they had been tagged. Pitchers had no compunction about establishing their ownership of the plate. If a batter hit a pitcher hard in his first two at bats, he could expect to be knocked down on his third. Perhaps more than once.

The poor umpires, with no backing from a centralized, powerful league, were often the targets of abuse. Faced with a profound incentive to favor the home team on close calls, the less sturdy often buckled. Most umps were white, and their color may have been their primary protection. It was common for those associated with black baseball to lament the lack of black umpires.[26] The lack of supply could have been related to the fact that black umpires were extremely vulnerable to abuse. Who would sign up for such a thankless task? Oscar himself once relayed a story indicating just how rough the umps had it, owing to intense players like him. He was in St. Louis with the ABCs in the early 1920s when an umpire, who was black, made a call Oscar didn't care for. "Stop robbing or I'll knock your block off!" Oscar shouted in the man's face. But this umpire had come prepared. "No, no, Mr. Charleston," he said, reaching into his shirt to reveal a pistol. "You wouldn't be a damn fool, would you?"[27] Multiple umpires, in fact, had reputations for packing heat when on the job.[28]

With rosters typically carrying only thirteen to sixteen players, virtually no professional or medical treatment available, no disabled list, and no guaranteed money, a man had to be tough—very tough!—to last in black baseball. He played through any injury he possibly could. If he was a regular, days off during the season were rare.

The pre-1920 ball was "dead," not so much because it was different from that used later by the big leagues (1920 conventionally marking the beginning of the lively ball era) but mostly because it was rarely thrown out of play, with the result that by the end of a game it was softer and often slightly misshapen. Only the very strongest batters could hit it far; that is why home runs made such an impression on observers and why small-ball strategy ruled the day. Every advantage went to pitchers, who, with no batter's eye in the background and no lights overhead in the deepening gloam, got to use a scuffed, dark, squishy ball—and could cover it with spit too. The only thing the batter had going for him was the fact that the pitcher may have thrown 130 pitches the previous day—or even in the first game of that day's doubleheader. The man on the mound had perhaps hurled a few hundred pitches that week alone. Fresh arms were few and far between.

Strikeouts and walks were comparatively rare; the aim was to put the ball in play. The teams best at executing in key situations were said to be playing "scientific baseball," the style embraced and honed by innovative managers like Foster and Taylor. "Scientific" ball teams bunted, stole, hit and ran, and used fine bat control to spray the ball where the fielders weren't. They executed fancy plays to move over runners. For example, with a runner on second a batter might square to bunt and the runner begin to move toward third. If the third baseman charged too hard and far, the batter would pull back at the last second and allow the runner to simply steal third with no one covering. If the third baseman held back, the batter would lay down the bunt, sacrificing the runner over and, if he was fast, possibly getting an infield hit.

Before 1920 the black game was generally referred to as "semi-pro" by the press. The label implies that there wasn't a lot of money to be made by anyone—at least if we can take owners like Rube Foster at face value. But during the six months of the season, and comparatively speaking, players did pretty well. They typically made between $100 and $250 per month at a time when the average working man's wage (for all races) was $50–$100 per month.[29] Bill "Plunk" Drake, Charleston's team-mate in 1921, remembered thinking that his $100-per-month salary was a "fortune," given prices at the time. "A T-bone steak was a quarter—biscuits a nickel extra. And if you wanted to eat soul food, why that was even less."[30] All the travel, normally by train, had its rewards too. (The rigors of the road would actually get worse later, when bus and car travel became the norm.) The well-dressed players, especially when they traveled by Pullman car (as Foster's American Giants usually did), gained prestige and were looked upon with admiration by their black contemporaries.[31] Young men who had grown up rarely venturing more than a few miles from their homes discovered new faces, new places, new social and existential possibilities. As Quincy Trouppe recalled, traveling the circuit of the Negro Leagues "revealed new vistas that were more educational than a doctor's degree."[32]

Of course, the travel was also tedious (most players passed the time playing poker), and the majority of hotels, even in the North, were segregated. The quality of black hotels was not infrequently atrocious, especially in the smaller towns, with bed-bugs, lice, and uncomfortable temperatures among the most common complaints. A lack of funds, a shortage of rooms, or both meant that players frequently slept two to a bed. Many a night was spent on the train or even outside. Whatever its compensatory advantages, everyday life in the Negro Leagues was no picnic.

Until 1920 black baseball was also characterized by its comparative lack of formal organization. There was no league to establish rules, determine a fair schedule, keep standings and statistics, hire umpires, promote games, prevent players from jumping teams, or build up a progressively larger fan base for member clubs. In 1920 Rube Foster, frustrated for years by these evident deficiencies, finally changed that.

• • •

On February 12, 1920, Foster convened a meeting of the leading owners of western black baseball clubs, along with a handful of top black sportswriters. They gathered at the Paseo YMCA in Kansas City, a couple of blocks away from the not-yet-famous intersection of Eighteenth and Vine. C. I. Taylor was present, along with the *Indianapolis Freeman*'s Elwood Knox and other representatives from Detroit, St. Louis, Chicago, Dayton, and Kansas City. Foster stunned them all by announcing that he had incorporated a new National Negro Baseball League in the states of Illinois, Michigan, Ohio, Pennsylvania, New York, and Maryland. His next announcement was even more surprising. Knowing that his rivals would suspect this new league was intended merely to benefit Rube himself, he said that he was prepared to have the newspaper men present at the meeting not only draft the league's constitution and bylaws, but also reshuffle the players on each team so there would be league-wide competitive balance. This seemed too good a deal for CI and the other owners to pass up. Rube's plan went forward, and he proved his good faith by allowing his young star Oscar Charleston to be transferred back to the Indianapolis ABCs.

Thanks to his old rival, then, C. I. Taylor was back in the game. His ABCs would be one of eight entries in the 1920 Negro National League (NNL), along with the Chicago American Giants, the Chicago Giants, the Cuban Stars of Havana, the Dayton Marcos, the Detroit Stars, the St. Louis Giants, and the Kansas City Monarchs.[33] The ABCs would play at the Indianapolis Indians' home grounds, Washington Park, and feature many of the same players that had formed the core of CI's fine ABCs teams of the 1910s, including Ben Taylor, Jim Jeffries, Specs Clark, Russell Powell, Dizzy Dismukes, and Dicta Johnson. The Indianapolis press promoted the squad as a likely contender for the league title. With Charleston in the fold there was little reason to think otherwise. Oscar was now clearly the man. Writers were beginning to refer to him as the "Black Ty Cobb" and as "one of the greatest colored players the country has ever known."[34] It was considered an act of extraordinary selflessness, and proof of his commitment to the common good of black baseball, that Rube Foster had let go such a "great drawing card," a man "idolized by the fans."[35] Indeed, sometime in 1920 a group of Chicago businessmen would travel to Indianapolis to present Charleston with a token of their esteem.[36]

League play would start in May. Taylor, eager to have his club in peak form by then, took eighteen players to Birmingham on March 29 for a month of spring training and exhibition games in the South. Once his crew was settled in Alabama, Taylor implemented a typically grueling spring training regimen. Players left for practice at eight in the morning. They would walk to the park, jog around the grounds a few times, and grind through a two-hour workout consisting of various baseball drills. After a break for lunch and showers, they would return to the field for an intrasquad game at two o'clock.

It was a schedule that probably did little to endear CI to his men, but it did result in victories. The ABCs laid waste to the South. Defying the demeaning travel conditions and disadvantages posed by Jim Crow, the ABCs went 17-1-2 against southern competition in the spring of 1920, drawing large crowds consisting of both black and white fans in New Orleans, Montgomery, Atlanta, and elsewhere. Oscar hit at least two home runs in this stretch. He also hurt his leg somewhere along the way. One might have expected him to get off to a slow start when the league season began. One would have been wrong.

The NNL officially commenced with a doubleheader between the ABCs and the Chicago Giants on May 2 at Washington Park.

Charleston went 1 for 4 in the first game of the historic affair, won by the ABCS, 4–2, in front of a crowd of six thousand–plus rooters "frantically enthused" by the return of their hometown club and the advent of a professional black baseball league.[37] In the second game Charleston laced a two-run triple in the second inning. When he came home to score on Ben Taylor's single, the excited fans proved their devotion by showering him with money. The ABCS won, 11–4.

Oscar scored another impromptu purse a week later in front of a home crowd of ten thousand. The ABCS were ahead, 4–2, in the ninth. In the top of the inning the Cuban Stars had two men on and two outs when José LeBlanc launched a missile to deep center. Oscar, two great catches already to his credit, turned and sprinted. An impossible distance later, with his back still to the plate, he leaped and snagged the ball out of the air. The fans were so elated that a number jumped out of their seats and ran to center field, where they congratulated their hero with fistfuls of money.[38]

Oscar had four hits during that day's doubleheader, and he went 8 for 21 and stole two bases in the first six games of league play—all with an ailing leg. Yet as good as he was on the base paths and as lethal as his bat had become, it was the glove that was building his legend. Against the Dayton Marcos on May 23 "Charleston made a sensational one-handed catch of a fly ball after a long run which seemed to take the 'heart' out of the visitors."[39] A few days later Charleston played so well in a contest versus the Monarchs in Kansas City that the *Kansas City Sun's* correspondent reported Oscar had "demonstrated the fact that he could possibly cover all three of the [outfield] positions at once."[40] Back home, folks came not just from Indianapolis, but also from outlying towns like Muncie, Kokomo, Anderson, and Logansport in the hope of seeing Charleston do something spectacular in center field.

By August Oscar's feats had led the Indianapolis press to find a better comparison among Major Leaguers than Ty Cobb. Oscar was now the "Black Tris Speaker."[41] In addition to being a better fielder, Speaker was also having a significantly better year than Cobb at the plate, so the comparison was all the more appropriate. The NNL wasn't yet in the habit of posting statistics, but we now know that Charleston put up a .353/.418/.517 slash line in 1920, which gave him an OPS (on-base percentage plus slugging percentage) 76 percent better than the league average. He also stole twenty bases. Speaker, who racked up doubles relatively easily thanks to the short, high right field fence in Cleveland's League Park, truly had nothing on him.[42]

Oscar was able to test himself against white big leaguers in early October. After the ABCs had finished their league season against the Monarchs in Kansas City, he and teammates James Raleigh "Biz" Mackey and Connie Day stopped in St. Louis to join the St. Louis Giants for a midweek two-game series against a barnstorming club consisting of St. Louis Cardinals regulars. The St. Louis Giants had finished sixth in the NNL at 32-40. The Cardinals had finished the National League season at 75-79 under manager Branch Rickey, good for fifth place. In these barnstorming games they were without Rogers Hornsby and one other regular but were otherwise mostly intact. Oscar homered in the first inning of the first game, helping the Giants win, 5-4, in ten innings. The next day Cardinals ace Jess Haines hurled a two-hitter, Oscar went hitless and committed an error, and the Giants lost, 5-0. One wonders whether Oscar's future employer Rickey was present at one or both of these contests and if this is when the relationship between the two men began.[43]

Good as it was, neither Charleston's performance nor the midseason addition of a new star in catcher Mackey—Roy Campanella's future mentor, acquired along with several other Texans when one of Taylor's friends, the owner of the San Antonio Aces, experienced financial difficulties—was enough to lift the ABCs above fourth place in 1920. CI had to have liked the crowds, which were the biggest any of the new NNL's clubs had ever seen, but he wasn't pleased by that finish. Nor was he pleased by the attitude of his superstar, with whom he once again started to lock horns. On May 22, when the ABCs took on the Dayton Marcos in Muncie, CI benched Oscar for "indifferent playing."[44] Oscar, for his part, resented some of CI's harsh methods, and he particularly resented CI's tightfistedness with gate receipts. The friction between CI and Oscar became public during the ABCs' four-game postseason set with a team of white All-Pros. After the first two games Oscar and two other ABCs quit the team. CI lashed out in the press. Oscar, he said, was not only the trio's ringleader, but he had also caused trouble all year. The adulation of the fans had swollen his ego, and Charleston refused to be content despite drawing a "lucrative salary" augmented by "neat sums in exhibition games."[45] But Oscar was not easily steamrolled. He released his own statement, claiming that Taylor had kept half the ABCs' total share of the exhibition gate in the previous Sunday's game against the All-Pros—an unconscionably large chunk, if true—and that this meanness, "along with other disagreeable features" of playing for CI, was the reason he had left the ABCs.[46] It didn't seem like these two strong-willed men would ever get along.

• • •

Still separated from Hazel, and with his playing status for the next league season unclear, after the conclusion of the 1920 season Oscar headed to Cuba to play winter ball, this time with the Bacharach Giants. He departed from Key West on November 16. His passport application, apparently filled out by trip organizer Edward Lamar, gives his height as 5 feet 8 inches. He is described as having a high forehead, brown eyes, a straight nose, and no distinguishing marks. The attached photo shows Oscar, in a heavy, double-breasted overcoat, looking straight into the camera. The intensity of his stare is discomfiting. This was a man one crossed at some peril.

The talented Atlantic City–based Bacharach Giants were the first black baseball team to play in Cuba since the ABCs had journeyed to the island five years earlier. The squad included four men who had starred for the club during the 1920 regular season: outstanding shortstop Dick Lundy, volatile third baseman Oliver Marcell, hard-throwing Cannonball Redding, and slight right-hander Red Ryan. For the trip to Havana Lamar had added Oscar and his ABCs teammates Connie Day and Specs Clark; the tall, light-skinned, future Hall of Fame catcher Louis Santop; St. Louis Giants center fielder Charles Blackwell; and an assortment of lesser players.[47]

The Negro Leaguers arrived in Havana just days after John McGraw's New York Giants—featuring a well-paid ringer named Babe Ruth—had left. The Giants had come to play in a preseason three-team "American Series" featuring McGraw's club and Cuban teams Habana and Almendares, but the Giants didn't take these games very seriously. Everyone took full advantage of Havana's hopping nightlife. McGraw spent most of his days at the horse track. Ruth, who had hit an astounding fifty-four home runs for the Yankees in the 1920 regular season, showed up two weeks late, blew a small fortune gambling on jai alai, and then refused to play in the final contest when series officials wouldn't increase his already outrageous $1,000-per-game paycheck. Yet the Giants still managed to put up a 9-4-4 record, and the appearance of McGraw, Ruth, Frankie Frisch, and other Major League stars on the island generated a wave of enthusiasm. Ruth managed to hit two home runs, three triples, and two doubles in just nine games. The Bacharach Giants—who were slated to play a few games in the American Series themselves before joining the Cuban Professional League—had an impossible act to follow.[48]

Unfortunately, the Bacharachs got off to a bad start, and things went downhill from there. In the six games they played in the American Series in late November, the team went winless. Oscar went just 4 for 22 in these games—and he was one of the team's better-performing hitters. When the thirty-fifth championship season of the Cuban Professional League opened on December 2, the Bacharachs were expected to make a better showing. They didn't. Loss piled upon loss, and disappointed fans increasingly stayed away from their games, a situation that meant less money for the players. Disgusted, Charleston, Santop, and Lundy decided they had had enough and quit the team. A couple of weeks later, their record standing at 4-12-1, the depleted Bacharachs were forced to forfeit the rest of the season.[49]

Oscar arrived back in Key West on board the *Miami* on Christmas Eve.[50] He may have been disappointed in his winter-ball income and the Bacharachs' record, and he may have feared gaining a reputation as a quitter, but at least during the Cuban League portion of the trip he had shown the island's fans what he could do on the diamond. He gained a reputation for fielding his position well, and one headline credited him with a catch of a line drive that was so spectacular the fans applauded with "*loco entusiasmo*" for several minutes.[51] Oscar also hit nearly .500 that December. He displayed little power, so the performance wasn't quite worthy of the Bambino, but Charleston's 1920 Cuban League showing was the first indication to Cuban baseball followers that he was a player to be watched.

• • •

Probably neither Charleston nor C. I. Taylor relished the prospect of a reunion for the 1921 season, even though CI had prudently placed Oscar on the ABCs' reserve list at the conclusion of the previous league year. So, undoubtedly with Charleston's consent, CI worked out a sale of Oscar's rights to Charlie Mills, manager of the St. Louis Giants. The *St. Louis Post-Dispatch* noted on January 21 that Charleston would play for the local Negro League team for the 1921 season, but CI kept things quiet locally. He knew this wasn't a move likely to be popular with ABCs fans.

The St. Louis Giants had never had it easy in their city, which was more southern in its spirit and customs than any other in the NNL. From 1909, when Mills, a bank messenger, gained control of the team, until 1919, the Giants had no home grounds and precious little local support. In the latter year, thanks to white financial backers, Mills was able to open a home park for his club. Rube Foster consequently invited St. Louis to join the NNL in 1920. But the price of building Giants Park was high: the terms Mills was forced to accept from his white financiers were unfavorable, and the park was inconveniently located a fair distance away from the city's largest black neighborhoods.[52]

Mills surely hoped that the signing of the NNL's biggest star would help him overcome these challenges. Oscar would put more fans in the seats at home and increase the gate for exhibition games played in places like Topeka and Carbondale. Mills decided to take further advantage of his new attraction by arranging a four-week spring training trip to the South, much as C. I. Taylor had done the year before. So on March 25 Charleston joined twenty-one other St. Louis Giants players on a special car to Mobile, Alabama. And just before he left Indianapolis for another six months or more, the still-married Oscar attempted to take care of a lingering piece of business by filing, a second time, for divorce from Hazel.

Like the ABCs in 1920, the Giants encountered little competition in the South, reputedly winning twenty of twenty-four contests on their swing through cities like Montgomery, Nashville, Atlanta, Chattanooga, and Mobile (spirited local lad Satchel Paige had no chance to see the team, as he was confined to reform school at the time). In Mobile, Charleston celebrated his first game in a St. Louis uniform by hitting two home runs.

That performance set the entire season's tone. If in 1920 it was Charleston's glove that had most made an impression, in 1921 his power came to the fore. Charleston ripped through the regular season with sustained ferocity. On May 12 he hit two home runs against the Chicago Giants, including the game winner in the bottom of the eleventh. On July 5 he slugged two homers off the Detroit Stars' Bill Holland, a quiet short-and-stocky control artist whom he had known since they were both boys in Indianapolis. Another two-homer game followed six days later against the American Giants and yet another two-homer performance against Rube Foster's club at the end of August.

Forget Cobb and Speaker. By May the nation's number one black newspaper, the *Chicago Defender*, was commonly referring to Charleston as the "colored Babe Ruth." That was the comparison, far more than any other, that would be most used in connection with Charleston during the 1920s. The *Kansas City Times* ventured that Oscar had now proved himself "the greatest negro ball player in the country."[53] Nor had his wandering from team to team or fallings-out with managers done anything to dampen Oscar's popularity. Far from it. Fans of opposing teams regularly greeted his entry into the batter's box with wild applause. On multiple occasions the *Defender* published his photo on its sports page.

At year's end Oscar led the NNL in home runs with fifteen (in 339 plate appearances). His slugging percentage was an otherworldly .736. Was this a home-field mirage? There is some reason to believe that the right field—and possibly the left field—fence in St. Louis was a short one, and upon examination Giants Park did aid Oscar's numbers: he hit ten of his home runs, and had a ridiculous .452/.534/.784 slash line, at home. But he still put up a slash line of .412/.484/.684 on the road. In other words, when playing in St. Louis, Charleston really *was* Babe Ruth. On the road he was just Rogers Hornsby.

The Giants Park fences could not have been too short, for they didn't stop Oscar from ringing up triples; he finished third in the league with 12. And they offered no help with stolen bases; Oscar finished second in the league with 32. The other statistics are just as remarkable: 104 runs scored (tops in the league—and compiled while he was batting third, not first, in the lineup); 91 RBIS (first); 17 doubles (tenth). All of this in just 77 league games. The 162-game equivalents would be 36 doubles, 25 triples, 31 home runs, 218 runs scored, 191 RBIS, and 67 steals.

If we take into account Charleston's stellar defense, his 1921 performance was one of the best years anyone in a Major League has ever had. And it took Charleston's fame to another level. "Were it not for his color," it was claimed in one long feature, Charleston "would be in the big leagues and would be classed as one of the 'greatest outfielders of all times.'" To see "this superman of the diamond in action" was "a rare treat." Charleston was credited not only with regularly making circus catches in the outfield, but also with perfecting the swinging bunt, which had to be fielded perfectly and on the run to have any chance of getting him out at first. His base running was daring, and if a catcher tried to block the plate when Oscar was coming down the line, well, "the catcher goes one way, his mask another, and the ball another."[54]

Oscar's 1921 season is all the more remarkable when one considers that he was not only going through a divorce proceeding, but also that he suffered the loss of his pretty twenty-year-old sister Clarissa, from pulmonary tuberculosis, in August.[55] Oscar missed at least two games to return to Indianapolis for the services.

Thanks to Charleston and underrated right fielder Charlie Blackwell—whom Oscar had gotten to know in Cuba and whose season may have been as good as Charleston's—the St. Louis Giants hung around near the top of the 1921 NNL race all year, finally finishing in third place at 42-32-1, a nine-game improvement over their 1920 performance. When the season closed, they again tested themselves against a St. Louis Cardinals barnstorming team. Branch Rickey's Cardinals had been much better in 1921, winning eighty-seven games, and the barnstorming club would again feature much the same squad that had split two games with the Giants the previous autumn, though still minus Texas native Rogers Hornsby, who at this point in his career was not keen to play in interracial contests. This time the teams booked a five-game series at Sportsman's Park, home to both the Cardinals and the Browns.

In the first game in front of a mixed-race crowd—whites seated on the third base side, blacks behind the first base dugout—

fourteen-game-winner Bill Pertica held Charleston to just one hit in six at bats as the Cardinals won, 5–4, in eleven. In game two, however, Oscar touched eighteen-game-winner Jess Haines for a double and a triple, and the Giants evened the series with a 6–2 win. A doubleheader was scheduled for the next Sunday.

That is when the St. Louis Giants' precarious financial situation finally caught up with owner Charlie Mills. A contractor who had made improvements to Giants Park back in 1919 had filed suit against the club months earlier, claiming that he had never been paid. His case was convincing enough that, prior to the Sunday doubleheader, a judge attached the day's gate to help pay the debt. One can imagine how that news went over with Oscar and his teammates, who were expecting to be paid out of game receipts. Deflated and perhaps more than a little unfocused, the Giants were no-hit in the first game of the doubleheader, losing 12–3. They lost the second game, as well, 9–6. George "Tubby" Scales later recalled how angry the Giants were at having to play for nothing. "Some slicksters were handling the affair, and that meant we were left in the cold," remembered Scales.[56] The planned fifth game was never played.

Such were the dramatics of everyday existence in the Negro Leagues. Things had to be taken in stride, and a man had to be ready to move on. With the opportunity to prove himself against the Cardinals and their fans by the boards, Oscar headed home to Indianapolis, where he and two of his St. Louis Giants teammates were eagerly added by C. I. Taylor to an ABCs squad then in the midst of the usual October series against white all-stars. However poorly they got along when put together for an extended period, neither Oscar nor CI was a man to hold a grudge when there was money to be made, a game to be won, or a reputation to be built. Oscar arrived in Indianapolis in time to play in the last two of these games. He homered in the first, an ABCs victory, but committed a key error in the second, an ABCs defeat. It was the last time Oscar and CI would stand on a diamond together.

Oscar's divorce from Hazel was finalized on September 15, 1921. The event came in the midst of a tough personal stretch for Charleston. Since 1918 he had been drafted into the army, separated and divorced from his wife, buried his father and a younger sister, and fought bitterly with his mentor. Fortunately, he had also risen to the top of his profession, and his popularity and reputation meant that baseball could now be a steady, relatively well-paying year-round affair—for as he long as his skills and his body held up.

No black teams or players were headed to Cuba in the winter of 1921, so, like numerous divorcés before and since, Oscar decided to decamp to California. After a decade of sporadic play the California Winter League had become a viable winter-ball option for Negro Leaguers the previous year. Owner Doc Anderson, a local businessman, had specifically built a ballpark—White Sox Park, located in Los Angeles at the corner of Anderson and Fourth Streets—for a team of black players known as the Colored All-Stars to use as its home grounds. Anderson's responsibility was to recruit the Negro Leagues. His partner, Joe Pirrone, night club owner and part-time ballplayer, lured white players from the Majors and Minors to serve as the competition. Oscar's former teammates Bullet Joe Rogan, Biz Mackey, and Zack Pettus had all played in California in the winter of 1920–21.[57] Mackey was headed back for the 1921–22 season, and perhaps it was at his urging that Oscar traveled west himself. It was Oscar's first trip to the Pacific coast since, in the spring of 1912, he had briefly been stationed at Angel Island as a mere fifteen-year-old who had lied his way into the army.

Charleston arrived in Los Angeles on Saturday, November 6, three weeks after the opening of the California Winter League season. The arrival of the "colored Babe Ruth," reported the Los Angeles Times, was expected to result in significantly larger crowds for games involving the Colored All-Stars.[58] The team Oscar joined was already very good. It featured Mackey, José Méndez, ABCs left-hander Jim Jeffries, Kansas City Monarchs left fielder Hurley McNair, and Monarchs first baseman George "Tank" Carr.[59] The team's competition consisted at first of ever-shifting groups of white players, most of whom were Minor Leaguers.

Observers were captivated by the Negro Leaguers from the outset. "If Cobb, Heilmann, Sisler, and Hornsby wish to be put out of conceit with themselves let the four form the nucleus of a team and tackle the colored lads over at the White Sox park," taunted Ed O'Malley in the *Los Angeles Times*. "One will get you five if you don't think they (The Big Four) will finish second."[60] And that was written before Charleston—"the heretofore unacknowledged and most sensational man in baseball"—arrived and, for the first time in his career, assumed managerial duties.[61] It was clear that the Colored All-Stars weren't going to be seriously tested by squads of Minor Leaguers.

Excitement was therefore high when it was announced in January 1922 that the Negro Leaguers would face the Meusel All-Stars in a seven-game series. This was a serious team. Southern California natives Bob and Irish Meusel had just faced each other in the World Series, with Irish's New York Giants emerging victorious over Bob's Yankees. Both Meusels had hit over .300 in the 1921 regular season. Their all-star team featured other fine hitters in Tigers first baseman Lu Blue (.308 in 1921), Boston Braves third baseman Tony Boeckel (.313), and Tigers catcher Johnny Bassler (.307). Their pitching staff was led by the Cardinals' Bill Pertica, whom Oscar had faced in St. Louis in October. The Meusels' lineup, said the *Los Angeles Times*, was the "strongest ever seen in Los Angeles," and "undoubtedly the strongest bunch that has ever been gotten together on the Coast."[62] The series was to be a fair fight.

Two thousand fans—many of them accommodated on the outfield grass—turned out for the first game between the Negro Leaguers and the Meusels' bunch in Los Angeles on Saturday,

January 14. They saw the Meusels blow a 2–0 lead in the bottom of the ninth when the Colored All-Stars mounted a three-run rally to claim the victory. Oscar went 1 for 4. In front of an even bigger, overflow crowd for Sunday's game Jim Jeffries took the mound for the second day in a row, and the Colored All-Stars lost, 7–6, to Pertica. Charleston, praised by the press for his "brainy" play, went 3 for 4 with two doubles and a stolen base.[63]

Games three and four were played the following weekend. In the former the Colored All-Stars took a 3–0 lead before Bob Meusel helped lead a game-tying comeback by lofting a triple over Charleston's head in center. Oscar got revenge in the seventh. With a man on second and the score tied at three, Oscar scorched a line drive past the head of pitcher Lefty Thomas, plating the go-ahead run. The Colored All-Stars hung on to win, 4–3. The next day the Negro Leaguers won another tight game, 5–4. The highlight was a Charleston triple to deep right-center (White Sox Park's center field fence was a whopping 546 feet from home plate). Many fans, reported the Times, were "of the opinion the swipe [was] the longest ever seen in Los Angeles."[64] The Colored All-Stars were now up 3–1 in the series, thanks largely to Charleston's play. "Oscar Charleston, the slugging demon of the St. Louis Giants . . . has been the hero of the series. His batting and fielding have been sensational."[65]

On Saturday, January 28, the Meusels slugged their way to a 15–10 victory. After starting pitcher Jeffries got crushed, Oscar relieved him; he also went 3 for 5 with two triples. What were supposed to be the final two games of the series were played on Saturday and Sunday, February 5 and 6. The first contest was won by the Colored All-Stars, 5–4, Oscar going 2 for 5 with a double, and the latter was taken by the Meusels, 5–2. That made the series 4-3 in the Colored All-Stars' favor, but with fans turning out and the games competitive, the teams kept scheduling more contests. Irish Meusel may have been the moving force behind these extra games. He reportedly wasn't "convinced that the Colored All-Stars are a better bunch of players" than his squad. Alas for Irish, the Negro Leaguers beat the Meusels in three of the four remaining games. The final series outcome was 7-4, Colored All-Stars.

The series against the Meusels was the feature of the 1921–22 California Winter League season, in which the Colored All-Stars went 25-15-1. Oscar lived up to his star billing, hitting .405 in seventy-nine at bats, including seven doubles and six triples. That batting average was second to that of Irish Meusel, who hit .425 in forty at bats. Bob Meusel hit .308. Neither Meusel could have left California that spring with any doubt that Oscar was their equal—or better. Reflecting on the showing made by Charleston and his teammates, the white Los Angeles press stated that Oscar had proven himself "without a doubt the second greatest living baseball performer in the entire universe, the great Babe Ruth being his only peer." Not one of the fourteen Major Leaguers who played in the winter league that year "ever approached an even footing in either fielding or work at the bat with that wonderful athletic outfielder and gentleman." The play of Charleston, Mackey, and the other Colored All-Stars had in fact been "inspiring to many of the local fans of both races."[66]

Before they left California, the Colored All-Stars barnstormed their way up the state. Charleston clipped for his scrapbook a *Sacramento Union* article reporting on one of their games against the Sacramento Senators. In that piece Pacific Coast League veteran Ross "Brick" Eldred is quoted by *Union* reporter Win J. Cutter as saying that "this boy Charleston was the best ballplayer he had ever laid eyes on." Cutter was skeptical, at first, but Oscar's performance made him a believer.[67]

On this day Oscar had apparently been in an entertaining mood. In the sixth inning, with the scored tied at one, he warned the third baseman that he was going to bunt—or "dump one." At the last second, he squared up and laid one down, but the ball went foul. So on the next pitch he pulled a liner past the first baseman for a double. Figuring, perhaps, that he owed the third baseman another chance, when he next came to the plate, Oscar again warned him that he was going to bunt. The third baseman moved in close. "This time he did it," wrote the fascinated Cutter. "Even though Pick was playing in on the grass, the dusky star was sliding across [the first base bag]" before the ball arrived. The All-Stars won, 2–1. Perhaps it was the philosophical note on which Cutter ended his game report that caused Charleston to save it:

> Bobby Burns wrote a whole mouthful of truth in his famous "A man's a man for a' that," and we're stringing with Bobby. What matters a man's color or creed, just so he be a man and delivers the goods. The colored race has produced some of the world's greatest athletes and some of them are champions today. There's one thing I cannot understand about organized baseball, and that is just why every nationality under the sun is allowed to play except the colored people, and they own some of the greatest ball playing talent in the world. Of course, it's organized baseball's business, in a way, but I have to smile sometimes when people tell me the war is over.[68]

• • •

As Oscar was showing off his skills to Major Leaguers in California, C. I. Taylor lay dying in Indianapolis. Taylor had taken ill in early February. It wasn't thought, at first, to be life threatening. A *Chicago Defender* item published on February 18, 1922, reported that his doctors believed he would recover.[69] But, as doctors so often are, they were wrong. On February 23 Charles Isham Taylor passed away peacefully at his Indiana Avenue home. His wife, Olivia; brothers Ben, Jim, and Johnny; and many other relatives were at his bedside. The cause of death was given as chronic myocarditis and bronchial pneumonia. CI was forty-seven years old.

In the opinion of journalist Arthur Williams, CI's health had been compromised by his indefatigable work on behalf of the new, fragile NNL. "He fought for baseball. He lived for baseball. He died for baseball," concluded Williams.[70] The third sentence might be an exaggeration (Williams referred obliquely to Taylor's having attended a league meeting in the weeks before he died, against the advice of doctors and friends),[71] but the first two certainly weren't. CI's rigidity and sternness might sometimes have rubbed his players the wrong way, but they were also among his great virtues. No one was more devoted to professionalism and craft in black baseball than C. I. Taylor. And few inside or outside baseball possessed his deep commitment to civic rectitude and the advancement of the black community. On the morning of Monday, February 27, thousands of Indianapolis citizens lined Indiana Avenue to pay their final respects at the Taylor home. The funeral at nearby Bethel AME Church was attended by Rube Foster and other NNL dignitaries, as well as Taylor protégés like Dizzy Dismukes.[72] A few months later the NNL owners voted to erect a monument in CI's honor and to memorialize CI with an annual "C. I. Taylor Day."[73]

On the day CI was buried, Oscar Charleston was, in all likelihood, still in Los Angeles. Even if he had been told of CI's sickness, the fact that it wasn't thought to be serious meant that neither he nor any of the others on the winter-league team had cut their trip to short to pay CI a final visit. As the years passed, Charleston would remember his mentor fondly and honor his memory whenever he could. He credited CI with teaching him how to manage a club, and in 1949 he named C. I. Taylor as the best Negro Leagues manager of all time.[74] The teams Charleston managed would often be compared to Taylor's in their hardnosed, heads-up, all-out style of play.

After CI's death ownership of the ABCs passed to Olivia Taylor. Managerial duties devolved to Ben Taylor. Fortunately for both, thanks to the financial mess in St. Louis, Oscar Charleston was allowed to return to his hometown team in 1922. It was arguably the best ABCs edition ever. Playing with black crepe on their sleeves in memory of CI, the 1922 ABCs were led by three of the best hitters in the game: Charleston, Biz Mackey, and Ben Taylor.

Charleston set the season's tone in the league-opening April 30 doubleheader against the Cuban Stars, in which he went 6 for 8 with a home run and a double. He didn't let up until the very end of the year. In the ninety-eight games for which we have box scores Charleston was held hitless in only sixteen, five of which came in the last seven games of the season. Although it was unreported, he appears to have had a twenty-eight-game league hitting streak from June 10 through July 25. During that stretch his slash line, over 135 plate appearances, was .425/.473/.708. Ben Taylor and Biz Mackey were nearly as excellent, with Mackey flashing tremendous power. The papers reported constantly on the wondrous home run pace he and Charleston were setting, while at ABCs home games cries of "Sock it, Charleston!" rang out from the stands.[75] Oscar loved it. If the game wasn't on the line, he would repay the fans for their adulation by doing a little hot-dogging in center. Crush Holloway, who manned right field for the 1921–23 ABCs and regarded Charleston as the best defensive outfielder he had ever seen, remembered that if Oscar "had time to get under a fly ball, he'd walk—he had it timed, he'd walk fast. And he'd do acrobatics. People used to come out and see him do his stunts in the outfield."[76]

Thanks to Charleston and Mackey, on July 15 the ABCs stood in first place in the NNL at 28-13. They arrived in Chicago for a five-game series against their eternal nemesis, Foster's American Giants, fresh off their second sweep that season of the St. Louis Stars (the new name of the St. Louis franchise, now under different leadership). With the ABCs threatening to run away from the pack, it was a crucial series, noted the Chicago press. "Foster's club must take four out of the five games played" to have a chance at the pennant. "Can they do it?"[77]

Yes, they could. The American Giants won the first four games of the series before the ABCs finally won in the fifth, when Oscar singled, stole second, and scored on Ben Taylor's single to center field in the tenth inning. Despite those series-closing heroics, Charleston went just 5 for 22 in these critical games, with no extra-base knocks. The ABCs remained in first place but only by a sliver.

During this series or shortly thereafter Ben Taylor hurt his arm, and Charleston was forced to take over at first base. The ABCs started an awful slide, going just 3-13 to start the month of August. The mojo was gone. It must have been a relief, at the end of the month, to escape the regular league circuit and head east, where the ABCs took on the Philadelphia-area Hilldale club (unofficially nicknamed "the Daisies") and the Atlantic City Bacharach Giants and played a few other exhibition games. When they returned from that trip, the ABCs started winning again, taking four out of five against Foster's team in Indiana, but it was too late. The American Giants won the league by a few percentage points. The ABCs finished third at 50-34-1. Both Crush Holloway and catcher Mack Eggleston later remembered the 1922 ABCs as the best squad on which they had had the opportunity to play.[78]

Oscar had certainly been tremendous. In ninety-eight games (including some that were not official league contests) Oscar hit nineteen home runs, eighteen triples, and twenty-four doubles. He also stole twenty-one bases. His 6.8 WAR was the highest yet compiled by a pure position player in black baseball. With the exception of the two-way Bullet Joe Rogan, who compiled 7.8 WAR in 1922, including 3.9 on the mound, Charleston was again the best player in the game.

In October the ABCs began their traditional postseason play against local white clubs. But after joining the ABCs for the first of these games, Oscar hopped on a train to St. Louis. This fall the St. Louis NNL team was taking on a Detroit Tigers barnstorming club, and as was by now quite clear, Oscar never passed up a chance to take on Major Leaguers. The Stars played the Tigers on October 2, 3, and 4 in St. Louis. These Tigers didn't have Ty Cobb or Harry Heilmann, but they did feature five other starting-position players, as well as a seventeen-game-winner in right-hander Howard Ehmke.

No series better exemplified the multiple ways in which Charleston, soon to turn twenty-six, could impact the game. In the first contest he went 2 for 4 with a stolen base off Ehmke. In the second he pounded left-hander Bert Cole for three hits, including a home run and a double. Cobb-like, Oscar twice baited Tigers pitchers into making bad throws to second by dancing off the base; on one of the errant throws to center field, he was fast enough to dash home. And twice, when on first with a man on third, his attempted steal of second allowed the man on third to score.[79] His exploits helped the Stars win two out of three.

• • •

In addition to his and the ABCS' fine showing, for Oscar the 1922 season was notable for three reasons. First, the string of personal losses wasn't over. His sister-in-law Anna—Roy's wife—died in mid-July, when Oscar was on the road in St. Louis. As with his sister Clarissa, the cause was tuberculosis. Anna was twenty-two.

Second, Oscar was unintentionally involved in the bestowal on a young rookie of one of the game's great nicknames. James Bell had latched on with his hometown St. Louis Stars at the beginning of the 1922 season. The Stars arrived in Indianapolis in early May for a four-game series. In the final game, with the Stars having already lost three times and down big again, Bell convinced his manager, Big Bill Gatewood, to let him take the mound. Using his curve, he managed to strike out both Ben Taylor and Charleston, who threw down his bat in disgust. Gatewood commented on how cool his skinny rookie was, someone else agreed that he was a "cool papa," and the moniker "Cool Papa" Bell was born.[80]

Third and most important, Oscar met someone. During the ABCS' late-season eastern swing he made the acquaintance of a pretty, petite, smart, and strong-minded twenty-seven-year-old teacher named Jane Howard. Their courtship was of the whirlwind variety. Soon after Oscar's season ended, he and Jane eloped to St. Louis. There, at noon on Friday, November 24, they were married by the Reverend C. A. Williams, pastor of St. Paul African Methodist Episcopal Church, at the home of one of Oscar's friends.[81] Oscar was once again a married man.

CHAPTER 5

Manager, 1922–1926

IF THE FAMILY OF Jane Howard, née Blalock, didn't live in Negroland, it at least resided in its suburbs. Jane's relatives weren't rich, but they were solidly middle class, comparatively well educated, civically active, and culturally aware. The socially respectable Blalocks were the kind of people to whom Oscar Charleston wished to attach himself. The kind of people he aspired to be.

The Reverend Martin Luther Blalock, Jane's father, was a native of Georgia and a graduate of Clark University. Born to a slave in 1864, with a white man as his biological father, Martin was well traveled and highly respected.[1] Rising steadily through the ministerial ranks, he had served congregations in California, Tennessee, Virginia, New Jersey, and elsewhere before landing in Harrisburg, Pennsylvania. By the time of his daughter's marriage to Oscar in November 1922, he was a presiding elder of the AME Zion Church's Harrisburg district. It was thought that Blalock might someday be made a bishop. He certainly looked and acted like an ecclesial authority. In surviving photos he invariably wears a suit and sports a thick mustache that drapes around his lips to the edges of his chin. The pictures suggest a formidable man with an air of Victorian propriety, even severity, about him.

The Harrisburg church where Martin served as pastor, Wesley Union AME Zion Church, was the spiritual home to the city's African American elite. Among its congregants was Esther Popel Shaw, a good friend of Martin's daughters who would later become recognized as a poet associated with the Harlem Renaissance.[2] Martin was assisted in his duties at Wesley Union by his wife Bettie, an Alabaman twelve years his junior. The couple owned a home at 12 South Sixteenth Street, a mile up the hill from Harrisburg's bustling downtown in an area that included a number of striving black professionals. In that narrow, red-brick, three-story row home Martin and Bettie raised four girls and three boys. Jane Grace, born September 29, 1894, in Kentucky, was their first.

Janie—the diminutive by which she was known to most people throughout her life—was educated in the Harrisburg city schools before taking a teaching certificate from the two-year program offered at the Harrisburg Training School for Teachers. She was more of a reader than an athlete, but as a young woman she played on a women's club basketball team, posing in one photo with Esther Popel and eight other members of the Philander Athletic Club team of 1915.

Janie had been an elementary schoolteacher for three years when on June 21, 1918, Martin and Bettie married her off to thirty-one-year-old LeRoy Layton Howard, a widely known and likeable man who came from a good family; his father had founded a black newspaper in Harrisburg in the 1880s and had eventually served as a deputy United States marshal in Washington DC. The Blalocks must have regarded this coupling as an exceptional match. Martin signaled his approval by marrying Janie and LeRoy at the family home.

Because married women couldn't teach in the Harrisburg schools, Janie resigned her position after tying the knot. Thankfully, LeRoy had fine prospects, having recently embarked on a career as the city forester. But tragedy struck quickly. According to family lore, on their honeymoon in Cuba LeRoy contracted the dreaded Spanish flu then raging throughout the world. Janie soon came down with the disease as well. At one point, as she lay in bed at her parents' home in Harrisburg, it was thought she would not survive the night. In the end, she pulled through, but LeRoy was not as fortunate. On October 13, 1918, he died of pneumonia.[3]

Thus did Janie, at the tender age of twenty-four, find herself a widow—and an exceptionally beautiful one. She was thin and barely five feet tall (she wore a size four shoe), with light skin, wavy hair, a high-pitched voice, and eyes full of light, eyes befitting a woman who read widely and possessed an active, curious intellect.[4] She was also introverted, reserved, and formal. Like her parents, she believed strongly in the importance of manners and decorum. "She was the disciplinarian" in the family, her great-niece Elizabeth Overton recalled. "She made sure you did things properly and by the book." Doing things the right way, at the right time, was a guiding philosophy for Janie. It was entirely in character when, late in life, she informed an elderly woman sporting a red hat that one did not *wear* red hats or red shoes after the age of fifty. Janie was tough "and always had spunk. She'd set anybody straight," said Elizabeth, who suspected that it was precisely because Janie saw in Oscar the same kind of feistiness that she was attracted to him.

Yet Janie was also warm and loving and deeply devoted to family, various members of whom she helped care for until she was no longer able.[5] Her great-great-niece Miriam Phields remembered that Janie would often sweetly sidle up to her as a child, making her fondness readily apparent, and that she was keenly attentive to the needs of others. Once, when she found out about a woman whose family had fallen on hard times, she hired the woman to clean her house. The work wasn't really necessary, since Janie kept an immaculate home, but she wanted to find a way to help the woman's family while allowing her to maintain her dignity.

Janie and her sisters—called "the three generals" by Elizabeth's brother because of their strong personalities—were all "big readers" who read every night, said Miriam.[6] Books were central to Janie's self-improvement ethic. Her interests did not, at least in her golden years, include baseball or any other sport, but she did believe in staying active. She walked everywhere—often taking Miriam with her and using these occasions to teach her young relative about the natural world—and even into her nineties she exercised regularly. Being active and useful lay at the core of Janie's identity; she hated nothing more than idleness. At the end of her life, when Janie was confined to a nursing home, Elizabeth begged the staff to give her something to do in order to lift her deepening depression.[7]

Janie relied on her faith and the strength of her spirit after LeRoy died. After her father took her on a recuperative trip to Niagara Falls, she continued to live in her parents' home and went to work as a clerk for the county recorder's office. Then, in September 1921, she left town to teach English and history at the Peabody Academy in Troy, North Carolina. About a year later she met the man who would become her second, and last, husband.

Just where that meeting took place is a matter of some question. When she was eighty-nine years old, Janie told Miriam that she met Oscar Charleston in North Carolina. It is possible that the ABCs swung through North Carolina on their eastern road trip in 1922, but there is no record of their doing so. They did stop in Janie's hometown of Harrisburg, however, on September 8 and 9, 1922, to play against the independent Harrisburg Giants, and it is highly likely that Janie's brother-in-law Bud Marshall, a black-baseball promoter, was involved in the arrangements to bring the ABCs to town (as he would often be in later years). In other words, it is possible that Janie's memory was faulty and that she met Oscar in Harrisburg shortly after she had returned from her North Carolina teaching stint.

No matter where they met, the courtship, as Janie also remembered to Miriam, was exceptionally short, even if one accounts for the fact that Janie was a widow. Oscar continued to play for the ABCs after they had rolled through Harrisburg in September 1922, and then in October he played in postseason exhibition games in the Midwest. Given that they were married in late November, this would have left Oscar precious little time in which to woo Janie. He must have been a fast worker.

Winning Janie's parents was a trickier proposition. Martin and Bettie were apparently not as enthusiastic about this potential union as they had been about the one with LeRoy. Or perhaps Janie simply knew they wouldn't approve of the match had she told them about it. In any case, she and Oscar eloped[8]—not to Indianapolis, as might have been expected, but to St. Louis, where Oscar had spent the 1921 season and where a month earlier he had played for the Stars against the Detroit Tigers barnstormers.[9] Percy Richards, a bartender who was presumably Oscar's friend, and his wife Millie opened their house for the Charlestons' quickie wedding ceremony on November 24. The next morning, November 25, directly after a celebratory breakfast, Oscar and Janie left for Key West, where they would embark on a ship bound for Havana. Their honeymoon—Janie's second in Cuba—would be combined with a season of winter ball.

• • •

Janie's new husband was daily becoming more famous throughout black America. But what was *he* like personally? Why was Janie, like so many others, attracted to Oscar Charleston—strongly enough, in her case, to risk angering her beloved family and throw in on a marriage after having known the man for only two months? Alas, unlike the case with Janie, we cannot repair to any of Oscar's friends or family members to answer these questions. We do have his scrapbook and photo album, though. We have the testimonies of many former players. And we have contemporaneous newspaper articles, which, as Oscar rose to superstardom in the 1920s, began more frequently to remark on his personal attributes and interests. The portrait that emerges is of a charismatic, likable man who was a natural leader.

Oscar was, to begin with, decidedly unlike the white player to whom, at this point, he had been most compared. Grantland

Rice's description of Ty Cobb as "an extremely peculiar soul, brooding and bubbling with violence, combative all the way" describes Cobb with a good deal of accuracy, but Charleston was nothing like that.[10] He was handsome, stylish, and—in stark contrast to Cobb—*charming*, gifted with an ability to win over people of all races and stations. As one of his friends observed, "Oscar has met the high and low, the rulers of the cities, the sheriffs of the wayside hick towns. He conquered them all and like Will Rogers he made them like it."[11] It helped that he was "a very impressive individual and a good-looking man," in the words of Stanley Glenn, Charleston's catcher on the Philadelphia Stars of the late 1940s.[12] He spoke and sang in a fine tenor voice, and he was always well dressed and clean-shaven.[13] William Nunn, writing in the June 20, 1925, *Pittsburgh Courier*, combined praise of Charleston's skills on the diamond with a paean to his personal qualities. "Oscar, it appears, has everything," wrote Nunn. In addition to being the greatest player of his generation, "he is a singer of rare ability, a writer of parts, a billiard player of more than ordinary skill and a happily married man. In short, Charleston is a rare specimen of one upon whom the gods have smiled in affable mood. Oh, he's a bird of a boy, is Oscar, and his personality—mysterious, inexplicable, indescribable, has won for him a warm spot in the hearts of each and every one of his players."[14]

This description reads like eulogy guff. But while Nunn may have exaggerated Oscar's positive qualities and ignored his vices, nothing we know challenges the essential validity of his claims. It's clear, for example, that Oscar was typically cheerful. He possessed a big, hearty laugh and a lively, if somewhat unrefined, sense of humor.[15] Both Schoolboy Johnny Taylor and Wilmer Harris even described him as jolly. "He laughed real easy," said Harris.[16] He liked to kid Taylor by rubbing his hands, which were as rough as "elephant's hide[,] . . . on my face," chuckled Taylor, "like a piece of Brillo, and laugh."[17] In Cuba, Oscar liked to amuse himself by waking up his roommate Willie Powell with a splash of water.[18] And he wasn't above entertaining himself and his teammates by hazing the youngsters. Cool Papa Bell recalled that as a rookie with the St. Louis Stars he would often dress in the same clubhouse as the opposing team, "with Charleston and those guys. They'd say, 'Where'd you get this new boy from?' They would push me out from under the shower, spit on me, step on me. They used to do that, see, just to try to get your goat."[19]

Such behavior doesn't sound very charming to twenty-first-century ears, yet it was commonplace at the time. Bell, in fact, admired and respected Oscar, who could be rough but wasn't a bully. "We had some ballplayers who were bullies," said Stanley Glenn, but Oscar wasn't among them. He was simply an authoritative, no-nonsense leader. "Nobody in their right mind was going to cross him. You could get it off your chest, but he was going to have the last word."[20] Sam Streeter, who played under Oscar on the Pittsburgh Crawfords, recalled Charleston as easy to get along with so long as one abided by his unbending rules.[21] Bill Cash, who played for Charleston in the 1940s, said much the same thing. "He was not hotheaded with us. He told us, 'You play my brand of ball or you don't play.' . . . All he wanted us to do: don't cross him. And nobody did."[22] "He was very strict," said Stars infielder Mahlon Duckett. "But very fair. Ninety-nine percent of the time he was right. You just couldn't get over on him."[23]

Oscar was quick to stand up for his friends and teammates. Larry Brown recalled a game in Cuba when an irrationally irate Adolfo Luque, hot-tempered manager of the team and a friend of Oscar's, "was fussin' and raisin' hell. 'Tell you what you do. You pack up, get your stuff,'" said Luque to Brown, with whom he was furious for something that wasn't Brown's fault. "I said, 'All right, I've got my ticket in my pocket, got my train fare back to Havana.' Oscar Charleston said, 'Well, we'll all just go home.' Luque says, 'Oh, no, oh no, oh no.'" That defused the situation. The team stayed intact.[24]

Oscar wasn't an intolerable braggart, but he certainly did not suffer from low self-esteem. "He believed in himself," said pitcher Andrew Porter. "You'd see him sitting around, talking about pitchers, and he believed he could hit anybody, play as good as anybody. And he could."[25] To dissipate his abilities was anathema to Charleston. He neither drank nor smoked, abstemious qualities that did not always endear him to his fellow ballplayers but were praised by members of the press.[26] These were only two of the most noticeable manifestations of his tremendous self-discipline, a quality he expected also to find in others. "He'd tell us, 'If I can't depend on you, I don't need you.' And he meant it," said Cash.[27] Punctuality was a fetish. Oscar would have agreed with Vince Lombardi that to arrive on time is to arrive fifteen minutes too late.

For all his impatience with nonsense, Oscar was nevertheless a good listener—someone, his players reported, you could confide in, even if he would not hesitate to lay into you on the diamond.[28] "I could always stand advice, especially from Oscar Charleston," said Duckett. "We got to be very close. Charlie was like a big brother to me. He used to take me under his wing. . . . We talked like men talk."[29] Still, Charleston remained private, even with friends like Duckett, who recalled that Oscar was slow to reveal much about his personal life.[30]

On the field, Charleston was rough, no doubt about it. Buck Leonard said he was among the worst offenders at coming in high and hard on slides. Newt Allen showed an interviewer a scar given him by a Charleston slide into third that knocked his glove off his hand—and the ball out of the glove. At the plate, the left-handed Oscar held his hands low and close to his body. He was twitchy, getting his timing by pumping his bat up and down and wiggling his right foot back and forth.[31] He could hit lefties, he had little trouble with breaking balls, and he sprayed the ball to all fields. His weakness lay in his temper. Pitcher Webster McDonald's strategy was to toy with Oscar long enough to "get him arguing with the umpire. . . . He'd keep looking back at him, you'd get him upset." Yet "if it was a close ball game," added McDonald, "then you've got to walk him."[32] The wise pitcher knew when not to push his luck.

He was a man's man, Janie's new husband, confident and happy, prickly and talented. More than anything, he was a competitor deeply invested in the quest to make a name for himself by mastering his craft. As Janie would soon learn, he did not regard getting married as any reason to let up.

• • •

The newlywed Charlestons hurried to Havana so that Oscar could take part in the 1922–23 Cuban League. He and several other black American players had been recruited there by Tinti Molina, a veteran manager with strong ties to black baseball in the United States, to join a new entry: the Santa Clara Leopardos, representing the capital of Las Villas Province, located in the middle of the island and boasting a population of about sixty-three thousand. By putting a team in Santa Clara, organizers hoped to broaden the league's fan base to include those who lived outside the Havana area, where the league's other three teams were based, and to capitalize on existing regional loyalties.[33]

Local product Alejandro Oms had played in America with the Cuban Stars East in 1921 and 1922 and acquitted himself well, hitting over .400 in both seasons combined. In December 1922 he was twenty-six. He had been joined on the Cuban Stars by another Santa Clara kid, Pablo Mesa. Mesa had hit about .300 in 1921 and 1922 and was just twenty-four. Oms and Mesa would flank Charleston in the 1922–23 Santa Clara outfield. Although they were the only Santa Clara natives on the team, their presence inspired enough local pride that, along with "Los Leopardos," the team acquired the nickname "Los Pilongos"—the Townies.[34] Besides Charleston, the team included other Negro Leaguers in infielders Oliver Marcell and Frank Warfield and pitchers Dave Brown and Bill Holland.

Because he had been busy getting married, Charleston missed the first few games of league play. But once he arrived, he raked, with fourteen hits in his first twenty-five at bats and twenty in his first forty. As a New Year's Day dispatch from the *Chicago Defender*'s Havana correspondent reported, Oscar was "setting the league on fire with his batting and at the present time he is leading the league in hitting, fielding, and base running."[35] On January 10, 1923, Santa Clara was in first place in the four-team league, and Oscar was leading the circuit with a white-hot .443 average.

For Charleston it must have been a welcome change to be finally experiencing team success in Cuba. But in the Caribbean no less than on the mainland, controversy seemed always to be at his side. Several weeks earlier league officials had banned Sunday morning games in Santa Clara in response to other teams' complaints that the fans at these games were too rowdy, sometimes raining bottles and other items onto the field. Yet on January 10 Santa Clara and Marianao had played a Sabbath-morn game anyway, Santa Clara winning, 8–5. Marianao, rather disingenuously, then filed a protest with the league, which stripped Santa Clara of its victory.

For a team that already thought the league and its three Havana-based clubs were biased against it, this was the final straw. The ruling confirmed Santa Clara's belief that it would not and could not get a fair shake. But it was still surprising when manager Tinti Molina withdrew the club from the league in protest. A few days of discussion followed, but the decision stuck. The team's fans regretted the decision yet "applauded the spirit" in which it was made, and the Santa Clara players accepted it as well.[36] Just like that, the season was over for the upstart Leopardos.

Although his season was cut short, Charleston had nevertheless taken an important step in building his Cuban League legend. He and Oms had led Santa Clara by hitting .418 and .411, respectively—first and second in the league. In twenty-one games Charleston had also slugged one home run, five triples, and seven doubles (he had the highest OPS in the league), while also stealing eight bases. He had made a wonderful impression— and not only as a player. He and his bride Janie had impressed Cuban observers by the way they carried themselves. On January 17, 1923, *La Prensa* reported on an interview it had had with Cuban baseball magnate Abel Linares. In the piece, which was accompanied by a large photo of Oscar and Janie, both handsome and nattily dressed, Linares announced that he had contracted with Charleston, "*el magnífico jugador*," to manage a club in the next league season. A translation of the article, apparently completed by Oscar himself, is pasted next to the original in Charleston's scrapbook. "Linares spoke to us with great enthusiasm concerning this wonderful player, who is one of the best all-around baseball players seen in a long time," wrote *La Prensa*'s correspondent. "Moreover, in Charleston there are fine personal qualities, and his wife, who is a teacher, and a very cultured woman, will assist him considerably in his affairs."[37]

As for the honeymoon, Oscar and Janie found time to enjoy the delights of life in Cuba in the winter of 1922–23, including, no doubt, the festive mood and more relaxed racial codes that made Cuba seem paradisiacal to many African Americans. Oscar's photo album contains pictures of Janie that were likely taken on this trip. In several she smiles, a little bashfully, as she poses with other young women, probably other players' wives, in their bathing suits. The album also contains a photo montage in which five pictures of Janie have been arranged in fan-like fashion. She sports bangs, a stylish bob, and a soft smile. In one of the photos she is reading a book. Life for the Charlestons was off to a good start.

• • •

Oscar and Janie arrived back in the States on January 19, 1923. With the Cuban League season cut short, time on their hands, and lost revenue to recapture, they headed for Palm Beach, where Oscar joined some of his ABCs teammates on the Breakers squad in the Hotel League.[38]

All had not been quiet on the home front while the Charlestons were in the Caribbean. In December 1922, at the NNL's annual meeting, ABCs owner Olivia Taylor had made the puzzling decision to trade Oscar back to Rube Foster's American Giants. Her underwhelming return in this swap consisted of four quite ordinary players. Olivia had also announced that Dizzy Dismukes would replace Ben Taylor, brother of her late husband CI, as the team's manager in 1923. Ben, with whom she had quarreled over money and team control the previous autumn, would be "sold or traded."[39] Then, in January 1923, it was said that Foster had received signed contracts for the 1923 season not only from Charleston, but also from speedster Jimmie Lyons and the brilliant Cristóbal Torriente. For a brief time it looked like Rube's club would have the best outfield in black baseball history.

Yet things were murky. The bespectacled Ed Bolden, postal worker and owner of the up-and-coming Hilldale club, had decided it was time for a separate professional black baseball league in the East. His new Eastern Colored League (ECL) was organizing in time for the 1923 season, and he and other eastern club owners were attempting to lure away players from the West. Signed contract notwithstanding, the *Pittsburgh Courier* speculated that Charleston and his ABCs teammate Biz Mackey would end up with Bolden's team in the Philadelphia suburbs. Another report further muddied the waters by stating that Charleston was in negotiations to *manage* a team in the East.[40] The *Defender* even said it was a "well-known fact" that Charleston wanted to manage.[41] Everyone knew that for Oscar, or for anyone else, managing wasn't in the cards with Rube Foster's American Giants. So rumors abounded that Charleston was going to "jump." The *Chicago Defender*, characteristically looking out for Foster's interests, tried to head off such an outcome by warning that the "public soon loses faith in a man whose signature does not amount to a hill of beans."[42]

In the meantime, not waiting to be sold or traded, Ben Taylor had agreed to manage a new club in Washington DC. Given his antagonistic relationship with his sister-in-law Olivia, he had no scruples over trying to sign away her ABCs stars, including Biz and Oscar. He found success with Specs Clark (who would soon drink himself out of professional baseball) and a couple of others, but not with Mackey, who did in fact go to Hilldale, and not with Charleston, who, formally at least, remained on board with Foster. In mid-March, Foster fired another shot across the bow by letting it be known that he had traded for Charleston only at Oscar's request. If he wanted now to go east, that was fine, but he wouldn't be paid as much there as he would be by Foster.

The surprise ending of this head-spinning mini-drama was that Oscar simply stayed with the ABCs. The reasons were not at first reported. Nor were the reasons why Charleston had requested a trade to the American Giants in the first place. At the time, it was rumored that Foster's cash, more than the nondescript players he had agreed to send to the ABCs, had persuaded Olivia Taylor to part with Charleston.[43] A year later, that suspicion was confirmed. Olivia had been deeply in debt to Foster and the NNL, and handing Oscar to Foster for a few players and some cash seemed to offer a way out of her difficulties. But after her team had been further diminished by the exits of Ben Taylor, Biz Mackey, and others, she had had second thoughts. Likely she agreed to pay Oscar a higher salary if he would return, and with the ECL raiding so many teams, Rube decided it was unwise to let the ABCs be totally destroyed. He and Olivia worked out a deal whereby Olivia would get a financial subsidy in 1923 and let Charleston go to the American Giants for the 1924 season.[44] None of this was known to the public in the winter and early spring of 1923. All that was certain was that Oscar had mysteriously remained with the ABCs without a fuss.

By March, Oscar and Janie had set up house in Indianapolis, where the Indiana Avenue neighborhood was enjoying its golden years. Bootleg liquor flowed freely behind the doors of the avenue's numerous soft-drink establishments. Gossip was shared just as freely in the avenue's many barber shops. Ragtime beats were giving way to the new jazz sound in the area's burgeoning entertainment scene. Even for those, like the Charlestons, who were sober and industrious, the hopping Indiana Avenue district was an exciting place to be young in 1923.

The couple had not been in town long before the ABCs' affable new manager, Dizzy Dismukes, took his club to West Baden for three weeks of spring training.[45] Without two of their three best players from 1922 (Biz Mackey and Ben Taylor), not much was expected of the 1923 ABCs. The *Defender* picked them to finish in the middle of the NNL pack, and Dismukes knew he faced an uphill battle. He had four capable outfielders in Charleston, George Shively, Crush Holloway, and Namon Washington, but he had to replace Taylor at first base. So he made the surprising decision to shift Charleston—despite the fact that he continued to be regarded as "without a doubt, the greatest outfielder in the game"—to first.[46]

The gambit raised eyebrows, but it worked. The ABCs once again started hot. In the season opener, an 8–7 ABCs win over the Detroit Stars attended by Indianapolis's mayor and nine thousand fans, Charleston made an error at his new position, but he also tripled and stole a base. (He hadn't been moved out of center because his wheels were going; that was still years away.) In the next game, another ABCs win, Charleston went 4 for 5 and hit a long home run over the right field fence that landed on the railroad tracks some distance beyond. The ABCs won their first nine games of the year. Their star first baseman, not yet particularly hot, was hitting .378 with two homers and two triples.

In early June, with the ABCs in first place, they suddenly found themselves short an arm when their star pitcher from Morehouse College, Charles "Sensation" Clark, was called home by an irate sister who said he was too young to be playing ball so far from his folks. Dismukes was forced to call on Oscar to take the mound against the St. Louis Stars, and he responded by giving up three hits and no runs over eight innings. Dizzy was pushing all the right buttons, and the *Defender* credited him with "keeping the morale and the fighting spirit of the club together," even though the ABCs were clearly undermanned.[47]

It couldn't last. In mid-June 1923 four straight losses to the Detroit Stars—one credited to Oscar, who was again called upon to pitch—knocked the ABCs down to third place, two and a half games behind the first-place American Giants. Up next was a five-game series against Foster's club in Chicago, where Charleston remained popular. ("The greatest finished ball player of today will find many admirers here," the *Defender* reported.)[48] The ABCs had not performed well, historically, against the American Giants in Chicago, especially when first place was on the line. That trend continued. Charleston went 8 for 21 in the series, but the ABCs dropped four out of five. In July they briefly clawed back to within a game of first place, but then they lost three out of five in another series with the American Giants. Dismukes decided to end the Charleston-at-first experiment and installed him in center field for the rest of the season. Oscar didn't miss a beat defensively, but the ABCs were done.[49] By August 4 they had sunk to fourth place. There they stayed, even as Charleston continued to pile up hits (he hit .364 on the year, ranking ninth in the league), home runs (eleven in league play, which ranked sixth), and stolen bases (twenty-five, best in the league).[50] On August 25, 1923, the *Pittsburgh Courier* carried his photo with the caption, "The greatest all-around player in organized baseball." Still baby-faced, Oscar stares into the camera with impassive eyes, cap tilted rakishly to the right.[51]

When the 1923 regular season ended, it was time to barnstorm. Per their silent arrangement, Olivia Taylor loaned Charleston to Rube Foster, who intended to use Oscar in the American Giants' postseason games against, first, white semipros, and second, the Detroit Tigers. In between these series Charleston was allowed to play for the NNL's Detroit Stars in a three-game series against the American League's St. Louis Browns. Once again he would get to test himself against white Major Leaguers.

The American Giants took care of business against the semi-pros, winning all three games.[52] Then, against the St. Louis Browns, Charleston helped the Detroit Stars win two out of three. The Negro Leaguers won the first game, 7–6. In game two Oscar and the Stars' twenty-two-year-old hotshot rookie center fielder, Norman "Turkey" Stearnes, clubbed five extra-base hits off Browns' sixteen-game-winner Elam Vangilder. In that contest Charleston had two home runs and a double, Stearnes had a home run and a triple, and the Stars again won 7–6. The Browns won the last game of the series, 11–8, but Charleston went long yet again. He finished the set 5 for 10 with three home runs, each at bat coming against legitimate Major League pitching.

Finally, Charleston returned to Chicago to play with the American Giants versus the Tigers. On October 21 the American Giants lost, 7–1, to a Detroit club featuring Bobby Veach, Harry Heilmann, and Heinie Manush (but, as usual, no Ty Cobb). Oscar went 1 for 4. The American Giants won the next day's game, but Charleston missed it. Another Cuban League season was about to begin. He had to get back to Indianapolis, pack his things, and sail with Janie to Havana.

• • •

Despite what Abel Linares had told the Cuban press back in January, Charleston did not return to Cuba as a manager in 1923–24. Instead, he rejoined the Molina-managed Santa Clara club, which would run out the same impressive outfield of Oms, Mesa, and Charleston but otherwise had been reinforced with additional black American stars. The Leopardos wore pinstriped uniforms, high pants, and socks with a broad white strip near the top. Palm trees fringed their home stadium, La Boulanger Park, which had a partially covered grandstand and a field-level shed for a dugout. From this home base Santa Clara would attempt to show that its surprisingly good but aborted 1922–23 showing was no fluke.

Molina's distinctively American team began its assault on the Cuban League in late October, and nearly from the beginning it overwhelmed its rivals. After the Leopardos swept a double-header against Almendares on January 13, their record of 36-11 had them so far ahead of second-place Habana—eleven and a half games—that fan interest had substantially waned. The league therefore decided to declare a TKO. Santa Clara was crowned champion, and a new, three-way championship season among Santa Clara, Habana, and Almendares commenced, with the best players from Marianao distributed among the other two Havana-based clubs. Santa Clara went on to win this second, Gran Premio Invernal season as well.

The 1923–24 Santa Clara championship team would over the years become regarded as the most dominant in the island's pre-revolutionary golden age—the equivalent, in the Cuban popular mind, of the 1927 Yankees in the American. The squad's players became legends. Roberto González Echevarría recalled his paternal grandfather smiling condescendingly when anyone praised the Cuban players of the 1940s and '50s. "He would then proceed to state categorically that [no one was] on the same level as the incomparable Oscar Charleston or Alejandro Oms," the Leopardos stars of his youth.[53] The team was feted in banquets, memorialized in postcards, and celebrated in a special set of baseball cards produced by a Havana tobacco company called Compañía Cigarrera Díaz.[54]

The 1923–24 Leopardos became an integral part of the Oscar Charleston legend, both in Cuba and in black America, for two reasons. The first was that Charleston was the league's most dominant player. The second was that he managed to ignite a truly spectacular fight.

If we count statistics compiled in both 1923–24 "seasons," Charleston led all his peers with thirty-six stolen bases and an OPS of .997. His .376 batting average was second best, as were his four home runs. His sixteen doubles ranked third. The Cuban press was full of admiration. One of the many Cuban cartoons clipped by Oscar and placed in his scrapbook is titled "El terror de los clubs." It depicts a giant, grimacing Oscar swinging a huge bat labeled "Santa Clara," while in the background three frightened little players labeled with the names of the other league teams flee for their lives. The caption notes that the likeable Charleston (*el simpático jugador*) was the sensation of the day (*la sensación de la temporada*). A long feature on Charleston from January 10, 1924, which Oscar placed in his scrapbook, recalls performances in which Oscar stole five bases and went 6 for 6 at the plate, with each hit coming off a southpaw. It calls him the "best and most complete player" in the league, a "perfect star" who combined intelligence, base running, slugging, fielding, and clutch play in a way never before seen.[55] Another article marvels at how Charleston scored from second on a deep fly ball to center field—a play, Oscar explained, he had been planning for days. He figured, correctly, that the infielder taking the cutoff throw would be caught completely off guard if he just kept running. For this heady risk-taking, this aggressive and exciting style, Santa Clara fans adored him. Everyone respected him.[56]

And that spectacular fight? It erupted on January 19 at Almendares Park in Havana during the first game of the Gran Premio Invernal season. Oscar, sliding with typical fury into third base, spiked Habana's Manuel Cueto, cutting him badly. As Cueto lay there in pain, his brother, a soldier, leaped out of the stands behind third base and charged Charleston. Soon, both Cuetos were taking swings at Oscar, and before long several other soldiers, or perhaps policemen, had run onto the field—either to join the fray, as the later legend has it, or to break it up, as is much more likely. (Contemporary Cuban news accounts refer to Oscar's getting into a fight with just one soldier.) Oscar defended himself as best he could and by all accounts acquitted himself well. A post-fight newspaper photo in his scrapbook shows him standing calmly next to a policeman, no worse for the wear. Manuel Cueto was not as fortunate; he was carried off the field by teammates and taken to the emergency room. Charleston was taken to the police station.

As news of the brawl spread, Oscar at first suffered badly in the Havana press, which published a number of articles accusing him of dirty play (Charleston proudly pasted some of these pieces in his scrapbook). The cartoonists had a field day, illustrating in comic fashion Oscar's slide into third, the chaotic fight that followed, and the punishment Oscar was to receive; one ends by showing him hanging from a noose labeled "Liga"— League. Rumors spread among fans that Charleston was nursing a vendetta against native Cuban players and that he had hoped to seriously injure one of them before he left the island that winter. Many citizens were outraged at the thought of a Cuban soldier being assaulted by an American player.

Yet Oscar had not only a legion of fans by this time, but also numerous well-placed friends. Both groups were quick to spring to his defense. A telegram reached him the next day, assuring him that all Santa Clara stood behind him. A friend named Salvador Castillo y León wrote Oscar a letter encouraging him to ignore the criticism being heaped upon him in the papers. Oscar had always been known for his "gentlemanly conduct." The Cueto injury was an accident—and in any case was part of the game when a fielder chose to block a base. The soldier Cueto, meanwhile, had "dishonored the uniform" and would be appropriately punished in a court of law. Castillo y León enclosed a flyer that fans were circulating in support of Oscar.[57] It repeated the claim that Charleston, well known for his gentlemanliness, was being ill-used by the Havana media for his role in the incident, and it called for fans to boycott the two newspapers—*El País* and *El Sol*—that were most strident in their criticisms of Charleston's play.[58]

Another of Oscar's friends, Hilario Franquiz, wrote to *La Prensa* on January 24 that Oscar was a "perfect gentleman" too "decent" and "cultured" to be legitimately suspected of intentionally trying to hurt someone. He conveyed with his letter one from Oscar, in which Charleston said (in Spanish, which he had picked up in a remarkably short span of time) that if he intended "to hurt a man, I would do it nobly," not by using his spikes. Anyone who knew Oscar would have known that much, at least, to be true. Nor was he prejudiced against Cubans. "I esteem a man as what he is, as a man, as a human being, without taking into account" ethnicity or other extraneous matters, wrote Oscar. After all, he and his fellow Negro Leaguers knew all too well what it meant to be judged on such terms.[59] Finally, Oscar met with representatives of the Cuban military, explained that he had been acting only in self-defense, and insisted that he meant no disrespect to the uniform of the Cuban Army, an institution for which, as a veteran himself, he had only admiration. In this meeting Oscar's charm and sterling social reputation once again served him well. His explanation was well received. The army even announced that it would discipline soldier Cueto for his role in the incident.[60]

The fight was a big deal, but Oscar was hardly scarred by the event. Besides memorializing it extensively in his scrapbook, he seems to have laughingly retold it far and wide once he returned stateside. The day Charleston got into a melee with a bevy of soldiers and spent the night in jail became a tale that would often be told, in various exaggerated forms, down through the years. Webster McDonald, who wasn't there, told Negro Leagues historian John Holway decades later that Oscar had whipped three men that day. "Grabbed one and swung him around and knocked the others down," said McDonald. Ted Page, who wasn't there either, told Holway, "There were a dozen or more soldiers, and he stretched them all over the park, just laying them out."[61] Oscar must have really enjoyed spinning this yarn. "He told us about how he was down in Latin America and there was one fight that they put him in jail overnight," said Wilmer Harris, recalling a conversation with Oscar that must have taken place in the late 1940s. "Said he rattled the cage all the time he was in there, scared 'em to death."[62] That was Oscar: perpetuating his legend—and always inclined to entertain himself by rattling cages.

Brawl aside, Oscar was very proud of the success he and his Santa Clara teammates achieved in 1923–24, reporting on the team's first-season championship to the *Pittsburgh Courier* in a January 1924 letter. Charleston relayed that Oliver Marcell was the team's leading hitter and that Bill Holland was its leading pitcher, before briefly noting a couple of his own statistics and accomplishments. "I mention Santa Clara, especially," he concluded, "not because I play with them, but because all of the players on the Santa Clara club are colored boys except Pitcher Dibut. And all the regular players are colored Americans except Oms and Mesa." For Oscar, Santa Clara's triumph was a triumph for Negro Leaguers. For African Americans.[63]

Oscar and Janie left Cuba on March 1, 1924.[64] On board their ship, listed just a few rows beneath them on the passenger manifest, was another internationally famous baseball man: New York Giants manager John McGraw, who was traveling with his wife, Blanche, and their son Stephen. One wonders whether the couples got to know each other during the passage. The McGraws, who regularly visited Havana in the winters, had been on the island for the last half of February.[65] They would have become well aware of Oscar's fame and abilities during that time, when Charleston and the Leopardos were finishing off their extraordinary year. It is not entirely inconceivable, in Havana's more relaxed racial atmosphere, that the McGraws and Charlestons had even mingled socially. (Charleston's photo album contains shots of Janie and him posing with white friends in social situations, including pitcher Adolfo Luque, then starring for the Cincinnati Reds during the regular season.)

One year previous, when McGraw had published a memoir of his three decades in baseball, he had said that Honus Wagner was the greatest player he had ever seen.[66] Years later, the rumor circulated in Negro League circles that McGraw had said *Charleston* was the best he had ever witnessed. If McGraw did say that, and if Charleston was the source of that rumor, perhaps he said it directly to Oscar as he sailed to Key West, having just watched Oscar lay waste to one of the world's better baseball circuits.[67]

• • •

While Oscar was burnishing his growing legend in the Caribbean, there were rumors back home that in 1924 Charleston would be going back to Chicago, where Rube Foster was getting rid of players who had complained about their salaries.[68] Certainly his rejoining the ABCS was out of the question. Because of Olivia Taylor's financial issues, and perhaps also her management style, the team was completely busting up. But a return to Chicago was not in Oscar's plans. Just a few days after the crazy brawl in Almendares Park, Charleston wrote the *Pittsburgh Courier* from Havana to announce that he had signed on to manage the Harrisburg Giants, a new entry in the Eastern Colored League.[69]

The decision to go to Harrisburg was probably not too difficult. Many players from the NNL, like Pete Hill, were migrating east. The ABCS were falling apart. Rube Foster and Olivia Taylor were fighting over Oscar's rights. The Klan was becoming so strong in Indianapolis that in November sixty-five hundred hooded members would march through downtown.[70] And Janie surely would be pleased to return to her hometown, where her parents, whatever their view of her marriage, would allow the Charlestons to live with them in the family home. Finally, Colonel William Strothers, owner of the Harrisburg Giants, had not only made Oscar a competitive salary offer, but he also wanted him to manage and put together his team. For Oscar, the situation could hardly have been more attractive.

Colonel Strothers was not a military man. Born in 1868 in Culpeper, Virginia, he was given the name "Colonel" in honor of his parents' employer (and, one suspects, former master). Strothers ran away from home at age eleven or twelve to work on a railroad gang. Eventually he landed in Harrisburg, where in 1896 he became the city's second black policeman. Later he owned a restaurant, barber shop, and pool hall, where perhaps from time to time some gambling may have taken place. Affable and talkative, Strothers was an active Freemason and stalwart Republican. He was also six feet tall and weighed about three hundred pounds, not the typical profile of a ballroom dancer, the fine art he taught to Harrisburg's young men and women.[71]

The Giants were formed by Strothers around the turn of the century. Ever since, they had played as an amateur or semipro outfit, occasionally fielding some fine clubs featuring tremendous players like Spottswood Poles, often remembered as black baseball's first great center fielder. But prior to the 1920s the Giants had never really hit, or even reached for, the big time. Now, given an opportunity to raise his club's profile and dramatically increase his revenues by entering the Giants in the ECL, Strothers jumped at the chance. Securing black baseball's most famous player as his manager was an incredible coup.

Columnist Fay Young prophesied in the *Chicago Defender* that Charleston would fail as a manager, but that was a minority report.[72] With Charleston in charge the eastern press built up Harrisburg's chances. In the new age of flappers and fast living, Oscar, after all, "seems to sweep things before him in much the same manner of the dance that bears his name."[73] Colonel Strothers did nothing to dampen expectations. "Reckon the Giants will have about the best team on record this year," he predicted on March 4, 1924, the day after Oscar and Janie returned to Harrisburg from Cuba.[74] He and Oscar quickly got busy securing transportation and players. They also chatted up journalists, Oscar showing off the eighteen-carat gold Elgin watch and fob given him by Santa Clara fans a few weeks earlier.[75] When he stopped by the *Pittsburgh Courier*'s offices in mid-March on his way west for a scouting trip, Charleston looked "the picture of perfect health, . . . announcing his weight as 201 pounds of solid bone, muscle, and sinew."[76] More cautious than his boss, he did not predict a championship for his team, but he did venture that they were the ECL's dark horse.

To make good on that claim Charleston aimed high, trying to wrest away young slugger John Beckwith from the Homestead Grays, for example. But his recruiting efforts brought back mostly middling players. (His former ABCS teammates Charles Corbett and Darltie Cooper, both pitchers, wrote asking for a job, and he signed them, taking pains to communicate through the press that he had not lured them away from his former employer.) In the short time he had between returning from Cuba and the opening of the ECL season, Oscar landed no truly high-quality talent. Forced to put his team together on the fly, during the first half of the 1924 season Charleston tinkered with his personnel, rotation, and lineup combinations. It eventually became clear that the team's strength lay in its outfield, where two players Oscar had inherited, Clarence "Fats" Jenkins and Herbert "Rap" Dixon, flanked him in left and right, respectively. The twenty-six-year-old, New York–born Jenkins was already famous in the black sports world for his excellence in the comparatively new game of basketball, a sport he continued to play in the winters (he and another Giants player, infielder George Fiall, were dubbed the "Heavenly Twins" by sportswriters for their work together on the hardwood). Dixon, just twenty-one, would ultimately impress Charleston so much that Oscar named him to his all-time team in 1949.

Charleston's power would come to the fore again in 1924. After helping his Santa Clara teammate Frank Warfield raise the U.S. flag in Darby, Pennsylvania, on opening day against Hilldale, Oscar doubled and homered to deep center. By July 9 he had reportedly already hit eighteen home runs. As of August 24, said the Harrisburg press, he had hit thirty-six. These numbers counted non-league games, contests against semipro and town clubs from the likes of Shamokin, Conshohocken, Kensington, and Wentz-Olney, but they were still perceived as astonishing. In one early August stretch against non-league teams Oscar hit seven home runs in three games, bagging three in a 15–0 shutout of Northumberland. Against a league team, the Brooklyn Royal Giants, at Carlisle, Pennsylvania, Charleston helped secure a Harrisburg victory with a home run to right that was "the longest hit that ever sailed over the ramparts of Biddle Field, according to gentry with dependable memories."[77] No one, it was said, had ever cleared that fence before.

With no other true star to help carry them, the Giants hung around .500 and fourth place in the ECL. But by mid-season they had shown well enough to excite fans and impress observers, most of whom hadn't expected much from a team that had to be constructed nearly from scratch. The *Pittsburgh Courier* praised Charleston for proving wrong those who had doubted his managerial chops. "Oscar Charleston and the Harrisburg Giants are coming into their own, and woe betide those weak sisters who cope with the Capitol City gangsters now," wrote Rollo Wilson. "They are on their way up and hitting in high. Watch 'em friends, watch 'em."[78] Oscar expressed optimism too: "If my pitchers hold out, and I think they are now going with creditable regularity, the Harrisburg Giants have a good chance to get into the lead."[79]

They didn't, but no matter. Harrisburg's fans were thrilled with the play of their new team and its rookie manager, who as of July 19 was leading the ECL with a .431 batting average. Harrisburg's rooters were so happy that July 23, 1924, was proclaimed "Charleston Day" at Island Park, the stadium in the middle of the Susquehanna River where the Giants and the white Harrisburg Senators both played their home games.[80] During that day's contest against Hilldale, Dr. Charles Crampton, a prominent African American physician, presented Oscar with a princely purse of $500 as a gift from the team's fans. Charleston smiled, thanked his benefactors, and was "given a warm reception by the large crowd."[81] He went on to double, walk, and steal a base, but Harrisburg lost, 7–2.

When the season ended in late September, Harrisburg stood in fifth place, the second division, at 30-31. Ben Taylor, who managed the league's Washington Potomacs, wrote in a lengthy postmortem of Harrisburg's 1924 performance that the Giants' infield defense and inconsistent pitching had betrayed them. Charleston, said Taylor, had not "made good yet" as a manager, but that was due mostly to the talent at his disposal. As a player, he continued to sparkle:

> I consider him the greatest outfielder that ever lived. I do not mention color, because I do not mean the greatest colored out-fielder, but the greatest of all colors. He can cover more ground than any other man I have ever seen. His judging of fly balls borders on the uncanny.
>
> He has a fine arm and is one of the fastest men in baseball. At bat he has few equals. A good bunter and an adept at the swing-ing style of bunting, and [he] is also a slugger par excellence. As a baserunner he has but one rival in the east, Frank Warfield.

"I might add," Taylor concluded, in a nod to his late brother, "that both [Warfield and Charleston] are graduates of the late C. I. Taylor" school of baseball.[82]

• • •

At the conclusion of the 1924 league year the ECL champion Hilldale club went on to play the Kansas City Monarchs in the first-ever Negro Leagues World Series. Charleston's Harrisburg Giants had a postseason series of their own to play: a best-of-seven set against the white Harrisburg Senators for the city championship.

For this postseason series the Senators would be managed by Nig Clarke. A former Major League catcher, Nig's real name was Jay Justin, but early in his career his dark complexion had led the era's ever-sensitive journalists to bestow upon him his nickname. A similar (and, to be fair, uncharacteristic) level of class was shown by the *Harrisburg Evening News* in previewing the series. The paper purportedly quoted Charleston, "whose smile is as captivating as his brilliant work in the field," as saying, "We is going to cut them Senators down to representatives in no time a-tall. Why boy, we knows we got the better team. And we knows we is gonna win. Ain't nature grand? Uh-huh."[83] Charleston's grammar and diction may not have been perfect, but it's doubtful he actually spoke in this exaggeratedly stereotyped manner.

Like the *News* reporter, the Senators may have underestimated Charleston. Whether out of gallantry, naïveté, or stupidity, the Senators agreed to a series rule that allowed either team to bring in, as ringers, any player it wished from the teams' respective leagues. Oscar took full advantage of this pact. He added to his otherwise unremarkable squad shortstop Dick Lundy, who had just hit .326 for the Atlantic City Bacharach Giants; third baseman Oliver Marcell, a hot-tempered and sometimes violent man who had starred for the Santa Clara Leopardos in 1923–24 before hitting .293 for the Lincoln Giants in 1924; and catcher John Beckwith, who had started the 1924 season with the Homestead Grays but had ended it with the Baltimore Black Sox, for whom he had hit .371. Oscar also added to his pitching staff Hilldale ace Nip Winters (23-6, 2.59 ERA). Those additions made all the difference. The Giants swept the series, Oscar going 6 for 15 with two home runs.

For Oscar, the triumph over the Senators was marred by a failure to control his temper, which erupted on Saturday, September 20, during the series' third game. In a tight contest, on Oscar's fourth trip to the plate, the home plate umpire rung him up on a called third strike. Enraged, Oscar turned and took a swing at the ump. He missed, but the umpire didn't, landing a counterpunch squarely to Charleston's jaw. The fans and players erupted, and it took the appearance of mounted policemen to restore order. Oscar was ejected. The same umpire worked the fourth and final game of the series, however, apparently without incident—a game for which Oscar, too, was back on the field.

Popularity had its privileges. A couple of months earlier two members of the Cuban Stars had assaulted umpires at Harrisburg's Island Park by throwing dirt in one umpire's face, throwing punches, and threatening them with baseball bats. It had taken mounted police to end that fracas as well, and after the game warrants were issued for the offending players' arrests. Oscar was already so popular in his wife's hometown that, in contrast to the Cuban Stars players, he suffered no legal consequences for his missed punch. For those keeping count, this appears to have been the fourth ballfield fight in which Oscar had by the fall of 1924 been involved. He had been playing professionally for eleven years. All four fights came in games featuring white players.

Charleston's 1924 season wasn't remarked upon at the time as markedly better than his typically lofty standard. But we can see now that it was one of the best baseball had seen or has *ever* seen. His OPS+ of 254 in league play was fifty-two points higher than second-place Bullet Rogan's 202. It was one of the best offensive seasons ever produced in the Negro Leagues (as of this writing, there is only one higher OPS+ among players with at least two hundred plate appearances in Seamheads' Negro Leagues database). In the fifty-four ECL games for which we have statistics Charleston hit fifteen home runs, five triples, and twenty-two doubles. To this production he added twenty stolen bases. His slash line was .405/.476/.780.

Would Charleston have fared as well against American or National League pitching and defense? Probably not. But even if we perform some mental discounting, his 1924 season is astonishing. Triple the counting statistics to get the 162-game equivalent: 45 home runs, 15 triples, 66 doubles, and 60 steals—in other words, a 126-extra-base-hit pace (subtract a couple if you would prefer to think in terms of a 154-game equivalent). No Major League player has ever had that many extra-base hits; Ruth holds the record with 119 in 1921. No one with *speed* has ever come close. The highest number of extra-base hits recorded by a player with at least 20 stolen bases is 99, posted by Larry Walker in 1997. The most extra-base hits Willie Mays ever posted was 90 (1962). Cobb's high was a mere 79 (1911).

Charleston's 1924 was so good that, even if we mark it down somewhat for the level of competition in the ECL, it is arguably one of the best all-around offensive performances ever witnessed. Furthermore, Oscar compiled his numbers while playing superb center field defense *and* acting as his team's manager. Has anyone ever had a better year?

• • •

Oscar told reporter Rollo Wilson in August 1924 that he intended to refrain from going to Cuba that winter. He wanted to concentrate on strengthening his Harrisburg club, he said. Perhaps Janie was pushing for a break in the couple's year-long baseball schedule. Oscar may also have been put off by Abel Linares's "czaristic control" over baseball in Cuba, which Dizzy Dismukes claimed was causing a number of Negro Leaguers to think about not playing on the island any more.[84] But Oscar proved unable to adhere to his summer plans. In October he and Janie returned to Havana, where Janie was a big enough celebrity in her own right that one paper ran a photo of her arriving from Florida. This winter Charleston would play with Almendares in the Cuban League.[85]

The Almendares Azules (Almendares Blues) of 1924–25 turned out to be little less powerful than the Santa Clara club of 1923–24. Managed by Adolfo Luque, the squad featured elite Negro League players such as John Henry Lloyd, Dick Lundy, Biz Mackey, and Bullet Joe Rogan. And just as Santa Clara had the previous season, Almendares opened such a lead that the season was finally stopped prematurely and the crown handed to the club. At that point, the team was 33-16 and had an eight-and-a-half-game advantage. The Azules' most exciting victory was probably one in which Oscar hit a game-winning line drive over the head of Santa Clara's Frank Warfield. The fans at

Almendares Park joyously carried Charleston off the field on their shoulders that day. They finally deposited him into the car that would drive him back to his hotel—but not before showering him with kisses. Their "frenzy" was such, according to one reporter, that "if the reader should now go to Almendares Park it is certain he will still find some of those fans shouting and acclaiming" their hero.[86]

Black baseball fans on the home front were not exactly restrained, but the passions of Cuban baseball fans were unparalleled. Charleston clipped for his scrapbook one short notice about a white player from the International League's Toronto club having been shot, at the ballpark, by a Havana sports editor. But it wasn't just the emotions that differed. The Cuban fields' dimensions were weird. The Blues' home diamond, Almendares Park II, which would be destroyed by a hurricane in 1926, was especially huge. The left field fence stood more than five hundred feet from home plate, and the right field fence was four hundred feet away. These obscene distances helped secure Charleston's legendary status in Cuba in three ways. First, he was one of the few hitters able to clear the right field fence with some regularity.[87] Second, the capacious outfield allowed speedy, instinctive fielders like Oscar to separate themselves from their peers. And third, the difficulty of hitting home runs meant that base running and defense were even more important. Other Cuban stadiums had somewhat similar, if not such extreme, dimensions and thus rewarded similar skills.[88]

Few players, of course, combined power, speed, and defense like Charleston. He stood out. "My uncle Oscar, as a boy in Belen, the renowned Jesuit prep school in Havana, used to sneak into Almendares Park on Sunday afternoons," remembered Roberto González Echevarría. "Until his death my uncle had engraved in his memory the figure of Oscar Charleston, the greatest player he had ever seen, sprinting through the outfield of that stadium."[89] He was not alone. By 1925 Oscar Charleston was a household name throughout the island nation.[90]

For the first time in years, however, Oscar was not unquestionably his team's best player in 1924–25. He started very slowly, and when the season ended, he had hit just .261, albeit with a league-leading four home runs. Had Oscar finally gotten tired? It's entirely possible; he had, after all, played ball every winter since the beginning of the inaugural 1920 NNL season, and he had competed in literally hundreds of spring-training, in-season, and postseason exhibition games in addition to official NNL, ECL, and Cuban League contests. Still, however fatigued he may have been, after Almendares was declared the 1924–25 Cuban League champion, Charleston signed up to play with a team composed entirely of black American players—the All-Yankees—in a special series of eight games against the All-Cubans. Commissioner Kennesaw Mountain Landis, on his way to Panama, stopped in to watch the series' third game on February 8. Oscar no doubt wished to impress the humorless autocrat; alas, he went 0 for 4. At least the Negro Leaguers won the game, 2–1.[91] That was Oscar's last game with the All-Yankees. He and Janie sailed for Key West on February 10. On board was the man as responsible as anyone for keeping Oscar and his fellow Negro Leaguers out of the white Majors. We can probably safely assume that the Charlestons and Landises did not fraternize.

Not that the Charlestons did not have prominent friends. Three winters in Cuba had given Oscar and Janie ample opportunity to build relationships with well-known persons in Havana, and they took full advantage. Over the previous twenty-plus years there had developed a strong network of cultural and economic ties between black communities in America and Cuba, and a small but noticeable number of American black writers, scholars, professionals, and businessmen had begun to live part time or permanently in Havana.[92] These men and women had helped form a cross-national group of Afro-Cuban elites centered around the Club Atenas, "Cuba's most exclusive cultural, social, and recreational organization among the colored people."[93] Founded in 1917, the club had strong ties to the Tuskegee Institute. Its members shared Booker T. Washington's commitment to racial improvement and moral and cultural uplift.

Oscar's fame and Janie's cultured background gave them entrée into this circle, which included a sports-loving businessman named James Martin and his journalist wife Margaret. James worked for the Simmons Mattress Company in Havana. Margaret had been born in Alabama. She had studied stenography, typing, and nursing before moving to New York, where she had met James and embarked on a career in journalism. The Martins and Charlestons became good friends; both Oscar's photo album and one of Janie's include many pictures of the couples together, and Oscar's scrapbook includes a Spanish-language copy of Margaret's article "The Negro in Cuba," which appeared in her correspondent W. E. B. DuBois's *Crisis* magazine in 1931. Margaret was, in the words of scholar Frank Andre Guridy, "an important point of contact between the Afro-Cuban elite and African American 'talented tenth.'"[94] One imagines that their friendship with the Martins was deeply rewarding to Oscar and Janie, neither of whom would have been satisfied by a life circumscribed by baseball alone, despite Oscar's year-round devotion to the sport.

• • •

Oscar returned to Harrisburg in February prepared to shape the second edition of his Giants into true contenders for the 1925 ECL season. While he rested his weary bones for a couple of months, he significantly strengthened his infield by luring Walter "Rev" Cannady away from the Homestead Grays and his old ABCs crony Ben Taylor from the Potomacs. Strothers, Oscar, and the black sporting press all expressed a belief that Harrisburg could compete for the league title.

There was much less confidence that the race would be fair. The main problem was the same one that bedeviled every Negro League: the man who essentially controlled the circuit also fielded a team. In the ECL that was Ed Bolden, owner of the Hilldale club. Bolden was a man who believed strongly in his own rectitude, but that meant little to the league's other teams, each of which was always ready to believe it would not be treated fairly. Bolden and the league's officials tried to allay these fears prior to the 1925 season by announcing that teams would have to play a minimum number of league games (widely varying numbers of official games having been a widespread complaint in 1924); that the first ten games between two league teams would be official games and any others classified as exhibition contests (confusion on this point having been another widespread complaint); and that umpires would be rotated and overseen by an independent supervisor (the quality and neutrality of umpiring having been a third, and indeed perennial, grievance).

These measures managed to keep the peace for less than two months. Charleston, not surprisingly, was the man who in mid-June threw a stick of dynamite into the ECL powder keg.

The Harrisburg Giants had gotten off to a splendid start in 1925. With Fats Jenkins leading off, Rap Dixon hitting in the two hole, Oscar batting third, and Cannady and Taylor following, Harrisburg had a terrific top of the lineup. The outfield defense was unparalleled. Catcher Bill Johnson later recalled, "I caught more men trying to come home after fly balls the two years I was in Harrisburg than in all my other years together."[95] By June 7, after sweeping a hot and humid doubleheader in Baltimore versus the Black Sox, Harrisburg had moved into first at 9-3. Two wins against the Bacharach Giants followed, in which Oscar was praised for his handling of his pitching staff and pinch-hitting moves—and for hitting a game-tying two-run homer in the tenth inning. Then, during a following series with Hilldale, Oscar made a strategic decision to bat the beehive.

In the Saturday, June 13, game of that series, which was played at Hilldale, three big decisions initially went against Harrisburg. All were apparently so egregious that the umpires reversed them on appeal, but those reversals only partially mollified Oscar and the Giants. When the two teams met the next day at Lancaster's Rossmere Park—where a loophole allowed professional baseball to be played on Sundays, despite Pennsylvania's Blue Laws—the Giants were still on edge. They were leading 6–2 after three innings when rain came. The downpour was brief, but to the dismay of the crowd and the fury of the Giants, the umpires, allegedly after conferring with Hilldale's management, called the game off.

Two days later Charleston sent a letter to Rollo Wilson at the *Pittsburgh Courier*. Oscar knew there was already a general belief among fans that the rules were frequently bent to help Hilldale. He intended to take advantage of that cognitive bias to create an uproar that put some pressure on the league.[96] He succeeded.

"I believe in the frank truth being exposed without fear of favor," wrote Oscar, deftly positioning himself as a courageous whistle-blower. "The Eastern Colored league [*sic*] is getting to be, or has gotten to be a farce. The public who is interested in the league and wish to see it strive is being hoodwinked and fooled out of their hard earned cash." He then detailed his complaints about the lack of clarity surrounding which games were official league contests, the poor umpiring, and the decision to call off the game in Lancaster. "Such things will ultimately mean the death of the Eastern Colored League, if there are no brakes applied quickly. Believing that you believe in the right, the truth and justice," wrote Oscar to Wilson, "I beg to submit these facts to you, hoping that you will deem it wise to denounce these evils through your column and offer remedies to the league authorities for the unnecessary evils that are existing at present."

The *Courier* published the letter on June 20, 1925, and despite a retort from Bolden on June 27, it found resonance and was reprinted in a number of other outlets. The *Courier* affirmed Charleston's charge that whether a game was a league contest or not was seemingly random, noting that in the previous week the Bacharach Giants and Harrisburg had played three games, yet none of them had counted as league battles for some reason. (Indeed, when one peruses the archives today, it is all but impossible to know how a given outcome will affect a club's official league record.) The sports editor of the *Baltimore Afro-American* also chimed in. "The question is, when do the Eastern league clubs play league games? That's what's got the fans around the circuit puzzled. First, it was published that the first ten games would count and now lo and behold, we find that they don't. Oscar Charleston of the Harrisburg Giants in an article last week is of the same opinion we are and have been for some time. When Hilldale wins it's a league game, when they lose it's an exhibition."[97] The inconsistency was maddening. Wilson reported in his June 27, 1925, *Courier* column that Oscar's letter "had started a fire which may burn down some of the weeds which are obstructing the growth of the Eastern League." He encouraged others also to stand up for the good of professional black baseball.

Others smelled conspiracy. William Nunn of the *Pittsburgh Courier* noted on July 4 that if Harrisburg won the 1925 pennant—an outcome that looked ever more likely—the Colored World Series would be a financial disaster from the perspective of the league's leaders. The moguls wanted the pennant winner to be Hilldale or another seaboard team, he concluded, and it therefore wouldn't be a surprise if the ECL tried to find a way to job the Giants out of the flag. The Harrisburg press, not surprisingly, fully agreed with Nunn's analysis. Umpires were giving the Giants the short end of the stick on the road, reported the paper, but that was only to be expected. Certain umpires, however, were ruling consistently against the Giants *at home.* And wasn't that mysterious?

Whether or not any of these charges were true, the Giants were energized by the controversy. With Oscar hitting over .500, they went on a hot streak that included three more victories over

Hilldale (though only two of these counted as league games) and two over the Potomacs. In an early July tilt against the Baltimore Black Sox the Giants won 16–14, Charleston winning the contest with his second home run of the game—a deep, opposite-field drive to left—in the bottom of the ninth. A reporter who rode with the Giants on their team bus during this period said they were as cocky and spirited a bunch as he had ever seen. Oscar had his men confident they could beat any team, anytime, anywhere. A white Harrisburg reporter said the Giants were playing Major League–quality baseball under Charleston's direction—indeed they were playing *better* than some Major League clubs. In the official league standings released on July 18, Harrisburg sat in first place, the "super-player" Charleston leading all ECL hitters with a .455 average and placing second in both home runs and steals.[98]

Slowly, though, and possibly with the aid of some creative accounting, Hilldale pulled away from Harrisburg as the season progressed. Everyone was frustrated. Oscar started displaying a quick hook with faltering starters. William Nunn pleaded with Bolden to send a list of the bona fide league games that had been played and would be played, and he all but accused Bolden of outright fraud. The Giants protested two losses to the Baltimore Black Sox on the grounds that one of the games' officials had not been sanctioned by the league's supervisor of umpires. Bolden charged Oscar with pushing a peacemaking player out of the way in one game so that *his* player (second baseman Dick Jackson) could duke it out man-to-man with Hilldale's Frank Warfield. "Charleston's poison tongue and foul tactics will never win the pennant," fumed Bolden.[99]

Even when it was clear what status a game had, it was just Harrisburg's luck to win the wrong ones, as on August 8, when Charleston went 2 for 2 with two walks and a sacrifice fly in an 11–4 exhibition win over Hilldale, only to see his club lose to Hilldale 5–3 in a league game a few days later. That loss left the Giants five games back of the leaders. "Such are the breaks of luck. When they count, we lose 'em and when they are not worth a hoot in Gehenna . . . we win 'em," sighed Charleston.[100]

In a time of such frustration there was nothing Charleston needed more than a good fight in a good cause. As the season entered its final month, Oscar allegedly hit the Bacharach Giants' Rats Henderson in the face after Henderson disputed an umpire's decision at home plate. Henderson and his teammate Oliver Marcell were ejected, but not Charleston, whom the home plate umpire credited with protecting himself and his partner. That episode infuriated Bolden. But even he would have had to admit that it was nothing compared to what John Beckwith, manager of the Baltimore Black Sox, did to an umpire in late July. After a loss in Harrisburg, Beckwith waylaid and brutally assaulted the ump as he left the field. A warrant was sworn out for Beckwith's arrest, and the league suspended him for a few games; a little later he quit the team and decamped to Chicago.

The Harrisburg Giants' chances for a league title essentially ended when they lost both ends of a doubleheader to Hilldale on September 19. When the 1925 league year concluded in late September, Harrisburg had tallied a record of 37-18, by the league's accounting, second to Hilldale's 45-13.[101] Charleston won both the batting crown (.430, officially) and home run crown (fourteen). All that was left was the postseason.

• • •

The talk was that Jim Keenan, owner of the ECL's woeful New York Lincoln Giants (7-39 in 1925 league play), was going to get together a "colored all-star team" to take on the New York Yankees in a six-game set at Yankee Stadium in October. Charleston and Giants pitcher Ping Gardner traveled to New York to help strengthen Keenan's team, which warmed up for the Bronx Bombers by taking on a squad of alleged "Philadelphia Professionals" at the Lincoln Giants' home park, the Protectory Oval in Harlem. The Giants beat the Philadelphians (for whom Judge Landis blocked Athletics spitballer Jack Quinn and catcher

Mickey Cochrane from playing) and a semipro team from Bayside, New Jersey, three out of three by a combined score of 26–5, as Oscar knocked the ball all over and out of the park.

The games with the Yankees never came off, but ten days later the Lincoln Giants did play a wild eleven-inning affair at Protectory Oval against a white "Bronx Giants" club that included a young Lou Gehrig in center field. The pride of Columbia University had just finished an outstanding rookie season with the Yanks, hitting .295 with twenty home runs. In front of the crowd of six thousand Gehrig helped the Bronx Giants win, 6–5, going 1 for 2 with a couple of walks. His older center field counterpart for the Lincoln Giants fared even better. Oscar homered in the sixth, doubled in the eleventh, and added two more hits and two sensational catches to his day's work.[102]

To see Oscar and his teammates play the likes of Gehrig must have been fascinating, but it would have been even more thrilling to see Oscar square off against the Babe.[103] They were by now the most popular and best players in their respective realms. Charleston's popularity was confirmed when, near the end of the season, Rollo Wilson asked his readers to submit their 1925 eastern all-star team. Charleston got more votes than anyone—212 votes out of 221 submissions. (He finished fourth in the managerial balloting, where Atlantic City Bacharach Giants manager John Henry Lloyd took the honors.)

As far as being the best? Today's reconstructed statistics tell an amazing story that only amplifies what people thought at the time. In seventy-one games (we are not restricted to official "league" games here) and 321 plate appearances, Oscar Charleston hit a Cobb-like .427 in 1925. His on-base percentage was a Ruthian .523; his slugging, a Bonds-ish .776. He ranked first among all black players in all three slash line numbers. He led in home runs with twenty. His fifty-one walks ranked fifth. Still speedy, he added seventeen steals. In the context of the Negro Leagues' overall offensive environment these numbers add up to an OPS+ of 228 (or 128 percent above average), a figure that again led the league by a significant margin. There was no better all-around player in the world, including—with emphasis on the adjective *all-around*—the great Babe Ruth himself.

Charleston had many excellent years remaining, but his seven-year span of Negro Leagues play between 1919 and 1925, during which he posted an OPS+ above 200 four times, constitutes his peak. It towers above his contemporaries in black baseball. He compiled a 1.143 OPS over those seven years—complemented by superlative defense and speed on the base paths. By OPS+, four of these years—1919, 1921, 1924, and 1925—rank among the top eight Negro Leagues seasons in the Seamheads.com database. Charleston's 1920 and 1922 seasons also rank among the top twenty-six. There aren't many better seven-year stretches in the annals of baseball history.

$\bullet\ \bullet\ \bullet$

After having taken no more than a few weeks off in the autumn of 1925, Oscar returned to Cuba. Switching teams yet again, for the 1925–26 Cuban League season he would play for the Habana Reds, a club that also featured Oliver Marcell, Cristóbal Torriente, Jud Wilson, and Martín Dihigo.[104] It was a strange year that began with three league teams—Habana, Almendares, and San Jose—but ended with just two after San Jose withdrew on December 22. Habana finished two games behind Almendares in the final standings, Charleston hitting .350 in just forty at bats.

For Oscar, the winter was more tragic than strange. He had been in Havana only a short time when he was informed of the death of his mother, Mary, from acute myocarditis, on December 4. She was fifty-three years old. Oscar returned to Indianapolis for the funeral, held December 15 at Simpson AME Church.[105] In his column, Rollo Wilson extended his sympathies to "the brightest star in baseball."[106]

Oscar had inherited from Mary his inclination to fight in defense of whatever he thought was his. He had also inherited from her his respect for civic engagement. In the years since

Oscar had left home, Mary had risen within the leadership ranks of the Ancient Knights and Daughters of Africa fraternal organization. In 1924 she had been elected national grand queen mother of the group's juvenile department at its convention in Cleveland, and the Indianapolis council had surprised her with a congratulatory reception in September of that year. In August 1925 Mary had presided over an organizational convention in Indianapolis. Her unexpected death must have come as a shock to Oscar and his seven living siblings.[107] Both of their parents were now gone, and both had died young.

By mid-February 1926 Oscar and Janie were back in Harrisburg. All winter there had been rumors that Colonel Strothers had lost a lot of money in 1925, that his Harrisburg Giants would be sold, and that Charleston would leave town for greener pastures. The first rumor was true, but the last two were not.[108] Strothers had decided to give it another go. In fact, his plan was to enter the Giants not only in the ECL, but in a second league, as well: a new circuit called the Interstate League (ISL). The league would ensure the Giants of several dozen more games and perhaps pique some interest, thought its clubs' owners, for the reason that three of its six teams were black and three where white.

In addition to Harrisburg, the other black teams in the ISL would also be ECL squads: Hilldale and the Bacharach Giants. The three white clubs would be based in Chester and Allentown, Pennsylvania, and Camden, New Jersey. The structural imbalance is perhaps clearer from today's vantage point, when we have a much better idea of just how good the best black players of the time were, than it was in the hazy present of 1926. That is, the white clubs almost by definition couldn't have been *too* good, for while the efficiency of organized baseball's talent identification and recruitment system in 1926 paled in comparison to what it is now, it was nevertheless not *completely* inefficient. Truly great white players weren't, for the most part, playing semipro ball any more. The ISL's final standings would prove the point.

In any case, with two leagues in which to compete Charleston got to work. By the end of February he was conferencing with Strothers and sending 1926 contracts to players. The stalwart Ben Taylor had been lost to the Baltimore Black Sox, which he would also manage, but Charleston had recruited a couple of Cuban players to join his club while in Havana, and essentially everyone else of importance was back. Despite Strothers's not having the financial wherewithal to host a spring training tour, by mid-April the Harrisburg Giants were ready.

The Giants kicked off the year by beating their city rivals, the Senators, on April 17, 14–5. Charleston went 3 for 5 with a stolen base. The next Saturday, against the York White Roses, Charleston hit for the cycle and stole a base in a 19–5 victory. Whether they were in the ISL or not, white semipro teams usually posed little trouble for the Giants. On April 28, after a 10–7 win over Williamsport in which Charleston's sole hit was a three-run homer, the *Harrisburg Evening News* reported that the Giants "are making a tour of the New York-Penn [league] and leaving a path of destruction in their wake." That continued when ISL play opened on Saturday, May 1, in Allentown; Harrisburg won both ends of the doubleheader, 14–6 and 16–4. In Lancaster on May 9 the Giants bludgeoned Chester, 23–6. In a mid-June double bill they destroyed the Brooklyn Farmers, 13–3 and 16–12. On July 21, at Island Park, the Giants steamrolled the Boston Black Sox, 17–2. Oscar went 3 for 4 with three stolen bases, and his home run to right was "the longest hit of the season into the right-field woods, where the ball landed out of sight."[109]

ECL opponents were a different story, but again Charleston spurred his club to a fast start, as the Giants led the league through May. Oscar had somehow been energized. His dynamism, and the dynamism of his players, was what stood out to observers. William Nunn noted that "Oscar Charleston, who has ofttimes been referred to (and justly) as America's 'King' of outfielders, white or colored, is still hitting home runs, beating out swinging bunts, throwing baserunners out at all stations and making spectacular catches, while Tris Speaker is ready to shelve his spikes and glove."[110] Rollo Wilson, who was based in Philadelphia, continued to marvel at Oscar as well. "Still the same urbane hustler as of old, the competent manager of the Harrisburg Giants, Oscar Charleston, strolled into the office the other day and gave us the season's greetings," he reported. "Oscar has a BALL TEAM and he is letting everyone SEE it."[111]

"Traveling at a terrific pace himself," noted Wilson, Charleston was "inspiring his men to superhuman efforts and the club is making the breaks go their way at all times."[112] However, Oscar increasingly edged into hotheadedness as the year dragged on. The Giants, whose pitching was always suspect, couldn't maintain their lead, and the players' frustrations—with the league, with the umps, and, one surmises, mostly with themselves—began to boil over. On June 10 Charleston spiked a Black Sox pitcher covering first, hurting him badly enough that he had to leave the game. Outfielder Rap Dixon tried to fight an umpire in Baltimore. Shortstop Rev Cannady was the year's worst offender. On June 27, in New York, Cannady slugged the home plate umpire in the jaw. About a month later Cannady exploded again. After a 3–0 loss to Hilldale in Philadelphia, he caught up to an umpire driving away after the game and threw a bat through his car window.

The Giants were far from the only team getting into confrontations like these, but they seemed to be involved in more than their fair share. The press, quite naturally, blamed Oscar. "It looks like Charleston is putting the pugilistic attitude into most of the Harrisburg players," commented the *Baltimore Afro-American*.[113] Even the sympathetic William Nunn was compelled to criticize Oscar's team. The Giants may be the "'squabblingest' baseball team of all time," he wrote. Nunn blamed the weak league administration for not fining Cannady and others for fighting with umpires—and for not fining managers like Charleston who encouraged such behavior.[114]

On August 14, at 18-16 Harrisburg sat in a disappointing fifth place, although this record put the Giants only four and a half games out of first. As usual the league's teams had played wildly varying amounts of games. Hilldale had played fifty-three, the first-place Cuban Stars had played twenty-five, and last-place Brooklyn had played but fourteen. In that respect the league was hardly less of a farce than it had been, by Oscar's lights, in 1925. Rollo Wilson lamented on September 4 that there was "about as much interest in the league as there is in the next performance of Halley's Comet."[115]

For the Giants that lack of interest may have been a blessing, for their 1926 league season ended with a whimper. The Bacharach Giants took both the ECL and the ISL pennants, and Harrisburg crossed the finish line at fourth place and third place in the two leagues, respectively (the three white teams finished last in the ISL). For Oscar the postseason was much more rewarding, not only because he again got to match up with top Major League talent, but also because, as time would prove, new career doors were opened.

• • •

In the autumn of 1926 Earl Mack, son of the legendary Connie, put together a bona fide team of AL All-Stars to do some postseason barnstorming, and both Hilldale owner Ed Bolden and Homestead Grays owner Cum Posey managed to get dates with the All-Stars on their schedules. Mack's club included true stars like Wally Schang (Browns) at catcher; George Burns (Indians) at first base; AL batting champion Heinie Manush (Tigers), Goose Goslin (Senators) and Al Simmons (Athletics) in the outfield; and the aging Walter Johnson (Senators) and up-and-coming fireballer Lefty Grove (Athletics) on the mound. To their usual clubs, both of which were already strong, Bolden and Posey added two Harrisburg stars: Oscar Charleston and the alcoholic red-ass for whom Oscar had traded in mid-season, John Beckwith.

Beckwith, nearly six feet tall and 200 pounds, was a bad man. A Kentuckian born in January 1900, he had made his professional debut in 1919. Since then he had made a reputation as a drinker, fighter, and fearsome slugger who was nevertheless athletic enough to play on the left side of the infield. So long as he refrained from waylaying umpires, any team would have been happy to add him. As for Charleston, one might have thought there was genuinely bad blood between him and Bolden at this point, owing to their very public 1925 contretemps and subsequent league controversies. But the lure of winning games versus Major Leaguers, and making money doing it, trumped such considerations.

The first two games took place on October 1 and 2 between Hilldale—a club that in addition to Charleston and Beckwith included Biz Mackey at catcher, Frank Warfield at second base, Judy Johnson at third base, and George Carr at first base—and the AL All-Stars in Wilmington, Delaware, and Darby, Pennsylvania, respectively. Oscar and Beckwith immediately earned their keep. Hilldale won in Wilmington, 3–2, behind Beckwith's game-winning homer in the eighth. In Darby it won again, 6–1, by lacing ten hits off Lefty Grove, while Nip Winters limited the American Leaguers to seven singles. Oscar, who never had much trouble against left-handers or fastballs, got the best of the future Hall of Famer Grove—who had led the AL with a 2.51 ERA and 194 strikeouts in 1926—by hammering one of the long-limbed southpaw's offerings into the right field stands in the fifth inning.

These games may have been exhibitions, but reputations and egos were still on the line. As Grove's teammate Jimmy Dykes later recalled, "Every game was played for keeps. . . . We wanted to beat those fellows as bad as they wanted to beat us."[116] Grove would retire as the finest left-hander the game had ever seen. But he preferred to pretend not to remember this contest—or any other in which he had played against Negro Leaguers. Decades later he told interviewer John Holway, "I have never played against blacks in my life."[117] (Oscar, on the other hand, certainly remembered and respected Lefty. Once, when he was asked whether an opposing Negro Leagues pitcher had better stuff than Grove, he responded, "Well, he owns a better curve than Grove—but, boy, he ain't got the same powder—no sir!")[118]

Immediately after Grove's pasting, Mack's All-Stars left for Youngstown, Ohio, where they would play the Grays, including ringers Charleston and Beckwith, the next day. One wonders whether the white and black men traveled the 365 miles together, talking about the crowds likely to greet them and the money they would consequently make, for the games in the West were even more highly anticipated than those in the East, in part because of Charleston's participation. Few Pittsburgh fans had ever seen Oscar play in person, noted the *Pittsburgh Courier*.[119] Thanks to a special train from Pittsburgh to Youngstown, eight thousand of them turned out for the Sunday, October 3, tilt, which the Grays lost to the white All-Stars, 11–6, in ten innings.[120] The Grays' cause was not helped when, in the tenth, their pitcher George Britt got into a fist fight with an umpire, and reliever Sam Streeter had to be rushed into the game without properly warming up. Oscar went hitless. The next day, before nine thousand spectators at Forbes Field, the Grays evened things up with a 6–5 victory behind the pitching of ageless fireballer Smokey Joe Williams, said to be fifty years old but actually a sprightly forty.

Next, the AL All-Stars, Charleston, and Beckwith moved on to Bloomsburg, Pennsylvania, where Hilldale awaited at the county fairgrounds. The two teams continued to show that they were about evenly matched. The American Leaguers won, 1–0, on Wednesday, October 6 (Oscar went 1 for 4), but Hilldale won, 3–0, on Thursday, October 7, its outfield, anchored by Oscar in center, depriving the All-Stars of what appeared to be several sure hits.[121] In the end Hilldale went 2-1 against the All-Stars in Bloomsburg and won five out of seven games overall. Oscar capped his season by traveling back to Pittsburgh to join the Grays in one last game versus the ECL's Colored World Series entrant Bacharach Giants. On Saturday, October

16, he helped lead the Grays to a 7–6 win by hitting a home run and two singles.

It's safe to say that at no time was Oscar intimidated by his AL company. He reveled in it. That much is demonstrated not only by the fine performances he etched in the historical record in games such as these, but also by the ones handed down to us orally as part of the Charleston legend. One interviewee recalled decades later that in one of the Bloomsburg contests Lefty Grove, doubtless with Oscar's earlier home run still fresh in his mind, aimed a fastball at Oscar's head. Oscar hit the dirt— and then charged the mound. Grove at first came forward, but at the last minute he ducked and dodged his assailant. "I knew you were yellow," yelled Oscar. "Why don't you fight like a man? I thought you weren't afraid of Negroes!"[122]

Ted Williams heard another of these stories. In his telling Oscar was facing Walter Johnson for the first time, perhaps in 1919 or 1920 at New York's Protectory Oval.[123] "I've done heard about your fast ball, and I'm gonna hit it out of here," Oscar boasted to the Big Train. Johnson made Charleston look silly in his first two at bats, striking him out both times. But by his third at bat Oscar had Johnson timed, and he pulled a fastball over the right field fence for the game's only run.[124]

Did Oscar really charge Lefty Grove? Where did Williams get his story about Charleston and Walter Johnson? It's quite possible neither event happened. It's also possible that if these events did take place, Johnson and Grove preferred not to mention them.

1. Janie Blalock (second from left, second row from bottom) and her teammates on the Philander Athletic Club of November 14, 1915, are all smiles. Janie's friend Esther Popel, future poet of the Harlem Renaissance, is seated in the middle of the bottom row. Estate of Elizabeth P. Overton.

2. Janie and her young Harrisburg students, sometime between 1915 and 1918. Estate of Elizabeth P. Overton.

3. A young Janie Blalock poses for a formal portrait. Estate of Elizabeth P. Overton.

4. (*opposite top*) Oscar Charleston (middle row, far left) poses with his Indianapolis ABCs teammates as a rookie in 1915. National Baseball Hall of Fame and Museum, Cooperstown, New York.

5. (*opposite bottom*) Oscar, pitcher Juan Padrón, and first baseman Leroy Grant played for the Royal Poinciana team, managed by Rube Foster, in the Palm Beach, Florida, Hotel League in winter 1917. This is the oldest photo of Oscar in his photo album. Courtesy of the Negro Leagues Baseball Museum.

Oscar   Palm Beach Fla.

Padrone   Levy Grant

6. Oscar Charleston (top row, third from right) and his 1922 Indianapolis ABCs teammates. Hall of Famers Ben Taylor and Biz Mackey (in that order) are standing to the left of Oscar (his right). National Baseball Hall of Fame and Museum, Cooperstown, New York.

7. (*opposite*) Janie and Oscar Charleston, probably in Cuba during the 1920s. National Baseball Hall of Fame and Museum, Cooperstown, New York.

8. Janie Charleston photo series, probably taken shortly after she and Oscar were married. Courtesy of the Negro Leagues Baseball Museum.

9. The legendary outfield that led the dominant Santa Clara club of the 1923–24 Cuban League: Pablo Mesa, Oscar Charleston, and Alejandro Oms. Courtesy of the Negro Leagues Baseball Museum.

10. Janie Charleston (right) with a woman identified as the wife of Oscar's Indianapolis ABCs teammate Dizzy Dismukes. Courtesy of the Negro Leagues Baseball Museum.

11. Oscar and Janie Charleston, dressed in style, as was their custom. Courtesy of the Negro Leagues Baseball Museum.

12. Janie Charleston and journalist friend Margaret Martin in Playa de Ponce, Puerto Rico, December 8, 1928. Margaret and her businessman husband James ran among the Afro-Cuban elite. Estate of Elizabeth P. Overton.

13. (*opposite top*) The more relaxed schedule in Cuba left time, occasionally, for players like Oscar to go swimming. Courtesy of the Negro Leagues Baseball Museum.

14. (*opposite bottom*) Oscar was pleased to have the sweet-hitting Clarence "Fats" Jenkins (left) flanking him in the Harrisburg Giants' outfield. Rap Dixon manned the other corner, giving the Giants the best outfield in the Negro Leagues during the mid-1920s. Courtesy of the Negro Leagues Baseball Museum.

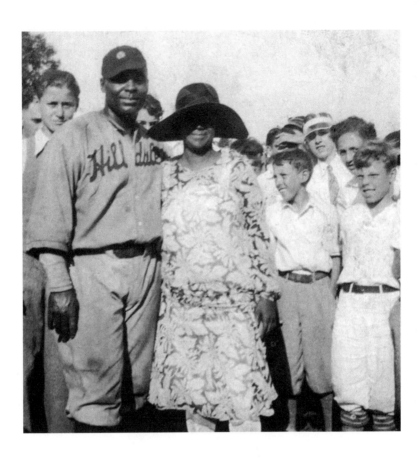

15. Transcendent Negro Leagues stars like Charleston were not heroes to black children alone, as this photo of Oscar with an unidentified woman, taken in 1928 or 1929, when he played for the Hilldale club based in the Philadelphia suburbs, demonstrates. Courtesy of the Negro Leagues Baseball Museum.

16. (*opposite top*) Heavyweight champion George Godfrey pretends to spar with Oscar, who was a huge boxing aficionado, for this publicity photo in 1928. Courtesy of NoirTech Research.

17. (*opposite bottom*) The 1930 Homestead Grays. Charleston kneels at the far right, bottom row. Owner Cum Posey, sporting his usual togs, is standing on the far right, while Smokey Joe Williams (fifth from left, top row) looms over everyone in the back. National Baseball Hall of Fame and Museum, Cooperstown, New York.

Homestead Grays of 1930
3-20-30

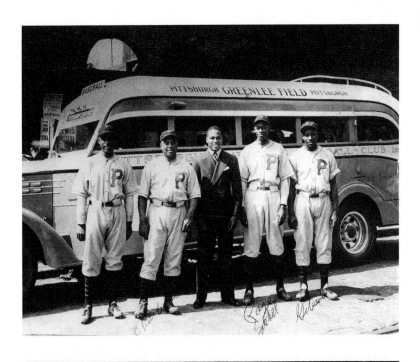

18. (*opposite top*) Five of the most accomplished athletes of the 1930s stand in front of the Pittsburgh Crawfords team bus (from left): Leroy Matlock, Oscar Charleston, boxer John Henry Lewis, Satchel Paige, and Josh Gibson. National Baseball Hall of Fame and Museum, Cooperstown, New York.

19. (*opposite bottom*) The champion Pittsburgh Crawfords of 1935 kneel for what has become an iconic photo in front of their famous bus, with Oscar kneeling at the front. National Baseball Hall of Fame and Museum, Cooperstown, New York.

20. (*above*) A smiling Oscar stands outside his friend Gus Greenlee's popular Crawford Grill in Pittsburgh, 1937. © Carnegie Museum of Art, Charles "Teenie" Harris Archive.

21. Pittsburgh Crawfords secretary John L. Clark and Oscar Charleston pause for a photo, sometime in the mid- to late 1930s. Estate of Elizabeth P. Overton.

22. (*opposite top*) West manager Andy Cooper greets East manager Oscar Charleston on August 21, 1938, at the Negro Leagues' East-West game at Comiskey Park in Chicago. Courtesy of NoirTech Research.

23. (*opposite bottom*) During World War II, Oscar (top row, third from right) worked at the Quartermaster Depot in south Philadelphia. He also played for and managed—more than four years before Jackie Robinson broke Major League Baseball's color line—the Depot's integrated baseball team, which played in the city's Industrial League. Courtesy of the Negro Leagues Baseball Museum.

24. Oscar and the infield of the 1943 Quartermaster Depot's team: Marvin Weinstein, Wendell Jenkins, and Eddie Brouillette. National Baseball Hall of Fame and Museum, Cooperstown, New York.

25. (*opposite top*) Web McDonald (left) and Joseph Hall (center) look on as in February 1945 Oscar Charleston signs his contract to manage the Hilldale entry in the short-lived United States League. National Baseball Hall of Fame and Museum, Cooperstown, New York.

26. (*opposite bottom*) Oscar, happy to be managing the Brooklyn Brown Dodgers of the United States League—while scouting for Branch Rickey's National League Dodgers on the side—poses during a game in May 1945 at Pittsburgh's Forbes Field. © Carnegie Museum of Art, Charles "Teenie" Harris Archive.

27. (*opposite top*) A young Philadelphia Stars player, the accomplished Dr. Hilda Bolden, and an appreciative Oscar in 1951 or 1952. Courtesy of NoirTech Research.

28. (*opposite bottom*) Charleston (far right), as manager of the Philadelphia Stars, poses with (from left to right) Kansas City Monarchs manager Buck O'Neil and umpires Sylvester Vaughn, Bob Motley, and Frank Duncan. Courtesy Bob Motley Family Archives.

29. (*above*) Indianapolis Clowns entertainer King Tut, Oscar, and second baseman Connie Morgan pose for one of team owner Syd Pollock's publicity shots in 1954. Courtesy of NoirTech Research.

30. Oscar's sister Katherine, shown
here with Commissioner Bowie Kuhn,
represented Charleston at his induction
into the National Baseball Hall of Fame in
August 1976. Courtesy of the Negro Leagues
Baseball Museum.

31. (*opposite*) A wooden statuette that Oscar
Charleston presented to his wife, Janie, as
a gift, probably in 1928 or 1929. Estate of
Elizabeth P. Overton. Photo by the author.

32. Probably taken in the early 1920s, this is one of the two photos of Oscar Charleston that his estranged wife, Janie, kept until her death. Estate of Elizabeth P. Overton.

CHAPTER 6

Leader, 1926–1931

BY THE AUTUMN OF 1926 Oscar Charleston, now thirty, had played professional baseball every winter since 1920. Yet his appetite for the game was apparently insatiable. During the winter of 1926–27 he and Janie returned to Cuba yet again. Once there, Oscar chose to spend his off days playing for the Preston sugar mill team, along with Frank Duncan, Dick Lundy, and Oliver Marcell, among other pros. Like other sugar mill squads, Preston frequently brought in Cuban League players, including Negro Leaguers playing in the Cuban League, as ringers. Preston in particular was "a powerhouse that could have challenged any team in the Cuban League," in Roberto González Echevarría's estimation. Charleston reputedly received $180 per month, plus expenses, to play for the club, in addition to his regular winter-ball salary. At the time, a Cuban sugarcane cutter made less than one dollar a day.[1]

Charleston was unusually eager to play in sugar mill contests, perhaps, because during this winter of 1926–27 he did not play in the official Cuban League but in a rival, independent league known as the Triangular. The moonlighting did not diminish his performance. He led the Triangular in hits, and his .404 batting average was the league's fourth best. It was a nice bounce back from the previous year's surprisingly pedestrian effort, but Oscar found the competition rather dull, much preferring a unified league with stronger teams.[2] Moreover, he was looking forward to another change of jersey for the 1927 season. He intended to forsake Janie's hometown Harrisburg Giants to play with Cumberland Posey's Homestead Grays.

Oscar broke this news himself in a letter published by the *Pittsburgh Courier* on New Year's Day. Posey had gotten to know Oscar better the previous fall, when Charleston and John Beckwith had barnstormed with the Grays. Like everyone else, Posey was impressed. Negotiations to bring Oscar to Pittsburgh commenced immediately, and by mid-December 1926 Oscar had signed a contract. He and Colonel Strothers had had some kind of disagreement, and Oscar told Posey that he wanted a change of scenery. Whether Janie gave her blessing to her husband's intention to move across the state is unknown, but since she was with Oscar in Cuba as terms were being finalized and when he announced his decision, she was probably not taken by surprise.

Oscar and Janie didn't leave Havana for Key West until February 13, 1927, so they were safely removed, for six weeks, from the uproar that followed Charleston's announcement. Posey was thrilled. He was already famous among black sports fans for the basketball prowess he had displayed at Penn State and subsequently on a Pittsburgh team called the Loendi Big Five. (Posey was inducted into the Naismith Memorial Basketball Hall of Fame in 2016, ten years after he was admitted into Cooperstown.) Signing Oscar would help him realize his goal of making the independent Grays one of the best black teams in the country. "Charleston is recognized as the World's Greatest Colored Baseball Player and is a tremendous drawing card," Posey wrote in the *Courier*, where he had a regularly recurring column. However self-interested this opinion might have been, it was echoed by the *Philadelphia Tribune*: "In Charleston the Grays are getting the man who is generally accepted as the greatest of our sluggers and outfielders. He is a colorful performer who attracts as much by his personality as by his unquestioned ability as a player. . . . He represents a high type of intelligence combined with remarkable physical endowments and a great deal of temperament, as well as temper."[3] Posey expected Oscar, outfielder Vic Harris, and catcher Buck Ewing to make his team highly competitive no matter who was in the other dugout or how volatile Charleston's temper really was.

Joining Posey was a risky move for Oscar. The Eastern Colored League had made clear that players who jumped their contracts would be banned from playing league ball for some years. If the Grays folded and the ECL owners held firm, Charleston would be marooned. But Posey wasn't done dealing. Charleston was leverage. Within days, Posey proposed to both the ECL and the western NNL a deal whereby the independent Grays would play four games per month at Forbes Field versus league teams, thereby making long-distance journeys for clubs traveling between the East and the Midwest more profitable. The Grays would no longer touch any league players, and league teams would agree not to raid the Grays. Posey would even send a few players to the Harrisburg Giants as compensation for Charleston—who, he reminded the owners, had already signed a contract.

The owners rejected Posey's proposal. They spread word that Posey offered huge salaries to lure players in and then cut those salaries after they had signed and burned their bridges. They also reaffirmed that jumpers like Charleston would be banned from playing in either major Negro League for five years. Posey laughed at such hypocrisy—the eastern clubs had built their squads precisely by stealing players from the West—and predicted that no such ban would ever be enforced. He reported that Oscar, too, was little worried about such threats; Charleston was "more concerned about the additional right hand pitcher whom the Grays will have this season."[4]

Rumors nevertheless continued to swirl. In late February it was said that the new Cleveland entry in the NNL wanted to make Harrisburg (which in the leagues' eyes still controlled Charleston's rights) the largest cash payment for a player ever seen and then offer Charleston the largest salary ever made by a league player, if the other owners would let it. Posey regarded this story as yet another league ploy intended to entice Oscar into changing his mind.

When Oscar and Janie arrived back in Harrisburg in early March, the confusion mushroomed. With all the rumors that were flying about, Ben Taylor, who was still managing the Baltimore Black Sox, smelled opportunity. He made contact with his old friend Oscar and convinced him to forget the Grays and sign a contract with Baltimore. He also persuaded Harrisburg to accept hard-hitting outfielder Jud Wilson in exchange. As Wilson was a major star in his own right, this was not only a reasonably fair trade, but also front-page news in the March 5 edition of the *Baltimore Afro-American*. Oscar allegedly wired the Baltimore owner to say that he would "give fans his best."[5] Yet the very next day the Harrisburg papers reported that Charleston would remain with the Harrisburg Giants in 1927 and that John Beckwith, whom Colonel Strothers had tapped to replace Oscar as manager when the news about Oscar's joining the Grays had broken, would remain the squad's skipper.

Even by Oscar's standards this was a dizzying offseason. What was going on? Carl Murphy, a reporter for the *Baltimore Afro-American*, decided to find out. He went up to Harrisburg, found Oscar at his "pretty" three-story home, and filed one of the more interesting articles about Oscar to appear in his lifetime.

The day after he had signed the contract with Taylor's Black Sox, Oscar told Murphy, he had had a change of heart. He felt bad about putting his friend Ben Taylor in "a bad light," but he was still considering going with the Grays, and in any case Janie did not wish to move to Baltimore (perhaps not only for family reasons, but also because Baltimore was a much more southern city, in its racial mores, than was Harrisburg). Shortly thereafter, Oscar said, he had decided not to go with the Grays, either, because despite Posey's assurances that the owners' threats were empty, such threats (and, it was later said, some wise friends' advice) had gotten his attention. He thought the leagues might well make an example of him if he jumped, and he knew that if they did, he would have no leverage with Posey over his future salaries.

Money was something Oscar did not feel he could take for granted, despite his history of being one of the game's best-paid players. In fact, when Murphy found him at home in Harrisburg, Oscar was in the midst of studying for a fingerprinting course he was taking by correspondence. He was on the seventeenth of twenty-two lessons, he said. Charleston imagined a future in which hundreds of fingerprinting experts would be needed. "A man can't play baseball forever," he conceded, "and he has got to have his eyes open, so that when his baseball days are over he won't be a candidate for the poorhouse."[6]

As it happened, Oscar would never need a career outside the game. But the same provident nature that led him to plan for such an eventuality meant that he was frequently on the move.

• • •

After the dust had settled, William Nunn wrote a patronizing piece in the *Pittsburgh Courier* criticizing Oscar for allowing Janie to sway his professional decision making; such conduct was not worthy of a man with "true guts."[7] Next to this article, in Charleston's scrapbook, is pasted another in which the author states that the "best men, as a rule, are the most deferential to women" and that a man who "dominates his wife" is a "bully." Was this Janie's attempt to ensure that Oscar not feel emasculated by Nunn's broadside? Or was it Oscar's own unpublicized response to Nunn—and his assurance of affection and fidelity to his wife? As we shall see, Janie may have had good reason to want such assurances.

Cum Posey, unlike Nunn, was amiable about the whole drama. Saying that Charleston "is a good man" and sending him "our best wishes for success," he released Oscar from his Grays contract and saved face by claiming that Oscar had wanted a long-term deal that he, Posey, was unwilling to sign in light of Oscar's relatively advanced age. Charleston would stay with Harrisburg for a fourth—and, as it turned out, final—season in 1927. Posey prophesied that he and new Giants manager Beckwith would get along just fine. "The only men who have an argument with either of these men are players who try to 'get by' without working hard at all times."[8]

That may have been true, but if an opponent was up for a fight, Oscar was willing to oblige. On May 6, in the fourth inning of the first game of the ECL season at Island Park, Oscar slid into first base. Maurice "Eggie" Dallard, brash first baseman for the opposing Bacharach Giants, stepped on him. Oscar made his displeasure known, Dallard took a swing, and the fight was on. After a few minutes of sparring in front of the capacity crowd, the bout broke up and the men shook hands. Neither player was ejected (but both were later fined twenty-five dollars). Oscar had been in a foul mood because in the previous inning the Bacharachs' Henry Gillespie had come in high and hot at third, spiking Beckwith in the chest and slashing his jersey clean through. Bloodied, uniform in shreds, Beckwith remained in the game. Harrisburg ended up winning, 4–1. It was just the kind of intense contest Oscar loved.

Two days later, in Brooklyn, Oscar confined his hitting to the plate, smashing two home runs and leading the Giants to a Sunday doubleheader sweep over the white Bushwicks. Although Rap Dixon was in Honolulu and no longer flanking Charleston in right, Harrisburg again had a good team and got off to a reasonably fast start in 1927. Yet the crowds at Island Park were depressingly small—so small that in at least one instance Colonel Strothers moved a couple of home games to Richmond, Virginia. Perhaps not many rooters were on hand, then, when Charleston hit the longest home run Island Park had ever seen—longer even than the one he had slugged the previous July. The drive came on Tuesday, June 21, against the Cuban Stars. In the eighth inning, with the Giants down two, Oscar drilled a pitch so deep to right field that it cleared the trees and nearly rolled into the Susquehanna. The Giants scored three more in the inning and won the game, 6–4. Wellington Jones, a white Harrisburg newspaper man who would ever after champion Oscar's abilities, tramped out into the bushes beyond the trees and found that the ball had traveled 464 feet, 9 inches.[9] No one has hit a ball that far at Island Park (now FNB Field) since. A local jeweler rewarded Oscar with a gold wristwatch.

The mighty blast broke Oscar out of a mini slump. His home run bat had previously been "somewhat impotent," remarked the press, but now the power returned.[10] He hit two doubles the next day and an inside-the-park homer the next. A little later, on June 28, his long triple helped defeat the Brooklyn Royal Giants, 9–8. "Charleston must get his daily extra base clout or he feels that his day is ruined," quipped the *Harrisburg Telegraph*. "And he gets them."[11] The next day he contributed a home run and a double to another Giants victory. On July 5 he singled in the winning run in the eleventh. The comparisons to Babe Ruth began again, and there was no more talk of a slump.

Oscar was amped. During a July 8 game against Hilldale in Darby, some fans decided to razz him. Oscar pointed to a row of bats: "These are the things that win ball games," he responded. Then he went out and singled; stole second when the pitcher, trying to keep him close to the bag, threw to first; homered to left; and hit a sacrifice fly—all while taunting and needling Hilldale ace Nip Winters.[12] When the 1927 season's first half came to an end, the Bacharach Giants had taken the flag, but Charleston was "still the greatest," said the *Pittsburgh Courier*. He was hitting .367, sixth in the league (Beckwith was fifth), and was "setting the East afire with his hitting and fielding." He had reportedly added fourteen homers too, a number that the *Courier* said was "a safe bet" to be leading the circuit (the ECL still didn't have its act together well enough to report official statistics).[13]

When the second half started, it was announced that Harrisburg was going to trade Charleston to Hilldale for Winters and center fielder Clint Thomas. Rap Dixon had returned to the Giants from Hawaii, and with his addition to the Giants outfield perhaps Strothers saw a chance to deal from a position of strength—and save a bit of money to boot. But the Colonel backed out of the deal at the last minute. He may have regretted not pulling the trigger. The Giants started the second half just 6-10 in league play, far behind the 16-7 Bacharach Giants, who humbled Harrisburg, 20–5, on August 14, one of those games in which Oscar was forced to take the mound. Harrisburg turned it on after that, but as the season came to an end in mid-September and the second-place Giants might have had a chance to catch the Bacharachs by winning a final series at Island Park, Strothers suddenly found—or so he claimed—that the diamond was being reshaped for football and was no longer his to use. Instead of scheduling the series elsewhere, and likely losing yet more money, he simply waved the white flag.[14]

The anticlimax was somehow fitting for the perennially dysfunctional ECL. And yet, although Harrisburg failed again to win a championship in 1927, the Charleston legend was taking root. There was the mammoth home run at Island Park. Oscar was the subject of one of the questions in a *Pittsburgh Courier* trivia quiz, in which "Who is Oscar Charleston?" appeared alongside such queries as "Who is Principal of Tuskegee Institute?" and "Who is the Editor of the Journal of Negro History?"[15] There were also half-mythical stories of amazing feats. Rollo Wilson relayed the following one in his August 20 column:

> The story goes that Oscar Charleston had been fanned three times in a game here in Philly against a neighborhood team. In the ninth inning, Beck, the Bludgeoner [John Beckwith], hit one over the right field fence.
>
> Charleston, coming up, was greeted with a wave of reverse applause. The Hoosier offered to bet the crowd that he'd smack one farther than his noble manager. FIFTY BUCKS was collected among the fans and Oscar covered it.

The pitcher sneaked over two strikes and then Charleston stepped out after a bad ball and smashed it over the center-field wall. Not only over the wall, but over the house tops across the street.[16]

That was the way they told it in Philly anyway.

• • •

As the 1927 calendar turned to October and the long, low southern Pennsylvania ridges became speckled with autumn color, it was again time for Oscar and other Negro Leagues stars to match up against the best white competition on offer. Charleston and John Beckwith traveled south to join Ben Taylor's Baltimore Black Sox in their set against an all-star team composed principally of players from the Baltimore Orioles, an International League outfit. In front of overwhelmingly white crowds of five thousand or more, the Black Sox had already won the first three games against the white all-stars when Charleston and Beckwith arrived. On the mild, rain-soaked afternoon of Sunday, October 9, the reinforcements from Harrisburg helped the Black Sox make it four straight with a 5–4 victory. A week later the all-stars fortified their lineup by installing Washington Senators star Goose Goslin in center field, but the Black Sox won again, 5–2, aided by Oscar's RBI single and long drive over the right field fence; Goslin went 0 for 4. The next Sunday, the increasingly frustrated all-stars traded in Goslin for the Cubs' hard-living fireplug Hack Wilson, who had tallied thirty home runs during the regular season. They also installed on the mound the Cardinals' Bill Sherdel, who had just won seventeen games for Branch Rickey's club. The changes made no difference. Wilson homered, but with the Black Sox down 7–6 in the ninth, a man on second, and Sherdel still pitching, Charleston singled, and Beckwith followed with a rocket to right, scoring Oscar with the winning run. Once again the quality of Negro Leagues baseball had been confirmed.[17]

Thanks to performances like these, a different tone began to become more prominent in the black press's baseball coverage. With so much evidence that black stars were clearly the equals of their white counterparts, some writers began to insist upon the obvious: blacks were excluded from the Majors for no reason other than racial prejudice. The *Baltimore Afro-American* argued that big league scouts often decided whom to sign by seeing how white players fared against the top-level competition offered by Negro Leaguers; Yankees ace Herb Pennock of Kennett Square, Pennsylvania, got his chance in the Majors only after he beat the St. Louis Stars, claimed the paper. Rollo Wilson also began to more forcefully campaign for black players in the Majors. "I believe the time is not so far in the dim future when Negroes will be playing on league teams openly and will advance just as far as their abilities warrant," Wilson prophesied. "Then it will not be necessary for men to assume a 'Cuban' or 'Mexican' or 'Indian' parentage or to 'pass' for a 'swarthy' white man. Unfortunately, it will not be this season or the next or the next. It will not come in time to benefit such great stars as Raleigh Mackey, Frank Warfield, Oscar Charleston, Rats Henderson, or John Beckwith."[18]

After Oscar had returned to Cuba for the 1927–28 Cuban League season, a correspondent for *El País* made the same argument, with respect to Charleston at least, at greater length. The piece was reprinted in the December 10, 1927, issue of the *Pittsburgh Courier*. It reveals much about how Oscar went about his craft:

> You may think I am exaggerating when I say that Ty Cobb has nothing on Charleston. I have seen Ty play for many years, and was one of the first to sing his praises, but I must confess that I fail to see where he is a better player than this noted colored star.
>
> I have tried time and again to find a weakness, and always with the same result, he measures up to the perfect athlete. At first sight, he appears too thick and heavy, but later one is sur-

prised to find that he carries not an ounce of fat, but is solid muscle. A bulky mass of steel, with the speed of lightning and the aggressiveness of a tiger.

Charleston, like all the great colored baseball stars, is always a gentleman, almost humble, always in good humor, but nevertheless dignified, and extremely dangerous if you try to make fun of him or get personal, as a Cuban once tried, to his sorrow. With the speed of a ballet dancer, Charleston turned and with a single punch sent him to the ground. Another time he was insulted without cause, and smiled all the while his assailant was trying to get in his deadly work, then without saying a word, and still smiling, this giant athlete punched once with his left hand, and his enemy was out like a light. During all this time Oscar never lost his temper and walked out of the park still smiling.

How could a *Courier* reader not regard Charleston as anything but an African American superhero after reading such testimony? The Cuban writer went on to paint a vivid portrait of Charleston's pure baseball skills:

When the opposing pitcher uses speed, Charleston is in his element and bats like a demon, and when the pitcher is a slow or curve ball artist, this perfect baseball machine adjusts himself to meet the conditions and with a confidence that fairly oozes from every part of him he will bunt, or pull a short hit that leaves the fans and the opposing players with their tongues sticking out. Many times, with two strikes called, when the ordinary player would try to kill the ball, I have seen him lay down a perfect bunt with a grace and skill that nothing but nerve and faith in his own ability could accomplish, then streak to first base like a scared deer, on those wonderfully developed legs that don't look as if they could carry that heavy frame with the speed that they do.

His fielding is of the highest class. Always good at pulling down flies, he studies each batter in a manner that few fans realize, but always, always, he is forever under the ball. When a hit is labelled "Home-run," he is off with the crack of the bat and with the speed of a grey hound he reaches the ball, and when he touches it, whether it be high or low, or on either side, the batter is out. . . .

For the reasons which I have mentioned, I call him the most dangerous and the most scientific hitter in Cuban baseball, and one of the best that I have ever seen in my life.[19]

Oscar was playing for a new team, called Cuba, when this piece was published. The club represented the latest attempt to establish a third league team that, alongside the venerable Habana and Almendares outfits, was financially and competitively viable. It included legitimate Negro Leagues stars in Charleston, third baseman Judy Johnson, catcher Larry Brown, and pitcher Willie Foster. But it was not as deep as previous clubs Oscar had played with on the island. The standings told the story, as Cuba finished with a 16-21 record, eight games behind Habana. That wasn't Oscar's fault. Although his hairline was now receding and his midsection visibly thickening, he posted typically fantastic numbers, stealing eleven bases and batting .350 with five homers, two triples, and six doubles in 120 at bats. Those home run and stolen base totals led the league. The *El País* writer had not exaggerated; at thirty-one, Oscar was still very much in his prime.

• • •

Oscar and Janie, sailing on the *Cuba* with their journalist friend Margaret Martin, returned to the United States on March 13, 1928. Things seemed never to remain quiet back home during their winters in the Caribbean, and this offseason was no different. A few weeks earlier Colonel Strothers had given up making a go of it in the ECL. The other teams had then held a draft of the Harrisburg Giants players, and Oscar had nominally become the property of the Atlantic City Bacharach Giants.

That outcome didn't suit Oscar. Once Janie and he arrived in Harrisburg, he looked up the Colonel and tried to change his mind. Strothers wavered for a bit under the spell of Charleston's charm, but ultimately he decided to hold to his original plan. Still not wishing to play in Atlantic City, Oscar considered his options. By the end of the month he had signed a contract to play with Harrisburg's chief rival, Ed Bolden's Hilldale Daisies, which had left the troubled ECL and could therefore sign whomever it wished. Despite his past run-ins with Oscar, Bolden was delighted to sign the player who was the best draw in black baseball. The team's fans were overjoyed. For his part, Oscar was likely attracted to Hilldale by the proximity of Bolden's club to his home in Harrisburg (105 miles away), the chance to star and win in a big city, and the opportunity to play with some old mates.

The Hilldale club was based in Darby, a suburb situated a few miles southwest of Philadelphia. The town itself was small, with a population under ten thousand, but it was in the middle of a large and growing metropolitan area that, like every other northern city, had seen a huge influx of African Americans since World War I. From 1900 to 1920 Philadelphia's black population rose from 63,000 to 134,000. By 1930 it would grow to 220,000.[20] Many of these individuals lived on the city's west side, whence they could easily get to Hilldale games. And many could afford such luxuries, since the region's black residents shared—if not equally, at least considerably—in the era's prosperity, at least until the Depression began to set in at the end of the 1920s. Hilldale was unquestionably Philadelphia-area blacks' home team.

The short (5 foot 7) and slight (145 pounds) bespectacled Bolden had been in control of the Hilldale club since 1910, methodically and efficiently guiding the squad from an obscure amateur nine into a major black-baseball force. Efficiency lay at the core of Bolden's bland personality. In 1904 he had left his job as a butler to take a clerk position at Philadelphia's Central Post Office, a job in which he excelled. Unlike other team owners, Bolden had no independent access to funds, and he was never accused of lighting up a room, but the same qualities that served him well in his occupation served him well in baseball. He was a family man, steady, serious, responsible, hard-working, self-righteous. Nicknamed "Chief" by the press, Bolden was also an anxious person who, the previous September, had suffered a nervous breakdown and been forced by doctors to take a leave of absence from both baseball and his post office job. Perhaps the signing of Charleston a few months later helped alleviate his distress.[21]

Indeed, Bolden had every reason to expect his club to sparkle on the diamond. Although Hilldale would play as an independent team in 1928, the squad was in no way inferior to the five others that remained in the ECL. Talent permeated the roster. Bolden had under contract catcher Biz Mackey, first baseman Rev Cannady, second baseman Frank Warfield, and starting pitcher Darltie Cooper—all former teammates of Oscar's—as well as shortstop Paul "Country Jake" Stephens and third baseman Judy Johnson. Johnson, like Mackey and Charleston, would one day end up in Cooperstown. Probably the club was the best in uniform east of the Alleghenies.

It was, however, a somewhat enlarged Oscar who took the field for Hilldale in 1928. As the *El País* writer had noted the previous winter, the thirty-one-year-old now carried a distinctly "heavy frame" (historian Geri Strecker has noted that Charleston's self-discipline often failed him when it came to sweets, especially pie).[22] The Pittsburgh press described him as "rotund" and "chunky."[23] Charleston could still run well, finishing second among Hilldale players in stolen bases with ten in 1928, and his base running daring and ability in the field still brought praise from the press. The *Chicago Defender* claimed, during the season, that he still "hits and runs like a youngster."[24] But the truth was that those extra pounds meant that Charleston's once-spectacular range in center field had diminished. From time to time he manned first base instead.

There was no question that the bat was still elite. On Easter, in a spring-training exhibition in Newport News, Virginia, Charleston smacked two home runs. In Hilldale's first "regular season" game in Brooklyn against the semipro Bushwicks, he drilled the first pitch he saw far over the right field fence; it was said to be the longest drive ever hit at Dexter Park, bringing the number of diamonds where Oscar was said to have hit the longest home run ever to at least four. Two-hit games, three-hit outings, and game-winning drives followed with numbing regularity—as on July 26 in Philadelphia, when Oscar stepped into the box with two men on and two out in the bottom of the ninth. The Bacharach Giants led Hilldale, 3–1. Ping Gardner, who in an earlier contest in a similar situation had struck out Charleston to win the game, was on the mound. "Over the fence, Charlie, over the fence!" roared the fans. Oscar fouled off Gardner's first offering. Wrong bat, he decided. Prolonging the drama, he strode to the dugout and selected a new piece of lumber. At length, he stepped back into the box. Gardner tried to bait him with a pitch outside the zone, but Oscar laid off. The next pitch was a fastball down the middle, and Oscar connected perfectly, launching the ball over the deep center field wall for a 4–3 Hilldale win in front of a deliriously happy crowd.

After that game Oscar was more frequently pitched around or flat out intentionally walked.[25] He was walked in all five of his plate appearances against the Cuban Stars on September 6 in Philadelphia. When teams did choose to challenge him in the last half of 1928, he usually delivered. Oscar had a two-homer game against the Baltimore Black Sox in August. He followed that a few days later with another two-homer game against Wentz-Olney, a white semipro team. The Homestead Grays, in town for a four-game series with Hilldale in mid-September, paid the price for not walking Oscar when he hit a homer, two triples, and a single in the series' third game. Hilldale took three out of four to claim what was billed as the state championship.

The ecstatic fans who surrounded the field—"a living wall of howling dervishes"—had never been more satisfied.[26]

Charleston was as heady, and violent, a player as ever. In a September matchup against the Brooklyn Royal Giants he managed to score after being caught in a rundown. Oscar was on third and had started for home on a ground ball to first. Recognizing that he was going to be out by a mile, he stopped and played for time while the runner on first advanced to third. Finally, Oscar was tagged—but the tagger dropped the ball. Oscar then broke madly for home, where his Indianapolis-born friend Bill Holland, the pitcher, was covering. Seeing his chance, and caring not a fig for friendship, he threw himself full force into Holland. Holland went flying into the dirt, the ball came loose, and Oscar was left standing on home plate, safe.

The Philadelphia fans ate it up. Oscar's photo album includes shots of him posing in Hilldale uniform with children and various unidentified women. Everyone beams. They are clearly thrilled to get close to the man to whom the Philly press, echoing the press everywhere else, still labeled "the greatest colored baseball star of all times"[27] and the "Babe Ruth of his race."[28] Late in the year, prior to Hilldale's big series with the Homestead Grays in Philadelphia, the papers ran a publicity photo of Oscar posing in sparring position with black heavyweight boxing champion George Godfrey, a photo that the pugilism-loving Oscar also included in his personal photo album. "Almost he is a legend," wrote Philadelphia-based Rollo Wilson of Oscar's status among black baseball fans.[29] There was no "almost" about it. At the end of the season Wilson selected Charleston as the baseball representative in his all-time black All-American Team. (Cum Posey was his basketball selection, and former Rutgers College star Paul Robeson—later to become somewhat more famous as a singer, actor, and activist—his football pick.)

Under the managerial leadership of veteran outfielder Otto Briggs, Hilldale largely fulfilled its promise in 1928. The team posted a 35-27-1 record against top competition. In fifty-nine games Oscar hit ten home runs, second only to Rap Dixon among eastern players and more than twice as many as any of his Hilldale teammates. His slash line was .346/.449/.605. Oscar may have been heavier, and hence not as utterly dominant as he once was, but in Rollo Wilson's opinion he remained "the greatest player in Negro baseball."[30]

• • •

As he had done the previous autumn, in October Charleston joined Ben Taylor's Baltimore Black Sox for a series of exhibitions at Maryland Baseball Park against a shifting team of Major and Minor League all-stars. This year those all-stars would include, at various times, Lefty Grove and Jimmie Foxx. As many as ten thousand fans showed up for these Sunday games, meaning that many had to be accommodated on the field. The white all-stars ended up winning the series, 3-2, but the Negro Leaguers hardly embarrassed themselves. For the Black Sox the highlight came on October 14, when they pounded Lefty Grove for eleven hits and worked him for five walks on their way to a 9–3 victory. In Grove's defense, he was saddled with an exceptionally incompetent catcher whose wild throws and erratic arm allowed the Black Sox to steal at least seven bases—four by Charleston alone. Oscar went just 2 for 11 in the series, however. Surely he was tired.

It had been Oscar's intention, in fact, to spend the winter in Harrisburg. He figured he would skip the Cuban League, which had been degenerating in recent years, to rest and figure out where he would play in 1929. Cum Posey wanted him badly. He recruited Charleston with gusto, thinking that if he could sign Charleston for his Homestead Grays, other stars would follow and put Posey in a strong position to enter league play on friendly terms. But Ed Bolden wasn't inclined to let Oscar go. He offered a three-year contract, reportedly longer than he had ever given anyone, for Oscar not only to play for but also to manage Hilldale going forward.

Oscar found Bolden's offer attractive—and energizing. First, he signed the multiyear contract, which offered him a hefty $375 per month for the 1929 season. Over the five-month season Charleston could thus look forward to making as much as the average American worker made all year, and he would augment that income significantly by what he made in Cuba, in exhibition games, and in gifts from fans. Second, he immediately changed his mind about not going to Cuba. He needed to find talent for what was now truly *his* team. On November 1, just a couple of days after his last game in Baltimore, he left to play ball on the island for the seventh winter in a row.

• • •

It may not have taken long for Oscar to regret his decision, for the 1928–29 Cuban League was yet another in which the league demonstrated its essential instability. Oscar returned to the Cuba club, which was now managed by Adolfo Luque and had gained Manuel Cueto, the infielder Charleston had so badly spiked back in 1924. The roster also still included Larry Brown and Judy Johnson, but it had lost Willie Foster and was not in any obvious way more talented than the previous winter's edition. This time Cuba did not even make it to the end of the season, withdrawing from the league on January 3. In 114 at bats Charleston hit .333 with four home runs, four triples, six doubles, and six stolen bases.

Having been on the fence about returning to Cuba at all that winter, the Charlestons did not linger once the club called it quits. They returned to Key West on January 5, 1929, and presumably spent the rest of the winter in Harrisburg, which they continued to call home. While Janie busied herself with the Girl Scouts, her Unity Social Club's annual charity ball, and substitute teaching (for which she was paid $5.79 per day), Oscar used these cold and dreary months along the banks of the Susquehanna to mold his Hilldale team, which in 1929 would compete in the new American Negro League (ANL), the Eastern Colored League ECL having folded.[31]

Roster construction was a task neither Bolden nor Charleston was inclined to treat with sentimentality. The men cut Otto Briggs, who had been with the team since 1917, to make room for Oscar's former ABCs teammate Crush Holloway. They added pitcher Cliff Carter. And, most significant, they traded stalwarts Paul Stephens and Rev Cannady to the Homestead Grays for catcher-infielder George Britt and the uber-versatile Martín Dihigo, whom they agreed to pay even more than Oscar at $400 per month. "Baseball is a big business and the Hilldale Corporation is conducting it along sane lines, hence the past and future turnover in talent on the suburban lot," wrote Rollo Wilson.[32]

The Dihigo deal was doubtless the fruit of Charleston's time in Cuba. The first Cuban player to appear with Hilldale, Dihigo had starred for the Habana club in 1928–29. Charleston had been his teammate on Habana in 1925–26 and had played against him every winter since 1922–23, when Dihigo made his professional debut at just sixteen years old. In his extraordinary versatility Dihigo was the Bullet Joe Rogan of Cuba; he could not only play every position, including pitcher and catcher, but could also play every position *well*. Blessed with speed, power, intelligence, coordination, and an intangible grace that marked him as a star from the moment one spied him on the diamond, Dihigo was a tremendous asset to any club. He also cared deeply about the social and political issues that were beginning to roil his native island. These qualities must have strongly attracted Charleston to Dihigo, and vice versa.[33]

With Dihigo in tow, Bolden's expectations—everyone's expectations—for Charleston's performance as both manager and player surged well beyond the bounds of reason. Hilldale now had its own "Ruth-Gehrig combination," said the *Wilmington News Journal*, a white paper that also talked up the talents of Wilmington's own former sandlotter, Hilldale third baseman Judy Johnson. (Connie Mack allegedly had said he would sign

Johnson if not for his color, which was "decidedly brown.")[34] Charleston himself boasted before the season opened that Hilldale would have the strongest unit in the ANL. Rollo Wilson fanned the flames with a long preseason profile of Hilldale in which he praised the club as the most popular and colorful team in the East and its new manager as "one of the shining stars of all time and all baseball. His name is Oscar Charleston and his big bat and fleet limbs have been the means of his being enrolled on the glory scroll. Big, aggressive, intelligent, highly efficient—that's Oscar, the Hoosier Hustler."[35] Yet another Wilson article, published in late April 1929, made much of Charleston's clutch hitting. It also noted that while Oscar now tipped the scales at 208 pounds, he was still fast, an opinion shared by others.[36] In that article Wilson stated: "I have lamped major league baseball for more than a score of years, years through which have paraded Clarke, Jones, Murray, Paskert, Felsch, Speaker, Cobb, Hooper, Lewis, Wilson and the stars of now. With the eyes of a critic I describe our hero thus: A base stealer like Carey, a slugger like Ruth, a fielder like Speaker, a thrower like Wilson, an eye like Sheckard, a brain like Clarke, a personality like Donlin. What more could you want in an athlete?"[37]

All of this buildup made Hilldale's slow start painful for its passionate fans—and intolerable for its owner. The Daisies were beaten by the Lincoln Giants in their home opener in Darby on April 27. The Bushwicks embarrassed them in Brooklyn, 15–1. Then the team lost two games to the Baltimore Black Sox at home in early May, despite Oscar's doubling three times in the first contest. Hilldale turned around and walloped the Wilmington Chicks, 11–5, in Wilmington on May 15, but Bolden had seen enough. The next day, just a few games into the league season, he fired Charleston as manager. Spitballer Phil Cockrell replaced him. This was Bolden's Steinbrenner moment.

Oscar had signed a three-year contract with Hilldale only a few months earlier. He could not have been happy, and he showed it on Friday, May 17, during a game in Philadelphia versus the Homestead Grays. Grays' catcher Buck Ewing, incensed by a call, got into a heated debate with the umpire. His manager, Cum Posey, ran onto the field to lend his voice to his catcher's protest. As the argument escalated, Ewing walloped the umpire. Enter Oscar, who, deciding that Posey and the Grays ought to abide by the umpire's indubitably just decision, let out some steam by landing a right cross to Posey's jaw.[38] It was classic Oscar: never let slip an opportunity to finish a fight, even if it isn't yours. Both Charleston and Ewing were suspended for a brief while.

Back in the lineup on May 26, Charleston helped Hilldale split a doubleheader with the Cuban Stars in New York by making a "star one-handed catch . . . in deep center field."[39] As of June 5 he was hitting .459, yet expectations were such that when in mid-June Hilldale got swept in a doubleheader and Oscar had only one hit and one stolen base on the day, the subhead in the *Baltimore Afro-American* read, "Mighty Oscar Charleston Fails to Impress as of Yore."[40] Charleston, noted the *Philadelphia Tribune* in a midseason review, "is the same colorful performer as of yore, but in actual work isn't up to past standards."[41] At the time, it was reported that he was hitting .379 with one home run, one triple, thirteen doubles, and five stolen bases in 103 at bats. It's tough at the top.

Hilldale finished the season's first half at 8-14. The team made a much better showing in the second half, when Biz Mackey and Paul Stephens rejoined the squad, and Oscar redeemed his allegedly poor start by hitting better than .400 and bashing six more home runs in league play. But the Baltimore Black Sox caught fire at the end of the year and won the second-half pennant, just as they had won the first. Another year had passed without Charleston winning a championship; this one, in light of those sky-high preseason expectations, was bitterer than most.

After the season ended in late September, Oscar, Judy Johnson, Paul Stephens, and outfielder Clint Thomas hopped a train to Pittsburgh in order to barnstorm with the Homestead

Grays. Oscar's fight with Posey back in May had apparently been forgiven—another piece of evidence that Oscar never held a grudge and that his charm was such that no one ever seemed to hold one against him. With the Grays, Oscar spent a week or two beating up on Pittsburgh-area teams before going west to Chicago for a five-game series versus the American Giants.

When the games were over, Oscar returned not to Harrisburg but to Philadelphia. He and Janie would not go to Cuba for the 1929–30 winter season. Instead, the great Oscar Charleston stayed in Philadelphia and worked, probably as a baggage handler.

. . .

The American Negro League proved to be even more fragile than the dysfunctional Eastern Colored League. Neither circuit was blessed by farsighted, charismatic, or deep-pocketed owners, and the catastrophic stock market crash of October 29, 1929, certainly didn't help matters. Complaining about high salaries, poor umpiring, and various other challenges they had been unable to overcome, the ANL magnates announced in March that their league was folding. The Hilldale club added that it would not operate either. Indeed, no professional black baseball league would operate in the East in 1930 or 1931, and while the legendary Philadelphia-area squad for which Charleston had played during the last two years *would* ultimately end up fielding a team in 1930, it was a very poor one.

Charleston had seen which way the wind was blowing. Well before the notices about the ANL and Hilldale came down, he had successfully made other arrangements. On February 22, under the headline "Signs!," the *Pittsburgh Courier* announced that Oscar had joined the Homestead Grays. "Our own king of swat and one of the most brilliant batters and fielders in baseball," now thirty-three years old, would play first base for Cumberland Posey's team, proclaimed the paper.[42] Charleston was the greatest black outfielder of all time, wrote Dizzy Dismukes a couple of weeks later;[43] during Oscar's ABCs days opponents had said it was like playing a team with four outfielders. But from now on, owing to his increasing weight and declining speed, Charleston's fielding talent would be displayed only at the "initial hassock" (as writers of the time loved to say).

Why did Oscar choose to go to Pittsburgh? There were other teams on the East Coast who would have loved to add him to their rosters, established teams in cities like Baltimore or New York—cities that probably would have been more acceptable to Janie. I can think of four reasons why Oscar chose to play in the bustling city of soot and steel.

First, Posey had probably offered Charleston an attractive salary, as he had done a year earlier. Having included Charleston on his barnstorming club in each of the last two postseasons, he knew from experience that Oscar was a strong drawing card.

Second, Posey was a college-educated family man from a prominent and wealthy Pittsburgh family. His father, Captain Cumberland Willis Posey Sr., was an engineer, entrepreneur, and investor who ultimately came to own the largest black-owned business in Pittsburgh, the Diamond Coke and Coal Company. His business success and civic leadership led to the Poseys' ascension into the "Old Pittsburgh" upper social class, or at least that class's black component. Cum, unlike his father, had decided to devote his life to sport, but he was very much Captain Posey's son with respect to his intelligence, consuming drive for success, and commitment to civic duty (for example, he later served on the Homestead Board of Education). Posey must have reminded Oscar of his mentor, C. I. Taylor. He was precisely the sort of person with whom Charleston always preferred to associate himself.

Third, Posey was putting together an excellent team; along with Charleston, Posey had lured from Hilldale shortstop Paul Stephens, third baseman Judy Johnson, and second baseman George Scales. Also under contract were stars like catcher Buck Ewing, the long-necked fireballer Smokey Joe Williams (now forty-four but still effective), and outfielder Vic Harris. This was a team that could win big.

But the fourth reason may have been for Oscar the most exciting: Posey was bringing in a new center fielder from Indianapolis, a kid by the name of Bennie Charleston. Genial and responsible, the youngest member of the Charleston clan had made a nice name for himself in the Indianapolis semipro circuit. It's possible that Oscar signed with Posey only on the condition that he give Bennie a chance. Thus, when the Grays decamped for Hot Springs, Arkansas, for spring training in mid-March, Bennie was in tow. "[He was] said by critics in the west to be a comer who will remind fans of his famous brother, Oscar," reported the *Courier*.[44] That was a highly dubious claim, but the excitement surrounding the Grays was hard to contain. As it turned out, Ben Charleston was not the rookie destined to make a name for himself with the Grays in 1930.

Major League teams, including the Pittsburgh Pirates, had been training in Hot Springs off and on since 1886. The Grays weren't in the famous spa town long before Oscar asserted himself as a team leader. Players gathered at 9:15 each morning for a five-mile jaunt through the hills. They could walk, or they could run. Judy Johnson served as the team's captain, but Oscar was the leader of the runners' group. At 11:15 the players ate. From 1:30 to 3:30 they practiced, drawing many curious, and sometimes prominent, onlookers both black and white. At 3:45 they took to the baths, and at 5:30 they dined. By the end of the spring this regimen reportedly had helped Charleston slim down to 180 pounds from the 214 he had carried in 1929.

In the meantime, the press built the Grays up, especially the new first baseman. "First base is now in the hands of the most competent player that has ever held down that sack for the speedy Pittsburgh colored club," claimed the *Pittsburgh Post-Gazette*.[45] "In addition to being an able player," wrote Chester Washington in the *Courier*, "Charleston is one of the most popular players in the game." While playing for Hilldale, Oscar had been "to

Philadelphians what Smokey Joe Williams was to New Yorkers when the latter was with the Lincoln Giants—their hero. Scores of school kids turned out regularly just to see Oscar perform. He was to them what Babe Ruth is to kids of a lighter hue. . . . Fans here are waiting expectantly to see the mighty Oscar scintillate on local diamonds."[46]

No pressure. Yet as a team the Grays managed to live up to their fans' high expectations. Near the end of March they left Hot Springs for a wandering tour of the South. They began with a game in Little Rock on their way to New Orleans, where they took on the Black Pelicans for two games. After that they drove to Texas, where they played in Marshall, Waco, Austin, San Antonio, Houston, and other towns. They then made their way back to Shreveport, Louisiana, before heading north and east toward Pittsburgh. Every day the Grays played at least one game, and most every day they found themselves taking the diamond in a new town not necessarily brimming with southern hospitality—towns where they were denied restaurant service and lodging, towns where the hotels and boarding houses in which they *could* stay were often so infested with bedbugs or lice that players preferred to sleep on chairs. Despite such hardships, the Grays pounded the competition in these contests. In the twenty-six games they played before their home opener at Forbes Field on May 10, they went 23-2-1 and outscored their overmatched opponents by a combined score of 246–74.

The Grays' mode of travel consisted of two brand-new Buicks. Nine members of the traveling party would cram into each car, which carried equipment boxes on the back and luggage racks on the side. As the Grays discovered after their games in Marshall, Texas, having nine tired young men spinning along at about seventy miles per hour on southern dirt roads at twilight was not a recipe for safety. On this evening they were headed for Shreveport. Oscar was driving the lead car, and Grays co-owner Charlie Walker, driving the second, was trying to catch up—for those who got to the next stop first got the best rooms.

The road was graded in such a way as to leave a small hump in the middle. As he tried to catch Charleston, Walker drifted into this hump and lost control. The car flipped. Amazingly, when the vehicle came to a rest, it was discovered that no one was hurt. The car was even still running, and the only real damage was to one of the fenders.

Soon, Walker and his passengers had their vehicle back on the road. Yet they had not gone far when they spied another auto flipped over in front of them. To their astonishment "it was our other car," recalled Judy Johnson. "Charleston had slid off the road and blew a tire. And the car went down in the ditch and rolled over three times. The cars had those old canvas tops then, and when those tops broke off, the men rolled out into the ditch. That's the only thing that saved their lives. Nobody got hurt! Nine men packed in there like sardines, and when the roof caved in they all just dropped out into the ditch. That was a miracle."[47]

As they recovered themselves, Oscar's teammates saw something strange in his clutches. In each hand Charleston held a piece of the Buick's wood steering wheel. He had never let go. Splinters from the rest of the steering wheel were lodged in his scalp. There they remained for several days, until Oscar reached a town that had a doctor whom he trusted to remove them.

• • •

Bennie Charleston survived the car crash, but he didn't survive Posey's critical scrutiny. After the Grays won two games against the St. Louis Stars on April 18 and 19, Posey sent Bennie home. He had an opportunity to sign a more experienced player to patrol center in Chaney White, and Bennie hadn't wowed him. What Oscar thought of that decision is unrecorded, but the team's play didn't suffer. The Grays kept blowing Minor League teams away in towns like Springfield and Akron, Ohio; Clarksburg (a 22–2 victory that included an Oscar home run) and Wheeling, West Virginia; and Jeannette and Charleroi, Pennsylvania.

In late May and early June the Grays reportedly put together a nineteen-game winning streak (again, *reportedly* bears emphasizing; it was virtually impossible to confirm such claims then, and it is certainly impossible to do so now).

For fans one of the downsides of following an independent ball club like the Grays was that no official statistics were compiled or recorded. Not a few games went unmentioned in the papers. And among those that were reported, box scores were often missing. The game accounts that do exist suggest that Charleston adapted well to first base. "The infielders seldom make bad throws when he's on the sack," noted one reporter. "Seemingly he is able to go under the surface of the infield and come up with the ball."[48] A writer for the *Philadelphia Tribune* said that Oscar was "furnishing the best work of the season" at first base.[49] By the end of the year, Judy Johnson and Paul Stephens were saying that Charleston was the best-fielding first baseman they had ever played with.

Owing perhaps to a left arm injury suffered on a slide into home plate, Oscar's bat had slipped a touch. Researchers have recovered statistics from only seventy-five Charleston plate appearances in 1930. In that sample Oscar hit .246 and slugged .385, far below his usual lofty standards.[50] Yet the Grays kept winning, and Oscar was an important contributor. In the club's home opener versus Youngstown, which to Posey's and Walker's delight drew more fans than any game the Grays had played the previous season, the Grays won, 10–1. Hitting in his customary third position, Oscar had three hits, including a triple and a first-inning line drive shot into the right field bleachers that left the grandstand shaking. A week later, in a 7–1 victory over Akron at Forbes, he doubled and homered. No Pennsylvania or regional team could offer the Grays any resistance, not even the Memphis Red Sox of the NNL, whom the Grays embarrassed in a lopsided three-game sweep. There was a good deal of excitement when the respected Brooklyn Royal Giants came to Pennsylvania in mid-June. But the Grays took four of five against Brooklyn, Smokey Joe Williams throwing a three-hitter in one contest and Lefty Williams throwing a one-hitter in another. Charleston added a walk-off single. Could anyone stop the Grays?

The famous Kansas City Monarchs, perhaps the strongest club in the west, would get a chance. Posey arranged to play the Monarchs for about two weeks straight in late July and early August. The clubs would meet in various locations in Ohio and Pennsylvania, including Forbes Field, before traveling back to Kansas City for a series of games at Muehlebach Field. The attraction of the series lay not so much in the fact that the Grays would finally be tested by a first-rate nine, but rather in the delightful fact that many of the games would be played at night. The Monarchs, thanks to their irrepressibly entrepreneurial owner, J. L. Wilkinson, had devised their own portable lighting system, which they had already tested in dozens of midwestern games. Twelve trucks carrying poles and towers and a sputtering, 250-horsepower generator would now bring light—not good light, not consistent light, not light high enough to actually illuminate high fly balls and pop-ups, but *light* dammit!—wherever the Monarchs went.

Thus it was that on July 18, 1930, the first night game in the East—and the first night game to occur on a Major League diamond—took place at Forbes Field. (It would be five more years until the Cincinnati Reds introduced night baseball to the Majors.) A crowd of roughly seven thousand turned out to enjoy the spectacle. As the contest headed into the bottom of the ninth, Chet Brewer, the Monarchs' starter, was protecting a 4–2 lead. The first two Grays batters reached. Then Oscar Charleston stepped to the plate. He laced a double to left, scoring both runners, tying the game, and thrilling the fans. In extra innings, precisely at midnight, Buck Ewing knocked in the winning run to give the Grays a 5–4 victory. No one at Forbes Field that evening would ever forget it.[51]

A week later, after having shown off the wondrous lighting equipment in games played in towns around the region, the

Grays and Monarchs faced off again at Forbes Field. In that game catcher Buck Ewing was replaced midway through by a local eighteen-year-old sandlot phenom named Josh Gibson.

The legendary tale of how Josh Gibson first joined the Homestead Grays—launching a professional career as the most prolific slugger the game has ever seen, not necessarily excepting Babe Ruth—has it that Gibson was plucked out of the stands by Cum Posey during the *first* night game at Forbes. In this telling Ewing had split a finger and outfielder Vic Harris, the putative backup, had refused to catch in the poor lighting conditions. Gibson was allegedly eating a hot dog when Posey spotted him in the stands and asked if he could catch. The rest was history.[52]

It didn't go down quite like that. Gibson, whose father had traded a life as a Georgia sharecropper for a somewhat more hopeful if no less grueling one as a steel worker, was toiling at the Edgar Thomson steel mills in 1930 and playing for a team called the Crawford Giants in Pittsburgh's semipro circuit in his spare time, as he had since 1928. The Crawford Giants had become very popular by 1930, sometimes drawing more than three thousand fans to their games. Young Gibson—or "Gipson," as the papers often spelled it—was, although raw, clearly their most talented player. Posey had had his eye on him for some time, and Charleston may have as well, if a later claim that he "discovered" Gibson can be trusted.[53] In any case, Gibson actually first joined the Grays during a doubleheader staged a little while earlier against a white semipro team from Dormont, Pennsylvania. On that day Ewing did in fact split a finger and was unable to continue. Posey brought in Harris from the outfield to catch in his place. At the same time he sent Harris's brother Rich by taxi to the field where Gibson was playing with the Crawford Giants. A few innings later Josh stepped out of the taxi and into the Grays' lineup. That was the end of Josh's sandlot days—and the beginning of a Negro Leagues career that would make him, after Satchel Paige, the best-known Negro Leagues player of all time.

Gibson may have been only eighteen, but his addition made a very good 1930 Grays team much better. In sixteen games against top competition he compiled an astounding slash line of .417/.444/.833. He hit *seven* home runs in those sixteen games. One of those, as we shall see, would serve as a cornerstone of his legend.

Oscar and the other veterans, especially Judy Johnson, took the coachable, likeable Josh under their wing. The baby-faced kid smiled a lot and loved to eat. He was 6 feet 1 inch tall and weighed around two hundred pounds. And he was already so strong that he was one of the few men Oscar couldn't physically manhandle. It was said that on the one occasion Oscar tried to do so, Josh got the better of him.[54] Few other men, if any, could claim as much.

Once added to the squad, Gibson began traveling with the team right away. He was present in Kansas City on August 2, when the Grays and Monarchs staged one of the most legendary contests in Negro Leagues history. Because they were playing under the Monarchs' dim lights, the story goes, team owners Posey and Wilkinson had made a special point of agreeing that neither pitcher would doctor the ball; things would be hard enough on the hitters as it was. But when Monarchs starter Chet Brewer put two men on base early, he began using an abrasive emery cloth to make the ball move. The Grays caught on, and their starter, Smokey Joe Williams, retaliated by roughing up his baseballs with sandpaper. Before long, both hurlers were cutting the ball with every tool at their disposal; Williams had "everything except a blacksmith's file" with him, reported the *Courier*.[55] The result of these liberties was an unforgettable pitcher's duel. Williams didn't give up a hit for the first seven innings, and the Grays hardly fared better against Brewer, who struck out the side in the seventh, eighth, and ninth innings. Finally, in the top of the twelfth, Charleston drew a walk and advanced to second before Chaney White's bloop hit plated him. Smokey Joe closed the game out in the bottom of the inning for a 1–0 Grays victory. He had struck out an astonishing twenty-seven batters—all but nine of those he had faced. Brewer had fanned nineteen.

The amazing game put a fitting capstone on the Grays' extended series with the Monarchs, in which they won the vast majority of contests (seventeen out of nineteen, according to journalist Chester Washington, although it should be noted that the Monarchs played many of these games without several key players owing to an auto accident of their own). The *Courier* credited Charleston's "heavy bat" for the team's success.[56]

The Monarchs dispatched, there was but one other team that could plausibly claim to be as good as the 1930 Grays: the John Henry Lloyd–led New York Lincoln Giants. The black sports press clamored for Posey and Lincoln Giants owner Jim Keenan to schedule a late-season series that would determine the champion of black baseball. While Posey and Keenan bickered about how to price the games, where to play them, and how to split the gate—an entirely typically dispute—tragedy struck Josh Gibson. On August 20, shortly after he had returned to town from Kansas City, his eighteen-year-old wife, Helen, went into labor. Complications arose. She gave birth to twins—a boy and a girl—and then suffered convulsions and lapsed into a coma. Hours later Helen died. Josh was crushed. But by early September, with Helen's mother and sisters caring for his newborn children, he was playing and traveling again with his new team to St. Louis (where the Grays were finally beaten in a series), Chicago (where they won four out of five and where the *Chicago Defender* welcomed Oscar by describing him in a photo caption as "extremely popular with the fans, especially the ladies"), and elsewhere.[57]

By September 13 Posey and Keenan had come to terms. The Grays and Lincoln Giants would meet at Forbes Field for a doubleheader on Saturday, September 20. They would then entrain to New York for a doubleheader the next day at Yankee Stadium. Two midweek games in Philadelphia would follow before the teams headed back to Yankee Stadium for four more games the following weekend. The winner of this ten-game set would claim the 1930 championship.

Charleston contributed a two-run dinger in the series' first contest, helping the Grays win, 9–1. He was upstaged in the second by a grieving Josh Gibson, who was sensational in launching a home run over the 462-foot-deep center field scoreboard; Josh also tripled. The Grays won that game in ten innings, 17–16. The next day in New York, playing before a crowd of eight thousand, the two teams split. A few days later, in Philadelphia, the teams again split. The series therefore stood at 4-2 Grays as it headed into the final weekend in New York.

The first Saturday game was taken, 9–8, by the Lincolns when Lefty Williams couldn't hold a three-run lead with two outs in the ninth. Prior to that meltdown, in the seventh inning, Charleston had collided with Lloyd and hurt his leg. He sat out the second game, which the Grays still won, 7–3. That made the series stand at 5-3, Homestead. But it was the tremendous three-run wallop hit in that second Saturday game by Gibson, a drive that contemporary observers said traveled an estimated 430 feet to left field, that has been more remembered. Over the years the distance on that shot would rise to 500 feet or more. Sometimes it even left the stadium completely. Josh's drive didn't go *that* far, but it did get everyone's attention.

The next day, the Lincoln Giants won game one, 6–2. Charleston could only limp around the field. It must have killed him, but with the championship on the line in game two, the tenth and final contest of the series, he decided to sit. The Grays were up 1–0 in the eighth against Lincoln Giants starter Bill Holland, who had also started the first game of the day, when the New York defense fell apart, allowing the Grays to score four more runs and put the game away. The final score was 5–2. It was far from his greatest series, but Oscar Charleston finally had a second domestic world championship on his résumé.

• • •

The leg injury Charleston suffered in New York did not keep him from doing what he usually did after the end of regular-season play: hook up with a black team playing white Major League all-stars. This time Oscar traveled to Chicago to join the American Giants, now managed by his close friend and mentor Dizzy Dismukes. The opposing all-star squad included the Phillies' Lefty O'Doul, who had hit .383 in the 1930 regular season, current Tigers great Charlie Gehringer, former Tigers great Harry Heilmann, and Senators first baseman Art Shires. Once again the Negro Leaguers, led by Oscar, his old Harris-burg teammate Rap Dixon, and Rube Foster's half-brother Willie Foster, proved themselves more than worthy competition. They won three of the four contests. Oscar lined three hits and drew a walk in their game one victory. Throughout the series his bat "wreaked havoc with the major men," wrote Randy Dixon in the *Philadelphia Tribune*.[58]

Cuba, too, was once again in the Charlestons' plans. On October 23, 1930, Oscar and Janie arrived in Key West, their presence noted in the local paper. The next morning they sailed for Havana, where Oscar joined the Marianao club and played alongside some rising white American players from the high Minors. The Charlestons' stay on the island was shorter than they intended. Cuba, thrown into economic crisis by the Depression, had been experiencing rising political unrest since the spring, and just weeks earlier President Gerardo Machado had suspended constitutional guarantees. Shortly after the season started, riots began breaking out. Students led violent demonstrations in cities throughout the island. Despite the danger that lurked on the streets, the players kept showing up for games, even as fewer and fewer fans were inclined to leave their homes. Oscar personally witnessed a few street skirmishes, and he was entirely on top of the situation, later giving his opinion on its causes and complexities to the stateside press. (His sympathies seem to have lain with Machado.)[59] But on November 24, after just three weeks of play and with Marianao holding a three-game lead, league play ended. All of the Negro Leaguers came home except Oscar and Janie, who hung around to tour other, safer parts of the island before arriving back in Key West on New Year's Eve. For Oscar, it was the end of an era. He had hit .373 for Marianao, but he would never play in Cuba again.

No one could or ever would say that Oscar had not left a lasting mark on Cuban baseball. With Alejandro Oms and Pablo Mesa he had anchored the most famous outfield in Cuban history for the 1922–23 and 1923–24 Santa Clara Leopardos. He had won three championships. And by the time he said his final goodbye to Cuba, he had become the nation's most famous and respected American player.

• • •

On December 9, 1930, Rube Foster died. Increasingly erratic and paranoid as the years passed, he had been committed to Kankakee Asylum in 1926 after attacking a friend with an ice pick. Although his family insisted he was harmless, Foster suffered from severe, often baseball-related, delusions until the day of his death. In January, at the annual meeting of the league he had founded, black baseball's eminences held a memorial service in Foster's honor. Among the speakers at Chicago's Vincennes Hotel that day were Cum Posey, Bingo DeMoss, Candy Jim Taylor, Dave Malarcher, and a host of others. Oscar, still in Cuba, was not present.

Foster's death seemed to symbolize, and perhaps foreshadow, the state of black professional baseball in 1931. The miserable financial realities of the Depression, a leadership vacuum, an inability to transcend short-term thinking, and the diverging interests of owners led many observers to believe that the Negro Leagues were doomed. In 1931 there would again be no major black league in the East at all. The western NNL soldiered on, but with teetering franchises and diminished hopes.

The only two clubs making money, it was said, were J. L. Wilkinson's Kansas City Monarchs and Cum Posey's Homestead

Grays. Not coincidentally, those clubs' owners were innovative, hard-nosed businessmen who ran tight financial ships. In the context of the Great Depression such an approach seemed the only way to survive. Salaries reflected the new, post–Jazz Age reality. Posey and his co-owner, Charlie Walker, doled out a total of just $600 per month in payroll during the 1931 season. Just two years earlier Charleston had made nearly two-thirds that amount on his own. Posey had decided by 1931 to trim per diems and travel expenses to the bone. And, very much in the vein of C. I. Taylor, he counseled his fellow owners to strengthen players' popularity with fans by requiring them to display middle-class decorum in public. "Club owners should fine players standing around the street in bedroom slippers, with no collar or tie; also for drinking in public after 12 o'clock at night or frequenting cabarets after 1 o'clock."[60] (For his part, the light-skinned Posey remained true to his upper-class Negroland heritage by usually dressing as if he had just left the links; he had a marked preference for knickers, cardigans, and golf caps.)

Oscar had no beef with such expectations. But it's possible he was miffed at Posey for another reason: being left off Posey's 1930 All-American team, which Posey announced annually in the pages of the *Pittsburgh Courier*. It was the first time since his rookie season that Oscar had not been a consensus choice (and usually *the* consensus choice) for such lists. For the prideful Oscar that omission must have been painful. With the young, powerful Josh Gibson's ascension, the truth was that he was no longer the center of attention, no longer unquestionably the best player on his team, as he had been for the last decade in St. Louis, Indianapolis, Harrisburg, and Philadelphia. Now he shared the spotlight.

At least he was playing on a very talented club. The 1931 Grays were widely expected to be even better than the 1930 edition. Judy Johnson had returned to a reorganized Hilldale outfit, but Jud Wilson, a rough man, hard drinker, and prolific slugger, had been signed away from the Baltimore Black Sox to take

Johnson's place at the hot corner. Gibson was now the full-time catcher. Ted Radcliffe—who both pitched and caught but did not yet have the "Double Duty" nickname later bestowed on him by Damon Runyon—was also added, as was outfielder Ted Page and former Chicago American Giants ace Willie Foster. Everyone else of consequence returned.

An incident from the 1931 Grays season puts Charleston's occasional on-field scuffles into perspective. New team member Page was assigned to room with his friend George Scales, who had recruited him to the team and whom many in the game regarded as a temperamental loudmouth and clubhouse cancer. After one road game Gibson was in the showers when Scales entered and began to berate Josh for dropping a fly ball. Page told Scales to lay off the kid, and before long the two men, stark naked, were duking it out. Page managed to dislodge one of Scales's teeth before Jud Wilson and George Britt could separate them. That seemed to end it, but minutes later a vengeful Scales charged Page with a knife and slashed him in the stomach. Fortunately for all concerned, the cut was superficial.

That night, Page and Scales—still rooming together!—slept facing one another on their shared bed, Scales with his knife under his pillow, Page with the small pistol he always carried at his side (during games he slipped the gun into his jockstrap). "We didn't get a wink of sleep that night," remembered Page, no doubt accurately. (The men made up the next day after Scales brought two girls back to the room.)[61]

Whatever their off-field difficulties, early in the 1931 season the Grays were hardly challenged. After training for ten days in Hot Springs in late March and early April they dominated a short slate of southern semipro and college opponents before swinging through St. Louis, where they took a series from the NNL's Stars. The competition they faced in and around Pittsburgh during the first couple of months was seriously substandard for what was clearly a Major League–caliber team. The

Grays' opponent for the Forbes Field home opener on April 18, for example, was the Pennsylvania Railroad club from Cleveland. The Grays won, 24–3 (Oscar had three hits, including two doubles, along with two errors). Other early-season opponents included clubs from Cumberland, Parkersburg, Alliance, and Bloomington, as well as various company teams from the region. The fact that one cannot immediately say in which states these towns were located speaks volumes. And how good could the club from Klein Chocolate have been?

This was not worthy competition for a team that had five future Hall of Famers in uniform. The only thing that gave such opponents a chance was the Grays' grueling (and therefore at least marginally profitable) travel schedule, which often included two games in two towns on the same day and on at least one occasion included *three* games in *three* towns on the same day.

Actually, a second factor also gave opponents a chance: the Grays themselves. For an increased fee the Grays would keep the game close. One Pennsylvania mining country team, feeling its oats, paid the Grays their higher, tight-game asking price of $200. The miners added that it was only fair, given that they intended to take the Negro Leaguers down. Oscar loved that. He offered to play the entire game one-handed *and* buy a steak dinner for the mining team if it won. He even offered encouragement: after watching the opposing pitcher warm up, he remarked, "If the kid has a fastball to go with his slowball, he might do O.K." Then he smacked three hits, including a home run, to help the Grays scratch out a 21–0 nail-biter.[62]

Eventually, the quality of opponents improved. The Cuban House of David—one of promoter Syd Pollock's gimmick teams—arrived in May. The Grays took two out of three from the bearded islanders, losing to Luis Tiant Sr. and his screwball.[63] Dizzy Dismukes's Cincinnati Valley Tigers came to town and were thrashed by the Grays in all three games. Then, in June, the Grays met up with another Pittsburgh team that was expected to provide more of a challenge: their young catcher

Josh Gibson's former team, the Crawford Giants, or as they were now simply known, the Crawfords.

Based in the predominantly African American Hill District that stretched northeast from downtown Pittsburgh and served as the locus of the city's vibrant black cultural life, during the previous several years the Crawfords had gradually separated themselves from the rest of the city's semipro pack.[64] For the 1931 season they had been given a jolt by the bankroll of William A. "Gus" Greenlee, owner of a neighborhood club and the most prominent figure in what was known as the "numbers racket"—an illegal but highly popular street lottery. In order to secure his political influence, have at his disposal another operation in which to launder numbers money, and perhaps simply help out some local boys, Greenlee had purchased a controlling stake in the Crawfords and was intent on turning it into a top-quality club. Thus far his prime acquisition had been southpaw Sam Streeter. In the Craws' June 1931 contest versus the Grays, Willie Foster beat Streeter handily, 9–0. That only hardened Greenlee's determination to strengthen the Crawfords as quickly as he could. As Cum Posey was about to learn, in an atmosphere in which no league existed to prevent raids Grays players were definitely not off limits.

• • •

After the June 1931 game against the Crawfords the Grays' schedule became markedly tougher. But they proved themselves up to it, and Oscar, placed in the leadoff spot by Posey for much of the season, had a bounceback year. In late June, when the Grays took two out of three from the Cleveland Cubs, Oscar had three hits in one game and two in another. He also played a pivotal role in helping Homestead prevail over Hilldale, a strong club that now featured Judy Johnson, Biz Mackey, and Martín Dihigo. The Daisies won three out of five from the Grays in games played in late June and early July at Forbes Field, Griffith Stadium in Washington DC, and Wilmington, Delaware. The

Grays evened things up by winning the sixth game, in Philadelphia, 6–3. And then Charleston gave them the season-series edge in game seven. With the Grays down 4–3 in Philly, he sent a screaming liner three feet over the right field fence for a two-run, go-ahead homer in the seventh. The shot was much admired in the press. Oscar had "explode[d] the dynamite lurking in his trusty willow," wrote the *Philadelphia Tribune*'s Randy Dixon.[65]

Big series versus the Baltimore Black Sox, Kansas City Monarchs, and St. Louis Stars followed, the Grays winning each of them behind strong pitching and a relentless offensive attack. In a late August doubleheader against the Monarchs played before five thousand–plus at Cleveland's brand-new Municipal Stadium, Oscar helped the Grays win the first game, 9–1, by pounding out four straight doubles followed by a single. In the second end of the doubleheader he singled and then walked twice, reaching base safely eight straight times. The fans also saw him "cover his position in a colorful manner."[66] Josh Gibson, Jud Wilson, and Smokey Joe Williams got at least as much ink in 1931, but Oscar was again doing his part. Reconstructed statistics show that he slashed .340/.394/.532, far better numbers than he had posted in 1930.

Posey couldn't have been more pleased. Charleston had in Posey's opinion proved himself the "greatest first baseman of all time" in 1931, after having previously worn the same crown as outfielder. All season long Oscar consistently dug out low throws, caught errant tosses almost literally off the shoulders of oncoming runners, and went back on pop flies with astonishing agility. Posey estimated that Oscar did not drop more than five balls in the more than 160 games the Grays played that year. Although he was substantially paunchier than he used to be, he could nevertheless still stretch so far—a skill confirmed by surviving photos—that he gained an extra step on runners. "Charleston's playing was like a man without nerves, it was a sensation every game," wrote Posey, who added that Grover Alexander, among other Major League players and ex-players, had "proclaimed Charleston the best ever in discussing the Grays' team with the writer."[67] Yankees scout John Monahan said that Charleston was the best first baseman he had seen outside the Majors. "Why don't you sign me?" Oscar asked Monahan from time to time. Both men knew the answer.[68]

When it was all said and done, the Grays, by besting every major opponent, could legitimately claim their second consecutive black baseball championship in 1931.[69] It was the first undisputed championship since Hilldale had defeated the Kansas City Monarchs in the 1925 Colored World Series, said Posey, the key word being *undisputed*. He reported that the Grays had gone 33-18 against "major negro teams."[70] No one challenged either claim.[71] (Five years later Posey still considered the 1931 Grays the greatest team in Negro Leagues history. Double Duty Radcliffe would also remember the team as the best for which he had ever worn a uniform.)[72] Charleston's rejuvenation was widely acknowledged. The *Chicago Defender* noted that he had had "the greatest season in his colorful career, according to critics watching his play."[73] Posey put Oscar back on his postseason all-star team.

Gus Greenlee was paying attention. Throughout the season he had worked to make his Crawfords more and more competitive. On June 27 the *Courier* had reported that two more stars had been signed by Greenlee's Crawfords: "Satchell and Perkins" of Cleveland. That was catcher Bill Perkins and a pitcher with the last name of Paige, both former teammates of Sam Streeter on the Birmingham Black Barons. The brief piece noted that Satchell's (for a good while his nickname was usually spelled with two l's) "chief asset is a fast ball."[74] Why, yes. Yes, it was.

On August 1, 1931, the Grays hitters got to see that fastball in person. They were playing the Crawfords in McKeesport, Pennsylvania, and had just crawled back from a five-run deficit to tie the score at seven when a tall, long-limbed, rail-thin young man strolled slowly to the mound to relieve Craws starter Harry Kincannon. Paige's hurling was eye opening. The press reported it as "masterful and sensational."[75] Satchel held the Grays in check, and the Craws won, 10–7. Posey put Paige on his All-America team. Greenlee had found something.

It wasn't just Paige who impressed Greenlee. In his effort to put together a first-rate club and make as much money as possible doing it, Greenlee was building his own ballpark in the Hill District on Bedford Avenue. To properly open this new park and fittingly launch a new era of fully professional Crawfords baseball in 1932, he needed a new manager. Why not the great Oscar Charleston, who not only had proved in 1931 that he still had plenty in the tank, but also remained "the best gate attraction in Negro baseball"? There was every reason to think Oscar would be interested. "The berth is well worth going after and arguing about," noted the *Philadelphia Tribune* in reporting on the possibility. After all, the Crawfords "will play all home games in their own modern park. Out of town travel will be in buses. All in all, the Crawfords loom as the best attraction in the tri-state district, which can be taken to mean that they will be the best paid."[76] That certainly sounded like the sort of situation that would very much interest the Homestead Grays' first baseman.

CHAPTER 7

Champion, 1932–1938

ON JANUARY 28, 1932, Oscar Charleston was named the new manager of the Pittsburgh Crawfords. Thus did he begin an association, and finally a close friendship, with Gus Greenlee—a man he would hail in his scrapbook as "the daddy of them all"—that would last until Greenlee died on July 7, 1952.[1] The next seven years would not be without their trials. Oscar would watch Greenlee's empire rise and fall, his marriage to Janie falter, his skills slowly erode, and his place as the black game's most popular player be usurped. But he would also emerge from these Pittsburgh Crawfords years with his first managerial championships and a hard-earned reputation as the unquestioned leader of the Negro Leagues' most famous club.

• • •

Oscar's new boss had been born and raised in North Carolina, the son of a locally prominent contractor who instilled in his sons a strong drive for achievement.[2] Two of those sons became doctors. Another became an attorney. Gus became the wealthiest and most famous of the brood by taking a somewhat different path. After dropping out of college, he became a bootlegger and racketeer. His father quite reasonably never approved of his wayward son's career choice, but to nearly all of black Pittsburgh Gus Greenlee was a hero.

Greenlee arrived in Pittsburgh on a freight train in 1916. After he was mustered out of the army following the end of World War I, he returned to the city and began to fatten his wallet by running liquor as a taxi driver. Soon, he found himself the owner of a speakeasy, and a decade or so later, in 1933, he opened the Crawford Grill on Wylie Avenue in Pittsburgh's Hill District. The restaurant was ideally located. Since the latter half of the nineteenth century the Hill had been a principal residence area for the city's African Americans, and by the 1930s half of Pittsburgh's 50,000–60,000 blacks lived in the neighborhood. Many, of course, were unemployed; in 1934 the combined rate of black unemployment and underemployment in Allegheny County reached 69 percent. Yet the Wylie Avenue commercial district stayed busy, offering a lively street life and plenty of night clubs in which Prohibition was not scrupulously observed.

Greenlee's Crawford Grill was the most popular spot on the avenue. Three stories high and open all night, among its customers the grill counted black and white, rich and poor, entertainer and working man, policeman and pimp, athlete and politician. The food was excellent; the jazz stylings of Count Basie, Duke Ellington, Cab Calloway, and Lena Horne even better. Art Rooney, owner of the Pittsburgh Steelers and a friend of Greenlee's, was a frequent visitor, and virtually every Negro Leaguer who came through the city hung out there. Greenlee often held court at the bar, gossiping with visitors and dispensing advice. He also dispensed financial help, for by 1932 he was the undisputed numbers king of Pittsburgh.

The numbers lottery was exceedingly popular in Pittsburgh, as indeed it was in many other cities. It was fun, easy, and cheap. To play, a bettor simply placed as little as a half-penny on the three-digit number of his choice. Then he watched to see if it hit, the winning number being determined by, for example, by the results of particular horse races.[3] A winning bet paid off at six hundred to one, tops. One needn't be a mathematical genius to see why the industry was attractive to risk-tolerant entrepreneurs like Greenlee. Even after runners, collectors, watchmen, heavies, politicians, and cops were paid off, the margins were pretty good. Men close to the action later guessed that Greenlee took in between $20,000 and $25,000 per day during the height of his business in the mid-1930s. For the time, and especially for the black community, that was a stunning sum, and Greenlee lived it up, encasing his 6-foot-3-inch, 200-plus-pound frame in expensive silk suits and treating himself to a new Lincoln convertible every year.

The numbers financed black baseball in the 1930s—or at least a sizeable chunk of it. Among Negro Leagues owners, the New York Cubans' Alex Pompez, who allegedly bankrolled Greenlee's Pittsburgh operation during its startup phase; the Newark Eagles' Abe Manley; the Memphis Red Sox' Tom Wilson; the New York Black Yankees' James "Soldier Boy" Semler; and Homestead Grays' co-owner Rufus "Sonnyman" Jackson were all numbers operators. Few other black businessmen had the capital to finance ball clubs, so those who weren't involved in the numbers, like Ed Bolden, were often forced to carry white partners. Then, too, a numbers man had a pressing need for a legitimate business front—like a baseball team.

They were racketeers, these men. They were not hard-core, murderous gangsters like Al Capone, but neither were they cuddly innocents merely forced by social circumstances into unorthodox occupations. No matter what social good they achieved with their profits, no matter how magnanimously they distributed their largesse, their numbers lotteries were inherently predatory, a fact a little too easily passed over by many Negro Leagues historians—not to mention the even less pleasant fact that many of the numbers men, including Greenlee, also profited from the sex trade.[4] Furthermore, those muscling in on their territory were sometimes dealt with in extralegal fashion. It would be surprising if any of these men did not have at least *some* blood on their hands.

The crazy-eyed Semler was the most reviled and mistrusted of the numbers-connected Negro Leagues magnates; Pompez and Greenlee were the most admired and respected. When historian Rob Ruck interviewed nearly one hundred members of the Pittsburgh black community in the early 1980s, he found only one person who displayed even a hint of hostility toward Greenlee.[5] But a man doesn't get ahead in organized crime without being cruel and calculating, and whatever his virtues, Gus was no exception. Art Rooney recalled being with Greenlee when he reneged on a promise to give one of his lovers some money; Gus brushed the woman off by telling her, "Last night was last night. When I'm hard, I'm soft. When I'm soft, I'm hard." (She responded by whipping an ashtray at, and narrowly missing, Gus's head.)[6] Judy Johnson claimed that Greenlee's men hijacked trucks carrying liquor for rival gang operations and that Gus had arranged for the murder of two small-time punks demanding protection money from neighborhood businesses.[7] Greenlee may have steered clear of loansharking, drugs, and protection, but there was little doubt he "could be mean and ruthless."[8] Still, if one stayed on his good side, those very qualities, paired with his native generosity, made Gus a pretty great owner to play for.

• • •

Greenlee had been involved with the Crawfords since the team's beginnings, donating funds for uniforms in 1926 to the boys who had formed the team and entered it in the city's recreational league as representatives of the Crawford Bath House, a local Hill institution. In just six years the ball club had come a long way. In the early months of 1932 workmen were busily constructing a new park for the team to call home. When finished, the red brick, $100,000 Greenlee Field was to seat 7,500 and include showers and dressing rooms for both the home and visiting teams—an important amenity, given that black clubs were not allowed to use those facilities at the Pirates' Forbes Field. Although within a few years the stadium would prove to be badly flawed, especially in its lack of a covered grandstand, initially most of the players loved it. More generally, for black Pittsburgh the construction of Greenlee Field during one of the darker years of the Great Depression was a source of pride and hope—as was the fact that the city would now have not one but two elite black baseball teams to call its own.

It wasn't only with the construction of his own ballpark that Greenlee had made it clear he wasn't fooling around. Bringing in Oscar Charleston as his new manager also sent a message. Beyond his playing ability and managerial experience Charleston was a savvy pick for two reasons. First, among the candidates for the job Charleston was the fan favorite. As the *Philadelphia Tribune* reported in announcing the news, Charleston was "conceded to be the best drawing card in baseball. . . . He has that rare style of performing which makes the old retired business man want to kick over the benches . . . or make the meek little school marm yell until she's hoarse."[9] Second, the selection of Oscar gave Greenlee's Crawfords substantial credibility in the player community. Among his peers, the well-networked Oscar was nearly as popular as he was among the fans. Coupled with Greenlee's ability to pay top-end salaries and the financial gut punches the putrid economy was dealing the other owners, including Cum Posey, handing Oscar the dugout reins meant that the Crawfords could compete for the finest black baseball talent around.

Greenlee made it Charleston's job to identify and recruit that talent, and backed by Gus's wallet, Oscar moved with characteristic alacrity. Within days of being named the Craws' captain he had obtained commitments from Satchel Paige, Sam Streeter, Harry Kincannon, Roy Williams, Double Duty Radcliffe, Bobby Williams, and Jimmie Crutchfield to join the club. (Roy Williams and Radcliffe had been Oscar's teammates on the 1931 Grays.) A couple of weeks later it was announced that Josh Gibson, who was best friends with Kincannon, would also abandon Cum Posey to join his upstart rival.[10] Rev Cannady, perhaps the best hitter in black baseball in 1931, came over from Hilldale, and Rap Dixon, now in the prime of his career, journeyed west to join his former Harrisburg Giants manager. The Crawfords would be a force to reckon with.

They would also travel in style. Greenlee procured for the team's use a brand-new Mack bus proudly emblazoned "Pittsburgh Crawfords Baseball Team" along its side. Upholstered in fine leather, the bus featured a seventy-nine-horsepower V-6 engine, carried seventeen men, and did sixty miles per hour. Such features seemed utterly luxurious by the standards of the Great Depression.[11]

By the time spring training arrived, Greenlee and Charleston had their new-look Crawfords more or less in order. Oscar drilled his men for ten days in Hot Springs before beginning a typically ambitious barnstorming tour across the South and Midwest. Over the six weeks of spring training the new bus's odometer topped five thousand miles as the Craws wandered through Louisiana, Texas, Nebraska, Kansas, Missouri, Iowa, Tennessee, and Alabama. The Craws played twenty-two games in those eight states, and everywhere they went they impressed the locals with the class of both their outfit and their play. Occasionally they reaped a big reward, as in Houston, where a woman known as Mother Mitchell, made rich by oil royalties, treated them to a royal roast beef and fried chicken feast at her spacious home. Mrs. Mitchell's mouthwatering homemade meal stood in stark contrast to the meager fare the players were usually able to secure when traveling south of the Mason-Dixon line.[12]

There was no question, throughout the spring exhibition season, who the Crawfords' star was. Out "west," in Missouri and Nebraska, Charleston's "showmanship at first, with his one-hand catches, was something new" for admiring fans.[13] In Marshall, Texas, there was "little doubt that fans will flock far and wide to see the Flying Hoosier" who had so impressed them when appearing there with the Grays the previous spring.[14] In Birmingham, reported the *Atlanta Daily World*, fans would behold in Charleston the man regarded as the "most colorful fielder and hitter in the game—anywhere."[15] Oscar excelled even in the Craws' snappy pregame shadowball routine.[16] Young Josh Gibson and the relatively unknown Satchel Paige were, at this point, cast as supporting players by the press; Jimmie Crutch-field and Rev Cannady were as apt to be highlighted in game accounts as were they, and Oscar still played the leading role.

Finally, on April 28, 1932, the Crawfords unofficially chris-tened the hastily constructed Greenlee Field by defeating a semipro team from Vandergrift, 11–0. The next day, April 29, the team officially opened its season, and dedicated its new ballpark, against the New York Black Yankees. It was a proud moment for Pittsburgh's African American community. Follow-ing a street parade and speeches by local dignitaries, includ-ing the mayor, Gus Greenlee entered in style. He arrived on the field to a standing ovation, wearing an immaculate white suit and riding in a red Packard convertible. Satchel Paige then took the mound against the Black Yankees' "Mountain" Jesse Hubbard. The two men fought a classic pitchers' duel until the Black Yankees finally broke through with a run in the bottom of the ninth to seal a 1–0 victory and spoil Charleston's official debut as the Crawfords' manager.[17]

In the folklore that emerged much later the 1932 Crawfords are sometimes nominated as the best black baseball team ever—even, perhaps, as the best team in all baseball history. After all, Paige, Gibson, and Charleston were all bound for Cooper-stown. Two other future Hall of Famers, third baseman Judy Johnson and left fielder Jud Wilson, joined the team midsea-son. And the supporting cast included exceptional players in Dixon, Cannady, and Ted Page, another midseason addition. But while the 1932 Craws certainly enjoyed plenty of success, they rather embarrassingly lost the season series to the Home-stead Grays, despite having viciously plundered Posey's squad. In the end the Grays went 35-22-1 against top competition, while the Crawfords went 32-26-1 (at the time the team reported an overall record of 99-36).[18] Charleston's gang was certainly much celebrated and feared, and at one point the club not only put together a sixteen-game winning streak, but also played those sixteen games within a span of just seven days. (That fancy Mack bus had seventeen thousand miles on it by late August.) Nevertheless, the Crawfords did not dominate the competition the way "history's best team" would have.

Charleston, now thirty-five years old, had a good but not great year, posting an OPS+ against top competition of 139. On January 2, 1932, Rollo Wilson's New Year's wish for Charleston had been for a fresh pair of legs.[19] Perhaps that bit of ribbing inspired Oscar, for after a late-May series against the Grays, the *Courier* marveled that Oscar remained a better base runner than anyone else on the diamond. "He knows when to go," noted the paper, implying that his advantage now lay more with his brain than with his legs.[20] That was true, remembered Jimmie Crutchfield: "When I played for him with the Crawfords, he was already old and fat. It was hard fat, but it was fat, and he couldn't run very well. Still, he stole a lot of bases, especially when we really needed one. He did it by getting a great jump, knowing which pitch to run on, and by using his sliding ability to avoid tags."[21]

Oscar also proved to be the fan favorite he was touted to be before the season started. He was the headliner when the Crawfords came to Washington's Griffith Stadium, home of the Senators, on June 1. And when the Crawfords went to Indianapolis for a four-game series against Candy Jim Taylor's ABCs in mid-May, his Indianapolis days and status as a favorite among the city's black fans was remarked upon by the white *Indianapolis News*.[22] A large crowd turned out for the Sunday, May 15, doubleheader, and a delegation of local dignitaries presented Oscar with "a handsome hand bag" as a token of the hometown fans' appreciation. Oscar, touched, said that "he was quite surprised as well as pleased with the token from Hoosierdom."[23]

Nevertheless, it was the emergence of Paige and Gibson under Charleston's watch that constituted the story of the season. Oscar has rarely gotten any credit for their development; he is at best a bit player in the standard biographies of both men. Yet perhaps, given the esteem in which he was widely held for his managerial skills and temperament, he ought to get a little acclaim for shepherding the two young men toward stardom. After all, just getting Paige to show up for buses and games on time was a monumental challenge, and the powerful but raw Gibson could have had no better model for how to attack pitchers than the man considered one of the greatest hitters of all time.

Charleston shared more and more of the spotlight with Satchel and Josh as the 1932 season progressed. Prior to the Craws' series against the Pilots in Washington DC, Satchel was saluted as a "smokeball pitcher with a world of steam."[24] In an eight-game late June series versus the Grays, Paige and Gibson were the Craws most praised by the Pittsburgh press. On July 16, at Greenlee Field, Paige won more fame by hurling a no-hitter against the Black Yankees. By the end of the season, it was the amazingly powerful Gibson, rather than Charleston, who was being called the black Babe Ruth—and for good reason. Although team statistics weren't reported until January 1933, the 1932 Crawfords kept careful records. Charleston played in more games than any other player—135. In 430 at bats he collected 104 runs, 156 hits, 22 doubles, 10 triples, and 13 home runs. He walked twice as much as he struck out (75 versus 37). Those numbers work out to a .363 batting average, .457 on-base percentage, and .551 slugging percentage—darn good production. Yet Josh's full line, in 123 games, consisted of 490 at bats, 114 runs, 186 hits, 45 doubles, 16 triples, 34 homers, 41 strikeouts, and 31 walks, for a team-high batting average of .380, an on-base percentage of .417, and a terrifying slugging percentage of .745. A torch had been passed, and while Oscar would remain a dangerous hitter for another four years, it would never be returned.

• • •

In late September and early October the Crawfords barnstormed with a Major League all-star team in Pennsylvania and Ohio. On September 27 in York, Pennsylvania, they crushed the all-stars, managed by Casey Stengel, 11–2. The next day they were hammered themselves by the all-stars at Greenlee Field, 20–8; Oscar had three hits and two home runs in that game, while RBI machine Hack Wilson homered for the all-stars. After three more games in which the Craws went 2-1, Charleston's club wrapped up the seven-game series with a doubleheader sweep in Cleveland on October 2. Oscar must have relished winning the managerial battle versus Stengel, then the Brooklyn Dodgers' first base coach.

The series was a fine way for the Crawfords to wrap up their inaugural season in the big time. For if the 1932 Crawfords weren't quite as transcendent as would come to be believed, no one lodged any complaints about their performance. The complaints were being lobbed at a different target: the black baseball magnates and their failure to put together a functioning league.

• • •

Getting a true league up and running was easier called for than done. The owners who might be drawn into an association were men used to exercising autonomous leadership in their various spheres. Most of them were not natural coalition builders. They had different levels of financial wherewithal, and in some cases they had formed partnerships with white booking agents or money men in order to keep their teams afloat, a situation that meant additional complications for any league structure. Furthermore, if a league wasn't characterized by mutual trust, if it didn't have enforceable authority over its members, and if it didn't have high exit costs, the lure of independent play often proved too strong to resist. Cum Posey had tried to form a new league in 1932 in spite of such obstacles, but his East-West League fell apart in the middle of the summer, in part because Gus Greenlee had refused to join.

In 1933 Greenlee decided to try his own hand at forming a circuit. Unlike Posey, as a relative newcomer on the scene Greenlee did not yet have many enemies. He also enjoyed enviable cash flow. These advantages, added to his natural likeability, provided enough of a foundation for Greenlee to launch a new Negro National League that spring, with himself cast in the Rube Foster role as league president. Besides the Crawfords the league would include the Chicago American Giants, Columbus Bluebirds, Baltimore Black Sox, Indianapolis ABCS (soon to move to Detroit and take the name Stars), the Homestead Grays, and the Nashville Elite Giants. Akron and Cleveland also both briefly fielded league entries.

The Craws started the 1933 NNL season with a bang by sweeping a doubleheader from the Elite Giants in Nashville on April 30. It was another opening day on which Oscar shined. He went 5 for 7 in the two contests with three home runs and a stolen base. The lineup around him was better than anyone yet could have known. Cool Papa Bell led off, Ted Page hit second, Oscar batted third, Gibson manned the clean-up spot, and Judy Johnson protected him in the five hole. Four Hall of Famers, in other words, filled the lineup's top five slots—and the one non–Hall of Famer, Page, would that year post a 139 OPS+ against top competition. (The thirty-three-year-old Johnson, in truth, was slipping; he would post a mere 74 OPS+ on the year.) Led by Charleston, a super fast outfield, the game's hardest hitter in Gibson, and its hardest-throwing pitcher in Paige, the Crawfords rolled through the season's first two months like the elite club they were. As of June 24 they reportedly led the league with an 18-7 record, thanks largely to Oscar's .450 batting average in sixty official at bats. Bell was hitting .379, Gibson .378, and Perkins .344. Nevertheless, the Crawfords could not shake the American Giants—which featured four future Hall of Famers of their own in Turkey Stearnes, Mule Suttles, Willie Wells, and Willie Foster—and in a July 8 game that decided the first-half pennant winner, rookie Sug Cornelius defeated Satchel Paige to put the Chicagoans over the top.

There were bigger problems than losing out on the first-half flag, though. It wasn't clear that Greenlee's new NNL would survive. Black baseball teams were chronically undercapitalized, and the catastrophically bad U.S. economy in 1933 made things even tougher (the year's GDP would end up only half what it had been in 1929). Various teams were forced to merge, switch cities, or drop out of the league entirely. The Craws themselves called off a series in Chicago in early July because of high travel costs. Many other games that were supposed to be played never were.

Fortunately, Greenlee had a bright idea—an idea that not only probably saved the NNL, but also proved to be the most popular event in Negro Leagues history: an all-star game pitting the stars of the East versus the stars of the West. The concept wasn't original; the first-ever Major League All-Star Game had just been staged in Chicago's Comiskey Park on July 6, 1933. But Greenlee knew a good idea when he saw one, and with Roy Sparrow, a black journalist for the *Pittsburgh Sun-Telegraph*, as his point man, he got to work. In early August it was announced that the East-West game, with participating players determined by a fan vote, was to take place at Comiskey on September 10.

Backed heavily by the *Pittsburgh Courier, Chicago Defender*, and other black newspapers, the idea instantly took off. Over the next few weeks, tens of thousands of fans eager to support their favorite players submitted their ballots. Sparrow drummed up publicity, scoring a coup when he got WGN Radio to do live interviews with Oscar Charleston and Willie Foster on the evening of September 9.[25] Foster was the American Giants' ace. Charleston's inclusion made sense in that he was the game's leading vote-getter. Despite the influx of new stars in Paige, Gibson, and others, the soon-to-be thirty-seven-year-old Oscar was still the black game's most popular player.

When the East-West game's first pitch was thrown by Willie Foster at three o'clock on Sunday, September 10, only twelve thousand fans were in the stands.[26] That was not quite the showing Greenlee and his associates had hoped for, but the weather forecast had been lousy, and when it started raining in the second inning, many fans were forced to scurry for cover. Drizzle continued throughout the game, but in nearly every other way the day was a resounding success. Fans showed up from across the country in their stylish best, and the players gave them an entertaining, hard-fought contest. The West emerged with an 11–7 victory. Oscar had no hits, but he was twice hit by a Foster pitch, and he and Lundy were said by the *Defender* to be the game's fielding stars.[27] Oscar also stole a base and scored a run. Henry Farrell, a white reporter, was plenty impressed: "The boy, Oscar Charleston, who played first base for the eastern team . . . could handle the same job on at least ten clubs in the big leagues," he wrote. "He handled the base with the grace and agility of Hal Chase. . . . He was hit twice by Foster. . . . Three other times Charleston hit the ball hard but the drives were taken."[28]

As for the 1933 pennant, Greenlee, Charleston, and the Craws were determined to win it—by whatever means necessary. Amid the stress of the race, Oscar, intense as ever, suffered a midseason meltdown. The Craws had played a doubleheader versus the Nashville Elite Giants in Birmingham on July 16 and lost both games. The next day, the two teams were playing in Chattanooga when a line drive hit by one of the Elites was ruled fair rather than foul. Oscar lost it. After having it out with the umpire, he ambled to the mound and took the ball. He proceeded to simply stand there staring into the heavens for a few minutes. Then he walked six straight men without throwing a strike, thus ensuring that the game be regarded as a farce. Along the way he loudly employed some language not fit for the drawing room. That season lowlight, for Oscar, was offset somewhat by his performance against the Philadelphia Stars at their Forty-Fourth and Parkside home grounds in an August contest. In front of a frenzied capacity crowd, and with the Craws down 3–2, Oscar hit a game-winning two-run homer off right-handed submariner Webster McDonald in the top of the ninth.

On September 30 and October 1 the Crawfords played the Nashville Elite Giants in a three-game series that would decide the second-half pennant, the winner to play the American Giants for the league championship. The Crawfords needed to win only one of these contests. After losing the first game at Greenlee Field, Oscar sent Satchel to the mound for the opening game of the next day's doubleheader in Cleveland. In front of just three thousand fans the Craws took a 4–2 lead into the bottom of the ninth, but the Elites managed to scratch across the tying runs off Paige before Oscar brought in Leroy Matlock to end the threat. Finally, in the top of the twelfth, Cool Papa Bell hit a screaming liner to deep center and flew around the bases for an inside-the-park home run, and Matlock closed the door in the bottom of the frame. Charleston had gone 2 for 5.

And then . . . there was no championship series after all—or at least none that was completed.[29] The Craws and American Giants met in Cleveland on October 8, 1933, and played to a 7–7 tie. But for the series' second game in Wheeling, West Virginia, such was the esteem in which the NNL championship was held that only seven American Giants players showed up. The game was played anyway—and predictably won by the Crawfords. That was enough for the remaining Chicago players; they refused to go on to Pittsburgh for the series' scheduled third game, and so the championship was forfeited to the Crawfords. It was the most anticlimactic of anticlimactic endings.

• • •

Oscar Charleston's reconstructed 1933 slash line, over 260 plate appearances, was .338/.397/.628, good for a 176 OPS+, second on the team only to Josh Gibson's 218. In October, as he turned thirty-seven, Oscar was invited by Memphis Red Sox owner Tom Wilson to join his California Winter League team of black all-stars along with Paige, Gibson, and others, but Oscar declined. He hung around Pittsburgh instead, predicting to a *Courier* reporter that the end of Prohibition, which came on December 5, would probably "help in the way of employment," but otherwise keeping a low profile.[30] By the time March 1934 arrived, Greenlee had successfully pulled together a reformed NNL that included eastern teams like Ed Bolden's Philadelphia Stars and Charles Tyler's Newark Dodgers, as well as Posey's Homestead Grays and the Bacharach Giants as associate members. The league even had a salaried commissioner in Oscar's friend Rollo Wilson, the respected *Courier* columnist who made his home in Philadelphia.

On March 25 Greenlee's flashy bus left for Memphis. It was laden with talented ballplayers who, given the country's economic situation, must have been delighted to be employed. Satchel Paige was on board, as were Charleston and veterans like Josh Gibson, Judy Johnson, Ted Page, Harry Kincannon, Sam Streeter, and the pure-hitting left fielder Vic Harris. Cool Papa Bell and Jimmie Crutchfield were picked up along the way. Soon, the club was rambling through the sunny South. The Craws lost an early exhibition game to Piney Woods College, 7–5, an outcome that received a lot of press back north. But it was an otherwise uneventful, if tiring, spring. An eleven-day mid-April spring swing through Texas had the Crawfords playing one or two games every day in towns like Jefferson, Tyler, Crockett, Nacogdoches, Henderson, Kilgore, Gilmer, and Longview. In none of these places was the team welcome in any public place. Yet after the Piney Woods loss the Craws won virtually every game they played.

When league play opened in April, Oscar was on his best behavior. In the opening series versus the American Giants in Chicago he didn't even complain when a questionable ruling put an American Giants runner who had been on first at third. Al Monroe of the *Chicago Defender* marveled that Oscar had not thrown a fit or even stepped onto the field to protest. "Truly, it was a commendable move made by Charleston and is one of many other things done in the series to show why Oscar is and should be called one of the game's great, if not greatest, figures and managers." It was easier to put up with bad rulings and the rigors of the road when one was playing for Gus Greenlee. Monroe gaped not only at Oscar's restraint, but also at Greenlee's largesse. Gus "must be a whale of a fellow to work for," wrote Monroe. "We observed the equipment his men are given to play with and, in comparison with many another club, his rates with the major leagues. Carrying no more than fifteen men Gus has supplied his club with more than two bats per player and then, they tell me, an order was placed for a dozen more."[31] Unlike other owners, Greenlee seemed Depression-proof.

A large crowd attended the Craws' home opening series versus the Philadelphia Stars in mid-May at Gus's namesake park. Oscar, whose career results in opening games were staggeringly good, led the team to a win in the first contest by hitting a two-run homer deep over the center field fence in the sixth inning. In the series' third game he smashed another long ball to help his Craws take two out of three from their cross-state rivals.

With Vic Harris supplanting Ted Page, the 1934 Crawfords boasted an even better first four in their lineup—Bell, Harris, Charleston, Gibson—than they had in 1933. The pitching depth was strong, too, with Satchel leading a staff that included Sam Streeter, Harry Kincannon, and the underrated Leroy Matlock, as well as William Bell and Bert Hunter. By the end of the year Paige would separate himself from this pack forever, but as of early 1934 it wasn't yet clear that he was the sure ace of the staff, and Charleston remained the Craws' headliner at least as often as Paige or Gibson.

When the *Washington Post* promoted a Sunday, June 10, game between the Craws and the Philadelphia Stars at Griffith Stadium, Oscar not only got top billing, with Cool Papa Bell and Satchel Paige second and third, respectively, but also was referred to as the "highest paid colored professional" in the game, a fact that was the result of Oscar's hard annual negotiations with Greenlee.[32] When the Crawfords rolled into Altoona in mid-June, the *Altoona Tribune* hyped them as being led by "that ever popular Oscar Charleston."[33] An ad in the *Philadelphia Tribune* promoting a doubleheader between the Craws and Bacharach

Giants on August 4 advised fans not to "miss seeing the Crawfords' two Babe Ruths, B. [*sic*] Gibson and Oscar Charleston."[34]

Not that Oscar was unwilling to share the limelight. He knew as well as anyone how popular Paige, especially, was and could be—and how much his presence could mean to the Craws' bottom line. When the club traveled to Harrisburg to play the Philadelphia Stars in a mid-July Sunday doubleheader, Oscar wrote a letter to his brother-in-law, promoter Bud Marshall, promising that he would start Satch. The *Harrisburg Telegraph* quoted Oscar as saying, "I sincerely hope Page [*sic*] is at his best because I want to let Harrisburg folks watch some really great hurling."[35] Alas, before a very large crowd (for Harrisburg) of nearly three thousand, the Craws dropped both ends of the twin bill to the Stars.

Oscar wasn't happy with how the last game ended; the Craws had just tied the game 1–1 in the bottom of the fifth on his triple and run scored when the clock struck six; by law, the game had to be discontinued. The score then reverted to what it had been at the end of the last completed inning, 1–0 Stars, an interpretation of the rules that Oscar vigorously disputed. Worse still, Oscar was hurting. Some kind of leg injury had nearly kept him out of these games in Harrisburg, where he remained extremely popular. He had played only in order not to disappoint the fans.

As the season wore on, Oscar missed a few games because of this injury, and with Judy Johnson also hurting, those absences didn't help the Craws' cause. They finished behind the American Giants for the first-half flag, but Oscar was still putting up fine numbers. When the first official league statistics were finally released on August 4, 1934, he was batting .318. That was fifth on the team behind Gibson's .369, Harris's .367, Johnson's .333, and Chester Williams's .319. Oscar also had four home runs, second on the team to Gibson's six, and three stolen bases, second to Cool Papa's five.

As the second annual East-West game neared on August 26, it was announced that Oscar would manage the East club and that his old ABCs teammate Dave Malarcher would manage the West. The fans had reportedly made it known that these were their preferences. Injury or not, they also voted in Oscar as the East's starting first baseman. The only player to get more votes than Oscar—narrowly—was his teammate Satchel Paige.

This was one game for which Satch was excited. By the time the East-West game rolled around, he had been absent from the Craws for a couple of weeks. Greenlee had loaned him to the House of David to play in the *Denver Post* baseball tournament, an event that had been taking place in the Mile High City since 1915 but had never before included blacks. Paige and catcher Bill Perkins were the only two African Americans on the House of David team, which was managed by former Major Leagues great Grover Cleveland Alexander. Satchel had pitched the bearded barnstormers to the title, striking out forty-four in twenty-eight innings, winning three games in five days, and defeating the Kansas City Monarchs' Chet Brewer, 2–1, to take the championship.[36] When he arrived in Chicago on the evening of Friday, August 24, Satchel was still jazzed. He started telling the press that he was not only ready to go all nine innings in Sunday's all-star game, but also that he had asked Oscar for permission to do so. He wanted to set a strikeout record. Charleston, as he must have had to do on countless occasions, resisted Satchel's salesmanship. With a number of other outstanding pitchers at his disposal, he decided to save Paige for a high-leverage situation.

Twenty-five thousand fans—including many celebrities, women, and (by one estimate) about five thousand whites— showed up at Comiskey Park on Sunday, August 26, to see their heroes battle.[37] For five innings no batter on either team could do much against the West's Ted Trent and Chet Brewer or the East's Slim Jones and Harry Kincannon. In the sixth inning, with the game still a scoreless tie, American Giants' star shortstop Willie Wells smacked a leadoff double off Kincannon. Oscar knew this was Satchel's moment. From his post at first base he made the call to the bullpen, and Satchel, in his inimitable way, strolled languidly to the mound as the crowd cheered wildly. He struck out Double Duty Radcliffe, then got fearful sluggers Turkey Stearnes and Mule Suttles to fly out to end the threat. Jud Wilson singled in Cool Papa Bell in the eighth to give the East a 1–0 lead, and when Jimmie Crutchfield ended the game by firing a strike to home plate to nab a tagging Mule Suttles, Paige had achieved a thrilling save (a term not yet in use). He and the rest of the club celebrated with a chicken dinner at the Grand Hotel Café, where Oscar and Dick Lundy treated the East team's two batboys, still wearing their Crawfords uniforms, to all the ice cream and cake they wanted.[38]

Alas, getting Paige back from Denver was not enough to lift the Crawfords to the second-half flag, which was taken by the Philadelphia Stars. The Craws' 47-27-3 total record for the year was the second best in the league but not good enough in either half to put them in line for a championship. The months of September and October 1934 nevertheless would contain two of the most memorable series of games the Pittsburgh Crawfords ever played.

The first consisted of a string of doubleheaders in which Paige continued to blossom into a full-blown superstar.[39] On Sunday, September 9, the Crawfords participated in a four-team doubleheader at Yankee Stadium. Battling the Philadelphia Stars in the second game of the day, in front of a raucous crowd estimated to be between twenty-five and thirty thousand, the Craws were no-hit by Slim Jones for six innings before Oscar broke through with a single in the seventh. They failed to score, but with Paige holding the Stars to a single run, the Craws tied the game in the eighth. Then, in the bottom of the ninth, the Stars loaded the bases against Satchel with one out. Paige struck out the next two men he faced—his eleventh and twelfth strikeouts of the day—to preserve the tie before the game was called because of darkness. Famous entertainer Bill "Bojangles" Robinson, a huge baseball fan, memorialized the duel by giving both Paige and Jones travel bags embossed with the words "the greatest game ever played."[40]

The Crawfords returned to Yankee Stadium on Sunday, September 30. This time thirty-five thousand fans showed up to watch Paige again battle Slim Jones and the Stars. Once again, Paige got the best of Jones, fanning eighteen Stars to lead the Crawfords to a 3–1 victory. In that game Oscar, even though his leg wasn't feeling right, tagged from third and scored on a high pop foul to catcher Biz Mackey when he noticed that no one was covering home. He also singled, doubled, and was intentionally walked. Nevertheless, there was no doubt who the Crawfords'—and black baseball's—biggest star was now. Satchel had stolen the show.

• • •

The only pitcher whose star was as big in his community as Paige's was in his was a charming, egotistical, hillbilly braggart christened Jay Hanna Dean. Like Paige, Dean was a supreme self-fashioner who had renamed himself Jerome Herman but was now universally known as Dizzy.[41] Also like Paige, Dean had risen to superstardom in 1934, leading the Gashouse Gang Cardinals to a World Series championship over the Detroit Tigers. Not one to be slow in capitalizing on a money-making opportunity—yet another trait he had in common with Satchel— Dizzy and his brother Paul had embarked on a barnstorming tour immediately after the World Series ended. The brainchild of chubby, mustachioed, oily promoter Ray Doan—nickname "Ding-Dong" and proud inventor of donkey baseball—for three weeks the Deans teamed up with local semipros in different cities.[42] Their opponents mostly consisted of Negro Leaguers, including, when the Dean All-Stars were in Ohio and western Pennsylvania, the Pittsburgh Crawfords. Dizzy and especially Paul were sore-armed from the Cardinals' long season, during which they had pitched about six hundred innings combined. But they were determined to make bank. In these exhibitions each would typically pitch a couple of frames to delight the fans before moving to some other position.

The Crawfords met the Deans at the end of their tour, starting in Cleveland. Twelve thousand fans showed up at League Park for a cold, drizzly night game featuring Paul and Diz versus Satchel, Oscar, Cool Papa Bell, Josh Gibson, Judy Johnson, and the rest of the Crawfords regulars. It wasn't a deadly serious affair; Paige and Dizzy mocked each other's deliveries on the mound, Diz took wildly hard swings at Satchel's fastballs, and there was plenty of clowning on both sides. But when he released the ball, each pitcher was all business. Oscar singled in the only run Dizzy allowed when he knocked in Paige, who had miraculously doubled. Satchel struck out thirteen before Oscar removed him, much to the crowd's chagrin. The game ended with the Crawfords winning, 4–1. The Midwest was still experiencing a bitterly cold autumn when the Deans and Craws met in Columbus on Monday, October 22. The Crawfords won again, 5–3, in a game highlighted by Paige's deliberately walking the bases loaded before striking out the side.

The final game of the series, and the final contest of the Deans' whirlwind, much-hyped tour, came the next day at Forbes Field. Dizzy and Paul had made something like $20,000 on the trip, but they were tired and grumpy. The weather was nasty. The small crowd of twenty-five hundred was energetic. So were the Crawfords. They eagerly looked forward to a series sweep over the white baseball world's new media darlings.

With two out in the bottom of the fifth, the Craws were down 3–1 when Vic Harris chopped a swinging bunt in front of home and was ruled safe at first. He then dashed to second on the catcher's wild throw. Dizzy, who was playing left field, came charging in to claim that Harris had run inside the first base line and thus was guilty of interference. The home plate umpire, overruling the field umpire, bought Dean's argument. Harris was out.

Now, Harris was not one of your mild-mannered, easygoing types (Buck Leonard thought he was "as rotten as anybody you ever saw in your life").[43] Enraged, Harris lifted the umpire's mask from the ground and smashed him across the face with it. The catcher then attacked Harris, and before long a full-blown melee was under way, with fans rushing onto the field to take what part they could. Just what Oscar did during the rumble was unreported, but as a man who in his teammate Ted Page's words "really enjoyed a good fight," surely he was in the middle of it all.[44] Ultimately, billy club–wielding police restored order, and the game continued. The Crawfords rallied for three runs in the bottom of the eighth thanks to a Charleston double (his second hit of the day), Gibson homer, and Judy Johnson triple, and they held on to win, 4–3.[45] It was a game, and a series, Oscar did not wish to forget. He clipped a photo of the brawl out of the *Pittsburgh Sun-Telegraph* for his personal collection.

The fight left no hard feelings between the Deans and the Negro Leaguers. Oscar liked Diz, placing a humorous excerpt from Dean's autobiography in his scrapbook. Dean, for his part, had high regard for Charleston. He heaped praise on Oscar in an August 1939 interview with the *Pittsburgh Courier*. After agreeing that Josh Gibson would be worth $200,000 in the Majors, he added, "Another guy I think could have made the grade in the majors was Oscar Charleston. He used to play against us in exhibition games. He could hit a ball a mile. He didn't have a weakness, and when he came up we just hoped he wouldn't get a hold of one. We just threw and hoped like hell he didn't send it out of the park."[46]

• • •

By spring 1935 Oscar had spent twenty seasons in the Negro Leagues. His on-field skills were not quite what they once were, although in 1934 he had managed to hit .322, get on base at a .410 clip, and slug .497, all of which made him, after Gibson, his team's second-best hitter. But his managerial skills had gotten better. What he lacked as a tactician he made up with passion and motivational skills; win or lose, "Charleston would take [the game] to bed with him and go through everything," said Bill Evans.[47] Oscar excelled at molding self-interested individuals into an all-for-one team.

The team-building process started with those exhausting spring training trips and their shared hardships and humiliations. Judy Johnson and Ted Page, dressed for an evening out, were advised by two men with a shotgun in one small southern town that "highfalutin n——" such as they were not welcome.[48] Once, when the Craws bus stopped at a restaurant in Mississippi, the players were advised by the staff to get out of state as quickly as they could; the local police were falsifying charges on traveling blacks so they could put them to work on the prison farm.[49] In both cases the team accepted the helpful locals' advice. On other occasions it was money, not immediate flight, that was extorted. A policeman might require an exorbitant bribe to look the other way about a traffic violation, or a restaurateur might require ten times the usual price for the grub he reluctantly made available.[50]

The fans were generally appreciative of the high-quality play teams like the Crawfords brought to their out-of-the-way parks, not minding seeing their hometown lads get beaten, but sometimes they could get a bit resentful. In one game in Arkansas the Crawfords were up big when Charleston decided to have a little fun. He was on first when Judy Johnson singled to right. On his way to third Oscar cut in front of second by a wide margin. The ump didn't notice but the fans did, and unlike the laughing Oscar, they didn't think his shortcut a bit funny. Someone threw a chair at Cool Papa Bell in the on-deck circle, which prompted Judy Johnson to leap into the stands in an unsuccessful attempt to find the perp. Bell expected a big fight after the game, but when an angry mob engaged the team as it left the park, Oscar "went nose-to-nose with the ringleader and backed him down." Gibson and Page stood right behind him.[51] Oscar had forged a true team.

Indeed, the players had no doubt that if and when fists started flying, their field general would be leading the charge. Ted Page didn't much care for Oscar, who he thought had "vicious eyes" like those of a lion or Old West gunfighter, but he sure as hell wanted him on his side if a fight broke out. Oscar, he said, was the fearless sort who when a brawl erupted would start hunting guys in the opposing dugout all alone.[52] Judy Johnson was another Craw who found Oscar too intense for his tastes. He remembered seeing Charleston once "grab an umpire by the throat and threaten to throw him up in the stands" at Greenlee Field. "Luckily for the umpire, we convinced him not to do that," said Johnson. But Judy nevertheless appreciated the fact that Oscar always had his men's backs.[53] Cool Papa Bell maintained that the team was leaving one ballpark when "some of the Ku Klux Klan tried to stop us. They had those hoods on their heads. Everybody was scared, except for Charleston. He just walked up and ripped the hood right off one of those guys. After that, none of them tried to mess with us." That story is almost certainly apocryphal, but it illustrates the fearful admiration that Oscar inspired in his players.[54]

It wasn't just the reality of racial oppression or the threat of violence that built up team spirit; hijinks helped too. When they traveled, players would put their food on racks above their bus seats. Harry Kincannon got on board after one stop with a bunch of fried chicken. He ate some and saved the rest, and to warn others from dipping into his stash he threatened them with a pistol he had gotten from Oscar (a gift from friends in Cuba). When Kincannon fell asleep, the pistol fell to the ground. Stealthily, the other players retrieved it, emptied the shells, and proceeded to wolf down the rest of Harry's chicken. They capped the caper by making a necklace of the leftover bones and tying it around Kincannon's neck. After he awoke, it didn't take long for the young pitcher to laugh along with everyone else.[55]

The Crawfords' exceptional togetherness paid off on the diamond. Cool Papa Bell believed the club won not only because it was talented, but also because it was highly connected. The

Craws didn't try to beat opponents simply by waiting for a Gibson or Charleston homer. They complemented their power game by exceeding at the fundamentals—by hitting the cutoff man, advancing runners, taking the extra base, and laying down sacrifice bunts. In other words, under Oscar's leadership they bought into the C. I. Taylor tradition of baseball as craft.[56] In Bell's mind that was why they experienced so much success versus Major Leaguers. The Craws had "great team spirit," said Judy Johnson.[57] "I'm very proud to have played for such a great team," said Jimmie Crutchfield. The Crawfords were a "team both on and off the field. We won together and we lost together. We laughed together and we cried together. We cared about each other. How could anything be any better than that?"[58]

Crutchfield's feelings were shared by many of the club's players, with one notable exception: Satchel Paige, whose solipsistic soul made him utterly immune from the contagion of team spirit. It must have been impossible for Paige and Charleston to understand one another. Satchel's celebrity certainly redounded to everyone's benefit. And although later some Negro Leaguers would claim he was not as good he was made out to be, in truth there is no doubt he was one of the most talented pitchers ever to play the game. Nevertheless, Satchel never stepped onto the field with anything but his own direct and immediate interests in mind—and those interests did not include the emotional satisfactions associated with team achievement, which to Paige meant almost nothing.

On dozens of occasions throughout his career, Paige, distracted by a fishing hole, a woman, or a better opportunity, was a no-show or latecomer to contests. Oscar was often given the task of ensuring that Satchel got from one place to another, especially when he was being advertised as the main attraction.[59] The energy required to keep Paige in line must have been tremendous. Heck, it was hard enough to keep Satchel on task even when he was on the field. Buck Leonard remembered one occasion when his Homestead Grays were playing the Crawfords in a Pennsylvania coal mining town. Satchel was playing right field when one of the Grays lifted a lazy fly ball in his direction. It was a sure out—except that Paige was over at the fence, getting a cigarette lighted by one of the fans.[60]

• • •

If Oscar and his Crawfords teammates believed they underachieved by not winning the NNL championship in 1934, they couldn't have thought their chances had become any better when in spring 1935 Paige decided to forsake the Craws—and jump a two-year contract—in favor of Bismarck, North Dakota, where a white auto dealer named Neil Churchill had offered Paige a handsome amount to pitch for his semipro club. With Vic Harris and Ted Page also departing the Craws, Oscar a year older at thirty-eight, and a fast-aging Judy Johnson now thirty-five, the 1935 club did not project to be nearly as powerful as previous years' squads. Expectations on the outside were that the team would be good, but no juggernaut.

Oscar, however, expressed nothing but optimism. He built up Josh Gibson, who was still just twenty-three (and who had allegedly hit sixty-nine home runs in 1934) and pitchers Bert Hunter and Harry Kincannon as players fully capable of carrying the team to success. He gave a statement to the *Chicago Defender* in which he said that the "batting of such men as Josh Gibson, the bronzed Bambino, will either keep us in or put us out of the close race which the teams will fight this year," and he championed the twenty-four-year-old Hunter's fastball and twenty-five-year-old Kincannon's curve.[61] Perhaps a little relieved to be rid of Paige drama, Oscar told the *Pittsburgh Courier*'s Chester Washington that he expected his club to be "a hustling, wide-awake ball club and one of the best teams he has ever had the privilege of managing."[62] The message to his charges was clear: the Crawfords weren't conceding anything.

Oscar put his bat where his mouth was for the Crawfords' home opener on May 11, 1935, against the Cubans. His two hits, including a home run, helped the Craws win, 6–5. By May 27 the Crawfords were 9-3 and in first place. Oscar was on fire, reportedly hitting one home run at Greenlee Field that went over five hundred feet.[63] In June he acquired another youngster, twenty-three-year-old Pat Patterson, to take over second base. That proved to be a brilliant move, as Patterson would go on to hit .389 for the season and help the Craws maintain their hold on the league's top position, even as Oscar missed a few games here and there with some kind of injury (perhaps the same leg problem that had bedeviled him the previous year).

After the Crawfords beat the Homestead Grays in both ends of a July 4 doubleheader in Pittsburgh, before a crowd of twelve thousand, they could lay claim to the first-half pennant. "The secret of success which brought the Pittsburgh Crawfords the first-half championship of the league," wrote Chester Washington, "is close harmony, team-play, a fine co-operative spirit and an appreciation of the leadership of Oscar Charleston, who has been given the very best that the men possess. It has made the Craws a different ball club than last year and Charley is to be commended for bringing to the Smoky City the first half title."[64] One would probably not be wrong to read into Washington's praise of the Crawfords' "co-operative spirit" a subtle swipe at Satchel.

The Craws posted a fantastic 24-6 record in the season's first half, but the second half didn't go as well for Charleston's club. On July 21 Oscar suspended Leroy Matlock, Roosevelt Davis, and Jimmy Crutchfield indefinitely for improper conduct off the field. That may have helped with team discipline, but it didn't help the Craws win games. After fourteen second-half contests the Crawfords were just 8-6, four and a half games out of first. It didn't count in league play, but they had even lost to a white semipro team in Chester, Pennsylvania, on July 16, an outcome that was described by the *Delaware County Times* as nothing short of stunning.[65] That was one game for which the Craws later got revenge. On August 5, playing again in Chester, Oscar helped lead the team to victory by rapping out three hits and stealing two bases—including a straight steal of home, much to the surprise of the *Delaware County Times* reporter, who estimated Oscar's weight at 255 pounds.[66] Oscar, eager to rub it in, even clowned on the base paths during that game—so much so that he unintentionally prevented Cool Papa Bell from getting an inside-the-park home run. Josh Gibson added two towering homers. The locals were very impressed.

The East-West game voting revealed that Oscar had new competition for the title of Negro Leagues' best first baseman in the Homestead Grays' Buck Leonard. A quiet, God-fearing twenty-seven-year-old from Rocky Mount, North Carolina, who had burst onto the scene the previous summer, Leonard and Oscar were diametrically opposed personalities. Buck never talked trash, never fought, and never risked spiking infielders on the base paths—a practice of Oscar's he didn't appreciate.[67] In the late 1930s and 1940s Leonard would team with Josh Gibson to make the Homestead Grays the juggernaut of black baseball. But in 1935 he couldn't yet unseat Oscar as the East-West game starter; Oscar won the polling by one vote.[68]

Charleston could not, however, manage the Crawfords to the 1935 second-half pennant. It wasn't that the team missed Paige so badly; Matlock was brilliant in his stead, posting a 1.52 ERA, and the rest of the staff was solid. No, Oscar's main problem was his first baseman; far from serving as a powerful complement to Gibson's thunder, Charleston hit just .273 and slugged only .399 over the year, offensive numbers that lagged far behind those posted by Gibson, Bell, Sam Bankhead, and Pat Patterson. As a result, the second-half NNL flag was taken by the New York Cubans, who were led by Oscar's former island teammates Alejandro Oms and Martín Dihigo, who also managed the squad. The Cubans' second-half victory set up a Crawfords-Cubans NNL championship series.

In their level of organization, publicity, and generated interest, black baseball's world series never managed to live up to those staged by the Majors. The leagues themselves simply didn't command enough respect for pennants to be viewed with awe, and the owners never stuck with one model long enough for fans to become invested. The 1935 series was no exception to the rule. The seven-game series started at New York's Dyckman Oval on Friday, September 13.[69] It bounced to Forty-Fourth and Parkside in Philadelphia the next day, then back to Dyckman Oval on Sunday before finally getting to the Crawfords' home city for games four and five on September 17 and 18. The schedule was so confusing that three of the four umpires went to the wrong stadium for game two, and the crowds were of only middling size. The players, nevertheless, were fully engaged. Legitimate blackball world series were rare enough that—for the players at least—to win one truly meant something. Plus, there was some real money on the line.

The Cubans landed the series' first punches, winning the first two games, 6–2 and 4–0. Leroy Matlock came back to blank the Cubans, 3–0, in the third contest, in which Oscar homered, but he was too gassed to stave off Dihigo in game four, losing 6–1 at Greenlee Field. Down 3–1 in the best-of-seven series, the Crawfords found themselves on the verge of elimination.

The next day Roosevelt Davis and Cool Papa Bell kept the Crawfords' hopes alive. Pitcher Davis went the distance for Charleston, unfortunately giving up a tying pinch-hit home run in the top of the ninth. But in the bottom of the inning Bell's aggressive base running led to a wild throw to third. He scampered home to give the Craws a 3–2 victory and narrow their series deficit to the same margin.

The following night play resumed in Philadelphia. Oscar started Bert Hunter, but the best he, Bill Harvey, and Matlock could do was to hold the Cubans to six runs. The Crawfords found themselves down 6–3 headed into the bottom of the ninth. Then Dihigo got cute. Instead of letting his splendid rookie pitcher Schoolboy Johnny Taylor try to close things out, the Cubans' manager took the mound himself. It was a defensible decision, given that Dihigo had that year posted a virtually identical ERA to Taylor's (2.77 and 2.78, respectively). But with Taylor pitching well it was probably unnecessary. Dihigo allowed light-hitting shortstop Chester Williams to reach base. Then Gibson got aboard. Still, Dihigo had gotten two outs, and the Craws remained down three runs, when Oscar Charleston stepped into the left-side batter's box.

The Forty-Fourth and Parkside ballpark had been the site of some of Oscar's most memorable moments. But he was nearly thirty-nine now, and overweight, and he had just struggled through his worst offensive season. Dihigo, at thirty, was in his prime. And all he needed was one out. The odds against Oscar winning this battle were so long that Cubans owner Alex Pompez and team business manager Frank Forbes were already counting out the winners' share of the money in the clubhouse. But Oscar wasn't finished. He timed a Dihigo offering perfectly and sent it sailing over the center field wall for a game-tying three-run blast. A disgusted Forbes threw a bundle of five hundred dollars across the room.[70] The Crawfords' Pat Patterson followed with a double, and when Judy Johnson, pinch-hitting, knocked him in with a single, the Craws had completed one of the most dramatic big-game comebacks the Negro Leagues had ever seen.

The next night, September 20, on the same diamond, the Crawfords were nursing a 5–4 lead in the top of the eighth when Josh Gibson and Oscar hit back-to-back home runs. Dihigo made an error that allowed another run to score, and the Craws held off a furious Cubans rally in the bottom of the ninth to complete a thrilling 8–7 series-clinching victory. This time there would be no controversy. The Crawfords—sans Satchel Paige—were the 1935 Negro National League champs.

Some days later, when the Craws returned to Pittsburgh, Greenlee feted them with a victory feast at the Crawford Grill. Art Rooney, Bojangles Robinson, and the singing Mills Brothers (such big fans of the team that they had their own Craws uniforms and sometimes worked out with the club before games) were all there.[71] It was a huge, happy affair, and Judy Johnson thought Gus took all the more satisfaction in the championship because it had been achieved without Satchel.[72] That was probably true of Oscar as well. As Cum Posey noted a few months later, "[by leading] the Crawfords to the championship with a team on paper that was the weakest they have had since 1931," Charleston erased many questions about his managerial ability.[73]

Later the NNL and the *Amsterdam News* gave a banquet in Harlem in honor of the Crawfords and Cubans. A photo from the September 28, 1935, edition of the newspaper shows Oscar, dressed nattily in a dark suit, posing with a soft smile along with league commissioner Ferdinand Morton (who had replaced Rollo Wilson in that post), Alex Pompez, Gus Greenlee, Newark owners Abe and Effa Manley, league secretary John Clark, *Amsterdam News* sports editor Romeo Dougherty, and Oscar's old friend Candy Jim Taylor, now manager of the Nashville Elite Giants. As one of the highest-paid men in the Negro Leagues; as a player who was still one of the most dangerous clutch hitters in the game; as the manager of a newly crowned champion; and as a man born in poverty now fully admitted to social equality with the NNL's titans, Oscar had good reason to be pleased.[74]

• • •

On the eve of the 1936 season Greenlee and Charleston received some unexpected good news: Satchel Paige was back. On April 21 he reported to the Crawfords, who were limbering up in Pittsburgh rather than in the South in order to save some of Greenlee's diminishing funds. Satch was already in midseason form, having pitched in the California Winter League over the winter. He showed off his strong right arm by pitching a no-hitter in an exhibition game versus the Akron Grays on May 3, a contest the Craws won, 11–0. And all spring he did his usual showboating, taunting batters and kidding with Gibson, behind the plate, to get in opponents' heads. Greenlee, meanwhile, salivated at the gate results the transcendentally popular Satchel was bound to bring. Already, reported Chester Washington, eastern markets were "Crawford-crazy," and the presence of Paige, "a natural showman . . . as spectacular as a circus and as colorful as a rainbow," would only make the team more popular.[75]

Satchel defeated the Cubans' Chet Brewer in the first game of a league-opening doubleheader at New York's Dyckman Oval on May 10. The Craws won both games that day by scores of 8–4 and 6–5 in front of seventy-five hundred fans eager to see a rematch of the previous year's NNL championship series. Gibson had three mammoth home runs; Oscar added two homers and a double himself, with his home run in the second contest giving the Craws the lead. On May 24, in Washington, the Crawfords beat Candy Jim Taylor's Washington Elite Giants, 10–8, after Charleston singled with one out in the eleventh and then scored on a Chester Williams triple. He added a double that day too.

When May 1936 ended, Oscar was hitting .429, according to official league statistics, ranking tenth among those with at least twenty at bats—but only fifth on his own team. Although .429 is .429, Oscar knew that he was slowing down. Perhaps because his leg was troubling him, he typically slotted himself fifth in the lineup now, and he didn't play every day, yielding at bats to a promising young protégé named Johnny Washington. Washington even started more games than did Oscar against top competition in 1936. It was the first year since he had gotten his start in 1915 that Oscar wasn't an everyday player.

The balanced Washington club edged the Crawfords and the Philadelphia Stars for the league's first-half flag, in part because outside of Gibson, Washington, and Charleston, none of the Craws had a particularly good offensive season; Judy Johnson was now a shell of himself, and new acquisition Dick Seay, although a wizard at second base, barely hit his weight.

No matter. Oscar's club started the second half hot and never took its foot off the gas. In late July the Craws were 8-2, and as of mid-August they remained in first with a 13-6 record; ultimately, they would finish with a 19-8 mark. Oscar continued to have his heroic moments, as when on July 26, against the Bushwicks in Brooklyn, he surveyed the scene with the Craws down 4–3, two outs, and a man on first. Inserting himself as a pinch hitter, he drilled a two-run homer over the fence, and the Craws held on to win, 5–4. Charleston even managed to hold Paige in line. As the *Harrisburg Evening News* noted in September, Charleston had "done much to tame the temperamental star this year," such that Satchel, for once, was actually participating in games for which his presence had been publicized.[76]

Charleston posted a remarkable 193 OPS+ in 1936, compiling a slash line of .373/.475/.672 in twenty-five games against top teams. But in part because he no longer started every day, his star—as a batter anyway—began to wane. Washington's flashy Jim West beat him out handily in the first base vote for the East-West game, scoring 8,274 votes to Oscar's 5,979. Oscar still won the managerial vote—for the East this time—by a huge margin, getting 18,837 votes to Candy Jim Taylor's 6,801. But Satchel led all 1936 East-West players with 18,275 votes, and neither Oscar nor any other player came close to that amount. Paige was the true star of black baseball now, the Negro Leagues' own Dizzy Dean. Oscar didn't play in the annual all-star game at Comiskey on August 23, but he did manage the East to an easy 10–2 victory in front of thirty thousand fans—the largest East-West crowd yet.

That East-West game almost didn't come off. Some eastern owners, in order to save money and play to their own fan bases, wanted to hold the game in New York. Greenlee, seeing how the game had prospered in Chicago and believing that it was best for black baseball if it remained there, was forced to step up at the last second and foot all the promotional expenses himself. In the end, only four teams sent players to the affair. And only three teams—the Grays, Washington Elites, and Crawfords—provided players for the NNL All-Star team that the circuit entered in the August *Denver Post* tournament.[77] Behind Paige's brilliant pitching, the All-Stars rather easily overcame their white semipro opponents to win the *Post* tourney championship on August 11.

Despite losing five of his best players for a good chunk of August, when the final day of the 1936 NNL season arrived on September 14, Charleston had guided the Pittsburgh Crawfords to the second-half pennant with a 19–8 record.[78] Alas, by this point the championship of the fraying NNL meant as little to the players as it did to the fans. On September 21 the Elite Giants won the first game of the title series in Philadelphia, but numerous stars were absent, including Oscar.[79] He and many others were off barnstorming again, figuring that the money they could earn on the road was worth more than the crown of a league that commanded little respect. No other series games were played. The NNL would have no official champion in 1936. Reconstructed records show that the Crawfords, at 43-31-2, had the best record against top competition.

The NNL's barnstormers, which included Charleston, Paige, Cool Papa Bell, and Leroy Matlock, among others, had actually stopped playing in league games prior to the end of the regular season. Backed financially by Greenlee and perhaps also Cum Posey and Tom Wilson, they were in Chicago on September 6, and they were scheduled to appear in Pampa, Texas, on September 17. Perhaps it was on this trip that future Washington Redskins quarterback "Slingin'" Sammy Baugh, playing for a club from Abilene, met Oscar. As Baugh later told an interviewer, before one game Oscar approached him and said, "I hear you're some kind of football hero, but if you get in my way, I'll cut you down." "He meant it," Baugh chuckled. "Believe me, he meant it."[80]

Later, the barnstorming all-stars returned to New York to play as members of their regular-season teams in a four-team doubleheader at the Polo Grounds, an event intended to raise funds for Sam Langford, an aged black boxer who was now almost blind and destitute—and a favorite of Charleston's, who clipped articles on Langford for his scrapbook. Then they returned to the road. October found them playing a five-game series in Iowa and Colorado against a quality team of Major League all-stars promoted by Ray Doan and led by Rogers Hornsby, who, like Oscar, was now forty. The Major League squad also included Johnny Mize, Big Jim Weaver, and, for one game in Des Moines, a teenage pitching sensation by the name of Bob Feller.[81]

It was a fascinating set. The games began in Des Moines on October 2, and Oscar got off to a hot start. He drove in Cool Papa Bell in the first inning with a single, and he tallied another RBI in the third with a double into right-center. This early success did not, nevertheless, put him in a good mood. Oscar had previously gotten some bad press on the trip when he pulled his team off the field in Kansas City—an umpire there had obstinately refused to reverse a called ball that Charleston insisted was a strike.[82] Now he got into a scrap with another ump. The altercation was not physical, but it got both teams riled up enough that fans streamed onto the field. After the police restored order, the Negro Leaguers went on to win, 5–2. Hornsby's team got revenge the next day in Davenport, winning 2–1 behind the pitching of the Cardinals' Jim Winford.

The series then moved to Denver. Satchel led the black all-stars to victory in the opener, pitching a complete game six-hitter and winning, 6–3. In the nightcap the Major Leaguers were ahead, 4–1, in the sixth when first Oscar and then Bell banged run-scoring singles to tie the game. Sammy Hughes's ground-rule double in the seventh gave the Negro Leaguers a 6–4 come-from-behind win.

The last game, on October 7, was back in Des Moines, where Bobby Feller, the seventeen-year-old boy from Van Meter, was already a legend in the making. The opportunity to see the high schooler pitch against Satchel Paige attracted a huge crowd to Western League Park; an hour before game time, 8:30 p.m., every seat had been taken, and overflow fans were standing on the field along the foul lines. Feller, who went three innings, struck out eight of the ten batters he faced. Paige struck out seven of eleven. Neither man gave up a run. But after Feller left, the Negro Leaguers broke through and ended up taking the game, 4–2, for their fourth win in five tries.

Charleston went 4 for 10 in the series. Perhaps he reflected that he had shown Hornsby a little of what he had missed by skipping those contests with the St. Louis Giants back in 1920 and 1921.

• • •

By the mid-1930s the exclusion of black men from organized baseball had become a more obvious and infuriating injustice than ever. Younger black sportswriters increasingly returned to the topic. White players, managers, and owners were more frequently asked by these younger black writers to give their opinions on the matter. Concentrated action to pressure the Major Leagues' white owners to remove the color bar began haltingly to take shape. Amid this effort Oscar Charleston's name arose repeatedly. Even at his advanced age the quality of his play gave the lie to anyone who claimed African Americans couldn't compete at the highest level.

In February 1933 Oscar's friend Rollo Wilson pointed out that "white league players live more comfortably and are better cared for," but "whether they have more real ability under like conditions than sundown athletes is debatable."[83] If Oscar Charleston, wrote Wilson, had come up under the same conditions, there was little doubt that he would be classed by all observers with Tris Speaker, Ty Cobb, and other legends. After two white players had come out against the color line, another black writer, Bill Gibson, put forward shortstop Dick Lundy and Charleston as examples of players who could step right into the big leagues as stars. A few weeks later Dan Parker, white sports editor of the *New York Daily Mirror*, wrote the *Courier*'s Chester Washington to give his support for ending the color line—and to point out that white owners were only too happy to take black fans' money.

After the first Major League All-Star game was held in July 1933, the *Chicago Defender* ran a picture of Charleston next to Babe Ruth and lamented that an "all-Race" team wasn't given a chance to compete. "Doesn't Charleston look about as powerful as Ruth? Wouldn't you rather see [Willie] Foster face the Babe than Lon Warneke or Hallahan? We at least predict that a team led by Foster and Charleston would kick the National League around just as the American league did."[84] In August, Yankees coach Cy Perkins singled out Vic Harris, Oscar Charleston, Dick Redding, and John Beckwith as black stars who could have been great big league players if given the chance. Following the first East-West game in September 1933, Henry Farrell wrote that if Lundy, Mule Suttles, or Oscar Charleston were white, they would be worth at least $100,000 in the bigs.[85] Farrell's long account of the game was reprinted far and wide in black newspapers, which knew it would make readers proud— and all the more committed to bringing about change.

Al Monroe argued in the *Chicago Defender* in October 1934 that the forthcoming World Series between the Gashouse Gang Cardinals and Tigers lacked legitimacy, given that blacks weren't allowed to compete. "I am wondering if 'Schoolboy' Rowe and the Dean brothers can gloat over their strikeout records and world's series wins over teams that failed to include Josh Gibson, Turkey Stearnes, Jud Wilson, Oscar Charleston and others in their lineup," he wrote.[86] The Gashouse Gang's star pitcher, Dizzy Dean, was no defender of baseball's segregation policies, even though he was an Arkansan not averse to using what even for the time was considered racially insensitive language. After the October 1934 postseason exhibition game in which his all-stars brawled with Charleston's team at Forbes Field, Dean heaped praise on his Negro League opponents and referred to Paige and Charleston, in particular, as "real major leaguers."[87] The following summer Diz told a radio audience that he would happily take his chances with an all-star black team versus a team of white all-stars.

Major League officials were unmoved by such observations, but the black sportswriters of the day kept up the rhetorical pressure. Lee A. Johnson of the *Indianapolis Recorder* implored Commissioner Landis to attend the 1935 East-West game and then to say, in all honesty, whether these weren't men who deserved to play in the Majors. "Look at Satchel Paige of the Pittsburgh Crawfords and Foster of the American Giants at Chicago and compare them with the Dean Brothers of the Cardinals or Rowe of the Tigers, or any of your famous hurlers. Look Oscar Charleston over at first base or at the bat and give him a fair break on your judgement of the caliber of baseball players, or have your best managers make the decisions for you."[88]

The success of Joe Louis in the ring and black athletes like Jesse Owens and Mack Robinson (Jackie's older brother) in the 1936 Olympics further fueled African American frustration at white baseball's obstinacy. Throughout that memorable Olympic year there were regular articles in the black press attacking Jim Crow laws and questioning why blacks were not allowed to compete on an equal footing with whites in baseball and other sports when they had shown how capable they were in the Olympics and in the ring. William Nunn noted in one *Pittsburgh Courier* column that even white writers were jumping onto this bandwagon. He quoted Chilly Doyle as writing the following in the *Pittsburgh Sun-Telegraph*: "Oscar Charleston could field around first base like Lefty Grimm, he could hit like Bill Terry, and he could run almost as swiftly as Arky Vaughan. . . . No, it isn't much of a compliment to baseball to have kept that act off the Big Time."[89]

Oscar followed it all. Back in 1920, when the first Negro National League had been formed, *Chicago Defender* journalist Dave Wyatt had predicted that "in the near future . . . Oscar Charleston will have to run bases protected by agile sons from all climes." Oscar had taken note of that prophesy, pasting it in his scrapbook.[90] Sixteen years later, still waiting for Wyatt's prediction to come true, at least in the United States, Oscar was happy to lend his name to the cause. In August 1936 the *Daily Worker*, a Communist newspaper, began its own effort to lift baseball's color ban. Given the paper's (correctly) suspected loyalty to Moscow and the sensitive geopolitics of the time, the *Daily Worker* was hardly an ideal vehicle for the fight for racial justice. Nevertheless, the NAACP, the *Chicago Defender*, and others, including white sportswriters Dan Parker and Jimmy Powers, rallied to its banner. The *Defender* of August 29, 1936, ran head shots of Martín Dihigo and Oscar Charleston with a caption that read, "Charleston, Satchel Paige, and other baseball stars barred from the major leagues have shown by their fine sportsmanship on and off the field that they are well worthy of recognition. That they are barred because of their color has been admitted by the powers that be in baseball and a move is being made to wipe out this practice."[91] The *Daily Worker*'s initiative had been "hailed" by players, said the *Defender*, including Johnny Taylor, Frank Forbes, Silvio Garcia, Dihigo, and Charleston.

Whether all or any of these players knew this effort was associated with communism is an open question. Charleston, after all, was a Republican. And unlike most revolutionaries, Oscar had a lively sense of humor. Cool Papa Bell recalled his responding to a waitress who said the restaurant didn't "serve n——" with the words, "That's fine, I don't plan to order one."[92] A well-worn line but significant in that Bell attributed it to Oscar. And as frustrated as he must have been by Jim Crow, Charleston related the following anecdote to Lewis Dial of the *New York Age*:

> Oscar Charleston, manager of the Pittsburgh Crawfords, tells a funny story on Clarence Palm, catcher of the Black Yankees. A Colored all-star team was playing a white all-star club down in Mexico; both groups were from the United States. Palm was at bat and a big white Texan named Pipgras was pitching. Pipgras threw a couple of fast ones at Palm's head which angered the colored boy, who walked out to the mound and beleaguered the white lad. Palm called him a big cracker and told him that

he was not in the United States now but down in Mexico, and another pitch like those would cause the cracker to have his head punched. When the Colored team returned to the States, Palm was the first man off the train, and who should be standing on the station platform but Pipgras. The colored boy quickly gathered his wits and realized he was again in Texas. Charleston said Palm went over to the white pitcher, tipping his hat, and said "Good morning Mr. Pipgras, how are you this morning? Do you still have that fast bucking curve?"[93]

Oscar himself was happy to push back against white men who took liberties, even when he was in the South. But on one occasion he decided that standing his ground wouldn't be a wise decision. It has often been repeated over the years, as a way of illustrating his ornery toughness, that Charleston once threatened to throw a professional wrestler from a train. That is true. But the point of the story, as told (probably) by Oscar himself, is that he was a fool for doing so.

It seems that Oscar was traveling by rail to Harrisburg sometime in the early 1930s when he took a seat opposite a burly white man. After Oscar sat down, the man looked up and told him he would have to move; he was saving the seat for someone else. Oscar, perhaps sensing racism at play, flatly refused to comply, telling the man that if he didn't let him have the seat, one of them was getting thrown out the window. At that the man gave a hearty laugh. Before anything else could happen, a railroad employee leaned in and asked Oscar if he knew who the man was. When Oscar said no, the employee told him it was Jim Londos, one of the most popular—and chiseled— professional wrestlers in the country. Oscar, taking another look at the Golden Greek, decided to find a different seat.[94]

• • •

Oscar Charleston's Pittsburgh Crawfords headed into the 1937 season with high hopes of again staking a legitimate claim to being the best team in black baseball. It seemed a good omen when, in March, Oscar won the numbers lottery run by his boss. "I guess you'll buy Gus out now," teased the *Pittsburgh Courier*'s "Talk O' Town" writer.[95] If only, Greenlee may have sighed in response. His Crawfords were not particularly profitable. They had played 132 games between April 25 and September 22, 1936, in front of crowds averaging 1,635 per game, and yet had barely made money, reported Greenlee's associate John Clark, largely because Gus put so many resources into publicity and payroll, plausibly reputed to be the highest in black baseball. Worse still, Greenlee had suffered a big hit in the numbers game (perhaps the very hit on which Oscar profited) and suddenly was short of cash.[96]

With funds tight, in spring 1937 Greenlee and Charleston reluctantly traded Josh Gibson to the Homestead Grays after their young star held out for more money. The deal sent Gibson and Judy Johnson to the Homestead Grays in return for catcher Pepper Bassett, who despite being only twenty-six had already attracted a gate following for his act of catching in a rocking chair.[97] Johnson preferred to retire than report to Posey's team, but even so, this must be considered one of baseball's most disastrously lopsided trades; Bassett would have a fantastic year in 1937 but would never be great, or even good, again.[98] Gibson, on the other hand, went on to hit a few hundred home runs for Cum Posey.

The consequences of the Gibson trade would not be felt for another year. Something else was to deal an even bigger blow to the Crawfords in spring 1937: foreign agents.

The Crawfords were training in New Orleans in April when a Dominican man named Dr. José Enrique Aybar, along with several of his associates, cornered Satchel Paige on the street. Aybar was on a recruiting trip.[99] His task was to find the best players possible for the Dragones de Ciudad Trujillo, a baseball team representing the Dominican Republic's capital city, recently renamed for the megalomaniacal dictator, Rafael Trujillo, who had taken control of the nation a few years earlier. Trujillo had made ample funds available to Aybar—not so ample that he could lure white players away from the Major Leagues but plenty to turn the head of a Negro Leaguer like Paige. Once Aybar, brandishing a pistol (in Paige's telling), had Satchel's attention, he offered the astounding sum of $30,000 for him and eight of his teammates to come play in the island nation. From that amount Satchel could take whatever he thought was his fair share. Much stronger men than Satch would have been unable to resist such an offer. Paige accepted and began recruiting.

News that Paige and others had jumped or would jump had already reached Greenlee and Charleston when, on or about Friday, May 8, two Trujillo men named Luis Mendez and Frederic Nina showed up in Pittsburgh looking for yet more players. They approached at least six—Ernest Carter, Chet Brewer, Barney Morris, and Chester Williams of the Craws and Joseph Strong and Raymond Brown of the Grays—with offers to play alongside Satchel in Santo Domingo, offering $150 in cash per player as a down payment, travel expenses, and $750 more per player when they arrived on the island.

Carter was among those who agreed to go. But the next day, May 9, he had second thoughts and decided to confer with his wife and Charleston. Oscar, who must already have been fuming over the losses of Gibson, Paige, and other key members of his squad, decided to make his feelings known. He caught up to Nina at a local hotel and, dispensing with introductory niceties, grabbed the diminutive Dominican by the throat. "I came here to whip you," Oscar growled, "but since you're so little, I won't do it."[100] Instead, he took him to the police.

A constable was prevailed upon to arrest both Nina and Mendez, and the two men spent the weekend in jail. When their irate lawyer showed up for their hearing on Tuesday, May 11, it was revealed that Mendez worked for the Dominican consulate in New York. Alderman A. M. Maloney, having received an admonitory phone call from the State Department, released both men on $500 bail as he tried to figure out whether any laws had actually been broken. The white Pittsburgh press thought the entire matter rather humorous.

Neither Oscar nor Gus Greenlee was laughing, of course. By the beginning weeks of the NNL season the Craws had been destroyed. They had lost nine men to Trujillo, including stalwarts like Paige, Leroy Matlock, Cool Papa Bell, and Sam Bankhead. The only experienced pitcher remaining was journeyman Barney Morris. Suddenly, Charleston was forced to scramble to put together a credible club. For half the season the Craws surprised and impressed with their gutty, heads-up play. Shockingly, they were in third place as of June 25, and on July 4 they stunned the Grays by winning both ends of the holiday doubleheader, 6–5 and 3–2. In the first game of that set, with the game tied in the bottom of the ninth, a man on third, and no outs, the Grays intentionally walked Henry Spearman and Bassett. The crowd chanted for Charleston, who although he now gave the lion's share of playing time at first base to Johnny Washington, was still capable of game-winning heroics. Indeed, he had won the Craws' 1937 season opener against the Washington Elites by belting a two-run homer in the eighth inning. But this time Oscar showed self-restraint by sending to the plate Chester Williams, who promptly hit a sacrifice fly to win the game.[101]

Pepper Bassett justified Charleston's interest in obtaining him, if not the price at which he had been bought. He came with a reputation as an excellent defender who needed to learn how to hit. And that he did, batting .444 with eight homers by the end of July. The *Pittsburgh Courier* called Bassett "another Oscar Charleston product, a hitting catcher who can line drive in the true Charleston manner."[102] Yet neither Bassett's emergence nor the no-name Crawfords' grittiness was enough to keep them afloat in the competitive NNL. By the beginning of August Oscar's team had slid back to fifth place, where it would remain. The 1937 Craws posted an 18-30-1 final record, easily the worst of any team Charleston had ever managed.

Oscar's star dimmed along with his club's fortunes. Biz Mackey beat him out in the vote for the East's manager in the annual all-star game in Chicago, denying Charleston a chance at a fourth straight East-West game managerial victory. And he finished a distant seventh in the first base voting, as Buck Leonard lapped the field. That wasn't too surprising, in that Oscar started himself only about one-third of the time in 1937, and when he did play, he was no longer his old self. In 1936 his hitting had still been stellar; in 1937 his OPS+ was a mere 85, or 15 percent below average. Oscar's days as an elite hitter were over forever. Not coincidentally, so too were the Crawfords' days as an elite baseball team.

• • •

Satchel Paige, Cool Papa Bell, and the rest of the players who had been lured to the Dominican in spring 1937 returned stateside in late July. They had won the island championship for Trujillo, but the experience had been unsettling. Trujillo's Dominican Republic had a totalitarian atmosphere, and that fall his troops would massacre fifteen thousand Haitian farmers in a horrific act of ethnic cleansing. So while the players were never in as much danger as they feared, they were plenty happy to get home. Once back in the States, they were greeted with a temporary ban from playing in both major black leagues. Fortunately, they had among their number the black game's most popular player in Satchel Paige. Before long, they were barnstorming as the Trujillo All-Stars, winning the *Denver Post* tournament, and generally making the crowd-hungry Negro Leagues owners daily soften a little more. By spring 1938, after the owners had deputized Oscar Charleston to assess the situation, the ban had been lifted.[103]

Oscar's patience with Paige had, however, been exhausted. He probably agreed with the *Philadelphia Tribune* writer who referred to Satchel in March 1938 as a "grade-A prima donna." Paige's decision to chase Dominican cash had completely destroyed Charleston's 1937 Crawfords. The two men's personalities were vastly different. And Oscar may well have resented Paige's unparalleled popularity. So when Satchel again held out for more money in the spring, the Crawfords openly discussed the possibility of instead trading him to the Philadelphia Stars. Schoolboy Johnny Taylor, formerly of the New York Cubans, was promoted by Charleston as a rising talent who could probably replace Satchel's production on the mound and do it more cheaply. He could also be counted on to stay with the team all season.[104]

Greenlee resisted the idea of going with Taylor instead of Paige. He liked Satchel, and he knew that no one was nearly as popular with the fans. Moreover, he was already experiencing financial difficulties; how was losing Paige going to help? But Gus had long since given Oscar final authority over the Craws' roster, and when Oscar stood his ground and Greenlee declined to intervene, Paige made other plans. He appears not to have done so gracefully. In late May, when Satchel was pitching for the Atlanta Black Crackers, Wendell Smith of the *Pittsburgh Courier* revealed that after Satchel left the Craws, his wife, Janet, a waitress at the Crawford Grill, had tried to persuade some of his former teammates to jump their contracts and join him. A furious Greenlee fired Janet as soon as he found out.[105] Satchel's days with the Crawfords were finished.

While this drama played out, Charleston tried to put together a contention-quality team. That wasn't going to be easy. First, it wasn't clear who would want to come or be allowed back from the contingent of Dominican jumpers. Second, Greenlee no longer had a financial advantage over other owners; in fact, he had to watch funds closely. So Gus and Oscar decided to hold open tryouts during spring training. And they decided to train in Pittsburgh, allegedly in order to get looks at local athletes whom they would miss if they were touring the South and to start winning back fans lost during the previous season's debacle, but probably simply to save money.

Training began on April 10, 1938, at the Center Avenue YMCA. Oscar's call for tryouts drew thirty young men, aged sixteen to twenty-seven, from all parts of the country. No stars were unearthed, but the episode is interesting in that it illustrates Oscar's passion for coaching and mentoring younger black players, the role that would increasingly become his primary identity. One kid hitchhiked to Pittsburgh from Meridian, Mississippi. Arriving dead broke, he had no chance to make the team, but Greenlee and Charleston took care of him anyway, ensuring that he received food and shelter. Oscar had a soft spot for all the young men who arrived, even though he thought only two or three had even a small chance to make the big time. He kept them around as long as he could, telling the *Courier*'s Wendell Smith, "We must do all we can to encourage these boys."[106]

By the time the season started, the Crawfords did not look like a very promising group. Gibson had been traded. Relations with Paige had been severed. Neither Cool Papa Bell nor Bill Perkins, among those who had jumped the team the previous year to play for Trujillo, returned to the fold. The team featured solid veterans in Matlock, Sam Bankhead, and infielders Harry Williams and Chester Williams, and it had rising youngsters in Johnny Washington, Pepper Bassett, Schoolboy Johnny Taylor, new outfielder Gene Benson, and new third baseman Bus Clarkson, but Charleston lacked elite talent.[107] Oscar's own expectations were modest. He allegedly predicted to one reporter that he expected the Craws to finish third in the league, and he cautiously ventured to the *Courier* that he thought he would have "a first division ball club this year."[108] That was as far as he, or anyone else, went. The Crawfords were, at best, rebuilding.

For much of the season Oscar's club overachieved. In Brooklyn, on May 29, the Craws swept the Bushwicks in a doubleheader, beating two former big league pitchers in Waite Hoyt and George Earnshaw. Buck Leonard remembered a 1938 game in Washington DC when, with the rain coming down and his team ahead, his powerful Homestead Grays pleaded with umpire

Mo Harris to call the game; Harris decided to let it go one more inning, during which Charleston hit a home run to send the Grays to defeat.[109] When the Craws met the Black Yankees on June 4 at Greenlee Field, first place was on the line, and a couple of weeks later they were still within a half game of second. They fell to third by June 25, but they had nevertheless managed to put together an impressive 13-7 record. Alas, in July things unraveled, owing in part to a six-game series sweep suffered at the hands of the Grays. It didn't help that, according to Wendell Smith, Schoolboy Johnny Taylor was "doing most of his pitching in night clubs."[110]

Oscar, now probably weighing in at some 250 pounds, regained some status in the eyes of Negro Leagues fans for his managerial job. The *Defender* claimed on July 30 that "everybody wants Oscar Charleston back as manager of the East club" for this year's East-West game.[111] Oscar beat out the Grays' Vic Harris in a close vote for the job of East skipper, with many fans "rallying to the Charleston banner in view of the fact that cheerful Charley took a team which was practically shot to pieces by desertions at the beginning of the season and developed a Pittsburgh Crawford Club which has to be reckoned with."[112] His East team lost, 5-4.

The Crawfords finished the 1938 year with an impressive 24-16 record, good for fourth place in the league and just four and a half games out of first.[113] They were supposed to play in a four-team playoff that would serve as a new kind of NNL championship series, but the Homestead Grays refused to participate. The failed series was a fitting symbol of the NNL's continuing dysfunction. Oscar was probably not surprised, but he must have been disappointed that his undermanned but feisty Pittsburgh Crawfords didn't get one last bite at the apple.

• • •

The Pittsburgh Crawfords years—1932 through 1938—were extraordinarily good ones for Oscar Charleston professionally, just as the years 1915 through 1931 had been. Although he was in his mid- to late thirties, he still hit .323 during that time span and was generally his team's second most dangerous hitter, after Josh Gibson. He led the Crawfords to an overall record of 265-197-13 versus major Negro Leagues teams during those years, and the club's winning percentage from 1932 through 1936, before it was busted up, was a robust .590. In his personal life, however, things were different. Oscar may have been popular, successful, and comparatively well paid, but none of that could save his marriage. At some point during this period, or perhaps just after, he and Janie became permanently separated.

Part of the trouble seems to have been that Janie didn't care much for baseball. The sport bored her. The life of a baseball player's wife bored her even more. Her husband would be gone for weeks at a time. Even when Oscar was in town for a home stand, instead of going to his games she would often while away the hours of the long summer days at the horse tracks. (Double Duty Radcliffe later recalled that Janie "wasn't a good mixer"—at least with ballplayers, one suspects.)[114] Oscar provided financially, so there was nothing much Janie *had* to do. But she was too conscientious to find idleness pleasing, too intelligent to be stimulated by shallow pursuits, too nurturing to find pleasure in a life of self-gratification. The situation gnawed at her, to the point that near the end of her life she confessed to her great-great-niece that her one real regret was the time she had wasted in the prime years of her life—years her husband had used to secure his reputation.

Oscar and Janie were well matched in some ways. They were both intellectually curious, tough-minded, strong-willed, and practical. But there were differences. An important one may have been their religiosity. Janie, daughter of a Methodist minister, was a practicing, no-nonsense Christian. Oscar, according to one ex-player, was an atheist. "He didn't believe in God," recalled Andrew Porter, who was shocked by how cavalierly Charleston spoke of the deity.[115]

More than one marriage has faltered over such a fundamental difference in first principles. But there was yet another problem: the ladies of Pittsburgh, not to mention those in other cities, were drawn to Oscar, and he was not always inclined to swat them away. There is no absolute evidence of marital infidelity prior to Oscar and Janie's separation, but a number of signs point in that direction. The impression John Holway got from his interviews with Oscar's teammates was that Charleston always had a "bevy of women" around him.[116] And Oscar included a few photos of other women in his scrapbook and photo album—including, for example, a 1927 concert program featuring a sultry Cuban singer named Gloria de la Cuesta, on which he added the note, "She's in New York now," and a large head shot of another pretty woman signed "Best Wishes to Oscar, From Evelyn."

The newspapers outed him too. Prior to the 1935 East-West game in Chicago, a reporter from the *Indianapolis Recorder* ran into Oscar, with "a beauty at his table," at the Grand Hotel.[117] Surely if that lovely woman had been Janie, she would have been named as such. And after a March 1938 car accident the author of the *Pittsburgh Courier*'s gossipy "Talk O' Town" column noted that Oscar had escaped the crash without injury in the same way he had "wiggled out of some love tangles."[118] If Janie wasn't separated from Oscar prior to the publication of these two pieces of innuendo, the second of which could hardly have escaped her attention, surely they hastened the end. Separated or not, Janie must have felt both betrayed and publicly humiliated.

Just when Oscar and Janie split isn't known. They were together as of Thanksgiving 1932, when they visited Janie's folks in Harrisburg. They visited Harrisburg together again during Christmas that year. Oscar and Janie were making their winter home in Pittsburgh at this point, renting a house on Hallett Street, a block south of Wylie Avenue, the Hill District's main thoroughfare. By 1937 Charleston had a home on Mahon

Street in the same neighborhood. But in all of the Pittsburgh city directories of this period, only Oscar is mentioned, so just when Janie left him is impossible to say (as early as 1935 she is mentioned as a member of the Unity Social Club in Harrisburg, so she was at least spending off-seasons there).[119] Cum Posey reported in December 1938 that Oscar was working in Monroe, Louisiana, for the winter. He did not mention Janie, and it seems unlikely that Oscar would have taken a winter job in the South if he and his wife were still living together.

Janie shows up again in the Harrisburg directories in 1940, although she may have returned to her hometown earlier. The story she later told is that she returned home to help care for her sick mother, Bettie. Soon, she took a job as a clerk with the country registration commission, a position she would hold until she retired decades later, and otherwise busied herself with family and civic affairs. Oscar, seeing that the marriage was irretrievable, filed for divorce on July 24, 1941, when he returned to Indianapolis as the manager of the Philadelphia Stars, but the case was dismissed in March 31, 1942. Janie probably contested the filing. She didn't believe in divorce, her niece Elizabeth Overton recalled. After all, her father was a Methodist minister. So Oscar and Janie remained legally married until his death in October 1954. They also remained separated.

CHAPTER 8

Scout, 1939–1947

Oscar Charleston's marriage might have been effectively over, but his playing career wasn't. Not quite yet. Oscar entered the 1939 season with a new club; new owners; new players; and a new, internationally famous traveling partner. The one thing that wouldn't change was his role as player-manager. Although he was now forty-two and sported a broad midsection he wryly called "sliding insurance," he planned to still take the field on at least a semi-regular basis.[1]

And why not? Oscar could do nothing now to sully his utterly secure reputation as a player. In 1935 African American radio pioneer Jocko Maxwell rhapsodized about Charleston on his popular radio show, "The Sportsman's Melody Parade," on WHOM in New York. Candy Jim Taylor, interviewed in July 1936, maintained that the greatest player, black or white, he had ever seen in his long career was Charleston.[2] The following April black umpire Johnnie L. Craig said the same thing: Oscar was the best he had ever seen.[3] Both Fats Jenkins and Bill Holland told Wendell Smith in 1938 that Charleston was the finest player they had ever had as a teammate. During this same period, as the need to reflect on and capture black baseball history began to dawn on journalists, William Clark, Rollo Wilson, Cum Posey, Lucius "Melancholy" Jones, Randy Dixon, and many others all selected Oscar for their all-time black nines, often concluding that he had been the greatest of all.[4] White Major Leaguers added their own testimony. In 1939 St. Louis Cardinals manager Ray Blades told the *Pittsburgh Courier*'s Wendell Smith that

"Charleston was one of the best ball players I have ever seen. . . . He could hit and field with the best of them."[5] Tigers slugger Hank Greenberg, in the midst of his 1940 MVP season, told black newspaperman Alvin Moses that Charleston hit the ball as far and hard as anyone who had ever stepped to the plate.[6] There was no dissent from these judgments.

Many of these observers had watched Oscar ply his craft in Pittsburgh over the last decade. But the Steel City would no longer be Oscar's baseball home. Gus Greenlee, hounded by the Depression, competitors in the numbers game, and bad luck, had been reduced to humbler circumstances and could no longer finance his beloved Craws.[7] He could not even properly maintain his beloved Greenlee Field, which by early 1939 was in the process of being dismantled to make way for a New Deal housing project. Thus, in mid-April 1939 Gus withdrew from the NNL. The Crawfords franchise was quickly awarded to a group of Toledo businessmen who had considerable experience in promoting the sport; in Oscar's words, they "took in baseball from the fungo stick to the rear end of the bus."[8] Their first move was to sign Charleston as the rechristened *Toledo* Crawfords' manager. The legendary Oscar, they figured, would help draw fans. But the Craws' new owners had another, even bigger card to play. One of their number was none other than the dazzling star of the 1936 Berlin Olympics: Jesse Owens.

Owens was the key to the whole deal. The Toledo group was not well heeled. Years later the daughter of the lead investor, promoter Hank Rigney, estimated that her father and Owens had both probably invested no more than fifty dollars in the venture.[9] With little margin to spare and the Depression refusing to lift, the Crawfords' new owners were betting in part on their promotional abilities, in part on Charleston's appeal to black baseball fans, and in much larger part on the extraordinarily popular Owens's ability to attract both black and white fans who would otherwise rarely if ever come to a baseball game.

Jesse Owens had grown up in Cleveland. By spring 1939 he was twenty-five and had a wife and three children, and he had been scrambling for several years to capitalize on the fame he had won at Berlin. For a brief while Owens had made good money as a celebrity spokesman (most notably for 1936 Republican presidential nominee Alf Landon), but as he spent freely and supported family members and old friends generously, his funds had rapidly diminished. In summer 1938 he had invested much of his remaining savings in a dry-cleaning company on Cleveland's east side, but the business failed to turn a profit. In the meantime, the Internal Revenue Service had put a lien on his home for failure to pay income taxes. The result was that in May 1939, shortly after he helped purchase the Crawfords, Owens filed for bankruptcy. The Toledo Crawfords' new co-owner had no head for business.[10]

Owens was, however, entirely willing to race for money, and money was what the Crawfords needed more than anything else. As early as July 1933, when the Pittsburgh Crawfords met the Chicago American Giants in Cleveland, Owens, the local high school phenom, had raced a man named Jimmy Johnson as part of the ballpark festivities.[11] In late 1936 Owens had raced professionally for the first time, beating a racehorse in Havana. And in 1938 Owens had put on racing exhibitions throughout the summer.[12] Jesse probably first met Oscar Charleston at that 1933 game in Cleveland. Now, during the 1939 and 1940 seasons, the two men would be traveling partners, cobbling together their livings by rattling across thousands of miles of countryside in Buicks and buses.

The usual program called for Owens to put on a running exhibition between games if a doubleheader had been scheduled or after the game if not. Jesse specialized in three stunts.[13] First, he would run a 100-yard dash against the fastest competition available, often spotting his rivals a considerable head start. Sometimes he would instead race a horse, in which case Owens would give *himself* as much as a forty-yard lead and would often further benefit when his equine competition was scared by the starter's pistol (a technique devised by promoters to increase Owens's chances of winning). Next, Jesse would dash around the bases, on the outside, against a four-man team running the bases as a relay squad. Finally, if possible, he would take on the 120-yard hurdles against a competitor running a straight 120-yard dash. Although he ran sometimes on muddy fields or on a sprained ankle—and almost always after enduring the grueling rigors of Negro Leagues travel—Owens usually emerged victorious, and he always earned the gaping crowd's admiration.

In his memoirs Owens looked back at this period as a degrading and humiliating way to have had to make a living, not recording Oscar's name or that of anyone else with whom he partnered in the baseball world. When he first was asked to race a horse, he "wanted to throw up," he recalled. He had hated every moment he was connected with Negro Leagues baseball. He had been treated as a "freak," and a poorly paid one at that.[14] More than three decades later it still made Owens "sick" to reflect on this period of his life.[15] He disingenuously made no mention of having owned a stake in the Crawfords, nor of the considerable publicity he obtained when his appearances were promoted.

Certainly Owens, the world-record-holding Olympic champion and national hero, racing horses in front of midwestern villagers does not strike us today as a particularly dignified way to have earned a buck. But this reaction anachronistically imports later values and understandings into a rougher and readier era. At the time, neither Owens nor anyone else gave any indication that such exhibitions were embarrassing.[16] White athletes had raced horses prior to Owens doing so, and on at least one occasion, in Louisville, white Olympic sprinting champion Helen Stephens joined Owens on the bill.[17] *Everyone* had to hustle during the Great Depression, and in truth Jesse Owens made *much* more money than did Oscar Charleston or other Negro Leaguers in the late 1930s, not to mention the average working man, black *or* white.

Although neither Owens nor his biographers mention Charleston in their accounts of this period—yet another indication of Oscar's virtual erasure from history—at the time Oscar was placed in the role of co-leading man with Jesse. The greatest track star of all time had been paired with the greatest Negro Leaguer of all time, it was said. Oscar genially played his role for all it was worth. Invariably the Craws' pregame press now emphasized, falsely of course, that the "Old Master" holding down first base was an incredible fifty-nine years old (when asked, Oscar pretended to be "touchy about his age").[18] That stunning "fact" made it all the more memorable when Charleston knocked long drives over outfield walls, or laced bases-loaded doubles, or even managed two triples, as he did in Louisville and Flint, Michigan.[19] Oscar even hammed it up during games, putting on displays of "eccentric base running" or taking the mound himself when victory was in the bag.[20]

Oscar was still trying to win—and the Craws usually did beat their semipro opponents—but it soon became clear that despite having decent talent on the roster in the form of School-boy Johnny Taylor, Harry Kincannon, Johnny "Needle Nose" Wright, Bus Clarkson, and Jimmie Crutchfield, the 1939 Crawfords team wasn't going to claim any championships. In fact, owing to their position well west of the NNL's other clubs, the Crawfords couldn't even get many league games. So at the end of the NNL's first half, the Craws, sporting a record of 4-5-1, withdrew from the league. The next day they were accepted as members of the more geographically appropriate Negro American League (NAL), in which they finished the season with a similar mark at 8-11-1. Oscar managed to hit a respectable .283 in this, his twenty-fifth year in the Negro Leagues, and he capped the season by managing an all-star NAL team at Yankee Stadium, losing 10-2 to a Josh Gibson–led NNL squad in front of seventeen thousand. But the distance between the graying, bulging Oscar and the game's contemporary stars was now dramatically apparent.

...

Sometime that off-season Oscar sensed it was time to move on. With no particular reason to remain in Pittsburgh, he returned to Indianapolis, where he moved in with his sister Katherine and reconnected with the four of his brothers who still lived in the city. Soon, he had been graced with a vision: he would bring first-rate black baseball back to the place of his birth. He would prove that he was a worthy student of, and heir to, his mentor, C. I. Taylor. He would show the hometown folks he had made good, that the poor kid running around the streets of the Indiana Avenue neighborhood had become not just a star ballplayer, but also a worthy business partner of the celebrated Jesse Owens, not to mention white movers and shakers. Oscar bought a stake in the Crawfords himself, and he convinced his partners to split the team's 1940 home games between Toledo and Indianapolis. "It is Charleston's ambition to have a team comparable with the ex-ABCs in color, pep, spirit, and fight," reported the *Indianapolis Recorder*. "He hopes to relive the days of his greatest glory through a constellation of young stars who loom as potential world champions."[21]

Putting together a competitive team was, however, going to be a huge challenge. First and most significant, as a player Oscar was done. He would play in exhibitions, he said, but he would no longer compete regularly in league games; for several years now he had preferred to hit only when the game was on the line.[22] (Jimmie Crutchfield recalled an occasion when the Crawfords were playing against a team of Major League all-stars. He heard Charleston on the bench, saying, "'I just don't get a thrill out of batting anymore unless there's someone on the bases.' He had popped up a couple of times. Sure enough, we got two men on against Big Jim Weaver, and Charleston said, 'Now this is what I've been waiting for.' And he doubled against the left-centerfield wall and waddled into second base.")[23] He therefore needed a new first baseman. Second, because the Craws' finances were known to be precarious, Oscar's most productive veterans had jumped ship for other clubs by the time spring training rolled around. The talent that remained was limited. Oscar knew it, even though he doggedly told the press that he expected his Craws to compete for the NAL pennant (founded in 1937, the NAL comprised the top black clubs in the Midwest). He spent the spring looking under every rock in the South and Southwest for undiscovered talent. In Atlanta he scored a huge find in a tall, skinny, raw country boy named Connie Johnson, whom he would help develop into a pitcher who would play professionally for more than twenty years, including five seasons in the Majors.[24] But not every find was a gem. One of Oscar's discoveries was a fifteen-year-old batboy from Dallas named Rusty Payne. Poor Payne spent his time booting the ball around the outfield; at one point he struck out in fourteen straight at bats, and he finished the year hitting .091. Another ballyhooed "find" came from the ring. Douglas Rhone was a Houston boxer who also pitched; he disappeared from the scene before he had even played in a league game.

As Charleston searched for ballplayers, Owens once again raced them—as well as local athletes, horses, motorcycles, and pretty much anything else that promised an entertaining contest. Syd Pollock, owner of the Ethiopian Clowns and promoter extraordinaire, had asked the Crawfords' partners to allow him to act as their and Owens's exclusive booker during the spring, and they wisely agreed.[25] From March 31 through mid-May 1940 Pollock kept the Craws menagerie constantly on the move. Starting in Miami, which Pollock's club claimed as its nominally "home" city, the Crawfords barnstormed first with the Clowns, then the Kansas City Monarchs, and then again with the Clowns, across the South from Florida to Texas to Virginia. Pollock cranked up his hype machine in publicizing the Craws' tour, even getting Fats Waller and his band to appear at their March 31 spring opener.[26] But with Jesse Owens's "streamline track exhibition" as their calling card, the Craws didn't need top-flight salesmanship. As an *Atlanta Daily World* columnist wrote, when Owens and the Crawfords came to town, the event was the equivalent, in quality, of a big Joe Louis fight or the East-West Negro Leagues all-star game. In cities like Atlanta, cameramen and autograph-hungry children trailed Owens everywhere he went.[27]

On May 26 Oscar's club won its first home game in Indianapolis versus the Chicago American Giants, 8–2, behind the pitching of promising Johnny Wright, a twenty-three-year-old fast establishing himself as the team's ace. It was a rainy, nippy day, which depressed turnout, but Charleston installed himself at first base for the occasion and received a warm ovation from the fans, many of whom he knew personally. Prices were kept low, at just forty cents for a grandstand ticket, and the team had sprung for brand-new, elegant dark uniforms that had "CRAW" running across their jerseys in block letters trimmed in white, with matching jackets to boot. One can tell, in reading through the old newspaper accounts, that Oscar fairly bursted with pride.[28]

But his team just couldn't compete. Oscar had missed badly on some of his scouting selections, especially among the position players. No one could hit a lick except for Charleston and rising shortstop Bus Clarkson, a Wilberforce College graduate who would ultimately become one of Oscar's best friends. In mid-June Oscar exasperatedly inserted himself back into the starting lineup. But the Craws were so hopeless—and funds, perhaps, so low—that at around the same time Charleston loaned Clarkson to the Newark Eagles.

Oscar remained popular. Pollock always played up his presence in pregame publicity, nearly putting him on the same level as Owens.[29] When the Crawfords toured the east in the late summer, the fans in Harrisburg (where his mammoth home run of 1927 was now remembered as having traveled seven hundred feet!) and Chester, Pennsylvania, hailed Charleston's return.[30] The *Chicago Tribune* called Oscar the "Negro John McGraw."[31]

When the Crawfords went to Birmingham to take on the Black Barons in July, the Barons' team president begged Oscar to help him draw fans by announcing he would play in at least one of the games at first base.[32] Owens hung with the team all season, continuing to race between or after both home and away games, leading clinics, often speaking for a few minutes to the fans, and generally lending his championship aura to the Crawfords' operation. And there were star-studded affairs like that of August 31, when Oscar and Jesse must have been proud to share the program for a benefit game in Detroit with Joe Louis, Bojangles Robinson, and Eddie Anderson ("Rochester" of the *Jack Benny Program*).[33]

Bob Motley, then seventeen and headed toward a future career as a flamboyant Negro Leagues umpire, remembered the Craws coming through Dayton with the St. Louis Stars during that summer of 1940. Placards advertising the Sunday game were hung all over town, and black Dayton was buzzing. Even Motley's uncle Samuel, "who never talked about sports, was all keyed up about it." Businesses normally open on Sundays closed early, and pastors made sure to keep their sermons short so that folks could stroll in their Sabbath finest to the affair. It was like a "festival," Motley recalled, with the ballpark so full that some people were seated on the tops of the dugouts. Even some white fans turned out to take in the contest. Motley remembered Connie Johnson starring on the mound that day for the Craws. And he remembered the fans chanting, "'Charlie, Charlie, Charlie,' for a stocky yellow slugger" who Motley later came to understand was the great Oscar Charleston. In Motley's recollection Charleston "crushed a towering triple that smacked off the centerfield wall, much to everyone's delight." It was the highlight of an afternoon that was essentially a communal gathering, a celebration, a site for the flowering of fraternity.[34]

One hopes that Oscar took satisfaction in helping to provide the occasion for such feelings, for the brand of baseball played by the Craws must have pained him terribly. He had brought major Negro League baseball back to Indianapolis, but it wasn't very *good* major Negro League baseball. The Crawfords finished in last place in the 1940 NAL with a 6-17 record. A Satchel Paige profile that appeared in that July's *Saturday Evening Post* must have only added to Charleston's distress. Ted Shane's piece treated the Negro Leagues as a joke. It quoted Oscar as saying that in black baseball, "We plays for home-run bunts." With respect to his former star pitcher's unreliability, Shane reported that Charleston had been "unable to checkrein" him and therefore "tore his kinky hair and took it." The article even described Oscar as a "gent of the old school of Negro players, who were given to beating up and razoring young rookies who presumed on their jobs."[35] Aside from the article's general condescension, it was the last claim that was too much for Rollo Wilson. He wrote an angry letter to the *Post* demanding a correction, but Shane declined to give him satisfaction.[36]

Fortunately, Charleston's reputation suffered little lasting damage from either this article or the Crawfords' poor showing in 1940. When he brought his club to Philadelphia in late August of that year, Newark Eagles' co-owner Effa Manley—a libidinous, biologically white woman who was raised by a black stepfather and chose to identify as black—asked Oscar if he would like to manage her team in 1941. Oscar said he would think about it.[37] Almost two months later columnist Randy Dixon speculated that Oscar would head the Philadelphia Stars in 1941.[38] It was becoming clear to everyone, apparently, that the once proud Crawfords were nearing the end of the line.

• • •

The Crawfords broke up after the 1940 season, never to play as a major Negro League team again. But Oscar wasn't done trying to make a go of it in Indianapolis. He rebuffed Effa Manley, acquired a new business partner in Charles Burnett (a ballplayer who had played the previous season for the now Minor League Indianapolis ABCs), and by January 1941 was ready to announce that he was launching a new team.[39] The San Blas Indians, as they were oddly named, would play as an independent club and make Perry Stadium their home grounds on Sundays when the Minor League Indianapolis Indians were out of town. Oscar had, yet again, to gather and mold a team.

Spring training took place in and around Sarasota, Florida. Oscar kept his eyes open for undiscovered talent. He met with more success than he had in Texas. Charleston signed a pitcher named Bernard Fernandez after the big right-hander led his Tampa semipro club to a victory over Oscar's squad, telling Fernandez, "If you can win with this team you got here against the team I got, I could give you a job."[40] On the same team he discovered another promising pitcher, little John Gibbons, who at 140 pounds was so thin that Charleston told him to "quit runnin' out there so much. I'll be able to read a newspaper through you after a while."[41] Both Fernandez and Gibbons would pitch in the Negro Leagues for several years, following Charleston from job to job.

Oscar emerged from the 1941 spring training jaunt with a roster of fifteen. As usual, he used the press to tell the fans they could expect hustle, hard work, and heads-up play, the blue-collar, old-school qualities he would forever most prize in any club—perhaps to the extent that he sometimes underestimated the importance of native talent.[42]

Stepping down to semipro ball could not have been easy for the prideful Oscar. Matters did not get off to an auspicious start when, in the San Blas Indians' doubleheader home opener versus the Brooklyn Royal Giants, Oscar's club got swept by scores of 1–0 and 8–1 before eighteen hundred enthusiastic fans. Oscar responded by doing what he did best: drilling his players, hard, in whatever practice time could be found between road games. Barnstorming with the Detroit Stars, the road took the Indians to little Indiana towns like Loogootee, to Toledo, and even to Hamilton, Ontario (for benefit games in support of British refugee children). By May 25 the team had improved enough that it defeated the Stars, 8–1 and 14–8, at Perry Stadium. The highlight was Benny Charleston's straight steal of home.[43]

Oscar was intent on running a tight ship, in the manner of C. I. Taylor. Much like Taylor, in fact, he concerned himself with the fans' behavior. In late May he lamented the illicit drinking going on in the stands, and he warned fans that henceforth the team would be stationing uniformed officers throughout the park in order to catch anyone violating the no-alcohol rule.[44] Then, just as it seemed Oscar might settle into a new life as the respected local leader of a semipro nine, at least partly fulfilling his original vision for restoring high-class baseball to the Indianapolis scene, opportunity knocked. Ed Bolden, now the owner of the NNL's Philadelphia Stars, had been looking for a permanent manager all season, after the previous one had been drafted into the army. The pressure was on, for the Stars had gotten off to a terrible start, and in the fragile Philadelphia market, as in most others, attendance, and therefore revenues, depended on performance.[45] Would Oscar Charleston, the man Bolden had impatiently fired just a handful of games into Hilldale's 1929 season, come to Philadelphia?[46] For Oscar, the chance to step back into the big time was irresistible. In early June he flew to Pennsylvania, stepping off a TWA jet and into the Stars' dugout as manager.[47]

Immediately, the Stars went on a four-game winning streak. Charleston was lavished with credit. It was an age that believed deeply—seemingly *needed* to believe deeply—in the ability of managers to shape the fortunes of teams through their strategic decisions and the sheer force of their wills. Given that premise, along with the indisputable fact that Oscar possessed a "dominant personality," it was easy for writers to claim it was Charleston's old-school methods and clever tactics that were making the difference.[48] "Noted as a hard and exacting but fair taskmaster, Charley has cracked the well-known whip," wrote Randy Dixon approvingly.[49] With another global military conflict on the horizon, the sort of martial discipline represented by Oscar was all the more appealing.

The club Oscar inherited in Philadelphia was more talented than the previous season's Crawfords outfit, but beyond its two best pitchers—hard-throwing Chet Brewer and curveball artist Henry McHenry—there were no elite players on the roster. The most talented of the position players—former Pittsburgh Crawfords Gene Benson and Pat Patterson—were solid, but hitting was an issue. After the Stars' short-lived winning streak ended, Oscar started making roster moves, releasing several players, bringing in replacements (including Fernandez and Gibbons), and searching for a formula that might get the Stars into the NNL's first division—or at least keep them out of the basement. He found a cook for Gibbons in an effort to fatten him up.[50] He spent time working with center fielder Benson, hitting fly balls over his head so he would learn to turn and sprint rather than watch the ball the whole way.[51] And he groomed the team's teenage middle infielder Mahlon Duckett, who was promising in the field but extremely weak at the plate.

On the occasions when he put himself in the lineup—for Oscar could still not refrain from playing from time to time—he tried to teach his charges some of the game's old tricks. In a June 21 game against the Baltimore Elite Giants at the Stars' Parkside Athletic Field, as an injured Roy Campanella watched from the stands, Oscar, playing first base, noted that Homer "Goose" Curry, who had singled, was lazily taking his time getting back to the bag. He quickly cut behind Curry, signaled to the second baseman to throw, and tagged a furious Curry out at first. Later, after walking, and with Pat Patterson on third, Oscar faked a steal to second, trying to draw a throw and perhaps get in a rundown that would give Patterson a chance to make it home. The play didn't work; Patterson, not yet hip to his boss's techniques, froze at third.[52] But the effort was entirely typical of the hyper-aggressive Charleston Way.

Even though Oscar was now forty-four, there were still heroic moments at the plate. After Oscar was elected to the Hall of Fame in 1976, a columnist in Kingston, New York, remembered when pinch-hitting for the Stars, Oscar had tripled to center-right in the top of the ninth to tie up a game against the local semipro team. In the top of the thirteenth, with a man on second and a right-hander at the plate, the Kingston manager instructed his southpaw pitcher to issue an intentional walk. Better, he thought, to pitch to the old, fat, left-handed player-manager on deck. Oscar promptly rapped a sharp single to center to give the Stars the lead and the win.[53] In a contest versus a semipro club in Chester, Pennsylvania, the score was tied 2–2 in the eighth when Oscar entered as a pinch hitter. "Fat and fifty," wrote one reporter, Charleston "waddled to the plate" and promptly smashed a single to center that drove in the go-ahead run, leading the Stars to an 8–7 win.[54]

Alas, despite such feats and Oscar's "keen knowledge of every maneuver known to baseball,"[55] when Benson and Patterson jumped the team in July whatever chances the Stars had of achieving a respectable league record went out the window. As the *Philadelphia Tribune* reported, "Oscar Charleston is here and he's doing all right with what he has to work with but even this veteran pilot must really stay awake nights trying to figure out ways and means."[56] Brewer and McHenry could only do so much. A wonderful photo of Charleston from this period, showing him managing from the dugout steps in Norfolk, Virginia, shows him looking a little sad and possibly even thinner than he had been.[57] The Stars finished with a woeful 15-46 record in league play. Whatever good Oscar had done in developing and finding talent, precious little of that work had as yet translated onto the field.

Oscar's boss, Ed Bolden, had seen enough. When the 1941 season ended, he dismissed, for the second time, the greatest all-around player in black baseball history from his managerial post.

• • •

When the Japanese attacked Pearl Harbor on December 7, 1941, Oscar found himself at loose ends. He was separated, without children, unfree to remarry, fired from his job, and unable to adhere to his vision of making a new life in Indianapolis. What was he to do? He had funds—or so Charles Decker, the sports editor of the *Evansville Argus*, reported, perhaps having been fed information from Charleston himself. Contrasting Oscar with Satchel Paige, Decker pointed out that while Satchel might be the highest-salaried black player, Charleston was likely the wealthiest. He had been the top drawing card in baseball before Satchel had arrived on the scene, and in Decker's estimation he had likely been the first $400-per-month man in the Negro Leagues. Charleston had "made a small fortune managing the old Harrisburg Giants," had never been a lavish spender, and even owned his own home in Pittsburgh, leaving him "well off financially." Paige might ultimately "surpass 'Cholly' but today Oscar is just about tops."[58]

To have a comfortable bank account was quite an achievement. But what the forty-five-year-old Oscar wanted was to get back to the top of the baseball mountain. The war years would make that difficult.

When Oscar registered for the draft on April 27, 1942, he was both out of the game and unemployed. Those savings, if they truly existed, must have come in handy. His two-story brick row home on Christian Street in Philadelphia, a few blocks south of bustling South Street and a few blocks east of the brown, polluted Schuykill River, was comfortable, but Oscar was restless. Fortunately, sometime that year Oscar found work at the Quartermaster Depot, located at Twentieth and Johnson Streets in south Philadelphia. Clothing and flags for the military were manufactured in the complex's yellow-brick Art Deco buildings.[59] The best thing about the Depot, besides the job security essentially guaranteed by the war, was that the colonel in command believed every worker ought to be an athlete.[60] Baseball was central to his sports program, and Oscar, naturally, was chosen to play for and manage the Depot club as it competed in the city's Industrial League.[61]

Or perhaps Oscar's selection as manger wasn't so natural, for the Depot team was integrated. A team picture in Oscar's personal photo album includes thirteen men, about evenly split between whites and blacks. Oscar, who appears by far to be the oldest man on the team, looks solemnly at the camera from eyes almost hidden by the white, pinstriped hat that conceals his gray hair. His marginalia includes the notation "1942–43." How many black men had managed a racially integrated ball club in America, even one that was only semipro, by 1942? It would be several years before Roy Campanella took over management duties for his Minor League Nashua team for part of a game, and nineteen years until Gene Baker became the first regular black manager of a team in organized baseball when he took the reins of the Batavia Pirates. One year earlier Jackie Robinson had been denied the opportunity even to *play* on the camp baseball team at Fort Riley, Kansas, by a racist captain.[62] It is not difficult to understand, then, why Oscar's role as manager of the Depot team, as humble as it may seem to us now, was of substantial importance to Charleston, who inserted a number of team pictures into his album. In one, taken on October 5, 1943, Oscar and the rest of the team's members sit at one of many long tables at Frank Palumbo's Restaurant, enjoying the Industrial League's annual awards banquet.[63] The only African Americans in the picture are Oscar and the other black Depot players.

The black *Philadelphia Tribune* certainly thought the Depot team represented a step forward for the race. In October 1943, under the headline "Democracy in Sports at Quartermaster Department," the paper ran a full-page spread of photos that emphasized the club's integrated nature. Oscar, referred to as "one of the 'immortals,'" is shown in the Depot's simple white uniform standing a little in front of three other players, two white and one black, arrayed to his left. The visual symbolism of his team leadership is not lost on the viewer.[64]

Even at forty-six, Oscar could still rake. On at least one occasion Charleston was named the Industrial League's player of the week.[65] The next year, on May 22, 1944, he was reported to have had a "few timely hits" in the Depot's 5–4 victory over Cramp's Shipyard.[66] It was all far, far from the big time, even the Negro Leagues' big time, but it was a hell of a lot better than crawling through the muck at Normandy or charging a hill in Okinawa.

Moreover, there were opportunities for a man who hustled. In addition to the Depot club, in spring 1944 Oscar managed a team of former Negro Leaguers working in the Philadelphia defense industry (a number of fine players had chosen the industry's relatively lucrative jobs over full-time baseball gigs) who moonlighted on weekends as the Cuban Yanks. By late June this barnstorming club had allegedly won twenty-two of twenty-four contests.[67] There were also opportunities for a man who persisted and never burned any bridges. In the latter half of May Oscar was invited by Ed Bolden to return to the Philadelphia Stars as a part-time coach. Bolden's team was again underperforming its talent, at least in his assessment, and he figured that Goose Curry, Oscar's replacement a couple of years earlier, could use the help.[68]

How Curry felt about this unusual arrangement we can only guess, but when he wasn't putting in a full day of work at the Depot, Oscar worked as a Stars coach for the remainder of the 1944 season, usually manning the first-base coach's box.[69] He saw firsthand how Gene Benson had developed into a top-flight defensive center fielder, and he helped Curry coach up young players like infielder Marvin Williams and catchers Stanley Glenn and seventeen-year-old Bill "Ready" Cash. Whether or not Oscar had much to do with it, the Stars played better after he arrived, turning in an official record of 21-18, good for third place in the NNL, and nearly winning the league's second-half flag.[70]

One more opportunity was about to present itself.

• • •

In May 1944 Oscar was included in a list of the top ten all-time black athletes presented by Judge Joseph H. Rainey at a special banquet given in Philadelphia at the Christian Street YMCA. Oscar, who was likely present, was included in Rainey's roster of greats along with Paul Robeson, Jesse Owens, and Joe Louis. The judge emphasized that these athletes had been "prime ambassadors of interracial goodwill."[71]

That must have meant a good deal to Oscar, for the oppression that had been suffered by his race, the progress his people had made, and the cultural heights they might reach all fascinated him. In his scrapbook he pasted newspaper articles and illustrations discussing, for example, lynchings, the Constitution's three-fifths clause, the gubernatorial veto of a compulsory education bill in South Carolina (a bill that would have meant educating black children), and a Depression-era hunger march on Washington. Other clippings focused on ancient Ethiopian civilization, the representation of blacks in Western art, and the achievements of Oscar's African American contemporaries in sports (other than baseball and boxing) and music (such as Lionel Hampton of Benny Goodman's orchestra). Additional insertions, with black high society as their subject, reveal both Oscar's racial hopes and his social ambitions.

It was in his own sport, Oscar believed, where he could contribute to the cause of racial uplift. As early as 1934 he had indicated to one writer that he wanted "more than anything else in life to help build up colored baseball."[72] Now, in 1945, as the fighting of white and black soldiers side by side in foreign lands drove African American demands for equal rights in their own country to their highest levels yet, Branch Rickey gave Oscar a chance to do even more: to help black players break into the Majors—and thereby fatally prick the bad conscience of white America.

Rickey had become the president and general manager of the Brooklyn Dodgers in 1942, after a twenty-three-year run as first the manager and then the general manager of the St.

Louis Cardinals.[73] During that time he had emphasized and systematized the identification and development of young players like no one before him. Rickey had invented the very idea of a Minor League farm system. Talent ruled, he knew, and to gain an edge on one's opponents one had to find—and control—more of it than they did. Rickey also knew that thanks to his own efforts in St. Louis, the Dodgers lagged far behind the Cardinals and many other clubs with respect to the Minor League talent the team could access. Where could an enterprising baseball executive find an edge? If that executive had guts, the answer was obvious.

In early 1943 at a hush-hush meeting of the board held at the New York Athletic Club near Central Park, the Dodgers' brain trust came to an agreement: Rickey would begin scouting black players, and when the time was appropriate, he would begin to sign them. The Dodgers would have to find "the right kind of player," one who didn't make racial waves, for neither Rickey nor any of his colleagues had any wish to be seen as, or be perceived as allied with, left-wing radicals.[74]

By instinct and conviction, Branch Rickey was a progressive Republican.[75] Although he was raised on a southern Ohio farm in humble circumstances, by the time he was a young man he had adopted early-twentieth-century WASP values as his own. A man very much in the Teddy Roosevelt mold, Rickey staunchly opposed the New Deal's expansive vision of the role the federal government ought to play in American life. Yet like many progressives, he was an inveterate meddler in others' lives, always ready to dispense advice, whether it was wanted or not, and completely confident in the validity of his own beliefs and principles. Rickey was also a believing Christian of the muscular, activist, Methodist, intensely moralistic type who cared little for theological niceties and distinctions.

All of this made Branch Rickey, on the one hand, a rather unlikely civil rights hero—though not the *most* unlikely, given his northern upbringing, his Christian faith, and his staunch belief in progress and America's destiny to be a leader in bringing light to the world. But still unlikely in that he hated the very idea of racial agitation; in that he would brook no suggestion that racism was or had been intrinsic to the American regime; and in that he believed strongly in the self-made man, that people made their own breaks, and that it was nobody's fault but their own if they didn't achieve their aims.[76] On the other hand, Rickey certainly did have an ego, and he found immensely appealing the idea that he—a Christian, an American patriot, and a Republican—might be the one to integrate baseball and thus vindicate all three of those positions against his, and America's, Communist, atheist, and Democratic enemies, especially because he truly and sincerely believed that the integration of America's national pastime was the right thing to do. There was one more thing: the maniacally competitive Rickey wanted nothing more than to win.

After he got the go-ahead from his board, Rickey beefed up his scouting staff, bringing on George Sisler as scouting supervisor and hiring a number of others, including J. Rex Bowen and Wid Curry Matthews, to join his trusted scout Clyde Sukeforth.[77] He assigned them to observe exhibition contests between Negro Leaguers and white Major Leaguers, where they wouldn't look so out of place. Through this process Rickey received reports on well-known, if now somewhat aging, stars like Satchel Paige and Josh Gibson, but none of them seemed right for what he had in mind. Paige, for example, was too independent and libertine, and Gibson was not immune to the temptations of nightlife.[78] When those outside the organization tried to identify players for him, he reacted angrily, especially if their motives were suspect. When black journalist Joe Bostic, who wrote for a radical Harlem newspaper, showed up at the Dodgers' spring training camp in Bear Mountain, New York, with pitcher Terris McDuffie and first baseman Dave "Showboat" Thomas, Rickey was furious. As Bostic requested, Rickey tried the men out, not wishing to give anyone the wrong impression. But he scolded Bostic for "using force" to achieve his, and the black community's, aims.[79]

By spring 1945 two years had passed as Rickey deliberately searched, to no avail, for the first black man to sign with the Brooklyn Dodgers. Part of the problem, he believed, was that it was hard for his white scouts to show up at Negro League games without arousing suspicion. It was even harder for them to get accurate inside knowledge about the character and background of any given player. Oscar Charleston and the United States League (USL) provided Rickey with a solution to this twofold dilemma.

The USL was not Rickey's idea. It was Gus Greenlee's, and it had swum into public view, at least the black public view, when Rollo Wilson announced its formation in January 1945.[80] Never one to play second fiddle, believing that the two existing black major leagues—the NAL and the NNL—were both poorly run and unpopular, and knowing that the war had brought relative prosperity to black communities in northern cities, Greenlee had decided to take another crack at starting his own circuit. By February 24 his plans were largely in place. Cleveland attorney John Shackleford, a former Negro Leaguer who was also a University of Michigan law school graduate, would serve as his league's president. The Pittsburgh Crawfords would be one of the league's eight franchises. Best of all, the greatest black player of all time, Oscar Charleston, would serve as the manager of the league's Hilldale club.[81]

The press played up Charleston's participation, with major black newspapers running long articles and accompanying photos. In the one that appeared in the *New York Amsterdam News*, Oscar signs his contract as former Philadelphia Stars pitcher Web McDonald, set to be Hilldale's business manager, and Joseph W. Hall, the club's white co-owner, look on. Oscar looks dapper and distinguished in his dark suit, white shirt, and tie.[82] In another photo Charleston, Hall, McDonald, and Shackleford sit in a circle at the Christian Street YMCA, talking over the new league and its plans.[83] Oscar's excitement is visible. It couldn't have hurt that he was supposed to receive one of the largest salaries, if not *the* largest salary, ever paid a black manager. In the end he received $500 a month.[84] That may not have been a record-breaking sum, but it was quite a step up from the Quartermaster Depot gig.

In early 1945, then, Oscar had been given the task of building yet another club from the ground up. By March 10 he had sent contracts to thirty players. At the same time, with so many men serving overseas and Oscar doubtless relishing another chance to coach up and develop young men, he announced he was looking for fresh talent. Oscar invited interested Philadelphia-area youngsters to try out for his team in April.[85] He also planned to scour the South—hitting Atlanta, Jacksonville, Tampa, Birmingham, and New Orleans—for overlooked arms, gloves, and bats. Already he had secured the services of several of his former Toledo/Indianapolis Crawfords, including Bernard Fernandez and John Gibbons.[86]

On April 16, 1945, under pressure from local politicians, the Boston Red Sox reluctantly gave tryouts to Negro League players Jackie Robinson, Sam Jethroe, and Marvin Williams, the last of whom was a member of the Philadelphia Stars. No matter how pro forma, these tryouts piqued Branch Rickey's interest. When Wendell Smith, the *Pittsburgh Courier* journalist who had helped make the Red Sox tryouts happen, came to Brooklyn shortly thereafter to meet with Rickey, Rickey asked for his report on the players. Smith delivered his opinion, and while he was there, the new USL came up. Rickey already knew about the league; Joseph Hall had approached him earlier that month about potentially placing a team in Brooklyn.[87] Furthermore, Smith learned, in his efforts to gain privileged access to black players Rickey was very much interested in placing a club in a black baseball league himself. He had even reached out, vainly, to the NNL and NAL.[88] Was there an opportunity here for a partnership?

Just a couple of days later, on April 19 and 20, USL representatives met in secrecy with Rickey in New York. There they made a deal. Rickey would partner with erstwhile Hilldale co-owner Hall to home a franchise called the Brooklyn Brown Dodgers at Ebbetts Field, and Oscar Charleston, bringing many of his recruits with him, would serve as the team's manager. Rickey would serve as an adviser to the league, which, besides Pittsburgh and Philadelphia, would place its other franchises in Toledo, Chicago, and Detroit. He would also publicly give the USL his blessing and do all he could to help make it a success.[89] In return the league would revise its constitution and policies in accord with some of Rickey's suggestions. Gus Greenlee, John Shackleford, and their colleagues were thrilled. With a powerful backer in Rickey, plans for each team to call a Major League park home, and the possibility of adding two more franchises in Boston and New York, their fledgling league had a bright future.[90]

None of these men, at least publicly, considered the notion that integration, which seemed increasingly like a plausible if still frustratingly elusive hope, might soon mean that all-black leagues would be rendered untenable. In fact, as Rickey would soon reveal, they hoped that the USL would eventually become a Minor League within the confines of organized baseball.[91] Regardless, Rickey viewed the USL as a way to scout Negro Leaguers more freely, to build organizational ties within the black community and start winning blacks' allegiance, and to make a little money at Ebbetts Field while the Dodgers were away—a priority never far from Rickey's mind.[92] Furthermore, with Oscar Charleston as his manager, he could easily leverage the knowledge, insight, and connections of the Negro Leagues' most respected figure. Just when Charleston learned that Rickey wanted him not only to manage the Brown Dodgers, but also to scout and advise on Negro Leagues players for the Major League Dodgers is unknown. Charleston never spoke about his role with the team. Nor did Rickey. But since Rickey believed he had little time to lose, in all likelihood Oscar had been brought into the loop by the time he joined Rickey for a head-turning press conference held at Rickey's Brooklyn office on May 7.

Flanked by Shackleford, Greenlee, and Charleston, Rickey kicked off the proceedings seated behind his large mahogany desk. Speaking at length, as was his wont, he announced to the two or three dozen reporters crowded in front of him that the United States League, a new black baseball circuit, had been formed and would begin its inaugural hundred-game season within a matter of weeks.[93] (The league's creation had been discussed in the black press for months, but it was nevertheless news to the white journalists present.) The Dodgers would sponsor a team in this new league, Rickey said, and it would have his full support. For unlike the two existing Negro Leagues, which were unprofessional, ill-run, corrupt "rackets," the USL would be characterized by the sort of order and rectitude befitting a major professional operation. The league's players would be treated better, have standard contracts, and play according to regular schedules.[94] Rickey was even going to do what he could to bring the league into a working arrangement with the Majors. The USL therefore represented a more promising step toward addressing baseball's race issue, he argued, than the Communist-inspired agitation for integration that was getting so much attention.

The general response was one of confusion, followed soon by anger. No matter how involved Communists might be in such matters, with black players now receiving at least token tryouts, politicians pressuring the Major Leagues to integrate, and much of the public souring on segregation, did yet another baseball league operating according to the rules of Jim Crow make any kind of sense? Numerous writers blasted Rickey for trying to make money off black baseball, or for wanting to control it, rather than doing what he could to make separate Negro Leagues unnecessary. Unsurprisingly, the magnates of the NNL and NAL were as upset as anyone. It was simply untrue that these leagues did not have contracts with their players or at least the vast majority of them (an untruth often repeated today). And it was hypocritical of Rickey to lecture his listeners about the existing Negro Leagues being "rackets" when Gus Greenlee, the former numbers king, was standing next to him.

The supremely self-confident Rickey was unfazed. He and his scouts now moved full speed ahead on their plan to identify and sign for the Dodgers the best black talent they could. In this effort Clyde Sukeforth, the taciturn Mainer, took the lead.

For his part, Oscar met directly with Rickey from time to time.[95] The two men must have seen much to like in one another. Both were teetotalers and Republicans, and as ambitious believers in the value of hard work, their personal worldviews were not dissimilar. While Rickey never seems to have mentioned Charleston in print, Branch Rickey III remembers that his grandfather held Oscar in high regard.[96] It was Sukeforth, probably, to whom Charleston usually reported, and it was Sukeforth who told *The Sporting News* in July 1951 that Rickey had "hired" Oscar because he "could get in clubhouses and find out facts in the colored leagues."[97] Oscar, Sukeforth added later, was invaluable to the entire effort. "He knew all the people in the colored league, and if we got interested in somebody, why, we'd call Oscar, and we could find out all about a boy, his habits, how much he'd been to school, what sort of boy he was."[98] That was the sort of inside information Rickey craved.

• • •

By the time of Rickey's press conference the Brown Dodgers had begun exhibition play. Sporting the same classic white uniforms worn by their white Dodgers counterparts, Charleston's Brown Dodgers played their first game on Sunday, April 22, 1945, at Harrisburg's Island Park, which had been leased for the season by one of the Hilldale club's owners to serve as a regular stopping point for league teams. The Brown Dodgers defeated the reborn Pittsburgh Crawfords, 8–7, that day, untying the score in the bottom of the ninth. But in all other respects the game represented an inauspicious start for Charleston and the USL. The day was chilly, and the Craws' bus blew a tire on the way to the game. As a result, the scheduled doubleheader became but a single contest, and only five hundred fans were on hand, Gus Greenlee and Joseph Hall among them. Given that the game featured eleven errors, the light crowd may have been a blessing.[99]

As things turned out, the USL never came close to living up to its promise of operating like a smooth-running, efficient machine. Like every black league before it, it was undercapitalized, and without a significant financial advantage the league could not lure top talent away from the NNL or NAL. The league's players may have enjoyed better contracts, from a legal perspective, but in seemingly every other respect their baseball lives looked essentially like those of the black players who had gone before them. The Brown Dodgers wandered around the mid-Atlantic and Midwest, playing exhibitions against Minor League teams like the Wilkes-Barre Barons, in which Oscar occasionally took a pinch-hitting turn, and league games in places like Indianapolis, Muncie, Hagerstown, and Newport News.[100] Interspersed with these affairs were contests held at Major League stadiums, including their league opener versus the Crawfords at Forbes Field on May 20—a gala affair with band, flag raising, and notable public figures that recalled the Crawfords' glory days—and their initial home game at Ebbetts Field on May 24. But the weather was bad all spring, and the crowds were disappointing. Given a little better luck, the league might have survived for a few years. But in 1946 the USL collapsed entirely.

Charleston didn't even make it to the league's ignominious end. After the first half of the 1945 season ended in late June or early July with the Crawfords in first place, Hall lost control of the Brown Dodgers to his partners, and Web McDonald was brought in to replace Charleston as manager and all but entirely revamp its roster.[101] In Rickey's opinion, Hall had "showed complete ineptitude" in running the team, failing to promote it well and repeatedly turning to Rickey for emergency loans in order to meet payroll.[102] Hall later sued Rickey in federal court for refusing to reimburse him for expenses he had incurred in moving his usl franchise to Brooklyn.[103]

Oscar's sympathies lay with Rickey. When he ran into his old friend John Clark at the Parkside ballpark in Philadelphia on August 18, Oscar said simply that the franchise had been "given to the wrong man." Now out of a job, Oscar planned "to return to his old job of watchman at one of the big Philadelphia plants," reported Clark, possibly referring to the Quartermaster Depot. But Oscar still had the baseball itch, and he expected to be back in the game, in some capacity, in 1946.[104]

Charleston may or may not have stayed on Rickey's payroll after the Brown Dodgers went through their shakeup. All we know for sure is that in 1945 he provided background information on multiple players to Rickey. Future Hall of Fame catcher Roy Campanella was one of the men on whom he provided an important perspective.

Rickey had taken an interest in Campanella after Clyde Suke-forth, sent by Rickey to scout pitcher Don Newcombe at a game in Jersey City between the Baltimore Elite Giants and Newark Eagles, had come back not only praising the Eagles' Newcombe, but also the Elites' strong-armed stocky catcher. A week later Rickey and his wife slipped into another Elites game incognito so that Rickey could take a look at Campanella in person. Suke-forth, Rickey decided, was on the money. Still, he and Clyde weren't entirely confident Campanella was one of the men they should target. Wasn't he too old? Campy was said to be only twenty-three, but surely that was a fib; he was too big and had been playing for too long.

Oscar, of course, knew Campanella's game well. By 1945 Roy had established himself as the best receiver in the Negro Leagues, excepting only Josh Gibson. Born to an Italian father and black mother in Philadelphia on November 19, 1921, Campy had loved baseball and endured taunts spurred by his mixed-race heritage from the time he was old enough to keep up with the older kids scampering along the streets of the Nicetown neighborhood in north Philadelphia. A preternaturally large and powerful teenager, he had graduated from sandlot ball to the Negro Leagues in 1937, at the tender age of fifteen. His first mentor had been Biz Mackey, Charleston's old teammate from the 1920s, and his teammates over the years had included numerous men well known to Oscar. All of these connections, along with Charleston's network of Philadelphia friends and acquaintances, would have made it possible for Oscar to conduct a thorough assessment of Campy's background.

Thus, when Rickey and Sukeforth summoned Oscar for his opinion, he was able to assure them that Roy's reported age was his real one. "That boy's not too old," he insisted. "He started early."[105] Oscar seems to have provided considerably more information on Campanella to the Dodgers than just a verification of his age, for Campanella recalled Rickey's telling him that Oscar had been assigned to "follow me around." As a result of this background work, Roy was "astonished" to "find out how much he knew about me."[106]

All of this came out at an October 8 meeting in Rickey's Brooklyn office.[107] The previous day Campanella had played in a postseason exhibition doubleheader against a team of Major League all-stars managed by Dodgers coach Charlie Dressen. Afterwards, Dressen told Roy that Rickey wanted to see him. He provided directions to Rickey's office, and the next day Campanella arrived a little before ten in the morning. Rickey was behind his desk, chewing a cigar. He shook hands with Roy and then sat there for four or five minutes, saying nothing, staring at Roy under his wild bushy eyebrows. It was the same approach Rickey had taken with another of his targets, Jackie Robinson, when they had met in the same office just a few weeks earlier, on August 28.

First Rickey asked Campanella how much he weighed. When Roy said he tipped the scales at 215 or 220, Rickey exploded, saying Roy couldn't possibly weigh that much and play ball. All

Campanella could do was to respond that he had been doing just that for years. Then Rickey asked Roy how old he was.

"I'll be twenty-four next month," Campanella responded.

"Are you sure that's your right age? I've been hearing about you for a long time, Campanella."

"Mr. Rickey, I don't know what I can tell you except that I was born on November 19, 1921. Today is October 17, 1945. That makes me twenty-four next month, and that's the truth. The God's honest truth."

After that, Rickey took over the conversation. He knew all about Roy, he said, thanks to Oscar Charleston, who had investigated his background thoroughly. "Mr. Rickey kept reading out of a little black book," Campanella would recall. Oscar had apparently done his job well.[108] Rickey liked what he had heard, he said. He liked that Roy, unlike (he claimed) many other Negro Leaguers, lived a healthy, clean life, was a good family man and hard worker, and got along well with others. Then he said: "You like to play with me?" Rickey was inviting Campanella to sign with the Dodgers.[109] But Campanella was so naïve, so unprepared for such a conversation, that he thought Rickey was referring to the *Brown* Dodgers of the USL. That prospect did not appeal to him at all. So he declined. He made $3,000 per year playing in the Negro Leagues and another $2,000 playing winter ball, he told Rickey, and he wasn't looking to alter that happy arrangement. Rickey, apparently not sensing Roy's confusion, asked him to promise he wouldn't sign a contract with anyone else before talking to him first, and Roy agreed. After four hours the meeting ended in a state of mutual misunderstanding.

The next week, Campanella was staying at the Woodside Hotel in Harlem with Jackie Robinson and other players with whom he was preparing to travel to Venezuela as a black all-star team. Jackie invited Roy up to his room to play cards. After a while he casually remarked that he had heard Roy had gone to see Rickey the previous week and that a few weeks prior to that he himself had done the same. He asked if Roy had signed to play for Rickey. Campanella scoffed. He had no interest in playing for the Brown Dodgers. Jackie asked if Rickey had ever mentioned the Brown Dodgers. When Roy admitted he hadn't, Jackie finally could contain himself no longer: he had signed to play not for the Brown Dodgers but for the Dodgers' farm team in Montreal. He was to be baseball's black pioneer. Finally, a chagrined Campanella realized his enormous mistake. He had screwed up his chance to beat Jackie as the first black man to play in the Majors since the color line had been firmly drawn at the turn of the century—and Roy always did believe he *would* have been the first, were it not for his confusion.[110] Had that been the case, Oscar Charleston may have gotten widespread credit for his role in the historic event.

Within days, on October 23, 1945, it was publicly announced that Jackie had signed with the Brooklyn Dodgers. Unlike Campanella, Oscar had nothing to do with Jackie's recruitment. "For Jackie we didn't need Oscar," said Sukeforth.[111] Jackie was already well known thanks to the extraordinary record of athletic achievement he had compiled at UCLA, and he hadn't really been in the Negro Leagues long enough (Jackie had played with the Kansas City Monarchs for only one year) for someone associated with black baseball to have a lot of insight into his character, especially an easterner like Oscar. The legend would nevertheless take root, however, that Oscar *did* play a role in Jackie's signing. Monte Irvin claimed that "Charleston suggested Rickey had to take Jackie over Campy and me, and he went ahead and did it, and he was right."[112] (Irvin's source for that claim was Gene Benson.)[113] The Hall of Fame even produced a Charleston bookmark stating that Oscar had recommended Robinson to Rickey.[114]

Robinson, Campanella, Don Newcombe, John Wright, Roy Partlow, and Dan Bankhead were the first six black men signed by Rickey's Dodgers. There is no direct evidence to confirm it, but Oscar almost certainly gave substantial input on at least some of these players. He may not have been terribly familiar with Newcombe. But he knew Wright very well; he had helped develop him into a top-flight hurler when he was a member of the 1939 and 1940 Crawfords. Partlow had pitched for the Homestead Grays, where Oscar had many relationships, for several years before moving in 1945 to the Philadelphia Stars, where Oscar had even stronger relationships. And Dan Bankhead was the brother of Sam Bankhead, one of Oscar's outfielders on the 1935–38 Crawfords. After they washed out of the Dodgers system, Partlow (1948 Philadelphia Stars) and Wright (1954 Indianapolis Clowns), both rejoined Charleston-managed clubs. Surely Sukeforth and Rickey leaned heavily on Charleston in backgrounding these crucially important early signees.

In any case, the evidence suggests that Oscar was the first black man ever to be paid to scout for a Major League team. His service for the Dodgers predated by four years John Donaldson's for the White Sox, by five years Judy Johnson's for the Athletics, and by eight years Quincy Trouppe's for the Cardinals, to name just a few other early black scouting pioneers.[115] It surely wasn't the one he would have most preferred, but Charleston did break a color line of his own.

$$\cdots$$

After his aborted stint with the Brown Dodgers, Oscar did not find it as easy to get back into the game as he had hoped. No one called with a coaching or managerial job for Oscar for the rest of 1945, or in 1946, or in 1947. His former boss Cum Posey died, at fifty-five, in March 1946; his former protégé Josh Gibson died, at thirty-five, in January 1947. The baseball integration drama played out before him in 1946 in places like Jersey City, where Jackie debuted for the Montreal Royals on April 18; in Nashua, where Campanella and Newcombe were breaking in; and in Three Rivers, Québec, where Wright and Partlow completed their seasons. Robinson put together a sensational debut season for Brooklyn in 1947. Oscar, at home in Philadelphia, bided his time.

With no dugout jobs on offer, Oscar took a different route back to the diamond. Sometime in 1946 he became one of the NNL's umpires, donning the black woolen suit, white shirt, black bow tie, and black shoes that constituted the official uniform of the time.[116] The job wasn't easy, as Oscar must have known as well as anyone. In a game on May 22, 1947, at Island Park in Harrisburg, Oscar's partner, the base umpire, quit the field after members of the New York Cubans would not stop arguing one of his calls. Charleston took over the "entire proceedings from that point in fine style," reported the *Harrisburg Telegraph*.[117] On July 27 Oscar worked a doubleheader at the Polo Grounds.[118] Two days later he was one of four umpires to work the all-star game held in front of 38,400 fans at the same park between the NNL and the NAL.[119]

By the end of that season Charleston was being recognized for his ability to project both serenity and authority when players and managers argued with calls. His technique was to hear them out, smiling (perhaps because the disputants reminded him so much of himself), and when they were finished, simply walk back to his position and order play resumed. He never let the complainants carry on for too long, and he never changed his mind.[120] Goose Curry was famous for throwing Piniella-ish fits when he didn't like a call. Philadelphia Stars pitcher Wilmer Harris remembered one game when Curry started to go off. Charleston was working behind the plate. Curry hadn't gotten beyond the top step of the dugout before "Charley didn't say a word, he just pointed. And Goose stopped right where he was, didn't make a peep. You could just see him telling himself, 'I'm not going anywhere near this.'"[121]

Perhaps Oscar would have been pleased enough to have continued working as an umpire. But as Christmas 1947 neared, the phone rang. For the fourth time in Charleston's life, it was Ed Bolden, offering a job.

CHAPTER 9

Legend, 1948–

INTEGRATION SPELLED THE DEATH of the Negro Leagues. Perhaps it needn't have. Perhaps, as was discussed at the time and has been much discussed since, the existing Negro Leagues could have been incorporated into the structure of (heretofore white) organized baseball, ultimately functioning as "historically black" leagues in much the same way that historically black colleges have functioned for decades. That seems to have been the hope of Oscar and others. It would have been a better outcome, probably, for the hundreds of African American players, coaches, managers, and umpires who made their livings in baseball. For as it turned out, the short-term effect of the long-awaited erasure of baseball's color line meant jobs, success, and (relative) riches for a few—and fewer jobs, less recognition, and less money for the many.[1]

The integration of organized baseball did not come as fast as blacks desired or deserved. Still, already by 1949 there were black players in every Class AAA and Class A Minor League circuit, and both Major and Minor League organizations were consistently purchasing the rights to players from Negro Leagues teams.[2] As the calendar turned from one year to the next in the post-Jackie era, the cream of the black crop was more and more thoroughly skimmed from the remaining black baseball teams. One result was the crumbling of the Negro Leagues. Another, paradoxical, one was that by the mid-1950s fewer African Americans were making their living from professional baseball than at any time since 1900.[3] That wasn't what anyone had wanted, but it was the reality.

Fan support for the Negro Leagues declined radically beginning in 1947, not only because Jackie Robinson and his exploits dominated people's minds, but also because the leagues came to be viewed by African Americans as a sort of peacemaking with segregation that now seemed embarrassing, even intolerable. Robinson himself heaped scorn on the leagues in a June 1948 *Ebony* article, criticizing everything from the pay to the bathrooms.[4] By the end of that year crowds were reportedly one-half to one-third of what they used to be.[5] After that season the rickety Negro National League called it quits. The New York Black Yankees folded. The once powerful Homestead Grays would henceforth play only independently. Abe and Effa Manley sold the Newark Eagles, which were temporarily relocated to Houston before finally ending up in Nashville. Beginning in 1949 a newly reorganized Negro American League incorporated those NNL clubs still left standing and split into Eastern and Western divisions. Gradually, it began to dawn on the remaining black-baseball owners that their business model must change. What profit there might be would henceforth come less from gate receipts and more from developing and selling players to the Majors.

Even that strategy was not enough to save black baseball. First, it meant selling off a team's best drawing cards, further reducing both fan interest and the quality of play. Second, while the demand among Major League teams for black players was growing—as it ought to have been, given the generally fantastic seasons blacks were producing at the levels at which teams were placing them—it wasn't growing fast enough to provide consistent, sizeable cash flow. Negro Leagues owners responded by slashing salaries, cutting corners, and ramping up already grueling travel schedules in order to go wherever the remaining fans were located. By 1950 the Baltimore Elite Giants were demanding foul balls back from the crowd and had taken players off salary to pay them a percentage of the gate instead—a practice that hadn't been seen in the major Negro Leagues for decades.[6]

This was the new, bittersweet world of black baseball in which Oscar Charleston managed Ed Bolden's Philadelphia Stars from 1948 through 1952. At a December 19, 1947, press conference, a gray-templed, gray-suited Oscar sat next to Bolden and signed a contract to return as the team's manager. He would replace the man who had replaced him in 1942, Homer "Goose" Curry, widely regarded as a clown by his players. (Some of them also thought Curry dealt crookedly with the team's finances.)[7] Bolden promised Oscar a free hand in shaping the club, and until his death in September 1950 he was true to his word.[8] The 1948–52 Stars were Oscar's team through and through. They were young, played hard, and were good citizens. Unfortunately, a team that was never especially talented—no Willie Mays, no Henry Aaron, no Ernie Banks came through the Stars before heading to the bigs—became less so as time went on. Oscar wanted badly to win one more championship.[9] The Stars would not give it to him.

In the five years Charleston managed the club in the late 1940s and early 1950s the Stars' full-season record was never better than fourth in their league. They finished fourth in the 1948 NNL, eighth in the 1949 NAL, eighth in the 1950 NAL, seventh in the 1951 NAL, and sixth—that is, last—in the 1952 NAL. It was a young club that seemingly got younger, and worse, each year as the best players jumped or were sold to Major League, Minor League, or Latin American teams. Roy Partlow, who had washed out of the Dodgers system after spring training in 1947 owing to run-ins with management; Gene Benson; Mahlon Duckett; and Henry McHenry—all veterans—anchored the 1948 Stars, but only Duckett returned for the 1949 season.[10] Oscar's friend Bus Clarkson and talented infielder Marvin Williams returned to the States and joined the Stars in 1949, but Williams didn't last the year, and Clarkson was sold to the Brewers midway through the 1950 season. The 1951 club, a true no-name outfit, had an average age of twenty-three.[11] The 1952 team's average age was reportedly just twenty-one, and it lost its best player, Ben Littles, when he died in a car accident in Muskogee, Oklahoma, in March of that year.[12] By 1951 the Stars' talent pool was so limited that Oscar's starting shortstop, Teddy Washington, had yet to even graduate from Camden High School. The following year, the starter at short was another eighteen-year-old kid named Dick Whittington.[13] These later Stars clubs were comparable to a mid-Minors team at best. These weren't the 1930s Crawfords.

But while there wasn't much depth, there *was* talent on these teams, even if it wasn't top-tier and even if it was sometimes very raw. Oscar got a thrill out of helping young black men get into organized ball. "I never got the chance to play in the majors because of the color-line," he commented to Wendell Smith. He was therefore committed to doing all he could "to see that these kids I'm managing get their chance. Everyone who goes up compensates in some way for me."[14] With that end in mind, one of Oscar's strategies consisted of constantly planting stories in the press about this or that player being scouted by a big league team.[15]

Harry "Suitcase" Simpson was the best of the Stars in the Charleston years. He left the squad after the 1949 season and debuted with the Cleveland Indians in 1951. Bus Clarkson, whom Oscar had hoped to groom for a managerial job one day, got his shot with the Boston Braves in 1952.[16] Catcher Charlie White hooked on with the Braves in 1954, and infielder Milt Smith made it to the Reds in 1955. Charleston was given at least some credit for the development of each of these men.[17] (White said that he "owed a lot" to Charleston for teaching him "a great many points" about the game during his time with the Stars.)[18] A dozen or so other Charleston finds and protégés carved out careers in the Minors of varying lengths, including Washington and Whittington, catchers Bill Cash and Stanley Glenn, shortstop Frank Austin, and pitchers Bill Ricks, Manny Cartledge, and Wilmer Harris. Despite the occasional whiff—as with the teenaged Bill Bruton, a future Braves standout who was brought to Stars training camp in 1948 by Judy Johnson but was present for only a week before Oscar sent him home—Oscar certainly proved he could scout.[19]

Oscar was happy for these men, but he must have looked wistfully into center field when the Stars barnstormed through the South with the Birmingham Black Barons in mid-1949. Eighteen-year-old Willie Mays was clearly something special out there; after he went 5 for 6 against the Stars in a game at Birmingham's Rickwood Field, Oscar made sure to tip his cap in appreciation.[20] And in 1952, when his team spent the beginning of the league season traveling with the Clowns, Oscar could not have helped but wish the eighteen-year-old shortstop who hit cross-handed, a kid named Henry Aaron, was wearing a Stars uniform.[21] Both men must have reminded him of himself. By July 1951 columnist Al Moses was comparing Mays to Oscar, noting that Willie's power, as well as "his natural love of the game" and "native baseball gifts," were positively Charlestonian.[22]

During these years old acquaintances were renewed as well. Oscar reconnected with his old business partner Jesse Owens in August 1948, when Owens, promoting his sporting goods line, raced Stars shortstop Frank Austin and a couple of other players during a game at Yankee Stadium. The two men sat together on the Stars bench, shooting the breeze and recalling the USO Camp Show in which both were supposed to have participated in 1945. The draft board had prevented Owens from going to Asia with the program, while the opportunity to manage in the United States League had kept Oscar home. "I really wanted to be on that one," sighed Owens. "So did I," responded Oscar.[23]

In 1950 forty-four-year-old Satchel Paige, then between gigs with the Cleveland Indians and the St. Louis Browns, sauntered back into Oscar's life. Still a gate attraction, Paige helped the Stars pump up their otherwise dwindling crowds by pitching for them that July and August in Philadelphia, Williamsport, Harrisburg, Buffalo, and Toronto. At least, he was *scheduled* to perform in each of those towns, as well as others. Satchel traveled not on the team bus but in his own Cadillac, to the top of which he had strapped a canoe. Sometimes, if Paige saw a lake, he would stop and do some fishing—and consequently be a latecomer or a no-show for the game. Before long, Oscar was keeping Satchel on task by traveling in the Cadillac himself.[24]

Satchel's time with the Stars was too brief to give the team much of a lift. But given all the obstacles the Stars faced—including, after 1948, having access to their nominally home grounds of Shibe Park only when the Athletics and Phillies were out of town, which therefore often meant staying on the road for two months or more at a time—Oscar was praised for his team's competitiveness. Joe Bostic, having seen the no-name Stars play at Yankee Stadium in May 1950, said they were "playing old Charlie's brand of ball. . . . They cashed every error the [Elite Giants] made and [the Stars'] hell-bent-for-leather hijinks was hustling them into making the miscues." Oscar would work miracles if he were given control of the Major League Giants, Bostic concluded.[25] Charleston was selected as the manager for the East in the 1950 East-West game (his club, a two-to-one underdog, lost 5–3), and he was entrusted with further control of the Stars by Dr. Hilda Bolden, Ed's daughter, when she inherited her father's share of the club after his death. Given the auburn-tressed, curvacious Hilda's prestigious status as the head of Parkside Clinic in Washington DC, not to mention her inclusion on the *Afro-American*'s list of the ten best-dressed women in America, Hilda's faith in him must have given Oscar great satisfaction.[26]

The next year Charleston's hometown friends honored him with "Oscar Charleston Night" on August 25, 1951, at Indianapolis's Victory Field. The outmanned Stars were crushed by the Chicago American Giants, 11–1, but Oscar was presented with gifts from Ted Sullivan, the Indianapolis Indians' business manager. Sullivan declared Charleston to be "one of baseball's true greats in every department," and he "lamented that his color kept him from stellar roles in the big leagues."[27] Of course, it wasn't too late for Oscar to be given a chance in the Majors. In

1949 black columnist Dan Burley had nominated Charleston for consideration as a Major League coach or manager.[28] And the *New York Amsterdam News* wondered aloud on September 8, 1951, why no team in organized baseball had at least hired Charleston as a scout.[29] It was a good question.

• • •

To play in the Negro Leagues in the post-Jackie era meant confronting, more or less on a daily basis, two especially salient facts: (1) the persistence of demoralizing and demeaning racial discrimination, prejudice, and violence; and (2) the necessity of spending a depressing percentage of one's life on a bus.

Occasionally the racial hatred was shocking, even for men who had known it all their lives. For example, there was the time when the Stars were in Cleveland, Mississippi, and they stopped for gas and heard some kind of commotion. When they asked the attendant what it was all about, he told them that a small black boy had been taken off his bicycle by a gang of hooligans and had an air hose shoved up his rectum, blowing him all to pieces. The Stars just shook their heads and got the hell out of there.[30]

Much more often, prejudice manifested itself in heckling and frustrating inconvenience. The players all heard, and remembered, the insults hurled from the stands, even as they trained themselves to ignore the noise. Mississippi was particularly bad, recalled one player, but it wasn't just the South where players encountered fan hostility.[31] Umpire Bob Motley thought he was called more names by whites while traveling through midwestern states like Indiana and Ohio than in Deep South states like Mississippi and Alabama.[32] "Negro ballplayers had a tough time" with certain fans, said Cliff Layton. The only strategy that worked was to wait them out. "If you would ignore them, they would settle down."[33]

Getting fed could be a serious challenge. After night games in small towns, no stores or eateries would be open, at least not where blacks where welcome.[34] Light-skinned and foreign players with accents were treasured for their ability to purchase food for the team in establishments that wouldn't serve African Americans.[35] The North was particularly difficult to navigate because, unlike in the South, it was frequently impossible to tell ahead of time whether one would be served or not. The only way to find out was to go into a restaurant, sit down, and see if a waitress came to take one's order.[36] Many a time the players were happy simply for the opportunity to purchase bread and cold cuts from a grocery store.[37] Buck O'Neil, who managed the Kansas City Monarchs during the years when Charleston managed the Stars, used to keep a book listing rooming houses that would accept blacks, along with information about the quality of their beds and meals.[38] *The Negro Travelers' Green Book*, which began publication in 1936 and listed restaurants, service stations, and private tourist homes that served blacks, met the same purpose. (The 1947 edition listed seven hotels open to African Americans in the entire state of Mississippi.) Whether in the North or South, bedbugs tortured the exhausted men in more than one of these establishments.[39]

And yet the players who suffered these indignities were invariably quick to point out that it wasn't all bad. "There were places where we could really enjoy ourselves—especially Birmingham and Memphis, where there were black-owned hotels and restaurants," said Jim Robinson. Harold Hair was proud to point out that players "stayed in the same hotels and ate at the same places as did the entertainers on the Chitlin Circuit." After games, said Hair, they often went out to clubs or to the movies, and in New York they stayed only a block and a half away from the Apollo. Buck O'Neil stressed that his Monarchs "stayed in some of the best hotels in the country. They just happened to have been black hotels." In other words, the black self-help tradition had not been without its successes.[40]

Travel stories dominated the recollections of former Negro Leaguers for the simple reason that their teams essentially belonged to the road more than they did to any one city. This was especially true in the post-integration era, when the remaining profit-making opportunities lay primarily in towns where black baseball was seen only a couple of times per season. And it was especially true of the Stars, who saw their Philadelphia gate receipts decline year after year after year. Traveling in a red, white, and blue 1942 Ford bus with the team's name painted on both sides, the Stars' schedule took them to big cities and small towns throughout the Northeast, Midwest, South, and Southwest.[41] In 1951 and 1952 they played more than 90 percent of their games on the road and did not debut at their nominally home grounds of Shibe Park until July.[42]

Oscar and several players usually took turns driving as the Stars rambled the country, putting up to sixty-five thousand miles per year on the old Ford, and putting *in* the occasional new motor, as they searched for gates that would pay their expenses and keep them in the game.[43] It was crowded on that bus, with seventeen men and their gear usually aboard, and it was inevitably stinky. As Bob Motley testified, "There is nothing worse than being stuck in tight quarters with a bunch of smelly ballplayers who have just completed a doubleheader on a hot summer day in a stadium that had no shower." The stench was made all the more pungent by the ointments, liniments, and tonics that the players used to treat their injuries. One of the more popular of these was called "goose grease," quite literally made with the rendered fat of a cooked goose. Kerosene oil and Epsom salts also had their uses in the home remedies that players had inherited from their elders. It all combined to form a nasal nightmare.[44]

Typically, players would sing, play cards, and tell stories as they bumped along from town to town, often boasting about the women they had bedded—or would bed in the next city.[45] "The guys liked bragging about their success in the bedroom," remembered Motley, "and always tried to one-up each other with exaggerated tales. Some had a different girlfriend in every town. Others preferred anonymous one-night stands. Some favored hookers. . . . Still others boasted of having two and three girls at a time."[46] Buck Leonard reported that many players ended up contracting syphilis and other STDs from prostitutes.[47] The Stars, thanks to their unusually high proportion of teetotaling, straitlaced, religious players, probably indulged in blue banter less than other teams. Other clubs teasingly called them the "saints."[48] That the Stars had a characteristic makeup was no accident. It reflected Oscar's own values and preferences.

The Stars' bus was often also the Stars' hotel, and during all-night trips someone would stay up with the driver to make sure he stayed awake.[49] Sometimes Oscar liked to give everyone a jolt. Multiple players remembered an occasion during which the team was driving through an awful thunderstorm on a treacherous mountain road. Suddenly, Charleston opened the bus door, leaned out, and shouted into the sky, "Hey, up there! Stop all that damn noise!" The players became deadly silent, as if God himself had been threatened. Oscar just burst out laughing.[50]

Teasing and kidding with his charges was part of Oscar's leadership style. He would make dinner bets with hitters on how many hits they would get. Too often, he won. "I'm getting too fat from the dinners you guys are buying me," he told them.[51] Over and over he asked junkballer Barney Brown if he was ever going to throw the ball *hard*. And he still liked to show off his strength; Stanley Glenn recalled that Oscar "could pick me right up like I was a baby," and Glenn was 6 feet 2 inches and 225 pounds.[52] More impressive yet were Oscar's hands. Not only were they so rough that Oscar could cut a ball just by rubbing it.[53] They were also so strong that he could twist the cover off a ball. These feats of a fifty-year-old left his players deeply impressed.[54]

By this time Oscar had definitely mellowed, never getting in fights or flying off the handle. Quincy Trouppe saw him as "relaxed," Harold Hair remembered him as a "nice guy," and James Robinson recalled him as "very mild" and "friendly."[55]

Motley, the umpire, thought Oscar was so calm that "you could have mistaken him for a man of the cloth."

> Unlike almost every other manager in the leagues, [wrote Motley] I never had one problem with Charleston. He was just a low-key kind of fellow who never raised his voice. If he did have a dispute about a call, he would simply walk up from the dugout and ask, almost in an apologetic tone, "What happened, ump?" Once I had explained the reason for my call he'd just nod or say, "Okay, ump," and go back to the dugout. He was the most calm and collected of gentlemen during some of the fiercest fought games, and I was always appreciative of his non-confrontational manner of managing.[56]

On one occasion Charleston and Buck O'Neil nobly helped Motley escape an angry crowd. In Motley's telling, after the final out of a game at Blues Stadium in Kansas City, a Monarchs loss, the fans expressed their displeasure by chucking Coke bottles at him. Either Oscar or Buck shouted to Motley to go out toward second base, where the fans' throws could not reach him, and when things did not immediately settle down, both managers came out of their dugouts and escorted Motley to safety over the center field fence.[57]

Oscar may have become less turbulent by the time he took the helm of the Stars in 1948 (a July 1948 game in which he was ejected and the game forfeited because he would not leave the field appears to have been an anomaly), but he had certainly not become a softy. Pitchers who failed to go all nine usually found Oscar handing them a ball on the bus after the game with a simple message: "It's your game tomorrow." Runners who didn't take the extra base would get a tongue-lashing.[58] Players didn't dare argue with him; players didn't dare be late; and between the lines players didn't dare do anything but play the game all out, as he had.[59] Oscar still went all out himself. Sometimes it was to comic effect, as when he pinch-hit in one 1948 contest and lined a gapper to right-center field. As he rounded second, Oscar—now with a forty-six-inch waist and weighing north of 250 pounds—stumbled and fell. He was forced to crawl his way to third base to complete the triple.[60] On another occasion, against the Brooklyn Bushwicks, he hit a long drive that would have been an inside-the-park home run for anyone else but was only a triple for the aged Oscar. When the next hitter hit a long fly ball to center field, a still panting Oscar was determined to score. Putting his head down and running as fast as his legs would take him, he bulled straight into the catcher, knocking off his mask—and knocking him out. "Charlie just stood up and dusted off his pants," recalled infielder Mahlon Duckett.[61]

There was a right way to play the game, Charleston believed, a way that he and other black stars had themselves received and honed, and it was his job to pass that way down to the rising generation. The players were grateful, because they were painfully aware that the little instruction they had received before turning pro had been inadequate. Hank Aaron bitterly recalled that "coaching was something for white kids."[62] Buck Leonard lamented that the Negro Leaguers "didn't have time for somebody to teach us fundamentals and inside baseball like the major leaguers did in the spring."[63] Stars pitcher Harold Gould claimed he was taught the definition of the strike zone by an umpire.[64] Numerous other players attested to the embarrassment they felt when they became aware of their ignorance. Oscar did his best to mentor them. According to Cliff Layton, Charleston "showed the guys how to play their position in a real professional way." He would go over base running techniques, swing paths, follow-throughs, and other nuances of the game that players might never have encountered. He was "a very intelligent man," said Layton, "who had great knowledge of the game."[65] Sometimes, at least, his advice helped, as when he was credited with helping the Stars' Mahlon Duckett and Harry Simpson blossom at the plate in 1948.[66] And sometimes he forged a deep connection. "He was like my dad," remembered Harold Gould. "I could never say enough. He was such a great man."[67]

Many of those who have written on the Negro Leagues have proceeded from the premise that the players must have been embittered by the experience. Lee Blessing's 1990 play *Cobb*, in which an angry Oscar Charleston challenges the Georgia Peach's understanding of himself, is a case in point. Generally, however, the premise that Negro Leagues players felt aggrieved and resentful is false, and it is certainly false with respect to Charleston.[68] Oscar dearly wished he had had the opportunity to play in the Majors, but no one recalled him as sulky or self-pitying. If Cool Papa Bell can be believed, what hurt him most was when he noticed that younger black players had no idea how good he had been.[69] Oscar himself confessed to the *Philadelphia Tribune*'s Malcolm Poindexter Jr. that he got "his biggest thrill . . . from hearing others talk of his sensational feats on the diamond."[70] He was proud that he had once hit two home runs in a game in Holland, Pennsylvania, and two more that went *just* foul, after a fan had asked him to hit four.[71] He was proud of having earned John McGraw's praise (if that never really happened, Oscar never corrected anyone).[72] And he was especially proud of having homered off Lefty Grove, in what Oscar believed was Grove's first time pitching against a black club, and of tearing up St. Louis Cardinals pitching in 1921.[73] He had proven himself against Major Leaguers. In 111 plate appearances Charleston had posted a tidy .347 batting average, .418 on-base percentage, and .806 slugging percentage versus big league pitching. He didn't need their or anyone else's validation.

Usually, when given the opportunity to promote himself, Oscar demurred. On May 1, 1948, Fred Wilson, of the *Delaware County Times*, was watching a Cubans-Stars game in Chester, Pennsylvania, with Lefty Vann, white longtime manager of the local semipro team against which Oscar's and other Negro Leagues clubs had played countless times during the last two or three decades. Vann took the occasion to give Wilson his all-time Negro all-star team. Coming to the outfield, he pointed at Oscar, standing in the third base coach's box, and said, "There's my center fielder." When Oscar came back to the dugout, Wilson and Vann called him over to ask who the team's left fielder ought to be; Oscar nominated Cristóbal Torriente. Wilson and Vann then told him the rest of their team. "You could have gotten a better center fielder," Oscar replied. When he disappeared into the dugout, Vann warned Wilson not to believe it. "He's the best I ever saw. He could hit 'em as far as Leonard or Gibson or anybody else."[74] Likewise, when Charleston, along with Ed Bolden, was asked to name his own all-time Negro Leagues team by the *Philadelphia Bulletin* in 1949, he chose Rap Dixon for center field and omitted himself entirely.

• • •

Oscar began frequently to be asked for his thoughts on this or that topic in the late 1940s. Were there any good prospects left in the Negro Leagues, asked the *Wilmington News Journal* in July 1948. Most assuredly, responded Oscar (described as a "quiet, scholarly individual"), naming his own center fielder, Harry Simpson, as one excellent candidate for the Majors. "The admission of Negro players into Organized Baseball was the best thing in the world for our leagues," he maintained. The entry of blacks into the Majors "revives interest in the game among our youngsters." He added that he thought Jackie Robinson a good clutch hitter and glove man and the best of the four blacks then in the Majors, and he believed that Satchel Paige, recently signed by the Cleveland Indians, would "be a good relief pitcher for them. . . . One thing about Satchel, if he says he's going to strike out fifteen men he strikes out fifteen men."[75]

When Ty Cobb was quoted in March 1952 to the effect that baseball was being ruined by a lack of fundamentals and the pampering of players, the *Philadelphia Tribune* spoke with Oscar to get his reaction. He agreed that baseball had changed, but he blamed the new economics of the game. Players used to play for love of the sport rather than money because there was so little of the latter to be had, he maintained. Kids would come for a tryout and hang around for nearly two weeks without payment ever being mentioned. "But now, they don't pull on a glove until somebody says how much." Charleston singled out Lefty Grove, Jimmie Foxx, Jimmy Dykes, and Jack Quinn as old-time Philadelphia Athletics who had craved the best competition so much they would play Negro Leaguers in postseason contests, even though for them the money didn't mean so much.[76]

Foxx seems to have been a particular friend of Oscar's. Once, after Grove had dusted him off in an exhibition, Charleston allegedly charged the mound. When Grove called to his first baseman, Foxx, for aid, Jimmie reportedly said he could hardly take the part of one friend against another.[77] In another story, this one told by Cool Papa Bell, an all-star black team was taking on Major Leaguers in Mexico City. The game was tied 4–4 in the top of the ninth when the Negro Leaguers took a two-run lead on Oscar's single. Foxx then tied the game with a two-run home run in the bottom of the inning. The game was finally called, allegedly because of darkness, in the twelfth, with the sun still in the sky and the score tied at six. When Charleston, Bell, and Foxx went to dinner that evening, Foxx admitted that the game shouldn't have been called. He also said he should have struck out before hitting his game-tying homer, but the ump had ruled a would-be strike three a ball. According to Bell, Charleston responded, "As usual, we Negroes get the short end. We do appreciate you though, Foxx. You're a friend and you've always given us the credit we deserve as ballplayers."[78]

Oscar was also given a platform on the race question. *Philadelphia Tribune* Charities included him in a public panel discussion of "Sports and the Negro" on January 20, 1952. Charleston didn't say anything profound or controversial, but he did insist that if the players of his day in the Negro Leagues "were still around, there would certainly be a goodly number of them being sought by the major clubs. For natural talent, they were unexcelled, but the opportunities of today weren't available."[79]

That such opportunities had finally arrived meant that by

the end of 1952 the talent in the Negro Leagues was seriously depleted. As Charleston worked in his off-season job as a baggage handler for the Pennsylvania Railroad, he debated whether he should continue with the Stars. The team was bad, the crowds were small, the travel was punishing, and he was tired.[80] In March 1953 majority team owner Eddie Gottlieb made the decision easy. The Stars were disbanding, he announced, and the players had been set free from their contracts. The financial losses were just too much. "If it were humanly possible to just meet expenses I'd run the club again," said Gottlieb. "But everything points to going in a hole like we've been doing season after season."[81] Oscar was probably relieved. He was immediately offered a job as manager for an unnamed southern team, but he turned it down.

• • •

Oscar sat out the 1953 season. He was living north of Center City in Philadelphia's Strawberry Mansion neighborhood, for decades home to some of the city's more affluent Jews and now, increasingly, blacks.[82] He may have checked out some of the performances of John Coltrane, who lived a few blocks to his south. He may have thought his days in baseball were over. But Syd Pollock wrote him on December 22, 1953, offering him a position as manager of the Indianapolis Clowns, and Oscar gladly accepted.

The Clowns had won the NAL championship in 1950, 1951, and 1952 but had relinquished their crown to the Kansas City Monarchs in 1953. Pollock thought Oscar—to his mind the greatest black player of all time—could put the Clowns back on top. Just as important, he thought Charleston could handle the players better than had his previous manager, Buster Haywood, who he believed was too soft on the men (a fault Haywood readily acknowledged).[83] As Henry Aaron had discovered in 1952, the Clowns were a wild bunch. They drank and hollered in the back of the bus as the team traveled from town to town, and once they arrived, they kept drinking—and looked for women, a particular passion of the team's dwarf comedian, Spec Bebop, who met with surprising success. "Women were all over that little guy!" marveled Aaron.[84]

Oscar knew the Clowns' operation well, having played against and barnstormed with Pollock's teams for many years. The Clowns pushed the margins of good taste; some felt they went well beyond those margins (although this was typically a judgment made in hindsight). The team's players no longer adopted silly African-sounding names, dressed weirdly, or painted their faces, fortunately. But they played an entertaining game of shadowball, and they employed three comedians—Bebop, the tall King Tut, and the white clown Ed Hamman—whose in-game routines came out of the vaudeville tradition. In 1953 they had taken their act a step further by employing a woman. Toni Stone had played several innings per game at second base. Pollock, who loved the draw she brought to the gate but did not wish to meet her demand for money (Stone would, in fact, be the highest-paid player in the NAL in 1954), now planned to sell her to another league team and to sign up two new women, Connie Morgan and Mamie "Peanut" Johnson, to replace her.[85] Charleston, he hoped, would mentor them.

Oscar took the train to Pollock's home in Tarrytown, New York, on January 22, 1954, to discuss with Syd the rest of his team's composition. He tried to get old mates Wilmer Harris, Bus Clarkson, and Joe Chestnut to join the club, but Negro Leagues ball no longer held the attraction it once did. Plus, the roster was already quite solid. Pollock was a charismatic, rough-around-the-edges hustler and bullshitter who kept a sharp eye on the bottom line. But he was also a good business strategist who was beloved by his players, had a decent nose for talent, and had scouts bird-dogging for him in various American and Latin American locations.[86] By early February quality players like Ray Neil, Ted Richardson, Dave Amaro, Erwin Ford, Henry "Speed" Merchant, George Wannamaker, and Orlando Lugo were on board.

What about the women? To balance the twin goods of maximizing both the team's entertainment value and its competitiveness, Pollock's plan for the 1954 Clowns was for Morgan to play second and for Johnson to pitch. Only one of them would be on the diamond at any one time, and each would play no more than two or three innings (Johnson often pitched only one). Morgan and Johnson certainly weren't jokes. Morgan, a nineteen-year-old Philadelphia native, was an excellent athlete—she played basketball too—and a good fielder with a strong arm. She had played for several years with a north Philadelphia women's baseball team called the Honey Drippers. Johnson, a twenty-two-year-old who grew up on Long Island and had attended New York University for two and a half years, could locate her pitches and get swings and misses with her curve ball. Surely they were two of the top female baseball players in the world. But later, politically correct mythology notwithstanding, they were primarily on the Clowns for publicity purposes, not because their skills were the equal of their male peers.[87]

Pollock decided to make Morgan his star. He invented a story in which Oscar had personally discovered Morgan on the Philadelphia ball fields and was incredulous when he saw that her arm rated with Major League infielders.[88] He arranged for Malcolm Poindexter of the *Philadelphia Tribune* to take publicity photos.[89] And he persuaded *Ebony* and *Our World* to run features on Morgan, Johnson, and the Clowns. Oscar happily played along, praising both women whenever he was given a chance and signing his name to whatever quotes Pollock came up with. All spring and summer, Pollock trickled out story after story about Morgan, and to a lesser extent Johnson and some of the male players, in papers across the country. The man knew his business.

Prior to the start of spring training, Oscar set about drilling Morgan into shape. "Oscar Charleston was my mentor," she later recalled. "Once the Clowns hired me and hired him, he took me off-season and taught me all he could about sliding and run-

ning the bases and, when it warmed a touch, hitting and fielding. He was a strict manager, not so you couldn't have fun, but
stern enough so you knew to get down to business. He had us
self-disciplined. Didn't talk much about the old days. He was
interested in winning here and now." Johnson, too, remembered
Oscar as being all business. "With Oscar Charleston, you either
played ball or you went home."[90] Neither woman had the power
or bat speed to hit particularly well, so Oscar encouraged them
to try to get on base with bunts and Baltimore chops.

Spring training began in Norfolk, Virginia, on April 12. Within
days the Clowns were barnstorming their way through the Car-
olinas. By May 3 they were in Key West with the Monarchs.
Then they turned around and barnstormed their way north
through Florida and the mid-Atlantic before arriving in Birmingham on May 15 to kick off the NAL regular season against
the Black Barons. The Clowns won the opener, 10–6, in a game
highlighted by a nifty stop by Morgan that led to a double play.
With Ray Neil and George Wannamaker leading the way, by
June 28 the Clowns were winning games at a .667 clip. They
still trailed the Black Barons at the halfway point, but thanks in
part to the pitching of Johnny Wright, who joined the team in
the season's second half, the club surged into first by the end of
August. The season's highlights included Oscar's managing the
East in the August 22 East-West game, a 6–4 loss, and pitcher
Dave Amaro's 11⅔ innings of no-hit relief in an 8–4 win in St.
Joseph, Michigan.

Syd Pollock's son, Alan, met Oscar in Kingston, New York, that
summer. What stood out, he remembered, was that "Charleston's
face matched his reputation. His eyes, clear and intense, below
bushy, defined eyebrows, radiated strength, confidence, knowledge. His smile was contagious. He was tall and stately. He had
the character and grace inherent to so many who spent their
lives on the road in black baseball. He was distinguished and
charming. He was competent and businesslike." When Syd told
Charleston that Alan wanted to be a center fielder, Oscar smiled

and put Alan next to him on the bench, giving him pointers as they watched Verdes Drake play the position for the Clowns.[91]

To have remained calm while serving as the ringmaster of the Clowns' traveling circus meant Oscar *must* have found some peace. His jobs included ensuring that the Clowns weren't financially cheated by their hosts via an artificially low gate count; keeping Tut and Bebop energetically engaging the fans through their various routines; dealing with Hamman, a flatulent former semipro player who was a minority owner of the team and a man after Pollock's own heart when it came to both publicity and money (Hamman absolutely refused to tip); working Pollock family members into the schedule, as on July 9, when the team took the day off to go see Syd's daughter Estelle and her husband Alfonso star in their own Broadway vaudeville show; serving as a father figure to the more youthful members of the club, especially the women, who appreciated their manager's loyalty; and, oh yes, winning games—at least half of them, as Pollock had demanded the previous winter.

Charleston managed it all even better than Pollock had hoped. His presence on the squad helped sell tickets, and by September 11 the Clowns had clinched the flag, giving Pollock his fourth NAL championship in five years and Oscar his first official championship since 1935. Both men were thrilled. Ever since he had stopped playing regularly, said Oscar, all he had wanted to do was lead another team to a pennant.[92] Soon, he and Syd had signed a contract to reprise their relationship in 1955.

Then, just days after he had finally returned to his Philadelphia home from his long season traveling with the Clowns, Oscar fell. He couldn't get up.

• • •

Somehow Oscar had lost his balance and tumbled down a complete flight of steps. At first it was thought he had suffered a stroke or that he had fallen because of an old spinal injury incurred while working for the railroad. It's possible his bones had been weakened by the cancer with which Oscar was ultimately diagnosed and which must have been the reason he had not felt well throughout the 1954 season. [93] Whatever the cause, the fall at his Sedgley Avenue row home left Oscar paralyzed from the belly button down. "I feel fine—what I can feel," he reported to Stanley Glenn when his former catcher visited him at Philadelphia General Hospital. It was a disorienting visit. Glenn had known Oscar for more than a decade and had never even seen him with so much as a cold. The man who had seemed so "strong and carefree" now lay in critical condition.[94] As optimistic as ever, Oscar told his visitors that he would shortly be up and about.[95] But hope that he would recover was soon extinguished. On Tuesday, October 5, Oscar Charleston died, just nine days shy of his fifty-eighth birthday.

A viewing was held at the Chew Funeral Home on Christian Street in south Philadelphia. "No church was big enough," thought Glenn (Charleston was probably not affiliated with a church anyway). With Oscar's sister Katherine there to represent the family, thousands of fans filed through to pay their respects, since "everybody knew Charleston." Energy seemed to radiate from Oscar's body, even in the coffin. "He looked like he was going to jump out of there and say hello to you," remembered Glenn. Another viewing was held in Indianapolis on Sunday, October 10, at the Jacobs Funeral Home. The funeral at Mt. Paran Baptist Church, where Oscar had married Hazel Grubbs back in 1917, was held the next day.[96]

Katherine and the rest of the family received telegrams, flowers, and messages of sympathy from a number of baseball figures, while public tributes poured in through the black press. "The blunt truth is that Charleston was a greater outfielder than Mays," wrote Russ Cowans in the *Chicago Defender*. "Charleston was the greatest outfielder I've ever seen," agreed Bingo DeMoss. "Oscar Charleston was the greatest ball player that ever lived," said Monarchs co-owner Tom Baird, not letting his membership in the Ku Klux Klan keep him from recognizing this truth, at least.[97] "The death of Oscar Charleston removes from this green earth the greatest all-round Negro ball player of all times," wrote Fay Young.[98] Just two months before Charleston's death, the great Honus Wagner had lent his own voice to the chorus. "I've seen all the great many players in the many years I've been around," said Wagner, "and have yet to see one any greater than Charleston."[99]

• • •

From about the time Oscar Charleston died, when the best young black players were no longer making a stop in the fast-fading Negro Leagues on their way to the Majors, until sometime in the 1970s, when there arose a coterie of new baseball researchers and scholars interested in blackball, the Negro Leagues were little talked about. For a generation, more or less, almost no one interviewed the veterans of black baseball. No one made documentaries or films about them. No one made them objects of historical study. No one put up statues or historical plaques. No one made or wore throwback jerseys. No one tried to compile the leagues' statistical record. No one paid honor to the leagues in any way at all. The era of segregated baseball was too close to the present, and too painful, to be considered fit for any of these purposes.

In the 1950s and 1960s about the only discussion of the Negro Leagues took place within the borders of nostalgic "remember when?" columns penned by older men in the black (and, occasionally, mainstream) sports press. Such writers wanted contemporary readers, especially younger ones, to remember the diamond stars who had preceded the now famous Jackie Robinson, Roy Campanella, Ernie Banks, Willie Mays, and the last generation of Negro League stars like Satchel Paige and Josh Gibson. Many of these scribes—writers like Sam Lacy, A. S. "Doc" Young, Russ Cowans, Sheep Jackson, and Ric Roberts—had seen men like Pete Hill, John Henry Lloyd, and Cannonball Redding play. If they hadn't, they nevertheless saw themselves as transmitters of the stories and knowledge handed down by the sportswriters who *had* seen those players in action. They did not wish for the history of the craft of black baseball to be lost. Charleston was probably mentioned more often than anyone in these reminiscences, but that didn't mean much in the larger world.

Various falsehoods and legends about Oscar sprouted during his afterlife. He became six feet tall or even 6 feet three inches.[100] He had threatened Ty Cobb and another player in Cuba, saying, "The first one that calls me a n——, I'm going to beat the hell out of you."[101] He had brought Jackie Robinson to Branch Rickey's attention.[102] His right arm was so much longer than his left that he could reach "halfway to second base" when he was playing first.[103] And so on. But authentic anecdotes and more sober assessments were also heard. Former Negro Leagues figures from Sam Lacy to Satchel Paige to Buck O'Neil to Turkey Stearnes, along with a host of lesser-known men, said he was the best player they had ever seen. A number of whites said much the same thing, just as so many had while Oscar was still alive. Former commissioner Happy Chandler said that Cobb and Charleston were the greatest ballplayers he had ever laid eyes on.[104] Ex-Reds pitcher Paul Derringer said Oscar was the toughest hitter he had ever faced.[105] Hollis Thurston, former Browns pitcher, asked Connie Johnson one day, "You know Oscar Charleston?" Johnson assured him he did—that Charleston, in fact, was the man who had brought him into professional baseball. Well, replied Thurston, "I've seen Babe Ruth and Foxx and all of 'em—that's the greatest hitter I ever seen. We barnstormed with him one year and he hit home runs every night! I ain't never seen nobody hit like that!"[106]

Ultimately, testimonies such as these helped usher Oscar into the Hall of Fame. In 1971 a Special Committee on the Negro Leagues was formed by Commissioner Bowie Kuhn. With Monte Irvin as its chair, and with men like Roy Campanella, Eddie Gottlieb, Judy Johnson, and Wendell Smith as members, the committee was charged with electing to the Hall one or two Negro Leaguers per year until its work was done—a slow-as-it-goes approach that did not exactly endear the Hall to the African American community. Satchel Paige, in 1971, was the committee's first selection. Josh Gibson and Buck Leonard were the 1972 choices, followed by Irvin in 1973, Bell in 1974, Johnson in 1975, and, finally, Oscar Charleston in 1976.[107]

The Hall's 1976 inductees were announced on February 10. Charleston would go in with umpire Cal Hubbard, Roger Connor (deceased), Fred Lindstrom, Bob Lemon, and Robin Roberts. Oscar's siblings—Katherine, Casper, and Benny were the only ones still alive—were thrilled, and the late Shedrick's widow Maude was excited too.[108] Yet although they all made their homes in Indianapolis, the Charlestons lived such quiet, unassuming lives that the Hall of Fame nearly failed to locate them. Only after *Indianapolis Star* columnist Bob Collins reported in June 1976 that "a search has turned up no heirs, no old friends," and lamented that Oscar would not have a representative at the ceremony unless the city sent someone itself, did Katherine finally come forward.[109]

When induction day arrived on August 9, Katherine and her husband George awoke at the palatial Otesaga Hotel on the shores of its namesake lake. The ceremony that afternoon was supposed to take place, as usual, on the stone steps of the National Baseball Library, but the threat of continuing rain forced the festivities inside to the Otesaga's ballroom. By the time the event began that afternoon, numerous people who had known Oscar were in their seats, including Judy Johnson, Cool Papa Bell, Buck Leonard, Bob Feller, and umpire Jocko Conlan. Wearing a green and white dress and a necklace of pearls, Katherine sat with the other inductees. With her hair combed straight back, she looked uncannily like her brother when she smiled, and she smiled often. At the moment, though, she was nervous.

A parade of dignitaries kicked things off: Dick Dozer, the president of the Baseball Writers' Association of America; Gerald Clark, mayor of Cooperstown; Shirley Povich, winner of the J. G. Taylor Spink Award and another man who had known Katherine's brother; and lastly the commissioner himself, Bowie Kuhn. All the Hall of Famers present were then introduced before Commissioner Kuhn finally came to the matter at hand. "The first plaque honors a man who John McGraw called the greatest player he had ever seen," said the commissioner, by way of introducing Charleston. "Jocko Conlan, who is here today, watched him play in Chicago and says he was as good as Tris Speaker. Cool Papa Bell, who you have just met, says that he was the Willie Mays of his day." He then read Oscar's plaque: "Rated among all-time greats of Negro Leagues. Versatile star batted well over .300 most years. Speed, strong arm, and fielding instincts made him stand out center fielder. Later moved to first base. Also managed several teams during 40 years in Negro baseball." A plaque can only say so much, but this was not only incomplete, but also rather misleading. It highlighted Oscar's versatility, for which Oscar wasn't really known, save for those rare occasions when he played multiple positions as an entertainment act. But there was no mention of his power. The Hall's writeup made Charleston sound like a singles hitter with a good glove.

Needless to say, Katherine didn't care. After Kuhn's introduction, she stepped up to the podium and took a full thirty seconds to compose herself. At length, in her sweet, high, grandmotherly voice, she explained, "I pause because this is the greatest delight of my whole life," putting emphasis on each of those last six words. "For twenty-two years I prayed and hoped that this day would come. He's well-deserving and I appreciate the privilege of being able to accept this plaque in the honor of my brother's name." Oscar's "life was baseball," concluded Katherine.[110] Baseball, finally, had noticed.

Epilogue

Enshrinement in Cooperstown recognizes more than it confers fame, especially for a Negro Leagues player who never spent a day in the Majors. After his plaque was hung with the rest, Oscar Charleston slipped once again into comparative obscurity. Had he lived longer and been blessed with children, he might have received the same treatment accorded Cool Papa Bell. Five years after Bell died, a special memorial was erected at his grave with a solemn ceremony attended by local dignitaries. Tributes were read from a sitting U.S. senator, the governor, and others. July 20, 1996, was even proclaimed "Cool Papa Bell Day" by the state of Missouri. In contrast, just five years after Katherine had represented Oscar in Cooperstown, the Indiana Baseball Hall of Fame was unable to locate any of Oscar's relatives for its own induction of Oscar.[1] There have been several temporary tributes and exhibits honoring Charleston and the legacy of black baseball in Indianapolis since that time. But when ABCs historian Paul Debono led the charge to get a permanent Oscar Charleston memorial erected in the 1990s, the best he and his allies could do was get a park renamed in Oscar's honor on the east side of town. That was in 1998, and despite the *Indianapolis Star's* efforts to retrieve Charleston's memory every few years, it seems that widespread recognition, even in his hometown, will forever elude Oscar.[2]

To wit: in 1999, *Washington Post* columnist Thomas Boswell, a purported expert on baseball, heaped sarcasm on *The Sporting News's* ranking of Oscar Charleston as the sixty-seventh best player of all time. "I'm truly tempted to research Oscar Charleston," wrote Boswell, who apparently couldn't be bothered to do so before filing his piece (the internet *did* exist in 1999). "Was he a nineteenth-century player? A Negro Leagues star? A legend in Antarctic sandlot ball?" He didn't need to look into who Oscar was or what he had done; it was obvious to Boswell that it was impossible for Charleston to have been better than such transcendent luminaries as Eddie Murray, Wade Boggs, and Paul Molitor.[3] Presumably, Boswell was made happier by the ESPN Hall of 100 approach, which still leaves out Negro Leaguers entirely, and by a 2003 *Sports Illustrated* article that named Charleston the thirteenth greatest sports figure—to have come from the state of Indiana. On that list Oscar came in one spot below Gil Hodges. And eight spots below Chuck Klein.

• • •

When it was announced that Oscar had been elected to the Hall of Fame, Elizabeth Overton asked her aunt Janie Charleston whether she had kept any memorabilia related to, or photos of, Cooperstown's newest member. "I hope not," Janie answered, in a tone that made it clear she did not wish to discuss the subject. Elizabeth pondered that answer for some time. She could never decide whether Janie meant she hoped she had given all of Oscar's effects to his sister Katherine, as she had intended, or whether she meant she did not wish to have any reminders of her late husband in her possession.

After the redoubtable Janie died on October 27, 1993, Elizabeth found that she had kept at least one item related to her marriage. Sometime in the late 1920s Oscar had given his wife a special gift. He had blown up a photo of himself standing at the plate, in a Hilldale uniform, and then had a Bethlehem, Pennsylvania, craftsman carve a silhouette of his figure. The photo was pasted to the front of the silhouette to make a small wooden figurine. On its back, Oscar had signed the gift "To Jane B. Charleston. From Oscar." Not an especially sentimental message, yet Janie had kept the present for decades—knowingly, in Elizabeth's estimation.

In summer 2017 I paid Elizabeth a visit to talk to her about Janie and collect some photos. We had a lovely conversation, and I learned much about Janie and her family, but other than the one pasted on the wooden statue, there were no further pictures of Oscar. The next day Elizabeth gave me a call. She had found another of Janie's photo albums, and this one included two pictures of my subject.

A few months later I dropped in on Elizabeth to see these images. One, of Oscar standing with Pittsburgh Crawfords secretary John Clark, a man who would go on to become an astute political journalist, I had seen before.[4] But the other was completely new. It showed a young, Jazz Age Oscar, probably right around the time at which he met Janie, leaning against a porch post and dressed casually in driving cap, sweater, tie, and pinstriped pants. Oscar gazes straight into the camera with a steady, cool, piercing stare. This was the man Janie had fallen in love with: well dressed, attractive, confident, strong. A man in the midst of establishing a record of athletic achievement that, if it were only more widely known, would be regarded as one of the finest such records in American history.

The eyes in that photo belonged to a man who didn't need others' approbation. Was Oscar Charleston underrated, misunderstood, and largely forgotten? What of it? For all the pain Oscar must have cost her, for all his absences, for all his too-human flaws, it didn't surprise me that this was one photo Janie had decided to keep.

ACKNOWLEDGMENTS

I humbly acknowledge, to begin with, the many researchers and historians who through their patient work have ensured that the legacies of those who were associated with the Negro Leagues would not be lost. I am grateful to them all, whether named here or not. I am especially grateful to those who generously gave their time and knowledge when I approached them, often in a state of desperate ignorance. John Holway, James A. Riley, Paul Debono, Roberto González Echevarría, Bill Heward, Neil Lanctot, and Bob Luke, in particular, kindly answered my questions, and Gary Ashwill pulled crucial statistical information from his unparalleled Seamheads.com database. Murray Polner and Lee Lowenfish not only patiently corresponded with me about Charleston's association with Branch Rickey, about whom both have written excellent biographies, but also took the time to connect me with others. Tim Rives, fine historian not only of the Negro Leagues but also of presidents, performed the same service while providing me with encouragement and feedback throughout this project. I am thankful for his friendship.

No less helpful were the various librarians and archivists who provided me with assistance. In this category I am happy to thank the wonderful Peter Clark, John Horne, and Cassidy Lent at the National Baseball Hall of Fame; Ray Doswell and the staff at the Negro Leagues Museum in Kansas City; Jeff Flannery at the Library of Congress; Cereese Woody at the Marion County records office; Clifford Muse and the staff at Howard

University's Moorland-Spingarn Research Center; Brittany Webb and Dejay Duckett at the African American Museum in Philadelphia; Jim O'Donnell, Ginny Sylvester, and the Interlibrary Loan staff at Arizona State University; the staff at the Indiana State Library; and Richard Buthod at the St Louis City Recorder of Deeds Office.

I started this project too late to speak with many former Negro Leagues players and their relatives. But I was fortunate enough to speak with Sam Allen, Harold Hair, Mamie Johnson, Cliff Layton, Jim Robinson, Carl Rogan, and Herb Walker. Satchel Paige's son Robert and Jackie Robinson's widow, Rachel, graciously took time to answer my questions, and Indianapolis native John Charleston kindly confirmed for me that he was *not*, as one newspaper had misreported, Oscar's son (or relation of any kind). Others in the baseball community who spoke to or corresponded with me included Carl Erskine, Branch Rickey III, and Ty Cobb biographer Charles Leerhsen. John Schulian was unbelievably generous, speaking with me on several occasions and sharing with me his extensive interview notes with Charleston family members and former players. But would one expect anything less from the creator of *Xena, Warrior Princess*?

Besides former players, there were precious few people still left to whom I could speak who knew either Oscar or Jane Charleston personally. One of them was Rodney Redman, whose aunt was married to Oscar's brother Shedrick. Another was Elizabeth Overton, Janie's great-niece and the keeper of the family history. Mrs. Overton unstintingly shared her family photos, memories, and insights; this book would be immeasurably poorer without her help, and I was deeply saddened to hear of her death in March 2018. Elizabeth's daughter, Miriam Phields, also helpfully provided additional crucially important information and context.

I was introduced to Mrs. Overton by Calobe Jackson Jr., Harrisburg historian par excellence. Calobe pointed me to important sources and nuggets of information about the Charlestons and Harrisburg generally. I was led to Calobe by Ted Knorr, Negro Leagues trivia master and premier historian of Harrisburg black baseball. I salute both men.

No one was more helpful or encouraging than Larry Lester, without whose decades of research and efforts on behalf of black baseball history this biography would have been impossible. Larry not only shared with me absolutely everything he had related to Charleston—letters, photos, articles, statistics—but he also introduced me to numerous others and championed this project in the Negro Leagues research community. He is one of the best men I know.

Many other acquaintances, friends, and colleagues helped me by sharpening my arguments, helping with research, sharing information, reading drafts, translating materials, and assuring me that I was not wasting my time. I would like to thank especially Eduardo Andino, Gregg Doyel, Frank Guridy, Leslie Heaphy, Tim Hoiland, Bill Kauffman, Jon Lauck, Will Luzader, Gary Mitchem, Rich Puerzer, Beverly Reese, Abigail Shelton, Carter Skeel, Sharon Skeel, Cecilia Tan, and Steve Wilson. I also extend heartfelt thanks to Rob Taylor and Courtney Ochsner at the University of Nebraska Press.

It is customary to say, right about now, that no one was more helpful than the author's spouse. I will not break with convention. No matter how much time—or money—I spent on this project, my beautiful wife, Kara, was never anything but utterly supportive. She even spent a week in the archives of the National Baseball Hall of Fame with me, diligently combing through files, and fell in love with Cooperstown as a result. By this point she knows nearly as much about Oscar as anyone in the world, whether she would or not! I am very blessed.

Anyone who writes about the Negro Leagues owes his greatest debt to the men (and women!) who played the game. They weren't unrecognized, at least in the black community, but they weren't recognized as much as they deserved. They weren't financially unrewarded, but they did not receive the remuneration enjoyed by their white counterparts. They weren't embittered, but they had a just claim to have received much better. They weren't superheroes, but they deserve our admiration and respect. I have grown through the study of their lives, and I am honored to have made their acquaintance.

APPENDIX

Statistical Record

The number of box scores and game results reported, or later discovered, in which Oscar Charleston played and/or managed is dwarfed by the many that were unreported or have been undiscovered (although it is surely true that the majority of games for which statistics and results are not extant consisted of contests versus semipro teams). The record, such as we have it, is therefore radically incomplete. Were we able to take into account all of his professional games, Charleston probably had, for example, at least three times as many plate appearances as reported here. In any case, note that the statistics below represent those compiled in games versus major competition only. Unless otherwise noted, all statistics come from Seamheads.com.

Batting

Year	Team	League	PA	2B	3B	HR	RBI	SB	AVG	OBP	SLG	OPS+
1915	Indianapolis ABCs	Independent	241	9	5	2	31	14	.258	.302	.371	99
1915–16	Indianapolis ABCs	Cuba, exhibition	77	1	1	0	6	2	.191	.253	.235	39
1916	New York Lincoln Stars	Independent	73	0	1	0	4	5	.344	.417	.375	124
1916	Indianapolis ABCs*	Independent	68	1	2	0	9	2	.293	.359	.379	120
1916–17	Royal Poinciana*	Florida Hotel League	45	0	0	0	1	1	.158	.273	.158	62
1917	Indianapolis ABCs	Independent	205	6	4	1	19	3	.292	.354	.388	146
1918	Indianapolis ABCs	Independent	171	8	8	3	46	13	.390	.437	.604	196
1919	Chicago American Giants	Independent	188	7	6	8	42	13	.409	.467	.671	245
1919	Detroit Stars	Independent	18	2	0	0	3	3	.313	.389	.438	134
1920	Indianapolis ABCs	NNL 1[1]	398	20	11	5	59	20	.353	.418	.517	176
1920	St. Louis Giants	Exhibition vs. Majors	18	1	3	1	4	3	.615	.722	1.385	612
1920–21	Atlantic City Bacharach Giants[2]	Cuba	62	2	1	0	4	3	.357	.410	.429	189
1921	St. Louis Giants	NNL 1	339	17	12	15	91	32	.433	.512	.736	249
1921	St. Louis Giants	Exhibition vs. Majors	23	2	2	2	10	0	.304	.304	.826	185
1922	Indianapolis ABCs	NNL 1	441	24	18	19	100	21	.375	.435	.676	195
1922	St. Louis Stars	Exhibition vs. Majors	13	2	1	1	1	2	.462	.462	1.000	281
1922–23	Santa Clara	Cuban League	90	7	5	1	22	8	.418	.483	.671	231

1923	Indianapolis ABCs	NNL 1	373	25	6	11	94	25	.364	.453	.591	168
1923	Detroit Stars	Exhibition vs. Majors	12	1	0	3	5	0	.500	.583	1.500	450
1923	Chicago American Giants	Exhibition vs. Majors	8	1	0	0	1	1	.333	.500	.500	193
1923–24	Santa Clara*[3]	Cuban League	282	16	4	4	33	36	.376	.464	.533	169
1924	Harrisburg Giants	Eastern Colored League	236	22	5	15	63	20	.405	.476	.780	254
1924–25	Almendares*[4]	Cuban League	153	10	4	4		0	.261		.458	
1925	Harrisburg Giants	Eastern Colored League	321	23	3	20	97	17	.427	.523	.776	228
1925–26	Habana[5]	Cuban League	40	3	2	2		0	.350		.675	
1926	Harrisburg Giants	Eastern Colored League	212	12	1	10	43	24	.308	.438	.568	173
1926	Hilldale club	Exhibition vs. Majors	24	1	0	1	3	0	.190	.292	.381	113
1926	Homestead Grays	Exhibition vs. Majors	13	1	0	0	2	1	.167	.167	.250	35
1926–27	Havana Reds[6]	Triangular (Cuba)	151						.404			
1927	Harrisburg Giants	Eastern Colored League	305	20	7	13	74	21	.399	.502	.694	209
1927–28	Cuba	Cuban League	155	7	2	5	26	11	.350	.481	.567	172
1928	Hilldale club	Independent	251	11	6	11	44	11	.348	.453	.618	184
1928–29	Cuba	Cuban League	114	6	4	4		6	.333		.561	
1929	Hilldale club	Independent	341	23	7	7	61	8	.360	.468	.571	150
1929	Homestead Grays[7]	Exhibition vs. Majors	15	2	0	0	2	0	.462	.533	.615	
1930	Homestead Grays*[8]	Independent	142	8	1	4	36	3	.290	.375	.468	

Year	Team	League	PA	2B	3B	HR	RBI	SB	AVG	OBP	SLG	OPS+
1930–31	Marianao[9]	Unico (Cuba)	51	0	5	0		4	.373		.569	
1931	Homestead Grays*	Independent	193	9	4	3	35	2	.343	.402	.491	
1932	Pittsburgh Crawfords	Independent	185	14	0	3	31	4	.350	.425	.494	139
1933	Pittsburgh Crawfords*	NNL 2[10]	260	17	6	13	60	5	.338	.397	.628	176
1934	Pittsburgh Crawfords	NNL 2	232	10	2	7	41	5	.322	.410	.497	156
1935	Pittsburgh Crawfords*	NNL 2	163	10	1	2	28	8	.273	.346	.399	87
1935	Pittsburgh Crawfords	NNL Champion Series	30	0	0	3	5	0	.308	.400	.654	196
1936	Pittsburgh Crawfords*	NNL 2	83	8	0	4	16	0	.373	.475	.672	193
1936	NNL All-Stars	Exhibition vs. Majors	4	0	0	0	0	0	.250	.250	.250	53
1937	Pittsburgh Crawfords	NNL 2	40	2	0	1	6	0	.250	.308	.389	85
1938	Pittsburgh Crawfords	NNL 2	1	0	0	0	0	0	.000	.000	.000	-100
1939	Toledo Crawfords	NNL 2/NAL	53	2	0	1	4	0	.283	.377	.391	116
1940	Toledo/Ind. Crawfords	NAL	16	0	0	0	2	1	.385	.500	.385	176
1941	Philadelphia Stars	NNL 2	3	0	0	0	0	0	.000	.667	.000	100
TOTAL			6,932	373	150	209	1,264	358	.352	.446[11]	.574[12]	100

Managerial

Year[13]	Team	League	Wins	Losses	Ties	Pct.
1924	Harrisburg Giants	Eastern Colored League	30	31	0	.492
1925	Harrisburg Giants	Eastern Colored League	48	24	1	.667
1926	Harrisburg Giants	Eastern Colored League	27	22	0	.551
1927	Harrisburg Giants	Eastern Colored League	41	32	0	.562
1932	Pittsburgh Crawfords	Independent	32	26	1	.552
1933	Pittsburgh Crawfords*	NNL 2	47	35	2	.573
1934	Pittsburgh Crawfords	NNL 2	51	29	3	.638
1935	Pittsburgh Crawfords*	NNL 2	49	22	3	.690
1935	Pittsburgh Crawfords	NNL Championship Series	4	3	0	.571
1936	Pittsburgh Crawfords*	NNL 2	43	31	2	.581
1936	NNL All-Stars	Independent	1	2	0	.333
1937	Pittsburgh Crawfords	NNL 2	21	33	1	.389
1937	NNL All-Stars	Independent	2	1	0	.667
1938	Pittsburgh Crawfords	NNL 2	22	21	1	.512
1939	Toledo Crawfords	NNL 2/NAL	12	16	2	.400
1940	Toledo/Indianapolis Crawfords	NAL	6	19	0	.240
1941	Philadelphia Stars	NNL 2	14	39	0	.264
1948	Philadelphia Stars	NNL 2	27	29	0	.482
1949	Philadelphia Stars	NAL	31	38	0	.449
1950	Philadelphia Stars	NAL	15	28	1	.349
1951	Philadelphia Stars	NAL	18	28	0	.391
1952	Philadelphia Stars	NAL	22	38	0	.367
1954	Indianapolis Clowns*	NAL	43	22	0	.662
TOTAL			606	535	17	.523

* Denotes that team credibly claimed a season championship.

    1. The Negro National League in its first, Rube Foster–driven incarnation.

    2. Includes statistics compiled in both the American Series and the Cuban Winter League.

    3. Includes statistics compiled in both the Cuban Winter League and the Grand Winter Championship.

    4. Statistics from Figueredo, *Cuban Baseball*, 159. The number given under plate appearances here represents at bats only, as Figueredo does not provide PA data.

Oscar also played in the American Series in Cuba following the Cuban League season, but those statistics are not available.

5. Statistics from Figueredo, *Cuban Baseball*, 165. The number given under plate appearances here represents at bats only, as Figueredo does not provide PA data.

6. Statistics from Figueredo, *Cuban Baseball*, 173. For this season Figueredo provides data only for at bats (the number given here under PAS), runs, and hits.

7. These statistics are courtesy of Larry Lester.

8. The 1930–31 statistics reported here are courtesy of Larry Lester. His database for these years is more complete than that of Seamheads.

9. Statistics from Figueredo, *Cuban Baseball*, 194. The number given under plate appearances here represents at bats only, as Figueredo does not provide PA data.

10. The NNL in its second, Gus Greenlee–driven incarnation.

11. Calculation does not count years for which walks are unavailable.

12. Calculation does not count year for which extra base hits are unavailable.

13. Managerial records for 1924 through 1941 are from Seamheads.com, with the exception of 1927, the records for which may be found, along with the records for 1948 onward, at the website of the Center for Negro League Baseball Research (CNLBR) at www.cnlbr.org. Note, however, that the Seamheads records count all games versus major competition, whether official league games or not, whereas the records from the CNLBR represent results from official league games only.

NOTES

Abbreviations

HOF. National Baseball Hall of Fame and Museum Archive and Collection. Cooperstown NY.

JSP. John Schulian Papers, in author's possession. Materials and notes from interviews conducted by journalist John Schulian in connection with his 2003 *Sports Illustrated* feature on Oscar Charleston, later included in his volume *Sometimes They Even Shook Your Hand.*

OCS. Oscar Charleston Scrapbook. Negro Leagues Baseball Museum. Kansas City MO.

SPL. Syd Pollock Letters, in author's possession. Letters from Syd Pollock to Oscar Charleston and other recipients in 1953 and 1954, owned by Larry Lester and shared with author.

BRP. Branch Rickey Papers, in Library of Congress.

Introduction

1. For more on the Clowns, see Pollock, *Barnstorming to Heaven.* Bill Heward provides a colorful personal account of life with the now integrated but even more ragged Clowns as they existed in the early 1970s in his *Some Are Called Clowns.*

2. From a Clowns program located in the Branch Rickey Papers at the Library of Congress. That Rickey was apparently still following the career of Oscar Charleston in 1954 says something about the relationship that must have existed between the two men.

3. "Big Crowd Expected for Monarchs' Game," *Joplin Globe,* September 5, 1954, 27.

4. "Monarchs Defeat Indianapolis, 6–4," *Joplin Globe,* September 11, 1954, 8.

5. W. Rollo Wilson, "Clowns Manager Succumbs at Fifty-Seven," *Pittsburgh Courier,* October 16, 1954, 12.

6. "Hospital Notes," *Joplin Globe,* September 12, 1954, 56.

7. This information comes from Charleston's death certificate and from the account of his death given by Bill Dallas in the *Philadelphia Evening Bulletin,* October 8, 1954. Dallas gets the time of death wrong, however.

8. O'Neil, *I Was Right on Time,* 25.

9. This error was not corrected even when Campanella's biography was brought out in a new edition by the University of Nebraska Press in 1995, a point I mention not to needle the press but to illustrate how obscure Charleston had by then become.

10. From Ted Williams speech at Cooperstown. Available at various websites. See, e.g., "Throwback: Ted Williams' Hall of Fame Speech," July 27, 2014, http://mlb .nbcsports.com/2014/07/27/throwback-ted-williams-hall-of-fame-speech/.

11. Peterson, *Only the Ball Was White*, 241–43.

12. Quoted in Holway, *Voices from the Great Black Baseball Leagues*, 120, 196, 54.

13. Bell quoted in Bankes, *The Pittsburgh Crawfords*, 54. McGraw's claim was first noted, it seems, by Chester L. Washington in his column in the *Pittsburgh Courier*, July 15, 1939, 16. The story of the wrestler is provided by Washington in "'Ches' Sez: Rap's Homer Beats Grays," *Pittsburgh Courier*, August 3, 1935, A4.

14. Larry Tye, when researching his biography of Satchel Paige, was told by radio station WGN in Chicago that its archives do not go back far enough to include the interviews with Negro Leaguers conducted in the 1930s and '40s.

15. See James, *Popular Crime*, and James and James, *The Man from the Train*.

16. James, *The New Bill James Historical Baseball Abstract*.

17. Quoted in Schulian, *Sometimes They Even Shook Your Hand*, 166.

18. James, *The New Bill James Historical Baseball Abstract*, 359.

19. Actually, he appeared on the October 1934 cover of *Colored Baseball and Sports Monthly*. This is the only exception I know of to James's claim.

20. James, *The New Bill James Historical Baseball Abstract*, 359–60.

21. James, *The New Bill James Historical Baseball Abstract*, 360.

22. McNeil, *Cool Papas and Double Duties*, 192.

23. James, *The New Bill James Historical Baseball Abstract*, 360.

24. James, *The New Bill James Historical Baseball Abstract*, 189.

25. Quoted in James, *The New Bill James Historical Baseball Abstract*, 189. See Trouppe, *Twenty Years Too Soon*, 118. Trouppe renders Borgmann's name as Bernie Borgan, and therefore James does as well. I am grateful to Branch Rickey biographer Lee Lowenfish for pointing out this error to me. Borgmann (given name Bernhard) was inducted into the Naismith Memorial Basketball Hall of Fame in 1961.

26. Quoted in James, *The New Bill James Historical Baseball Abstract*, 189.

27. Quoted in Peterson, *Only the Ball Was White*, 12.

28. Benson quoted in Holway, *Black Diamonds*, 79.

29. James, *The New Bill James Historical Baseball Abstract*, 175.

30. James, *The New Bill James Historical Baseball Abstract*, 177–78.

31. James, *The New Bill James Historical Baseball Abstract*, 192.

32. James, *The New Bill James Historical Baseball Abstract*, 192.

33. David Bodenhamer and Robert Barrows lamented in the mid-1990s that Indianapolis "does not know well its own rich history." *Encyclopedia of Indianapolis*, 2.

34. McNeil, *Cool Papas and Double Duties*, 192.

35. See the Oscar Charleston page in the Seamheads database at http://www .seamheads.com/NegroLgs/player.php?ID=134&tab=2. WAR is a comprehensive

measure of player value that takes into account, at least theoretically, both offense (including base running) and defense.

36. See Golenbock, *Bums*, 114, and King, "Campanella Not Antique but Modernizer," 3. My thanks to Neil Lanctot for leading me to these sources.

37. McNeil, *Cool Papas and Double Duties*, 172.

38. Ribowsky, *A Complete History of the Negro Leagues*, 87.

39. Ribowsky, *A Complete History of the Negro Leagues*, 277.

40. Ribowsky, *The Power and the Darkness*, 45–46.

41. Leerhsen, *Ty Cobb*, 331. Leerhsen documents the violence characteristic of baseball during the Cobb era in numerous other places throughout this biography.

42. Gregory, *Diz*, 63.

43. Charleston's scrapbook (OCS) and photo album (held by the Negro Leagues Baseball Museum in Kansas City MO) attest to this judgment. The scrapbook includes numerous boxing-related clippings, including a Cuban newspaper story about Charleston going into the ring himself in Cuba. This fight took place in late 1925 and featured Oscar versus a Spanish wrestler-turned-pugilist named Andres Castanos. The author of an article previewing the fight (in OCS) claimed that Oscar "is an excellent boxer and uses his left hand with extreme efficiency. Charleston boxes as well as he fields flies. He hits very hard." Oscar's brother Roy was a locally prominent and successful fighter in Indianapolis.

44. John Schulian, telephone interview, November 7, 2015. Schulian's article on Charleston is the best piece ever written about the man. It is collected in Schulian's *Sometimes They Even Shook Your Hand.*

45. Rodney Redman, telephone interview, December 28, 2015; Mamie Johnson, telephone interview, August 12, 2015; James Robinson, telephone interview, December 28, 2015; Cliff Layton, telephone interview, August 21, 2015.

46. Will, *Men at Work*, 4.

47. See, e.g., McNeil, *Black Baseball out of Season*, 4.

48. William Brashler, for example, uses this players-as-victims trope in his biography of Josh Gibson (*Josh Gibson*, xv).

49. As Monte Irvin writes in his memoir, "On Saturday or Sunday [black fans] went to a game and saw players the same color performing well on the baseball diamond. That made them feel pretty good and just generally uplifted their spirit" (Irvin with Riley, *Nice Guys Finish First*, 66).

50. As Dodgers scout Clyde Sukeforth states explicitly in Golenbock, *Bums*, 114. Even so, as Branch Rickey III pointed out to me, the claim that Charleston did recommend Jackie to Rickey has become embedded enough in the game's mythology that it is repeated on the back of a National Baseball Hall of Fame bookmark featuring Charleston.

51. Genovese, *Roll, Jordan, Roll*, xvi.

52. Genovese, *Roll, Jordan, Roll*, 394.

53. Genovese, *Roll, Jordan, Roll*, 451.

54. Genovese, *Roll, Jordan, Roll*, 279.

55. O'Neil, *I Was Right on Time*, 44–45, 9.

56. Rogosin, *Invisible Men*, 68.

1. Batboy, 1896–1912

1. Until I obtained her death certificate from the Marion County authorities, my research had led me to believe that Mary was the second child of Albert Thomas, born circa 1835, and his wife Harrett (possibly Harriett), born circa 1851. We find this Thomas family in the 1880 U.S. census. In addition to Mary, the children of this household included (in order) Steve, Shed, Corniel, and Ed. Albert was a laborer, and Harrett kept house. Neither could read or write. Despite the different parental names given on Mary's death certificate, it's hard to dismiss the idea that this was the Thomas family in which Mary was raised. First, this is the only census record listing a black Mary Thomas living in Tennessee and born in 1872 to parents who were also both born in Tennessee. (The Charleston family entry in the 1900 census also says that both of Mary's parents were born in Tennessee; hence the importance of this criterion.) Second, the district in which Albert and Harrett Thomas lived is about fifteen miles north of the city of Nashville, and that is the city from which Tom and Mary Charleston later emigrated to Indiana. Third and most important, Mary Charleston named one of her sons Shedrick. That's a distinctive name, to say the least, and the Mary Thomas who was raised by Albert and Harrett had a brother named Shed. Add it all up, and it's hard to believe that we don't have the right Mary here. My guess is that her biological parents were Jeff and Martha, as the death certificate states, but one or both died or became very ill, and consequently at a young age Mary went to live with relatives near Nashville.

2. The 1900 census gives the wrong birth months for Oscar's brothers Shedrick and Berdie, and his brother Casper is unmentioned.

3. Quote from Anna Charleston Bradley's letter to Larry Lester, relayed by email to author, August 12, 2015.

4. Rodney Redman, telephone interview, December 28, 2015.

5. Alvin Moses, "Beating the Gun," *Philadelphia Tribune*, February 24, 1945, 12. Ric Roberts, "Oscar Charleston: Now in Baseball Hall of Fame," *New York Amsterdam News*, August 28, 1976, 15.

6. The claim would be odd but not unthinkable. Larry Lester himself is not sure how much stock to put in Anna's statement, pointing out that African Americans were sometimes owned by American Indians and that claims of Indian ancestry are sometimes motivated by financial considerations.

7. Clark and Lester, *The Negro Leagues Book*, 36.

8. Anna's letter has never been published or subjected to public discussion. King, *Native Americans in Sports*, 78.

9. On Williams, see "Negro League Pitcher May Have Had Cherokee Blood," November 21, 2014, http://www.philly.com/philly/sports/phillies/Negro_League_pitcher_may_have_had_Cherokee_blood.html.

10. James Riley claims that Mary's father was a carpenter who had worked on construction projects at Fisk University in *The Biographical Encyclopedia of the*

Negro Baseball Leagues. (Riley provides no specific source for this information and could not recall where it came from when I contacted him.) Holway, *Blackball Stars*, 100, is the source for the claim that Tom was a construction worker. It is not clear where Holway got this information, but the censuses all list Tom as a laborer, so it is plausible enough.

11. The 1920 census says that Mary was born "about 1875," but her death certificate gives her birthdate as March 6, 1872. The Charlestons, their neighbors, or the census takers themselves were, depending on one's point of view, either charmingly or exasperatingly inexact about such quotidian details as birthdates.

12. I believe that the Charlestons arrived in Indianapolis in 1896 for two reasons: (1) the first year in which they are known to have lived in Indianapolis is October 1896, when the newspapers mentioned the birth of a new son, and (2) in contrast to later editions of the city directory, the Charlestons are not listed in any directory prior to 1897, a fact that implies they moved to Indianapolis in 1896 too late to be included in that year's edition. It is possible that the 1896 directory (or even earlier ones) missed them, but given the consistency with which they were listed thereafter, it isn't all that likely.

13. Bodenhamer and Barrows, *Encyclopedia of Indianapolis*, 1.

14. Bodenhamer and Barrows, *Encyclopedia of Indianapolis*, 63.

15. See Bodenhamer and Barrows, *Encyclopedia of Indianapolis*, 55.

16. Bodenhamer and Barrows, *Encyclopedia of Indianapolis*, 6–7.

17. Bodenhamer and Barrows, *Encyclopedia of Indianapolis*, 55.

18. Bodenhamer and Barrows, *Encyclopedia of Indianapolis*, 98–99.

19. Bodenhamer and Barrows, *Encyclopedia of Indianapolis*, 47. See also Williams, *Indianapolis Jazz*.

20. The 1900 census puts Oscar's birthday in February 1896, not October. This is wrong. Oscar's sister Katherine, to whom he was very close, recorded his birth as October 12, 1896, on his death certificate. This, too, seems to be a mistake. Except when trying to join the army or, later, to get army-related benefits, Oscar always gave his birthday as October 14, 1896.

As for Oscar's birthplace, the house on Yandes is long gone, and just what the right address was is a question. The address given by the *News*, 287 Yandes, is different from the one given by the *Indianapolis Journal* (299 Yandes) on the same date. And both are different from the address given for Thomas Charleston in the 1897 city directory, which was 289 Yandes. In any case, today all but twenty feet or so of the weedy, crumbling street stretches behind a barbed-wire fence on private property. An 1895 city ordinance ordered some of Indianapolis's streets to be renumbered, but the address of 287 (or 289 or 299) Yandes seems to have been given under the old system, as the north-south Yandes then had its southern terminus right about where the east-west Second Street would have come through had it been extended from the west. This same part of Yandes Street appears to be numbered 1200–1299 today.

21. William McKinley was elected to the U.S. presidency in November 1896. In October the contest between him and Bryan had reached its highest level of intensity. A

1934 article placed by Charleston in his scrapbook confirms that his parents did indeed name him after the Republican candidate (see Irwin N. Rosee, "Charleston Helps Build Colored Baseball League" in ocs). This is not surprising, for as Emma Lou Thornbrough notes, until the New Deal Indianapolis's "black voters . . . had always been loyal Republicans" (quoted in Bodenhamer and Barrows, *Encyclopedia of Indianapolis*, 8).

22. Apparently because the Guffin Street address is the one given in the 1900 census, it is sometimes claimed that Charleston grew up there. (Today Guffin Street is known as Bundy Place.) But the city directories make it clear that the Charlestons lived in at least ten different places before Oscar enlisted in the army in 1912. From Oscar's birth until he was four, the Charlestons lived in the Martindale neighborhood and after that in the Indiana Avenue neighborhood, but no one address and no one street was home for very long.

23. The 1900 census tells us that Tom and Mary had by that time had six children together, five of whom were still living. These would have been, in order, Roy, Berl, Shedrick, Oscar, and Casper. It's possible, even probable, that the sixth (deceased) child had been born in 1894, the missing year in the every-other-year childbirth schedule the Charlestons followed. This would make Oscar the fifth-born child, with six siblings coming after him (Casper, Clarissa, Thomas, Katherine, Benjamin, and James). Later press accounts usually claimed that Oscar was the seventh of eleven children, and presumably this information came from Oscar himself. The eleven-children claim is true, as it is the number given by Mary herself on James's birth certificate. But Oscar was not Mary's *seventh* child.

24. Quoted in Bodenhamer and Barrows, *Encyclopedia of Indianapolis*, 23.

25. See Bodenhamer and Barrows, *Encyclopedia of Indianapolis*, 64.

26. Bodenhamer and Barrows, *Encyclopedia of Indianapolis*, 64.

27. Quoted in Bodenhamer and Barrows, *Encyclopedia of Indianapolis*, 203.

28. Tarkington, *Growth*, 2.

29. Tarkington, *America Moved*, 144.

30. "Bicycle Fork Broke," *Indianapolis Journal*, May 15, 1899, 8.

31. "Mary Grabbed an Ax," *Indianapolis News*, August 24, 1901, 6.

32. "He Could Not Pay the Fine," *Indianapolis News*, September 3, 1901, 9.

33. "Boy Caught in the Store," *Indianapolis Journal*, July 25, 1900, 8.

34. "County Courts' Record," *Indianapolis News*, November 7, 1900, 8.

35. "The Court Record," *Indianapolis Journal*, November 8, 1900, 3.

36. "The Court Record," *Indianapolis Journal*, January 9, 1903, 8.

37. See "Julia E. Work Training School," at www.in.gov/iara/2547.htm.

38. "The Julia E. Work Training School/Brightside Orphanage 1899–1937," accessed at www.rootsweb.ancestry.com/~inmarsha/brtsd.html.

39. "Pie-Eating Contest," *Indianapolis Journal*, September 2, 1902, 10. The paper actually reports that it was *Ben* Charleston, not Berl, who was in the contest, but Ben was not yet born. The address given for this "Ben Charleston" matches that of the Thomas Charleston family, so we know it was one of the Charleston boys. My guess is that a reporter's scrawl of the unusual name Berl was printed as Ben.

40. "Ash Gets Shade in Ten-Round Contest," *Indianapolis Freeman*, December 16, 1911, 7.

41. "In the Field of Sport," *Indianapolis Freeman*, June 29, 1912, 7.

42. "The New Crown Garden," *Indianapolis Freeman*, July 13, 1912, 5.

43. "In the Field of Sport," *Indianapolis Freeman*, November 16, 1912, 7.

44. "Boxing Contest at the Indiana Theater," *Indianapolis Freeman*, November 23, 1912, 6.

45. Ridley, *From the Avenue*, 27.

46. For portraits of Indiana Avenue supporting this line of interpretation, see McWhorter, *Winning the Race*; Bolden, *Indiana Avenue*; and Ridley, *From the Avenue*.

47. Both Thomas Howard Ridley Jr. and Oscar Robertson provide these details. See Ridley's *From the Avenue* and Robertson's *The Big O*. There is no reason to believe that the Indiana Avenue–area homes in which the Charlestons lived had amenities that differed from the pattern.

48. Bolden, *Indiana Avenue*, 21.

49. Quoted in Bolden, *Indiana Avenue*, 22.

50. Ridley, *From the Avenue*, 44.

51. Ridley, *From the Avenue*, 43.

52. Bodenhamer and Barrows, *Encyclopedia of Indianapolis*, 879.

53. Bodenhamer and Barrows, *Encyclopedia of Indianapolis*, 2.

54. Bodenhamer and Barrows, *Encyclopedia of Indianapolis*, 6, 78.

55. Oscar's sister Katherine said that his highest educational level was the eighth grade in the questionnaire she filled out for the National Baseball Hall of Fame in 1976 (Oscar Charleston Files, HOF).

56. "Canol" (rather than Conoyer) is the name given in the account provided in "Local Baseball Pioneer Dies," *Indianapolis Recorder*, June 2, 1934, 2.

57. Some sources say that Oscar was 5 feet 11 inches or taller, but official records like his World War II draft card list him at 5 feet 8 inches. Photographs of Oscar standing next to other players also suggest that 5 feet 8 inches or perhaps 5 feet 9 inches was his true height.

2. Hothead, 1912–1915

1. See "Fort McDowell" at www.militarymuseum.org/CpReynolds.html.

2. Gay, *Satch, Dizzy and Rapid Robert*, 24.

3. "Baseball is now played in every part of the Philippine archipelago, and the number of persons actually engaged in it is remarkably high. Practically every school in the islands has a team and some more than one. Thirty or more provinces have their provincial leagues among the schools, and these are supplemented by inter-provincial leagues." In "Filipinos Play Baseball," *Lompoc Journal*, October 10, 1914.

4. "June 25, 2008: At SABR in Cleveland," June 26, 2008, http://www.whyilikebaseball .com/2008/06/june-25-2008-at-sabr-in-cleveland/.

5. Quoted in *Pittsburg Press*, March 22, 1903, 32.

6. William E. Hills, "Baseball in the Philippines," *New York Times*, February 13, 1916.

7. Information about the Manila League comes from Geri Strecker's biography of Grover Baichley. See her article "Grover Baichley" at www.sabr.org/bioproj/person/588aaf60.

8. Quoted in Holway, *Black Giants*, 69.

9. Syd Pollock, for whom Oscar worked when he managed the Indianapolis Clowns, claimed, in the brief biography of Charleston that he wrote in 1954, that Oscar started playing for the regimental team in 1912. He probably got this date from Oscar, as according to a February 5, 1954, letter from Pollock to Charleston (SPL), the bio was compiled from information Charleston provided to Pollock.

10. "Brownies Trim 24th Infantry While Manila and Army Tie," *Manila Times*, February 9, 1914, 11.

11. Geri Strecker states that the Marines were replaced because they had shipped out. See "Grover Baichley" at www.sabr.org/bioproj/person/588aaf60.

12. Quoted in Holway, *Blackball Stars*, 167.

13. These numbers represent batting average, on-base percentage, and slugging percentage respectively. When these statistics are presented in this fashion, it is called a batter's "slash line" or "triple-slash line."

14. "Rogan was the ace of any pitching staff," said Lester. "No relief pitcher need apply. A high average hitter who had power, and showed speed on the bases. Perhaps the only player, besides Martín Dihigo, capable of leading the league in most wins, lowest ERA, most strikeouts, most home runs, most RBIs, highest batting average, all in the same season. A dual triple-crown threat. It's criminal to think Bullet Rogan is not the greatest player of all time." Quoted in McNeil, *Cool Papas and Double Duties*, 183.

15. Ted Page, Charleston's teammate on the Pittsburgh Crawfords, is one source for the claim that Oscar didn't smoke or drink. See Holway, *Blackball Stars*, 101. On Oscar's insistence on punctuality, see Schulian, *Sometimes They Even Shook Your Hand*, 171.

16. Holway, *Blackball Stars*, 58.

17. Motley, *Ruling over Monarchs, Giants, and Stars*, 69.

18. "Mud Hens Put Up Good Game at League Grounds on Sunday," *Manila Times*, March 16, 1914, 2.

19. "Gloom Pervades the Camps of Brownies and Twenty Fourth," *Manila Times*, March 29, 1914, 7.

20. For example: "Rogan, the comedian catcher on the Batangas organization, was in the game every minute as usual, scoring two of the runs registered for his side, and generally handing out a line of talk that kept the fans on the titter." "Army and Cits Were Week-End Winners," *Manila Times*, April 27, 1914, 10.

21. "24th Slaughters Manila; Army Shuts Out Filipinos," *Manila Times*, May 10, 1914, 6.

22. "Notes of the Games," *Manila Times*, May 17, 1914, 7.

23. "Notes of the Games," *Manila Times*, June 14, 1914, 6.

24. "Sports of All Sorts for All Sorts of Sports," *Manila Times*, June 30, 1914, 12.

25. This information comes from Geri Strecker's biography of Joseph Coffindaffer. See her article "Joseph Coffindaffer," at www.sabr.org/bioproj/person/c6fd7724.

26. Charleston *may* have appeared in one game for Manila in mid-January 1915. It is unlikely, but I have not been able to definitely rule it out.

27. See Jefferson, *Negroland*.

28. For information on Loving, see Yoder, *In Performance*. Loving's constabulary band frequently played concerts in Manila, and it often showed up for weekend games at Nozaleda Park. That may have been where Charleston made his acquaintance.

29. These numbers come from a profile of Charleston published by veteran sports writer W. Rollo Wilson in the *Pittsburgh Courier's* Sunday Magazine Section on March 17, 1951 (in OCS). Wilson surely got this information from Oscar himself. The *Manila Times* of February 2, 1915, lists Charleston as finishing first in preliminary heats in both the 120-yard hurdles (18.2 seconds) and 220-yard dash (23.6 seconds), but times in the final events were not given. See "24th Infantry Wins the Trials," *Manila Times*, February 2, 1915, 5.

30. The article from the *Manila Times* was published in the *Indianapolis Freeman* on January 1, 1916 (in OCS).

31. Dizzy Dismukes, "Dismukes Names His 9 Best Outfielders," *Pittsburgh Courier*, March 8, 1930, 14. This article was placed in OCS.

32. "ABCs and Reserves Play at Northwestern," *Indianapolis Star*, April 9, 1915, 10.

33. The family now lived at 1812 Mill St. The house, most of the street, and any trace of Northwestern Park are all gone today.

34. See Lester, *Rube Foster in His Time*, 22–24.

35. I have compiled this list from information available at Seamheads.com, the best data source for Negro Leagues players.

36. Twenty-eight players have been inducted into the Hall of Fame primarily for their achievements in the Negro Leagues.

37. "ABCs Shut Out the Reserves by 7–0 Score," *Indianapolis Star*, April 12, 1915, 10.

38. Debono, *The Indianapolis ABCs*, 41. Butler died in 1934, at the age of seventy-seven, dead broke and having long since faded from public life.

39. Bill Holland told this story to John Holway. See Holway, *Black Giants*, 73.

40. See, e.g., "Colored Choirs Contest Friday," *Indianapolis Star*, May 13, 1917, 22. The portrait of Taylor here is drawn based on information taken from numerous contemporary newspaper articles, but see also Debono, *The Indianapolis ABCs*, 30–71, inter alia.

41. James, *The New Bill James Historical Baseball Abstract*, 176.

42. "ABCs Lose to the All Leaguers before Large Crowd—Pitcher Charleston Looks to Be a Wonder," *Indianapolis Freeman*, April 24, 1915, 5.

43. The "black Ty Cobb" is a designation often wrongly implied to have been more or less exclusively used for Charleston. In addition to Lyons, for example, center fielder Spottswood Poles was also frequently referred to as the "black Ty Cobb."

44. "Colored Boys Slug Ball, Beating All-Stars, 14 to 3," *Indianapolis Star*, April 26, 1915, 8.

45. "The Fast and Hard Hitting Out Field of the ABC Ball Team," *Indianapolis Freeman*, June 19, 1915, 4.

46. "Cuban Stars Defeat the ABCs in Flashy Game," *Indianapolis Star*, June 28, 1915, 8.

47. "Merits Have Been Hitting Ball Hard; Play ABCs Sunday," *Indianapolis Star*, June 4, 1915, 10.

48. "ABCs in Form and Merits Have No Chance," *Indianapolis Freeman*, June 12, 1915, 4.

49. Wilmer Harris interview, July 1, 2003, in JSP.

50. "Notes of the ABC's and Lincoln Stars," *Indianapolis Freeman*, August 21, 1915, 4.

51. Quoted in Russ Cowans, "Russ' Corner," *Chicago Defender*, June 7, 1952, 16.

52. Dizzy Dismukes, "Dismukes Names His 9 Best Outfielders," *Pittsburgh Courier*, March 8, 1930, 14.

53. "ABCs Win at Fort Wayne," *Indianapolis Star*, September 15, 1915, 8.

54. "ABCs Trim Gunthers," *Indianapolis Freeman*, July 17, 1915, 4; "Notes of the ABCs," *Indianapolis Freeman*, July 17, 1915, 4.

55. Information on Kauff is taken from David Jones's excellent SABR Bio Project article on Kauff. See "Benny Kauff," at http://sabr.org/bioproj/person/4a224847.

56. "Notes of the ABCs," *Indianapolis Freeman*, July 17, 1915, 4.

57. These figures are by my count. For what it's worth, Taylor reported an overall 71-26-3 record going into the game on October 24 against Donie Bush's All-Stars. Since they had played a few games before Oscar arrived and I am probably missing a few games, Taylor's claim is probably not *too* inflated.

58. "Champagne Velvet" was the name of a pilsner made by the team's sponsor, the Terre Haute Brewing Company. The brand, allegedly quite popular in Indiana during the first half of the twentieth century, has been revived by Bloomington's Upland Brewing Company.

59. Seamheads.com gives a triple-slash line of .293/.385/.437 for Ben Taylor, .298/.385/.382 for Shively, and .214/.365/.274 for DeMoss. Those lines translate to OPS+s of 172, 156, and 106, respectively, meaning that Taylor, for example, had an on-base-percentage plus slugging percentage (OPS) 72 percent above that year's Negro Leagues average (a figure that in the statistic OPS+ is always set at 100). Although these are the best statistics we have, keep in mind that they should be taken with a grain of salt, as box scores are sometimes incomplete or contradictory, and some are missing entirely. Charleston's OPS+ in 1915 was 125, or 25 percent above the average.

60. "Stars Play ABCs," *Indianapolis Star*, September 21, 1915, 11.

61. "ABCs and Stars Play Double-Header," *Indianapolis Star*, September 26, 1915, 21.

62. "ABCs Too Fast for Minor Leaguers," *Indianapolis Star*, September 27, 1915, 9.

63. "Chance for All-Stars," *Indianapolis Star*, October 1, 1915, 13.

64. "Southpaw in Shape," *Indianapolis Star*, October 2, 1915, 13.

65. "Stars and ABCs in a Drawn Battle," *Indianapolis Star*, October 4, 1915, 8.

66. See Scott Simkus, "ABCs vs. Donie Bush All-Stars, 1914," agatetype.com, December 5, 2006.

67. "Work for All-Stars," *Indianapolis Star*, October 12, 1915, 13.

68. "Williford at Indiana," *Indianapolis Star*, October 13, 1915, 10.

69. "Russell Beaten in Mound Duel," *Indianapolis Star*, October 18, 1915, 10.

70. "ABCs Beat All-Stars," *Indianapolis Freeman*, October 23, 1915, 7.

71. "Crandall to Be in All-Stars' Lineup," *Indianapolis Star*, October 24, 1915, 18. The statistics at Seamheads.com show that Redding had compiled a 1.06 ERA over 119 innings in 1915. At the time no one had such numbers at hand of course.

72. Bush claimed that DeMoss missed the tag. The *Chicago Defender*, in its game report, states squarely that "Scanlon called what should have been an out safe." October 30, 1915, 7.

73. My account of this game is taken from the following articles: "Last Game Taken by the All-Stars," *Indianapolis Star*, October 25, 1915, 14; "Race Riot Is Balked by Police," *Indianapolis Star*, October 25, 1915, 1; "All-Stars Take Last Game," *Indianapolis Freeman*, October 30, 1915, 7; "Fight Ends ABC Game," *Chicago Defender*, October 30, 1915, 7.

74. "American Giants in Fierce Riot at Hoosier City," *Chicago Defender*, July 24, 1915, 7. The title of the article was sensationalist; there had been an on-field fight but no riot.

75. Leerhsen, *Ty Cobb*, 328.

76. "Race Riot Is Balked by Police," *Indianapolis Star*, October 25, 1915.

77. "Race Riot Is Balked by Police," *Indianapolis Star*, October 25, 1915.

78. The text of Taylor's wire was published in "In the Field of Sport," *Indianapolis Freeman*, October 30, 1915, 7.

79. This was the *Chicago Defender*'s view of the matter: "Charleston came to DeMoss' aid," it reported (October 30, 1915, 7).

80. "Charleston's Unclean Act—He Is Very Sorry," *Indianapolis Freeman*, November 13, 1915, 7. Oscar surely wrote this letter himself, as it bears the style of his later letters.

81. "Mr. Charleston," *Indianapolis Freeman*, November 13, 1915, 4.

82. "Manager Taylor Regrets ABC Trouble," *Chicago Defender*, November 6, 1915, 7.

83. "Charleston Dropped by the ABC Club," *Indianapolis Star*, November 26, 1915, 8.

84. For statistics and information about the ABCs' trip to Cuba, see Seamheads .com, from which these numbers are taken, and Nieto, *Early U.S. Blackball Teams in Cuba*. Note that Nieto's statistics differ slightly from those on Seamheads.

85. "Baseball Verdict Withheld," *Indianapolis Star*, December 8, 1915, 2; *Indianapolis Star*, December 9, 1915, 13.

86. "Baseball Color Line Is Drawn by Police as Result of Fight," *Indianapolis Star*, December 5, 1915, 11.

3. Riser, 1916–1918

1. The papers may have declined comment because another two games were scheduled that apparently never took place. The Lincoln Stars also played the Chicago American Giants for the "championship" in 1915. Without a league structure in place, such championship series were usually quite contestable. Regardless of their legitimacy, they often functioned well as ploys for ginning up attendance.

2. James, *The New Bill James Historical Baseball Abstract*, 175. "Oscar Charleston was the greatest center fielder, they say. Before him they say there was a guy named Spottswood Poles, but after him they say that Charleston was the greatest," reported Cool Papa Bell, as quoted in Rust, *"Get That Nigger off the Field,"* 36.

3. Holway, *Blackball Stars*, 6.

4. "Catholic Protectory Oval," agatetype.com, February 28, 2011.

5. "Harlem's Shifting Population," *Gotham Gazette*, Citizens Union Foundation, August 27, 2008.

6. "Lincoln Giants Adds [*sic*] Another Brace of Victories to Its Brace," *Indianapolis Freeman*, May 20, 1916, 4.

7. "Lincoln Stars Trim Mike Donlin's All-Stars," *Indianapolis Freeman*, June 3, 1916, 7; "Food for Fans," *Indianapolis Freeman*, June 3, 1916, 7.

8. "Lincoln Giants Adds [*sic*] Another Brace of Victories to Its Brace," *Indianapolis Freeman*, May 20, 1916, 4.

9. "Food for Fans," *Indianapolis Freeman*, June 3, 1916, 7.

10. This is the record Seamheads.com gives them.

11. "Lincoln Stars Break Sox Winning Streak," *Chicago Defender*, July 15, 1916, 5; "Baseball," *New York Age*, July 13, 1916, 6.

12. "Lincoln Stars Lead in Championship Contest," *Chicago Defender*, July 22, 1916, 9.

13. "Lincoln Stars to Play with Taylor's ABCs," *Indianapolis Star*, July 20, 1916, 10.

14. "Charleston and DeMoss Added to Taylor's Team," *Indianapolis Star*, August 5, 1916, 13.

15. "Battle of Baseball Wits," *Chicago Defender*, August 25, 1916, 5.

16. Such incidents do seem to have been treated more lightly in black baseball at the time, in part because there was no league to mete out and enforce disciplinary measures. In 1917 an enraged Babe Ruth rushed off the mound to attack home plate umpire Brick Owens. He took several swings and landed a left to Owens's neck before a policeman escorted him from the field. Ruth was suspended for ten days. See Creamer, *Babe*, 139–40.

17. Figures are by my own calculation, which includes games absent from the Seamheads.com database.

18. "Thousands Bet on Coming Series," *Chicago Defender*, October 21, 1916, 6.

19. "We are very sorry this happened," reported the *Freeman*, "as it will in the end hurt the men who are trying to build the game up. We can not see how it is that a team like this comes down here and tries to destroy the peace we have been having all season by a lot of bulldozing actions. . . . When the umpire told Mr. Foster to leave the field, he should have left without a word" ("Third Game of Series Forfeited to ABCs," *Indianapolis Freeman*, October 28, 1916, 7).

20. "Taylor's Team Out to Clinch Series for Colored Title," *Indianapolis Star*, October 28, 1916, 15.

21. "Rube Foster Speaks," *Chicago Defender*, November 18, 1916, 9.

22. "Notes of the Game," *Indianapolis Freeman*, November 4, 1916, 7.

23. "C. I. Taylor and His Base Ball Club," *Indianapolis Freeman*, December 16, 1916, 7.

24. "C. I. Taylor and His Base Ball Club," *Indianapolis Freeman*, December 16, 1916, 7.

25. This profile of William Grubbs is primarily drawn from information about him published from time to time in the *Indianapolis Recorder* during the first third of the twentieth century. The quotes are taken from two articles: Lee A. Johnson, "W. E. Grubbs, Long Time Principal in Indianapolis Public School System," *Indianapolis Recorder*, June 22, 1935, 8, and "Wm. E. Grubbs, Retired School Principal, Dies," *Indianapolis Recorder*, February 29, 1936, 3.

26. "Concert of Real Merit at Corinthian," *Indianapolis Recorder*, November 7, 1914, 8.

27. "Charity Benefit, May 4th," *Indianapolis Recorder*, Aril 18, 1914, 4.

28. "News of the Colored Folk," *Indianapolis News*, August 24, 1918, 5. For more on Alberta Grubbs, see also especially "Rites for Mrs. Grubbs," *Indianapolis Recorder*, November 22, 1930, 2.

29. The exploits of Miss Hazel are mentioned in a number of *Indianapolis Recorder* notices. See, e.g., "Ethical Culture Society," *Indianapolis Recorder*, December 12, 1914, 2; "Around the Churches," *Indianapolis Recorder*, April 22, 1916, 5; "News of the Colored People," *Indianapolis News*, August 19, 1916, 13.

30. "Daily Vital Statistics," *Indianapolis News*, January 10, 1917, 16.

31. Hazel may have accompanied him, but I doubt it.

32. Yardley, *Ring*, 185–88. Like Oscar, Lardner had a connection to Donie Bush. Lardner was a cub reporter for the *South Bend Times* and bird-dog scout when Bush was coming up with the city's Central League team. He tried to interest the Cubs, White Sox, and Red Sox in purchasing Bush's contract, but they all ignored him. The Tigers drafted Bush in the next off-season. See "Me, Boy Scout" in Bruccoli and Layman, *Some Champions*.

33. O'Neil, *I Was Right on Time*, 23–25.

34. McNeil, *Black Baseball out of Season*, 20.

35. "The American Giants," *Kansas City Sun*, February 3, 1917, 2.

36. "Charleston did not play his usual game at Palm Beach," reported the *Indianapolis Freeman*, March 24, 1917, 7.

37. "Death in the Game," *Indianapolis Freeman*, February 24, 1917, 7.

38. Taylor is referring to Harry Hooper of the Boston Red Sox, whose reputation for excellent defense was not well deserved, if modern estimates of his defensive value are accurate.

39. Quoted in Irvin with Pepe, *Few and Chosen*, 100.

40. "Parade to Precede the ABCs-Giants Diamond Fray Today," *Indianapolis Star*, April 21, 1917, 14.

41. "Penographs from the Taylor-Foster Bill," *Indianapolis Freeman*, August 25, 1917, 1.

42. According to Seamheads.com, Oscar had an OPS+ of 146. Lloyd's OPS+ was 175, Ben Taylor's was 140, and Hill's was 142.

43. Quoted in Holway, *Black Giants*, 124.

44. "Our Champions Hit Ball Hard and Win Scrap," *Indianapolis Star*, September 23, 1917, 46.

45. "Charleston's Catch Saves It in the Sixth," *Chicago Defender*, June 30, 1917, 11.

46. "Taylor's ABCs Play Fifteen Innings to Tie with Foster's Giants," *Indianapolis Star*, August 4, 1917, 13.

47. "Eighth Inning Rally Defeats Taylor's 9," *Chicago Defender*, August 11, 1917, 10.

48. "Colored Stars Play 15 Rounds to a Tie Score," *Detroit Free Press*, August 4, 1917, 9.

49. Quoted in Holway, *Voices from the Great Black Baseball Leagues*, 46.

50. "Rube Foster's Giants and Taylor's ABCs Banqueted," *Indianapolis Freeman*, August 11, 1917, 7.

51. Hazel is not listed in the 1920 city directory. Oscar is still listed as living at his parents' home.

52. The fan was quoted in a Russ J. Cowans column in the *Defender*. The elderly fan added that "Lyons was one of the best players I've ever looked at. . . . He was a good hitter, a fine fielder and a daring base runner. He was always doing something for the entertainment of the crowd" ("Old Timer Talks Baseball As It Was in Other Days," *Chicago Defender*, August 1, 1936, 14); John W. Head, "ABCs to Play Team in Havana," *Indianapolis Star*, January 12, 1918, 12.

53. John W. Head, "ABCs to Play Team in Havana," *Indianapolis Star*, January 12, 1918, 12.

54. Quoted in "Thirteen Men Report at First Practice of ABCs," *Indianapolis Star*, March 26, 1918, 11.

55. "Dayton Marcos Meet ABCs This Afternoon," *Indianapolis Star*, April 7, 1918, 45.

56. "Taylor's Nine Shuts Out Dayton Marcos Again," *Indianapolis Star*, April 16, 1918, 10.

57. "Taylorites Divide Double Bill with the Cubans," *Chicago Defender*, May 25, 1918, 9; Dave Wyatt, "Base Ball!" *Indianapolis Freeman*, March 31, 1917, 7.

58. "Taylor's ABCs Defeat Anderson," *Indianapolis Star*, May 31, 1918, 13.

59. "Airplane to Drop Some Balls Where Soldiers Perform," *Indianapolis Star*, May 29, 1918, 10.

60. The details here are taken from Gearhart's firsthand account, which he gave to the *Star* when he had sufficiently recovered. "Maj. Gearhart Describes Fall of Airplane That Killed Capt. Webb," *Indianapolis Star*, June 24, 1918, 3.

61. "Ball Game Postponed When an Airplane Falls in Park Killing U.S. Aero Captain," *Indianapolis Star*, June 3, 1918, 9.

62. "Cubans and ABCs in 11 Inning Tilt; Donaldson Quits Indianapolis," *Chicago Defender*, June 29, 1918, 13.

63. "Cubans and A.s to Play Two Scraps," *Indianapolis Star*, July 21, 1918, 57.

64. "Giants-ABCs Deadlocked in Eleven Innings," *Chicago Defender*, August 3, 1918, 9.

65. Ira F. Lewis, "The Greatest Play I Have Ever Seen," *Chicago Defender*, March 1, 1919, 9.

66. "Dixon's Wild Peg Paves Way for ABC Victory," *Chicago Defender*, August 3, 1918, 9.

67. "Just Like Cobb," in OCS.

68. "American Giants Defeat ABCs in Washington," *Chicago Defender*, August 3, 1918, 9.

69. "A.s to Play Red Caps in Double Bill," *Indianapolis Star*, August 18, 1918, 41.

70. "Taylor's Squad Wins Two Games," *Indianapolis Star*, August 19, 1918, 8.

71. This information is taken primarily from Scott, *Scott's Official History of the American Negro in the World War*.

72. "Ball Players Take Optimistic View of Situation on Battlefields of France," *Chicago Defender*, August 17, 1918, 9.

73. Simkus, *Outsider Baseball*, 266.

74. Simkus, *Outsider Baseball*, 265–66.

75. Double Duty Radcliffe, for example, said that Negro Leagues baseball in the 1930s and 1940s was about AAA level. Monte Irvin compared the quality of play in the Negro Leagues to high AAA (Ron Cook, "Secret Stars," *Pittsburgh Press*, September 9, 1988, D1), and Simkus's research suggests that is about right. Carl Erskine agreed: "I say that the Negro Leagues were better than AAA. They would have fared very well against AAA, but not so well against the Majors" (Carl Erskine, telephone interview, August 21, 2015).

In part because they were so heavily invested in the mystique of training and technique, and so aware of how little coaching they had received compared to their white peers, some black players were surprised when they discovered that whites were not their clear superiors on the diamond. Quincy Trouppe first saw white players play in 1933, three years after his own professional career had started. "I was never so let down," he recalled. "I had grown up accepting the idea that white baseball was superior to black. I was expecting to see a ball club of white players perform in a way much superior to the caliber of baseball I had been playing" (Trouppe, *Twenty Years Too Soon*, xiii).

76. Torriente posted an OPS+ of 210 in 1918. Oscar's OPS+ was 196.

4. Star, 1919–1922

1. Quoted in Holway, *Voices from the Great Black Baseball Leagues*, 48.

2. Quoted in Debono, *The Indianapolis ABCs*, 82.

3. Quoted in Holway, *Voices from the Great Black Baseball Leagues*, 48–49.

4. Quoted in Debono, *The Indianapolis ABCs*, 82.

5. "American Giants Open Sunday," *Chicago Defender*, April 12, 1919, 11.

6. "Giants' Recruits Work Hard," *Chicago Defender*, April 5, 1919, 11.

7. "American Giants Open Sunday," *Chicago Defender*, April 12, 1919, 11.

8. James, *The New Bill James Historical Baseball Abstract*, 177–78. For a biographical essay on Torriente, see Bjarkman and Nowlin, *Cuban Baseball Legends*. See also Holway, *Voices from the Great Black Baseball Leagues*, 78.

9. Robert Peterson seems to have been the originator of the misconception that Torriente moved Charleston off center, rather than the reverse. See *Only the Ball Was White*, 245. Peterson also mistakenly has Charleston and Torriente coming to the American Giants in 1918 rather than 1919.

10. "American Giants Win Opener," *Chicago Defender*, April 19, 1919, 11.

11. "American Giants Win Fourth Straight Victory," *Chicago Defender*, May 17, 1919, 11.

12. "20,000 Fans See Cuban Stars and Am. Giants Divide Honors," *Chicago Defender*, June 7, 1919, 11.

13. "American Giants Blank the Detroit Stars," *Chicago Defender*, June 21, 1919, 11.

14. "American Giants, in 10th, Drop Hilldale, *Chicago Defender*, August 30, 1919, 11.

15. "25,000 See Am. Giants Cop Doubleheader," *Chicago Defender*, August 30, 1919, 11.

16. "American Giants Defeat Cuban Stars," *Chicago Defender*, July 12, 1919, 11.

17. William White, "25,000 See Am. Giants Cop Doubleheader," *Chicago Defender*, August 30, 1919, 11.

18. "American Giants Trim Dayton Marcos," *Chicago Defender*, September 20, 1919, 9.

19. "Downs Hearne," in OCS.

20. By Seamheads.com's calculations, Charleston compiled 5.9 WAR in 1919, and Torriente, 5.7.

21. "Oscar Charleston, Giants' Crack Center Fielder," *Chicago Defender*, in OCS.

22. The park was named after John Schorling, Rube Foster's white business partner. Schorling was Charles Comiskey's son-in-law. The park had served as the White Sox's Major League home from 1901 to 1910.

23. In Indianapolis a new version of the ABCs, owned by Warner Jewell and known as "Jewell's ABCs," had filled the void left by Taylor's retirement in 1919. They weren't very good, but in October they managed to schedule the traditional postseason Sunday games against white all-stars, and they excitedly announced that Charleston—expected "to prove a big attraction"—would join them for these contests, along with former ABCs George Shively and Todd Allen. Charleston missed the first of these games, but he did play in one or two of the ones that followed.

24. See, e.g., Luke, *The Baltimore Elite Giants*, 91.

25. Quincy Trouppe recalled a 1931 game between the St. Louis Stars and Indianapolis ABCs in which an umpire's call in the twelfth inning led to the fans going wild, "throwing seat cushions and chairs onto the field and coming down out of the stands" (Trouppe, *Twenty Years Too Soon*, 29).

26. See, e.g., "Demand for Umpires of Color Is Growing among the Fans," *Chicago Defender*, October 9, 1920, 6.

27. Quoted in "Oscar Charleston Tells One," *New York Age*, July 3, 1925, 6.

28. Irvin with Riley, *Nice Guys Finish First*, 72.

29. U.S. Bureau of Labor Statistics, *War and Postwar Wages, Prices, and Hours*. Wages went up significantly for all workers during World War I. The average ballplayer salaries reported here are my estimates based on various testimonies and newspaper reports. Jules Tygiel says that the average Negro Leagues salary was "far more" than the average black worker made at the time (*Baseball's Great Experiment*, 20).

30. Quoted in Holway, *Voices from the Great Black Baseball Leagues*, 30.

31. Rogosin, *Invisible Men*, 71.

32. Trouppe, *Twenty Years Too Soon*, xiv.

33. Numerous black baseball teams were known as the Giants, in one variation or another. The reasons for this practice are not entirely clear, but it seems that some of the earliest black clubs used the name in an attempt to capitalize on the popularity

of the white New York Giants and that later clubs used it not only for the same reason, but also as a way to signal to readers of newspapers and publicity materials that they were a black team.

34. See, e.g., "Taylor's Club to Have Many Stars Again This Year," *Indianapolis Star*, February 21, 1920, 9; "A's Have Fast Club in Line," *Indianapolis Star*, March 19, 1920, 15; and "ABCs to Meet Chicago Giants in Two Scraps Today," *Indianapolis Star*, May 2, 1920, 26.

35. "'Rube' Assigns Players to Giants," *Chicago Defender*, March 20, 1920, 9. See also Dave Wyatt, "Success of the League Is up to the Fans," *Chicago Defender*, April 3, 1920, 9.

36. "Who's Who in the Baseball World," in OCS.

37. "ABCs Win Opener," *Indianapolis Freeman*, May 8, 1920, 4.

38. "Great Playing Beats Cubans," *Indianapolis Star*, May 10, 1920, 12. Not a few of these fans likely had bets riding on the game's outcome.

39. "ABCs Win 2 Games from Dayton Marcos," *Indianapolis Star*, May 24, 1920, 9.

40. Charles A. Starks, "Local Fans Swamp Association Park Day after Day to See Local Games," *Kansas City Sun*, June 5, 1920, 8.

41. See, e.g., "Two Out in Ninth, Two on, Charleston Smacks Homer and A.s Cop, 8–6," *Indianapolis Star*, August 6, 1920, 11, and "A.'s Take to the Road after Games with Islanders," *Indianapolis Star*, August 21, 1920, 10.

42. Bill James points out the doubles-inflating nature of League Park in *The New Bill James Historical Baseball Abstract*, 468.

43. Rickey biographer Lee Lowenfish thinks it likely that Rickey attended at least one of these games and/or those played between the St. Louis Giants and Cardinals after the end of the 1921 season. See Lowenfish, *Branch Rickey*, 126–27.

44. "ABCs Are Beaten," *Indianapolis Star*, May 23, 1920, 28.

45. "A.s and All-Pros Change Lineups for Game Sunday," *Indianapolis Star*, October 15, 1920, 12.

46. "Two Sides to Story," *Indianapolis Star*, October 16, 1920, 10.

47. See "1920/21 Bacharach Giants in Cuba: Passport Applications," agatetype.com, November 27, 2007.

48. See Bjarkman, *A History of Cuban Baseball*, 139. Statistics are taken from Seamheads.com.

49. See Bjarkman, *A History of Cuban Baseball*, 115; Figueredo, *Cuban Baseball*, 137–40; and González Echevarría, *The Pride of Havana*, 169–70. Again for statistics I rely on Seamheads.com.

50. "Selected Passenger Lists and Manifests" (available at ancestry.com) is the source for Oscar's departure and arrival information, here and throughout this book.

51. "Un Juego de Carreraje en Almendares," in OCS.

52. Gary Ashwill, "Giants Park, St. Louis 1919–1922," agatetype.com, September 15, 2010.

53. "St. Louis Giants a Fast Club," *Kansas City Times*, April 28, 1921, 11.

54. "Uncanny Speed and Wonderful Hitting Power Have Made Oscar Charleston Super-Man of Diamond," in OCS.

55. Pitcher Bill Holland, who was from Indianapolis, recalls Clarissa's beauty and early death in Holway, *Black Giants*, 69.

56. Quoted in Holway, *Black Giants*, 57.

57. In addition to newspaper reports, I rely heavily on McNeil, *The California Winter League*, for the information presented in this section. I also draw from information provided by the Center for Negro League Baseball Research, online at www .cnlbr.org, and from Geri Strecker, "Winter Baseball in California."

58. "All-Stars Tackle Calpaco Today," *Los Angeles Times*, November 26, 1921, 25.

59. Carr supplemented his time playing ball in Los Angeles with occasional acting work in the movie business. See "George Carr, Movie Actor," agatetype.com, August 12, 2007.

60. Ed O'Malley, "Ouch!" *Los Angeles Times*, November 22, 1921, 38.

61. "Base Ball," in OCS. The Colored All-Stars were also sometimes called "Charleston's Bear-Cats."

62. "All-Stars Meet Meusel's Majors," *Los Angeles Times*, January 12, 1922, 32; "Meusels Will Swipe Apple," *Los Angeles Times*, January 13, 1922, 22.

63. "Base Ball," in OCS.

64. "Major Stars Nosed Out," *Los Angeles Times*, January 23, 1922, 24.

65. "Major Stars Would Claim Lost Laurels," *Los Angeles Times*, January 27, 1922, 31.

66. William Mells Watson, "Oscar Charleston King of Swatters throughout Season Hits .405, Fields .960," *California Eaglesports*, March 4, 1922, 6.

67. Win J. Cutter, "All-Stars Win Brilliant Ball Game," *Sacramento Union*, in OCS.

68. Win J. Cutter, "All-Stars Win Brilliant Ball Game," *Sacramento Union*, in OCS.

69. "C. I. Taylor Very Sick," *Chicago Defender*, February 18, 1922, 10.

70. Arthur Williams, "C. I. Taylor, Veteran Manager and Baseball Club Owner, Dead," *Chicago Defender*, March 4, 1922, 10.

71. So said the *Chicago Defender* a few years later in "Baseball on Trial; Zero Hour Arrives," March 31, 1928, 9.

72. Arthur Williams, "C. I. Taylor, Veteran Manager and Baseball Club Owner, Dead," *Chicago Defender*, March 4, 1922, 10.

73. "Colored League Plans Monument for Taylor," *Indianapolis Star*, December 12, 1922, 10. The NNL's fine sentiment extended beyond its administrative capabilities. As far as I know, no monument was ever erected, and no "C. I. Taylor Day" was ever announced.

74. *Pittsburgh Courier* columnist Ches Washington, probably getting the story directly from Oscar, wrote in the *Courier* of March 19, 1938, that while Oscar was playing for the ABCs, C. I. Taylor told Charleston he was "going to make a manager out of him some day" (16). Oscar selected Taylor as his all-time manager as part of an all-star team he selected for the *Philadelphia Bulletin* in July 1949.

75. So recalled Morris Taylor in "The Sport Trail," *Indianapolis Recorder*, February 18, 1928, 6.

76. Quoted in Holway, *Voices from the Great Black Baseball Leagues*, 66. Holloway's recollection must have been accurate, for Cool Papa Bell, among others, offered

a similar memory, telling James Bankes that Charleston would sometimes catch fly balls behind his back or in other difficult positions and that he would even do a flip or somersault while the ball was in the air. See Bankes, *The Pittsburgh Crawfords*, 56.

77. "ABCS Open Crucial Series against Foster," *Chicago Defender*, July 15, 1922, 10.

78. Holway, *Black Stars*, 220; Holway, *Black Giants*, 21.

79. "Tigers Drop Two Games to St. Louis Stars," *Chicago Defender*, October 14, 1922, 10.

80. See Gary Ashwill, "Cool Papa's Rookie Season," agatetype.com, July 15, 2016. There are multiple versions of how Bell got his nickname, but this one seems to be the most plausible. See Holway, *Voices from the Great Black Baseball Leagues*, 115.

81. An undated newspaper clipping announcing the marriage is pasted in OCS. A marriage license obtained from St. Louis County gives the precise date of the wedding. Oscar's friend was Percy Richards, a man in his late twenties who in the census of 1920 was said to be a bartender. Oscar, fudging, gave Richards's address as his own on his marriage license application. He had perhaps met Richards while playing for the St. Louis Stars in 1921. He may have even lived with him.

5. Manager, 1922–1926

1. Elizabeth Overton, Janie Blalock's great-niece, confirmed in a personal interview (December 7, 2017) that Martin Blalock had a white father and a black mother.

2. I am indebted to Harrisburg historian Calobe Jackson Jr. (telephone interview, January 13, 2017) and Elizabeth Overton (personal interviews, July 26, 2017, and December 7, 2017) for some of the following information on and context surrounding Janie, LeRoy Howard, and the Harrisburg of their era.

3. LeRoy's death came just eight months after pneumonia had also claimed the life of Janie's younger brother, Martin Luther Blalock Jr.

4. This, as well as many of the details that follow, we know thanks to Elizabeth Overton and Elizabeth's daughter, Dr. Miriam Phields (Elizabeth Overton, personal interviews, July 28, 2017, and December 7, 2017; telephone interview, July 9, 2003, JSP; Miriam Phields, personal interview, August 5, 2017). Elizabeth was largely raised by "Aunt Janie" and lived with her for many years as an adult. For Miriam, Janie served as a kind of grandmother figure.

5. Elizabeth Overton, telephone interview, July 9, 2003, JSP.

6. Miriam Phields recalled that Janie took *National Geographic* and other magazines and "there were always books in the house, so much so that I remember as a teenager going to someone else's house and thinking it was odd that they didn't have any books" (personal interview, August 5, 2017).

7. Although she may have rebelled against her preacher father by marrying Oscar, Janie's personal revolt never extended to her father's Christianity. She maintained a confident, straightforward belief in God her whole life, and she was an energetic member of the church, especially while her father was alive. She even taught Sunday school for a time. On at least one occasion, soon after she married Oscar, she persuaded him to come with her to the services. "Knowing Grandpa Blaylock, I'm sure you had to go to church to be accepted," explained Elizabeth Overton.

8. According to Elizabeth Overton, eloping was a family tradition. It is her understanding that the children found it easier to gain Blalock's forgiveness than his permission (personal interview, July 26, 2017).

9. Indianapolis was probably out of the question because Oscar's September 15, 1921, divorce decree stipulated that he not remarry for at least two years.

10. Quoted in Leerhsen, *Ty Cobb*, 25. Leerhsen's biography leads one to believe that Cobb was in more fights, on and off the field, than Charleston and that he certainly instigated more. And this is the impression left by a biographer who is trying to rehabilitate Cobb as much as the evidence allows.

11. "The Most Interesting Negro Ball Player," in OCS.

12. Stanley Glenn, telephone interview, July 1, 2003, JSP.

13. Stanley Glenn, telephone interview, July 1, 2003, JSP.

14. William G. Nunn, "Diamond Dope," *Pittsburgh Courier*, June 20, 1925, 12.

15. Along with the testimony of those who knew him, the many humorous clippings Charleston placed in his scrapbook speak to his love of a laugh. One such piece, fairly typical in its substance, reports that the manager of the Hattiesburg Black Tigers fired every one of his players after they lost, 17–1, to the Atlanta Black Crackers—except himself. The manager explained that since he scored his team's only run, he deserved to stay in uniform.

16. Harris's judgment comes from his interview with John Schulian (telephone interview, July 1, 2003, JSP). Taylor is quoted by Holway in *Black Giants*, 190. William Brashler's characterization of Charleston as "dour" is just one of the many examples of how the secondary literature has gotten Oscar's personality wrong (Brashler, *Josh Gibson*, 29).

17. Quoted in Holway, *Black Giants*, 190.

18. Holway, *Black Diamonds*, 48–49.

19. Quoted in Holway, *Voices from the Great Black Baseball Leagues*, 115.

20. Stanley Glenn, telephone interview, July 1, 2003, JSP.

21. Holway, *Black Giants*, 50.

22. Bill Cash, telephone interview, June 30, 2003, JSP.

23. Mahlon Duckett, telephone interview, July 1, 2003, JSP.

24. Quoted in Holway, *Voices from the Great Black Baseball Leagues*, 213.

25. Andrew Porter, telephone interview, July 3, 2003, JSP.

26. Either Oscar or Janie clipped and put in OCS the following item: "The time has about gone for the hard-drinking ball players to get together and spread propaganda about players on the club who do not drink. Many players like to knock such men as Lloyd, Charleston and other great players and call them 'snitches' because these men will not drink, but Lloyd and Charleston have seen many come and go and will see many others fall by the wayside." A long article on baseball and alcohol in the April 3, 1926, *Pittsburgh Courier*, used Charleston as a prime example of how shunning drink could lead to sustained success: "One of the outstanding characters of the diamond who shuns liquor is that great and colorful king of the diamond, Oscar Charleston, fielder supreme, the peer of whom is yet to be located. Year

after year Oscar has gone on piling up achievements which make him a place in the hall of fame of Negro baseball for all time, aiding the game by his clean and sane method of living and playing the game" ("Liquor—and the Havoc It Has Wrought in the Ranks of Baseball's Big Stars," 14).

27. Bill Cash, telephone interview, June 30, 2003, JSP.

28. Stanley Glenn, telephone interview, July 1, 2003, JSP.

29. Mahlon Duckett, telephone interview, July 1, 2003, JSP.

30. Mahlon Duckett, telephone interview, July 1, 2003, JSP.

31. Several sources apply here, but see Wilmer Harris, telephone interview, July 1, 2003, JSP, and Mahlon Duckett, telephone interview, July 1, 2003, JSP.

32. Quoted in Holway, *Voices from the Great Black Baseball Leagues*, 78.

33. Santa Clara had a reputation as a strong baseball town. In support of earlier teams—including one named Tosca, during a delightful period that saw some Cuban ball clubs named after operas—fans had formed a *charanga* (a sort of musical cheer group), and a town candy maker had produced team baseball cards. Santa Clara was also home to a lathe operator, Noel Pegudo, who was Cuba's most popular bat maker. Much of the information here about Santa Clara comes from González Echevarría, *The Pride of Havana*, 171–73, and Skinner, "Twice Champions," 35–42.

34. "Los Pilongos" literally means those baptized in the same font.

35. "Charleston Leads Players in Cuban National League," *Chicago Defender*, January 6, 1923, 10. That superb fielding wasn't taking place exclusively in center field; early in the season especially Oscar alternated there with Oms. When he wasn't in center, he patrolled right.

36. From a January 17, 1923, article in *La Prensa* included in OCS (the translation is either Oscar's or Janie's).

37. Article in *La Prensa*, January 17, 1923; in OCS.

38. This was according to Buck O'Neil, who first saw Oscar there. See *I Was Right on Time*, 23–25. According to O'Neil, Rube Foster was also in Palm Beach in 1923.

39. "Charleston to Am. Giants; Dismukes to Manage ABCs," *Chicago Defender*, December 16, 1922, 1.

40. "Easterners Organize a New League," in OCS.

41. "Rube Foster Goes Eastward; Giants to Train in Texas," *Chicago Defender*, February 3, 1923, 10.

42. "Pitchers Brown and Rile Jump to the Outlaws," *Chicago Defender*, February 17, 1923, 10.

43. "Figured in Recent Charleston Trade by Am. Giants and ABCs," in OCS.

44. This came out when a January 4, 1924, letter from Dizzy Dismukes to Olivia Taylor was made public. "Baseball Players Well Paid, Said Mrs. Taylor," in OCS.

45. Oscar's photo album contains several photos of Janie lounging in a field and in front of a bungalow with a woman identified as "Mrs. Dismukes." Dizzy isn't known to have ever married, so it's possible this is a later misidentification.

46. "Oscar Charleston Shifted to Infield by Dismukes; Shively in Centerfield," *Pittsburgh Courier*, April 14, 1923, 3.

47. "Dizzy Pace Set by ABCs in National League Race," *Chicago Defender*, June 9, 1923, 10.

48. "Indianapolis Here for Five Games and Fight for First Place," *Chicago Defender*, June 16, 1923, 8.

49. Oscar was credited with a running shoestring catch that was the "feature play of the day" on July 15 and with robbing a batter of a home run in straightaway center on July 16. "ABCs Win, 7 to 2," *Indianapolis Star*, July 16, 1923, 10.

50. Oscar even reportedly outmaneuvered Rube Foster in one 1923 contest. In a tight game Foster replaced a straightaway hitter likely to hit the ball toward Oscar in center field with a right-handed pull hitter. Oscar, knowing that this particular pinch hitter always took the first pitch, waited until just before the second pitch to switch positions with the left fielder. Sure enough, the hitter drove the ball deep into left field territory, and Oscar was there to snare it. The story is told in "Charleston Is Alone at Out Guessing Rube," in OCS.

51. "Holloway Leads ABCs in Hitting with Average of .329, 'Oscar' Has 11 Homers," *Pittsburgh Courier*, August 25, 1923, 6.

52. In the first game Oscar hit a "lollypop" home run to deep center that "fans won't forget in some time." "City Championship Race Tightens; Fosters Win 3," *Chicago Defender*, October 6, 1923, 9.

53. González Echevarría, *The Pride of Havana*, 113.

54. González Echevarría, *The Pride of Havana*, 178.

55. Alferio R. Noriega, "Sobre Oscar Charleston," January 10, 1924, in OCS.

56. "La labor personal de Oscar Charleston," in OCS.

57. Letter in OCS. Janie was certainly in Cuba at this time, as Castillo y León asks Oscar to remember him to her.

58. "A los fanaticos de Santa Clara." Flyer in OCS. I assume this was the flyer enclosed by Castillo y León.

59. "Charla con los fanaticos," in OCS.

60. "Charleston no ofendió a nuestro ejército," in OCS.

61. Quoted in Holway, *Blackball Stars*, 107.

62. Wilmer Harris, telephone interview, July 1, 2003, JSP.

63. The letter was reprinted in "Giants Have Great Manager," *Harrisburg Courier*, February 3, 1924, 5.

64. Santa Clara authorities had planned to hold a banquet in honor of Charleston, Linares, and their achievements with the Leopardos once the Gran Premio Invernal concluded; a charming letter from municipal representatives assured Oscar of the city's "love and admiration" and "sympathy and friendship," as well as its best wishes for Janie. But Janie was apparently not feeling well, so she and Oscar decided not to hang around for the festivities.

65. Charles C. Alexander says that McGraw and Blanche left New York in mid-February 1924 "for a couple of weeks of relaxation in Cuba" (*John McGraw*, 253).

66. McGraw, *My Thirty Years in Baseball*, 201.

67. That McGraw said Charleston was the finest player he had ever seen has been repeated numerous times in the secondary literature. The earliest mention I can find

of such a claim comes in a July 15, 1939, column by Chester L. Washington in the *Pittsburgh Courier*. Washington says that "many, many years ago," when McGraw was watching Charleston play for the ABCs, he remarked that he "could use that fellow . . . if I could put a coat of white paint on him" (16). This is probably apocryphal, at least in this wording. In 1912 the *Philadelphia Inquirer* ran a long feature on José Méndez in which Hans Lobert is quoted as saying that Méndez would help the Phillies win the pennant if he could be given "a good coat of white paint." See Gary Ashwill, "Black Diamond 1912," May 8, 2011, agatetype.com. But it is certainly possible that McGraw told Charleston personally that he was the best he had ever seen (an assertion he made with respect to a number of players).

68. "Foster's Ire Aroused over Ball Players' Charges," in OCS.

69. "Giants Have Great Manager," *Harrisburg Courier*, February 3, 1924, 5.

70. McWhorter, *Winning the Race*, 42.

71. I am grateful to Rich Puerzer for gathering Strothers's story and sharing it with me. Puerzer presented on Strothers ("Colonel Strothers and Black Baseball in Harrisburg") at the 2017 SABR Jerry Malloy Negro League Conference. See also Ted Knorr, "1890, Colonel William Strothers Founds the Harrisburg Giants," at http://blog.pennlive.com/gloryoftheirtimes/2006/11/1890_colonel_william_strothers.html, and "Baseball Leader Taken by Death," *Harrisburg Telegraph*, July 14, 1933, 1, 13.

72. "Fay Says," *Chicago Defender*, February 2, 1924, 9.

73. "Hoodle-le-hoot!" in OCS.

74. "Giants Planning for Big Season; Manager Arrives," *Harrisburg Evening News*, March 4, 1924, 15.

75. This gift is discussed in "El regalo a Charleston," in OCS.

76. "Charleston Returns from Cuba—In City," *Pittsburgh Courier*, March 15, 1924, 6.

77. "Brooklyn Nine Engage Giants in Double Bill," *Harrisburg Evening News*, July 15, 1924, 15.

78. W. Rollo Wilson, "Eastern Snapshots," *Pittsburgh Courier*, July 5, 1924, 7.

79. Quoted in untitled article, *Harrisburg Courier*, July 13, 1924, 2.

80. The Senators of the AA Eastern League still play their home games there today.

81. "Hilldale Trims Harrisburgh [*sic*] on Charleston Day," *Indianapolis Freeman*, August 2, 1924.

82. "Ben Taylor Calls Oscar Charleston of Harrisburg World's Greatest Fielder," *Baltimore Afro-American*, February 7, 1925, 6.

83. "Senators Ready to Enter Arena for City Crown," *Harrisburg Evening News*, September 16, 1924, 15.

84. William Dismukes, "Dismukes' Diamond Dope," *Pittsburgh Courier*, November 15, 1924, 7.

85. The caption to a photo of Oscar in an Almendares uniform in OCS says that Oscar was playing for Almendares in 1924–25 "because Santa Clara does not need his services." Surely this was a wry joke.

86. See "El juego mas emocionante . . . ," in OCS.

87. González Echevarría, *The Pride of Havana*, 151.

88. González Echevarría, *The Pride of Havana*, 152.

89. González Echevarría, *The Pride of Havana*, 152.

90. González Echevarría, *The Pride of Havana*, 162–63.

91. See "Cubans Honor Judge Landis," *Atlanta Constitution*, February 10, 1925, 8. In his "Eastern Snapshots" column of February 14, 1925, in the *Pittsburgh Courier*, Rollo Wilson reported that Frank Warfield and Cristóbal Torriente had both hit home runs while Landis watched from his box, causing Landis to call them over and thank them "for the double thrill" (6). But neither Warfield nor Torriente hit a home run in the series, and neither had so much as a single on February 8. See Nieto, *Early U.S. Blackball Teams in Cuba*, for box scores from all eight games.

92. Guridy, *Forging Diaspora*, 2. This discussion of the Afro-Cuban community in Havana and of the Martins (below) relies on Guridy's work.

93. Margaret Ross Martin's words, quoted in Guridy, *Forging Diaspora*, 75.

94. Guridy, *Forging Diaspora*, 161.

95. Quoted in Holway, *Blackball Stars*, 109.

96. That this was indeed his intention is evidenced by the fact that the *Philadelphia Tribune*'s Lloyd Thompson, in "Charleston Is Now on Other Side of Fence," later said as much, and Oscar put the piece in ocs.

97. "Sports Mirror," *Baltimore Afro-American*, July 4, 1925, A7.

98. William G. Nunn, "Diamond Dope," *Pittsburgh Courier*, July 18, 1925, 12.

99. "Bolden Tries to Defend League and Players," *New York Amsterdam News*, July 29, 1925, 6.

100. Quoted in W. Rollo Wilson, "Eastern Snapshots," *Pittsburgh Courier*, August 15, 1925, 13.

101. Those records of course do not account for the huge number of non-league games in which Charleston and everyone else toiled day after day after day. For example, on September 9 the Harrisburg papers reported that the Giants had a total record of 121-32, a figure that surely wasn't exactly accurate but that does give some idea of the grind of a black baseball season.

102. William E. Clark, "Little World Series for Bronx Title," *New York Age*, October 24, 1925, 8. The two teams met again on November 1, the Bronx Giants winning, 8–7, to claim the semipro championship of the Bronx. But neither Gehrig nor Charleston played in that second game. Sometime near the end of Gehrig's career Oscar clipped a photo of the Iron Horse with the caption "Gehrig Nears End of Trail" for ocs.

103. In July 1940 Alvin Moses reported on a conversation he had allegedly had with Ruth in 1933. Ruth had reminisced, claimed Moses, about playing with Earl Mack's All-Stars against the Homestead Grays, during which time he concluded that "Vic Harris and Oscar Charleston would make any big league team" (*Atlanta Daily World*, July 8, 1940). Unfortunately, no record of Ruth's playing with the Mack All-Stars has been found. What *has* been found is a 1933 *Pittsburgh Courier* interview with Ruth in which the Babe says some kind things about the Negro Leagues in general. Near the end of that piece big leaguer Cy Perkins is quoted as saying essentially what Moses attributes to Ruth. Thus, Moses in 1940 was probably misremembering

or misreading that old *Courier* article—and attributing the interview to himself. In short, if Ruth and Charleston ever squared off, I have found no record of such a game.

104. Even in Cuba there was controversy over who retained Oscar's rights. Prior to this season Almendares reportedly, but unsuccessfully, attempted to keep Oscar from switching teams. See "El famoso player Oscar Charleston," in ocs.

105. I am speculating here. Charleston's at bats for this Cuban season are so limited that his returning to Indianapolis is likely the reason why, and Wilson implies without directly stating that he left the team to come home.

106. W. Rollo Wilson, "Eastern Snapshots," *Pittsburgh Courier*, December 26, 1925, 12.

107. Charleston's stint with Habana was probably limited in length not only because he returned to Indianapolis in midseason, but also because he jumped the team to play on independent clubs before the end of the season. Others, including Dick Lundy, jumped the league as well.

108. Regarding the loss of revenue, one problem was that it was relatively easy to watch games from various vantage points around the park without paying. Strothers had many non-paying customers.

109. "Giants Defeat Black Sox by 17 to 2," *Harrisburg Evening News*, July 22, 1926, 20.

110. William G. Nunn, "Diamond Dope," *Pittsburgh Courier*, June 12, 1926, 14.

111. W. Rollo Wilson, "Eastern Snapshots," *Pittsburgh Courier*, May 22, 1926, 15.

112. W. Rollo Wilson, "Eastern Snapshots," *Pittsburgh Courier*, May 15, 1926, 15.

113. "Baseball," *Baltimore Afro-American*, August 7, 1926, 7.

114. William G. Nunn, "Diamond Dope," *Pittsburgh Courier*, August 14, 1926, 15.

115. W. Rollo Wilson, "Eastern Snapshots," *Pittsburgh Courier*, September 4, 1926, 15.

116. Quoted in William Jackson, "Tribe Manager Recalls Negro All-Time Baseball Immortals," *Cleveland Call and Post*, June 17, 1961, 4C.

117. Quoted in Kaplan, *Lefty Grove*, 120.

118. Quoted in Chilly Doyle, "Chillysauce," in ocs. This column was apparently published in the *Pittsburgh Gazette Times* circa 1930. I have changed "suh" to "sir" in the quote here. Oscar also clipped a photo of a September 1940 photo of Grove for ocs.

119. "Huge Crowds to See Grays Battle Big Leaguers," *Pittsburgh Courier*, October 2, 1926, 14.

120. Some sources say that three thousand fans, not eight thousand, turned out for this game. Such reporting discrepancies are not uncommon.

121. "Big Leaguers Fall before the Negroes," *Mount Carmel Daily News*, October 8, 1926, 5.

122. Quoted in Bankes, *The Pittsburgh Crawfords*, 58. Bankes's interviewee was a man named Johnny McBride, who was white and a former batboy. It is not clear if McBride was there that day or whether he had this story secondhand. The latter seems much more likely.

123. The *Pittsburgh Courier* claimed much later that Charleston had hit a home run off Johnson at this park in 1920. In the *Courier's* telling Charleston drilled a 1-2 pitch over the center field wall—after pointing at the wall, Ruth-style. It seems

likely that even in 1920 if this had really happened, it would have been reported. "Banks, Flood, Williams among 'Cleanest,'" *Pittsburgh Courier*, August 12, 1967, 15. (For another version of the story, see Ric Roberts, "Oscar Charleston: Now in Baseball's Hall of Fame," *New York Amsterdam News*, August 28, 1976, 15.)

124. Holway, *Blackball Stars*, 97.

6. Leader, 1926–1931

1. González Echevarría, *The Pride of Havana*, 193–94.

2. "Charleston to Play with Grays Next Year: Famed Outfielder Writes Courier He Is Enjoying Big Year," *Pittsburgh Courier*, January 1, 1927, 19. This article reprints a letter from Oscar to *Courier* staff writer Ira Lewis in which Oscar gives his opinions of that winter's baseball in Cuba.

3. Cum Posey, "The Sportive Realm," *Pittsburgh Courier*, January 1, 1927, 18; "Oscar Charleston Joins Cum Posey! Charleston with Grays Is First of Season's Major League Baseball Deals," *Philadelphia Tribune*, January 8, 1927, 10.

4. Cum Posey, "The Sportive Realm," *Pittsburgh Courier*, February 5, 1927, 12.

5. "Black Sox Get Charleston: 'Babe' Wilson to Harrisburg in Exchange," *Baltimore Afro-American*, March 5, 1927, 1.

6. "Charleston Is Still Property of Harrisburg," *Baltimore Afro-American*, March 12, 1927, 1, 15.

7. William G. Nunn, "Women in Baseball," *Pittsburgh Courier*, in OCS.

8. Cum Posey, "The Sportive Realm," *Pittsburgh Courier*, March 26, 1927, 18.

9. Wellington Jones, "Welly Jones: The Old Timer," *Harrisburg Telegraph*, July 28, 1938, 17. The drive exceeded by about twenty-five feet a celebrated home run hit by Babe Ruth at the park.

10. "Home Run Drive by Charleston Defeats Rivals," *Harrisburg Evening News*, June 22, 1927, 19.

11. "Giants Slug Way to Second Win in a Row," *Harrisburg Telegraph*, June 29, 1927, 16.

12. "Charleston and Perez Slam Out Home Runs as Slugging Senators Defeat Hilldale," *Chicago Defender*, July 14, 1927, 10.

13. "Still the Greatest," *Pittsburgh Courier*, July 16, 1927, 16.

14. The Giants also would have had to convince league officials to award them three victories against the Baltimore Black Sox, who they said had forfeited the games by failing to show in Harrisburg for a second-half series. As it happened, the league was not forced to rule on the matter. One strongly suspects that Strothers was simply finished. See "Harrisburg Giants Will Not Compete," *Harrisburg Telegraph*, September 20, 1927, 17.

15. "How Much Do You Know about Your Own Race," *Pittsburgh Courier*, August 20, 1927, 13, 17.

16. W. Rollo Wilson, "Sport Shots," *Pittsburgh Courier*, August 20, 1927, 17. This story is also told, with the same essential details, in an undated clipping included in OCS.

17. Later in October 1927 Charleston, Beckwith, and Jud Wilson, among others, were supposed to play with the Bacharach Giants in a series of contests against Earl

Mack's All-Stars in Atlantic City, Philadelphia, and Newark. Mack's club was reportedly going to include big stars like Harry Heilmann, Lefty Grove, and George Burns. I was not able to find evidence that these games were ever played. See "Bees to Play All Stars in Late Series," *Philadelphia Tribune*, October 20, 1927, 11.

18. W. Rollo Wilson, "Sport Shots," *Pittsburgh Courier*, January 15, 1927, 13.

19. "They Like Oscar Charleston Down in Cuba," *Pittsburgh Courier*, December 10, 1927, 17. The original, November 14, 1927, *El País* version of this piece, along with a typewritten translation, is included in ocs. I would guess that the translation of the article is Oscar's own.

20. Wolfinger, "African American Migration."

21. On Bolden, see Lanctot, *Fair Dealing and Clean Playing*, 17ff. On Bolden's nervous breakdown, see "Edw. Bolden Has a Nervous Breakdown," *Baltimore Afro-American*, October 1, 1927, 9.

22. See Strecker's comments on "Oscar Charleston General Thread" at www.baseball-fever.com/archive/index.php/t-58644.html.

23. "Grays Have Many Road Games This Month," *Pittsburgh Courier*, July 14, 1928, B5; "Expect Charleston in Game Tonight against Poseymen," *Pittsburgh Press*, September 21, 1928, 51.

24. "Still Going Good," *Chicago Defender*, July 21, 1928, 9.

25. That Oscar was pitched around or walked more frequently is the sense one gets from perusing game accounts and box scores. The box scores collected by Gary Ashwill show that Oscar's overall walk rate went up only slightly.

26. "Hilldale Is Greatest Ball Team," *Baltimore Afro-American*, March 16, 1929, A4.

27. "Veteran Outfielder and Star Pitcher Will Play for Daisies; Report Soon," *Philadelphia Tribune*, March 29, 1928, 10.

28. "Diamond Dust," *Mount Carmel Item*, March 30, 1928, 12.

29. W. Rollo Wilson, "Charleston and Dalty [*sic*] Cooper Sign with Hilldale," *Pittsburgh Courier*, March 31, 1928, A4.

30. W. Rollo Wilson, "Sport Shots," *Pittsburgh Courier*, September 29, 1928, 18.

31. The American Negro League comprised Hilldale, the Baltimore Black Sox, the Homestead Grays, the Lincoln Giants, the Bacharach Giants, and the Cuban Stars. It was not a very different lineup from the one featured in the ecl in previous years.

32. W. Rollo Wilson, "Sport Shots," *Pittsburgh Courier*, February 9, 1929, 12.

33. I take much of this information from González Echevarría, *The Pride of Havana*, 180–81.

34. "Sportographs," *Wilmington News Journal*, March 21, 1929, 21.

35. "Hilldale Is Greatest Ball Team," *Baltimore Afro-American*, March 16, 1929, A4.

36. The *Pittsburgh Post-Gazette* noted that Charleston, "while of the roly-poly type of player, . . . possesses amazing speed" ("Colored Stars Will Play with Hilldale," June 18, 1929, 19).

37. W. Rollo Wilson, "Oscar the Great," *Norfolk New Journal and Guide*, April 27, 1929, 5.

38. W. Rollo Wilson, "Thru the Eyes of W. Rollo Wilson," *Philadelphia Tribune*, April 15, 1944, 12. Wilson, writing retrospectively, adds that Posey "never won a fist fight."

39. "Cuban Giants and Hilldale Split a Doubleheader," *New York Age*, June 1, 1929, 6.

40. "Cuban Stars Twice Wallop Hilldale," *Baltimore Afro-American*, June 15, 1929, 17.

41. "Daisies Show Life to Beat and Tie Cubans," *Philadelphia Tribune*, June 20, 1929, 10.

42. "Signs!," *Pittsburgh Courier*, February 22, 1930, 15.

43. Dizzy Dismukes, "Dismukes Names His Nine Best Outfielders," *Pittsburgh Courier*, March 8, 1930, 14.

44. "The 1930 Edition of the Grays," *Pittsburgh Courier*, March 22, 1930, 15.

45. "Grays Leave Spa for New Orleans," *Pittsburgh Post-Gazette*, March 27, 1930, 15.

46. Chester L. Washington, "'Ches' Sez," *Pittsburgh Courier*, April 5, 1930, 16.

47. Quoted in Peterson, *Only the Ball Was White*, 11–12.

48. "Grays Possess Hitting Power as Well as Strength in Field," *Greenville Record-Argus*, June 20, 1930, 7.

49. W. Ardes, "Short Snaps," *Philadelphia Tribune*, August 7, 1930, 10.

50. Judy Johnson told a reporter in 1976 that Charleston moved to first base because of this injury and could no longer throw well; indeed he could not even straighten his left arm fully. See "Charleston Makes 'Hall,'" *Wilmington News Journal*, February 11, 1976, 23.

51. Oscar memorialized this game extensively in his scrapbook, including a column by *Pittsburgh Post-Gazette* sports editor Havey Boyle in which Boyle wrote that Charleston, "that great colored athlete with the Grays," told him he preferred playing under the sun, "although," Boyle added, "he manages to star by night as he does by day" ("Mirrors of Sport," in OCS).

52. The first version of this story was propounded by Rollo Wilson in the September 27, 1930, edition of the *Pittsburgh Courier* (14). Hardly a word in Wilson's account was true, but already Gibson, like Charleston before him, evoked mythicization.

53. "Discovered by Oscar Charleston seven years ago, Gibson is one of the mightiest sluggers in baseball" ("Homestead in Two with Bushwicks," *Brooklyn Daily Eagle*, May 18, 1939, 21).

54. Brashler, *Josh Gibson*, 26.

55. "Smoky Joe Scores 27 Strikeouts," *Pittsburgh Courier*, August 9, 1930, 15.

56. "Bat Helps," *Pittsburgh Courier*, August 2, 1930, 15.

57. "All-Round Player," *Chicago Defender*, September 6, 1930, 8.

58. "Sport Sidelights," *Philadelphia Tribune*, October 16, 1930, 11.

59. See "Charleston Back Home from Cuba," in OCS. Charleston also clipped and kept a September 23, 1934, profile of Machado in exile, as well as his obituary.

60. Cum Posey, "Looking over the Baseball Horizon," *Pittsburgh Courier*, March 21, 1931, 15.

61. Page quoted in Holway: *Black Giants*, 59–60, and, *Voices from the Great Black Baseball Leagues*, 158.

62. Dale Landon and George Wiley, "1930s Mine League Part of 'The Great Past,'" *Indiana Gazette*, November 10, 1976, 34.

63. The House of David baseball team was a barnstorming group of ethnically mixed, luxuriantly bearded players putatively representing a tiny, Michigan-based reli-

gious sect. By this time they had gained considerable fame, and Pollock had traded on that fame by convincing a group of Cuban players to grow beards and perform under the name of the Cuban House of David.

64. See Mark Whitaker's *Smoketown*, which offers a vivid narrative of black Pittsburgh during this period.

65. "Hilldale Drops Two to Homestead Grays," *Philadelphia Tribune*, July 16, 1931, 10.

66. William G. Nunn, "Divide Close Pair in Cleveland Arena," *Pittsburgh Courier*, September 5, 1931, 14.

67. Cum Posey, "'Cum' Posey's Pointed Paragraphs," *Pittsburgh Courier*, January 2, 1932, 13.

68. Quoted in Andy Dugo, "Dick Goldberg Who He No. 16," *Pittsburgh Post-Gazette*, August 14, 1968, 24.

69. The Seamheads database shows the Grays going 22-13-1 against top competition in 1931, second in winning percentage among major black baseball teams to Hilldale's 30-11 record.

70. Cum Posey, "Grays Undisputed Champs; Team Play Won—League Looms," *Pittsburgh Courier*, October 10, 1931, 15.

71. One encounters in the literature statements that the 1931 Grays compiled a 136-17 record and that Gibson hit seventy-five home runs. Neither of these claims was made at the time, and Posey's actual, plausible claim of a 33-18 record versus major competition means that the first assertion, at least, is obviously false.

72. Kelley, *The Negro Leagues Revisited*, 11.

73. "Still an Ace," *Chicago Defender*, September 26, 1931, 8.

74. "Crawfords Sign New Stars," *Pittsburgh Courier*, June 27, 1931, 15.

75. "Paige Stops Grays as Crawfords Cop, 10 to 7," *Pittsburgh Courier*, August 8, 1931, 15.

76. "Oscar Charleston Boomed to Pilot Pitts. Crawfords," *Philadelphia Tribune*, December 17, 1931, 10.

7. Champion, 1932–1938

1. Stanley Glenn reported that Oscar and Gus "were very good friends." Telephone interview, July 1, 2003, JSP. Oscar also clipped for his scrapbook part of a newspaper column in which Greenlee is praised, along with J. L. Wilkinson, as unique among owners in trying their best to treat players fairly. Greenlee is quoted as saying, "I think the player has a right to as much money as I can afford to pay him, and I am not in the game to kill off and underpay the men who draw the crowds through the gates. I want to make money out of it and I want the players to get a decent living." No wonder Oscar loved the man.

2. The discussion about Greenlee and the Crawford Grill that follows draws primarily from Ruck, *Sandlot Seasons*; Bankes, *The Pittsburgh Crawfords*; and contemporaneous newspaper articles.

3. Bob Luke explains how the numbers game worked, at least in Baltimore: "To play the numbers a person placed a bet in the form of three single-digit numbers,

such as 692, with a writer, who met a pick-up man between noon and one o'clock. The pick-up man took the money and the numbers to the banker's headquarters, which could be an office, kitchen table, or dining room, depending on the banker's finances. Throughout the process, lookout men kept an eye out for the police, both uniformed and undercover. Each day bankers agreed to use the results of three horse races at an East Coast race track to determine the winning numbers. They totaled the parimutuel payout on the horses that won, placed, and showed in each of the three races. Say those totals came to $26.30 for the first race, $29.70 for the second race, and $22.00 for the third race. The bankers selected the number in the units place in each total—in this case, 6, 9, and 2—to determine the winning combination" (Luke, *The Baltimore Elite Giants*, 108).

4. Leonard with Riley, *Buck Leonard*, 105; Tye, *Satchel*, 71.

5. Ruck, *Sandlot Seasons*, 149–50. Gus was known for helping struggling neighborhood families pay grocery or coal bills, for distributing hundreds of turkeys on Thanksgiving and Christmas, and even for helping put some local kids through college. In many ways he really was a community asset.

6. Ruck, *Sandlot Seasons*, 148.

7. Bankes, *The Pittsburgh Crawfords*, 20, 79.

8. Bankes, *The Pittsburgh Crawfords*, 79, 66.

9. "Charleston Is Elected Captain," *Philadelphia Tribune*, January 28, 1932, 11.

10. Rogosin, *Invisible Men*, 53.

11. One of the primary benefits of the new bus may have been that Oscar was no longer called upon to drive, an activity he undertook with much the same aggressive recklessness he displayed on the base paths. When Boston Braves pitcher Fred Frankhouse rode with Oscar from Pittsburgh to Altoona in the 1930s, Oscar took the mountain curves at such wild speeds that Frankhouse declined to return with him. "You scared the devil out of me," he told Oscar (quoted in Holway, *Blackball Stars*, 113–14). Charleston had his driver's license temporarily suspended by Pennsylvania in July 1932, and a few years later, on March 5, 1938, he almost killed Gus Greenlee and Crawfords secretary-publicist John Clark when he skidded off the road near McConnellsburg, Pennsvylania, into a tree. The three men were fortunate to walk away from that wreck with minor injuries.

12. Bankes, *The Pittsburgh Crawfords*, 22.

13. "Crawfords Back, Set for Test," *Pittsburgh Courier*, April 30, 1932, 15.

14. "Wiley Wildcats Turn to the Diamond," *Atlanta Daily World*, March 22, 1932, 5.

15. "Black Barons Open against Pittsburgh Crawfords," *Atlanta Daily World*, April 13, 1932, 5.

16. Bankes, *The Pittsburgh Crawfords*, 68.

17. See Bankes, *The Pittsburgh Crawfords*, 23–24.

18. The records reported here versus top competition come, per usual, from Seamheads.com. Ruck, *Sandlot Seasons*, 157, is the source for the 99-36 claim.

19. W. Rollo Wilson, "Sport Shots," *Pittsburgh Courier*, January 2, 1932, 12.

20. William G. Nunn, "Sport Talks," *Pittsburgh Courier*, June 4, 1932, 15.

21. Quoted in Bankes, *The Pittsburgh Crawfords*, 57.

22. *Indianapolis News*, May 13, 1932.

23. "ABCS Leave for Series with Montgomery and Birmingham Nines," *Indianapolis Recorder*, May 21, 1932, 2.

24. "Pilots Lose to Detroit Wolves," *Washington Post*, June 1, 1932, 13.

25. Lanctot, *Negro League Baseball*, 22–23. Foster and Charleston were reportedly interviewed by a second radio station as well.

26. The figure of twelve thousand is according to most sources. One source estimated the crowd at closer to twenty thousand.

27. "He Usually Got on Base," *Chicago Defender*, September 16, 1933, 9.

28. "Charleston, Lundy, Suttles Ranked as 'Major League Timber,'" *Pittsburgh Courier*, September 16, 1933, 15. The writer is identified as Farrell in "Paid Tribute," *Pittsburgh Courier*, September 23, 1933, 15.

29. *Pittsburgh Courier* reported on October 14, 1933; "Baseball Moguls to Meet in Philly Next Month," *Pittsburgh Courier*, January 27, 1934, 15.

30. "Repeal Hits the 'Avenooe'!" *Pittsburgh Courier*, December 9, 1933, 6.

31. Al Monroe, "Speaking of Sports," *Chicago Defender*, May 19, 1934, 16.

32. "Negro Nines Clash at Stadium Today," *Washington Post*, June 10, 1934, 17.

33. "Game Slated at 5 O'Clock," *Altoona Tribune*, June 14, 1934, 6.

34. *Philadelphia Tribune*, August 2, 1934, 12.

35. "Battle Royal When They Meet," *Harrisburg Telegraph*, July 11, 1934, 10.

36. See Tye, *Satchel*, 89–90, and "Satchel Paige Hurls Bearded Nine to Title," *Indianapolis Recorder*, August 25, 1934, 7.

37. Chester L. Washington, "Sez 'Ches,'" *Pittsburgh Courier*, September 1, 1934, 15.

38. "Bat Boys Responsible for East Team's 1–0 Victory," *Chicago Defender*, September 1, 1934, 15.

39. Gay, *Satch, Dizzy, and Rapid Robert*, 75.

40. Gay, *Satch, Dizzy, and Rapid Robert*, 76.

41. I rely on Gregory, *Diz*, for biographical information about Dean.

42. Gregory, *Diz*, 122–23.

43. Leonard with Riley, *Buck Leonard*, 45.

44. Bankes, *The Pittsburgh Crawfords*, 55.

45. Edward F. Balinger, "Near-Riot Marks Deans' Exhibition Here," *Pittsburgh Post-Gazette*, October 24, 1934, 15.

46. Quoted in "Discrimination Has No Place in Baseball . . . These Cubs Agree," *Pittsburgh Courier*, August 12, 1939, 16.

47. Quoted in Rogosin, *Invisible Men*, 80.

48. Bankes, *The Pittsburgh Crawfords*, 89

49. Bankes, *The Pittsburgh Crawfords*, 88.

50. Bankes, *The Pittsburgh Crawfords*, 89.

51. Bankes, *The Pittsburgh Crawfords*, 89.

52. Bankes, *The Pittsburgh Crawfords*, 54.

53. Bankes, *The Pittsburgh Crawfords*, 87.

54. Bankes, *The Pittsburgh Crawfords*, 54. The Klan story just doesn't sound very plausible. Bell places it in Florida, for one thing, and I am unable to find a time when he and Oscar were in that state together. For another, except for ceremonial occasions, when the white hoods were on, the mob usually meant business. Nor did the Klan usually conduct that business at ballparks in full view of the community.

One other occasion when Oscar stood up for his team was recounted by a *Cumberland News* columnist. It seems that decades earlier Oscar's Harrisburg Giants had come to town to play the local nine. The Cumberland pitcher had discovered that he could get quite a little extra movement on his pitches by stitching a nutmeg grater into the webbing of his glove. When a suspicious Giants player demanded that the mitt be examined, the pitcher refused. The Cumberland manager then ran onto the field to demand that the Giants clam up and play ball. If they didn't, he threatened, they wouldn't get a dime from the gate. Oscar's response was to pack up the bats and leave. C. V. Burns, "Sport Slants," *Cumberland News*, May 18, 1948, 9.

55. Bankes, *The Pittsburgh Crawfords*, 91.

56. Bankes, *The Pittsburgh Crawfords*, 91.

57. Quoted in Bankes, *The Pittsburgh Crawfords*, 67.

58. Quoted in Bankes, *The Pittsburgh Crawfords*, 92.

59. Eddie Gottlieb said that on tours he promoted, he arranged for Oscar to room with Satchel in order to prevent Paige from slipping away. Rust, *"Get That Nigger off the Field,"* 49.

60. Leonard with Riley, *Buck Leonard*, 42.

61. "Crawfords See Big Year in Baseball," *Chicago Defender*, May 4, 1935, 11.

62. Chester L. Washington, "Sez 'Ches,'" *Pittsburgh Courier*, May 11, 1935, 14.

63. Al Abrams, "Sidelights on Sports," *Pittsburgh Post-Gazette*, May 29, 1935, 20.

64. Chester L. Washington, "Giving Chicago the Once-Over," *Pittsburgh Courier*, July 20, 1935, A4.

65. Negroes Can't Find 'Babe' Mitchell's Tosses; Lose, 5–1," *Delaware County Times*, July 17, 1935, 11.

66. "Chester Loses," *Delaware County Times*, August 6, 1935, 10.

67. See, e.g., Leonard with Riley, *Buck Leonard*, 46, 55.

68. Oscar also held off Cum Posey to be named the West's manager (both the Grays and the Crawfords being moved to the West team in 1935) and thereby obtain the opportunity to skipper a club that included six future Hall of Famers, not counting himself. (The East's squad included five future Cooperstown inductees.) Joe Louis, fresh off his title bout of August 7 at Comiskey Park, threw out the game's first pitch at three o'clock. The East then got out to a fast four-run lead, but the West clawed back to tie things up with three runs in the sixth and one in the seventh. When the game entered the bottom of the eighth, Oscar, having gone 0 for 3 and having made an error trying to catch a hot throw from Double Duty Radcliffe in his patented one-hand style, had already allowed Leonard to take his place. Some of the fans grumbled that he had done wrong to start himself—despite winning the vote—over Leonard. Others criticized his failure to pinch-hit lefty Turkey Stearnes in the fourth inning

when right-hander Leon Day had taken the mound for the East, relieving Slim Jones. Fortunately, Mule Suttles made those criticisms academic when he blasted a three-run homer off Martín Dihigo into the right-center field stands in the bottom of the eleventh, giving the West an 11–8 victory and Oscar his second straight East-West managerial win.

69. I am grateful to Rich Puerzer for sifting through the inconsistent media coverage to provide a coherent account of this series: "The 1935 Playoff Series: The New York Cubans vs. the Pittsburgh Crawfords," presentation delivered at SABR Jerry Malloy Negro League Conference, Pittsburgh, August 7, 2015.

70. Forbes told John Holway this story. See Holway, *Black Giants*, 5–6, and Holway, *Josh and Satch*, 82. Note, however, that Forbes appears to be an unreliable source for the game's details (and for much else).

71. Bankes, *The Pittsburgh Crawfords*, 85.

72. Bankes, *The Pittsburgh Crawfords*, 73.

73. Cum Posey, "Pointed Paragraphs," *Pittsburgh Courier*, December 21, 1935, 13.

74. Joe Bostic, "Thousands See Defeat of Cubans and Stars," *New York Amsterdam News*, September 28, 1935, 12.

75. Chester L. Washington, "Sez 'Ches,'" *Pittsburgh Courier*, May 9, 1936, 14.

76. "Teams in Game at Middletown," *Harrisburg Evening News*, September 4, 1936, 13.

77. Lanctot, *Negro League Baseball*, 54.

78. The team found controversy near the season's end when it was accused by *New York Daily Mirror* columnist Dan Parker of throwing a game against the Brooklyn Bushwicks. Gibson had apparently dropped a pop fly when the Bushwicks had the bases loaded in the bottom of the ninth. Bettors found that fishy, but popups were Josh's kryptonite. Commissioner Landis, going well beyond his authority as usual, even reportedly met personally with members of the Craws in order to check the story out. Parker soon retracted his claim, however, saying he had gotten a bad tip. See Rogosin, *Invisible Men*, 114–15. Oscar certainly had his flaws, but no man was ever less likely to throw a game.

79. W. Rollo Wilson, "National Sport Shots," *Pittsburgh Courier*, September 26, 1936, A5.

80. Quoted in Bankes, *The Pittsburgh Crawfords*, 59. Baugh placed this encounter at the 1936 *Denver Post* tournament. But Oscar did not compete in that event, so if this discussion did in fact take place, it probably happened during the all-stars' late-season trip to Texas.

81. I rely primarily on Timothy Gay's excellent summary for the story of this series in *Satch, Dizzy, and Rapid Robert*, 162–66.

82. "Charleston Leads Men off Field in K. C.," *Philadelphia Tribune*, October 1, 1936, 11.

83. W. Rollo Wilson, "Sport Shots," *Pittsburgh Courier*, February 18, 1933, 14.

84. "One Was There—Delivered; Others Deserved Berth," *Chicago Defender*, July 15, 1933, 9.

85. Farrell is quoted in Bill Gibson, "Hear Me Talkin' to Ya," *Baltimore Afro-American*, September 23, 1933, 23.

86. Al Monroe, "Speaking of Sports," *Chicago Defender*, October 6, 1934, 16.

87. Al Abrams, "Sidelights on Sports," *Pittsburgh Post-Gazette*, October 25, 1934, 15.

88. Lee A. Johnson, "Shooting the Works," *Indianapolis Recorder*, August 10, 1935, 12.

89. William G. Nunn, "Your Turn Now, Pitt!" *Pittsburgh Courier*, August 15, 1936, A5.

90. Dave Wyatt, "Sweeping Educational Campaign in Baseball." Article in OCS.

91. "Battle to Lift Ban on These and Other Stars in Baseball," *Chicago Defender*, August 29, 1936, 13.

92. Quoted in Bankes, *The Pittsburgh Crawfords*, 58.

93. Lewis R. Dial, "The Sport Dial," *New York Age*, September 12, 1936, 9.

94. Chester L. Washington, "Ches Sez: Rap's Homer Beats Grays," *Pittsburgh Courier*, August 3, 1935, A4. Harry Beale told the same story, at less length, in the same issue of the *Courier* ("Local Sport Slants," A5), so he and Washington must have gotten it at the same time.

95. "Talk O' Town," *Pittsburgh Courier*, March 27, 1937, 9. The column reports that Oscar had won in the "sweepstakes." I am presuming that this was a reference to the numbers.

96. Leonard with Riley, *Buck Leonard*, 79.

97. "When the game would start [Bassett] would sit down in that rocking chair catching, but if somebody tried to steal second base he would get out of the chair and throw the man out at second and then sit back down. He did that for a couple of innings each game as a gate attraction for a year or two. But that was all show business" (Leonard with Riley, *Buck Leonard*, 81).

98. Bankes, *The Pittsburgh Crawfords*, 67.

99. Tye, *Satchel*, 110–16, has the best discussion of this affair. Other details are taken from newspaper accounts.

100. Quoted in Rogosin, *Invisible Men*, 166–67.

101. Oscar could not, however, resist the urge to get in a fight. On June 16 he was fined twenty-five dollars by Greenlee, acting in his capacity as league president, for getting into a scuffle with an umpire. Four other players and managers were also fined that day, as Greenlee tried to take some modest steps toward containing violence on the field, especially against umpires.

102. "'Pepper' Bassett, with Batting Avg. of .444 Is Helping Craws' Cause," *Pittsburgh Courier*, July 31, 1937, 16.

103. The league seems to have deputized Oscar to report on the players who jumped to San Domingo in 1937. No player deals, as of January 31, 1938, were allowed until he submitted his report. Just what any of this meant is not clear, but Oscar seems to have played at least a pro forma role in determining the jumping players' eligibility going forward. "Colored League Shapes '38 Plans," *Pittsburgh Post-Gazette*, January 31, 1938, 16.

104. "Satchell Paige Might Come to Stars," *Philadelphia Tribune*, March 17, 1938, 13.

105. Wendell Smith, "Smitty's Sport Spurts," *Pittsburgh Courier*, May 28, 1938, 17.

106. Quoted in Wendell Smith, "Grays Take Lead in Spring Drills with K.C.," *Pittsburgh Courier*, April 23, 1938, 17.

107. The 1938 contract between Taylor and the Crawfords called for him to be paid $400 per month between May 15 and October 1. It was signed by Taylor, Greenlee, and Charleston (as witness). The four-page document disproves the notion that Negro Leagues players did not have formal contracts. Image in author's possession.

108. "Here's What Rival Managers Predict on Eve of League Lid Lifters," *Pittsburgh Courier*, May 14, 1938, 17.

109. Leonard with Riley, *Buck Leonard*, 94–95.

110. Wendell Smith, "Smitty's Sport Spurts," *Pittsburgh Courier*, July 16, 1938, 16.

111. "Allen Sure to Start in Classic," *Chicago Defender*, July 30, 1938, 9.

112. "Charleston-Harris in Hectic Battle for Managerial Honors," *Pittsburgh Courier*, August 13, 1938, 16.

113. This record comes from the Center for Negro League Baseball Research. See http://www.cnlbr.org/Portals/0/Standings/Negro%20National%20League%20(1920 -1948)%202016-08.pdf. Seamheads has the Crawfords at 22-22-1.

114. John Schulian, telephone interview, November 7, 2015.

115. Andrew Porter, telephone interview, July 3, 2003, JSP. Porter, however, is the only ex-player who remembered this about Oscar.

116. Holway quoted in Bill Lee, "Charleston Was Born Too Late," *Hartford Courant*, August 15, 1976, 116.

117. Lee A. Johnson, "Shooting the Works," *Indianapolis Recorder*, August 17, 1935, 12.

118. "Talk O' Town," *Pittsburgh Courier*, March 12, 1938, 9.

119. As of March 2, 1935, Janie was still active in the Unity Social Club of Harrisburg. She is mentioned as a member in the March 2, 1935, edition of the *Baltimore Afro-American* (Tad Winchester, "Society in the East," 10).

8. Scout, 1939–1947

1. "Charleston in Action at Dexter Sunday," *Brooklyn Daily Eagle*, May 26, 1939, 19.

2. Chester L. Washington, "'Ches' Sez: 'Candy Jim' Talks Shop," *Pittsburgh Courier*, July 25, 1936, A4.

3. Chester L. Washington, "Sez 'Ches': Calling All Strikes," *Pittsburgh Courier*, April 24, 1937, 16.

4. Bill "Bojangles" Robinson, very likely a friend of Oscar's, selected Charleston for the mythical Negro Leagues Hall of Fame prior to a ceremony honoring the leagues' all-time greats at Yankee Stadium on July 2, 1939. Robinson, Joe Louis, and Cab Calloway had each been asked to pick five or six players. "Negroes to Honor Stars," *New York Times*, July 2, 1939, S2.

5. Quoted in Wendell Smith, "Owners Will Admit Negro Players If Fans Demand Them—Cards Pilot," *Pittsburgh Courier*, August 19, 1939, 16.

6. Alvin Moses, ". . . Beatin' the Gun," *Indianapolis Recorder*, October 5, 1940, 16.

7. "Sammy Bankhead Will Play with Toledoans," *New York Amsterdam News*, April 22, 1939, 19.

8. Quoted in "Oscar Charleston to Manage Strong Toledo Nine in NNL," *Pittsburgh Courier*, April 22, 1939, 17; Cum Posey, "Posey's Points," *Pittsburgh Courier*, April 22, 1939, 17.

9. John Wagner, "Swayne Field Was Full of History," *Toledo Blade*, October 5, 2001. See http://www.toledoblade.com/Mud-Hens/2001/10/05/Swayne-Field-was-full-of -history.html.

10. I take this biographical information about Owens largely from Baker, *Jesse Owens*.

11. "Big Crowd to Watch Chi-Craw Battle," *Pittsburgh Courier*, July 22, 1933, 15.

12. "Doubleheader and Jesse Owens at Park Monday," *Lima News*, June 4, 1939, 15. Dr. Charles Greenlee, Gus's son, told historian Rob Ruck (*Sandlot Seasons*, 157–58) that Owens traveled with the Crawfords, racing men and horses for a while in 1936. This does not appear to be true. Owens spent the spring, summer, and much of autumn 1936 qualifying for the Olympics, racing in the Olympics, and finally being celebrated across the nation for his performances in the Olympics. Later he stumped for Alf Landon. The *Pittsburgh Courier* covered both Owens and the Crawfords extensively in 1936 but never mentioned Owens racing or even being present at a Crawfords game.

13. I have pieced together this account of Owens's time racing with the Crawfords from newspaper accounts of the time.

14. Owens with Neimark, *Blackthink*, 49–50.

15. Owens with Neimark, *I Have Changed*, 71.

16. It was quite the contrary, as Baker points out in *Jesse Owens*, 143.

17. "Jesse Owens Dazzles Louisville People," *Atlanta Daily World*, September 8, 1939, 5.

18. "Paige's All-Stars vs. Crawfords," *Indianapolis Recorder*, September 9, 1939, 14; "Charleston in Action at Dexter Sunday," *Brooklyn Daily Eagle*, May 26, 1939, 19.

19. Wendell Smith, "Time Out!" *Pittsburgh Courier*, May 13, 1939, 17; "Crawfords in Two Victories over Clowns," *Chicago Defender*, July 1, 1939, 8; "Crawfords Beat Cubans," *Chicago Defender*, June 24, 1939, 8.

20. See, for example, Bill Cooper, "Negroes Down Heck Ross, 10–5," *Des Moines Register*, July 18, 1939, 8.

21. "Toledo Crawfords Here Sun., May 26 at Stadium," *Indianapolis Recorder*, May 18, 1940, 14. I am admittedly reading between the lines of contemporary newspaper articles in speculating about Oscar's deeper motivations.

22. Bankes, *The Pittsburgh Crawfords*, 59.

23. Quoted in Peterson, *Only the Ball Was White*, 242. Similarly, Connie Johnson remembered Oscar, as a manager, playfully hollering, "Hey! Somebody get on! Let ol' Charleston hit!" (quoted in Kelley, *The Negro Leagues Revisited*, 119).

24. See Johnson's account of coming to play for the Crawfords in Kelley, *The Negro Leagues Revisited*, 114–16.

25. See "Ethiopian Clowns Eye Another Big Season," *Atlanta Daily World*, February 20, 1940, 5; "Ethiopian Clowns to Play Busy Schedule," *Atlanta Daily World*, March 21, 1940, 5.

26. "Ethiopian Clowns Score in Ninth to Win Frank Merriwell Tilt 1–0, *Atlanta Daily World*, April 7, 1940, 8.

27. Lucius Jones: "Slant on Sports," *Atlanta Daily World*, April 7, 1940, 8, and "Jesse Owens Turns Horse Race into Farce with Easy Victory," *Atlanta Daily World*, April 22, 1940, 5.

28. "Craws Win Opener 8 to 2 as Murky Weather Prevails; St. Louis Has Strong Team," *Indianapolis Recorder*, June 1, 1940, 12.

29. For example: "Jesse Owens, despite his worldwide fame, will have to divide the spotlight with another national favorite, Oscar Charleston," in "Jesse Owens' Advent to Atlanta Recalls Great 1936 Performance," *Atlanta Daily World*, April 14, 1940, 8.

30. "Three Attractions in Double Bill Here," *Harrisburg Evening News*, August 20, 1940, 12.

31. "American Giants Meet Toledo in Two Games Today," *Chicago Tribune*, August 11, 1940, 25.

32. "Crawfords at Birmingham Sunday July 7," *Chicago Defender*, July 6, 1940, 23.

33. "National Mayors Ass'n to Hold Meet This Week," *Chicago Defender*, August 31, 1940, 4.

34. Motley, *Ruling over Monarchs, Giants, and Stars*, 31–34.

35. Shane, "Chocolate Rube Waddell," 80.

36. Ed Harris, "Humbly Ungrateful," *Philadelphia Tribune*, August 15, 1940, 11. Rollo's opinion that Oscar did not bully players was a "minority" one, wrote Shane in response to Wilson (according to Harris). However, the historical record definitely favors Wilson's point of view, even if it was not one shared by everyone.

37. "M'ley Seeks Charleston for Pilot," *Philadelphia Tribune*, August 29, 1940, 12.

38. Randy Dixon, "The Sports Bugle," *Pittsburgh Courier*, October 19, 1940, 17.

39. Burnett was just a couple of months removed from a horrific accident. He was driving a car packed with other members of the ABCs when, blinded by the lights of an oncoming vehicle, he lost control and smashed into a utility pole. The ABCs' manager, William Earl Smith, was killed in the crash, and several players were seriously hurt. "Richmond Crash Victims Show Stubborn Gains," *Indianapolis Recorder*, October 12, 1940, 1.

40. Quoted in Kelley, *The Negro Leagues Revisited*, 79.

41. Quoted in Kelley, *The Negro Leagues Revisited*, 131.

42. "Sunday's Twin Bill to Take Lid Off for Gala Season of Baseball at Perry Stadium," *Indianapolis Recorder*, May 10, 1941, 14.

43. See primarily "San Blas Indians Nod Twin Bill as Oscar Charleston Comes Home," *Indianapolis Recorder*, May 17, 1941, 14; Wesley O. Jackson, "San Blas Indians vs. Detroit Stars Sunday," *Indianapolis Recorder*, May 24, 1941, 14; "Locals Down Detroit Stars 8–1, 14–8 in Double-Header," *Indianapolis Recorder*, May 31, 1941, 12.

44. "Locals Down Detroit Stars 8–1, 14–8 in Double-Header," *Indianapolis Recorder*, May 31, 1941.

45. "Takes Over Reins as Bolden Makes 'Victory' Shift," *Philadelphia Tribune*, June 12, 1941, 9.

46. John Gibbons remembered that "Charleston got a phone call from Philadelphia and they wanted him to come to manage the Philadelphia Stars," so it doesn't

seem as if it took Oscar long to decide to take the job (quoted in Kelley, *The Negro Leagues Revisited*, 132).

47. The Indianapolis press was slow in reporting Oscar's departure from his own team. The papers had recently taken to referring to the San Blas Indians as Oscar Charleston's Indians, and they continued to do so for some time, not noting until June 21 that Oscar Charleston's Indians no longer retained the services of the man for whom the team had been named. "Indians Rout St. Louis Team 6–5 at Stadium," *Indianapolis Recorder*, June 21, 1941, 14.

48. "Homestead Grays to Meet Cubans in Gotham, June 28," *Norfolk New Journal and Guide*, June 21, 1941, 13.

49. Randy Dixon, "Sports Bugle," *Pittsburgh Courier*, June 21, 1941, 16.

50. Oscar gave the cook Gibbons's two dollars per day in meal money, according to Gibbons (Kelley, *The Negro Leagues Revisited*, 133).

51. Holway, *Black Diamonds*, 79.

52. "Stars Tumble Grays, Elites," *Philadelphia Tribune*, June 26, 1941, 9.

53. Charles J. Tiano, "Sportside," *Kingston Freeman*, February 15, 1976, 31.

54. "Stars Win Out in Final Frame as Breaks Help," *Delaware County Daily Times*, August 9, 1941, 13.

55. "Oscar Charleston Puts New Life in Philadelphia Stars," *Altoona Tribune*, June 21, 1941, 6.

56. "Ed Bolden Would Like to Trade—But Nobody Else Is Willing or Able," *Philadelphia Tribune*, July 17, 1941, 9.

57. "Leads Philadelphia Stars," *Norfolk New Journal and Guide*, July 26, 1941, 13. Oscar's draft card of April 27, 1942, lists him at 185 pounds, so it seems he really had dropped some weight.

58. Charles Decker, "Sports Perusals," *Evansville Argus*, August 15, 1941, 3.

59. The buildings remain in use, but visitors are discouraged, as the site now houses defense-related government agencies.

60. "Every Worker an Athlete Is Quartermaster Program," *Philadelphia Inquirer*, June 6, 1943, 33.

61. We know Oscar was the manager from a remark made by W. Rollo Wilson in "Thru the Eyes of W. Rollo Wilson," *Philadelphia Tribune*, April 8, 1944, 13.

62. See Rowan with Robinson, *Wait Till Next Year*, 74.

63. "Industrial Loops Honor Teams," *Philadelphia Inquirer*, October 6, 1943, 36. Oscar's Quartermaster Depot did not win the league in 1943, nor any awards. It is interesting, in hindsight, to note that while Oscar was by far the most professionally accomplished person present, his name is not mentioned in the *Inquirer* account.

64. "Democracy in Sports at Quartermaster Department," *Philadelphia Tribune*, October 2, 1943, 13.

65. W. Rollo Wilson, "Thru the Eyes of W. Rollo Wilson," *Philadelphia Tribune*, June 26, 1943, 12.

66. Untitled article, *Philadelphia Tribune*, May 27, 1944, 9; "Quartermaster Wins, 5–4," *Philadelphia Inquirer*, May 23, 1944, 17.

67. The Cuban Yanks were owned by Joe Hall and Whitey Mazer; Hall comes into our story below ("Cuban-Yanks Sign Two Hurlers, Fielder," *Philadelphia Tribune*, June 24, 1944, 12). Oscar may have helped create this team. He was said to be its manager when it came to play the re-formed Pittsburgh Crawfords in Harrisburg on July 2, 1944, even though he ended up not appearing in that game, probably because of his new duties as coach for the Philadelphia Stars (see below). "Twin Bill Listed on Island Sunday," *Harrisburg Telegraph*, June 29, 1944, 19. He is said to have "assembled" the team in "Crawfords Have Veteran Pitchers to Face Cubans," *Harrisburg Telegraph*, July 1, 1944, 7. But he is not listed as being with the team when it appeared in Bethlehem, Pennsylvania, on June 3. "Bethlehem Tops Cuban Yankees of Harrisburg," *Allentown Morning Call*, June 4, 1944, 9. On players taking defense jobs over baseball gigs, see, e.g., Luke, *The Baltimore Elite Giants*, 82.

68. W. Rollo Wilson, "Thru the Eyes of W. Rollo Wilson," *Philadelphia Tribune*, June 3, 1944, 12.

69. This is according to Charlie Biot, interviewed in Kelley, *The Negro Leagues Revisited*, 99. Stanley Glenn told Kelley that Oscar was the "real man behind [the Stars]" at this time, even as a coach (Kelley, *The Negro Leagues Revisited*, 154).

70. In fact, the Stars believed they had won the flag, but Cum Posey successfully argued that a game his Grays lost to the New York Cubans was an exhibition rather than a league contest. See Luke, *The Baltimore Elite Giants*, 55.

71. Don Deleighbur, "Behind the Play," *Philadelphia Tribune*, May 13, 1944, 12.

72. Irwin N. Rosee, "Charleston Helps Build Colored Baseball League," in OCS.

73. Where not otherwise noted, I draw for information on Rickey primarily from Lee Lowenfish's excellent biography, *Branch Rickey*, as well as from Jules Tygiel, *Baseball's Great Experiment*.

74. Lowenfish, *Branch Rickey*, 326.

75. The following is my own interpretation of Rickey's personality, character, and motivations.

76. See, e.g., Lowenfish, *Branch Rickey*, 78.

77. Lowenfish, *Branch Rickey*, 327.

78. Lowenfish, *Branch Rickey*, 350.

79. Lowenfish, *Branch Rickey*, 362–63.

80. W. Rollo Wilson, "Through the Eyes of W. Rollo Wilson," *Philadelphia Tribune*, January 13, 1945, 13.

81. Oscar had been invited to join an all-black USO Camp Show for an overseas trip in February, but he was not able to go (see chapter 9 below). See Edward Bennett, "Draft Board Threats, Age, Illness, Split USO Unit," *Baltimore Afro-American*, February 3, 1945, 8, and "The Sports Notepad," *Baltimore Afro-American*, February 10, 1945, 18.

82. "Charleston Set to Manage Hilldale Outfit" and "Oscar on the Dotted Line," *New York Amsterdam News*, February 24, 1945, 12A.

83. "Baseball Men at YMCA," *Philadelphia Tribune*, February 24, 1945, 12.

84. The amount is confirmed by a check put up for auction in 2010; the check sold for $35,000. See "Managing the Brown Dodgers," January 3, 2016, at https://oscarcharleston.com/category/brown-dodgers/.

85. "'Dales Eye Talent for U.S. Campaign," *Baltimore Afro-American*, March 17, 1945, 18.

86. "Hilldale Club Scours South Seeking Stars," *Philadelphia Tribune*, March 17, 1945, 13.

87. Branch Rickey, "Memorandum to Harry Walsh," November 29, 1947, in BRP, Box 33, folder titled "Brooklyn Dodgers General, 1946–47."

88. "U.S. League Opens May 20," *Chicago Defender*, April 28, 1945, 7; Manley and Hardwick, *Negro Baseball*. The Manley and Hardwick book provides a useful if not always reliable, and certainly self-interested, account of the USL's formation.

89. "Robinson, Williams and Jethroe 'Standing By': U.S. Loops Gets Rickey's 'Blessings' at Secret Meeting: Brooklyn Franchise Added to League," *Pittsburgh Courier*, April 28, 1945, 16.

90. Wendell Smith told a somewhat different story about how the Greenlee–Rickey–USL connection came about. According to Smith, Greenlee had been negotiating with Rickey to place a USL franchise at Ebbets Field as early as 1944. Rickey ultimately offered Ebbets on a rent-free basis, said Smith, who also made it sound as if Greenlee was the one who gave Rickey the idea of signing black players for the Dodgers. On hearing this idea, Rickey allegedly asked Greenlee to identify good prospects for him, and with Smith's help the two men compiled a list with Jackie Robinson's name on top.

Surely some of this story is true; it is not implausible, for example, that Rickey asked for Greenlee's advice on players, but if Greenlee and Smith suggested Robinson, they were but two among many to do so. It is also possible that Rickey had connected with Greenlee about the USL well before April 1945. See Wendell Smith, "Wendell Smith's Sports Beat," *Pittsburgh Courier*, July 19, 1952, 14.

91. "United States League Plays in Three Cities Sunday, New Rules, Plans Devised in Official Meeting," *Cleveland Call and Post*, May 19, 1945, 7B.

92. Joseph Hall said that Rickey also saw the Brown Dodgers as a way to "test public sentiment regarding Negro baseball players" (quoted in "Rickey Sued for $15,000," *Sioux Falls Argus-Leader*, October 1, 1947, 1).

93. Lowenfish, *Branch Rickey*, 365–66.

94. Tygiel, *Baseball's Great Experiment*, 47.

95. Sukeforth said that Oscar spoke directly to both him and Rickey about Roy Campanella (Joe King, "Campanella Not Antique but Modernizer," *The Sporting News*, July 18, 1951, 3). He also implies that Oscar spoke directly with Rickey in Golenbock, *Bums*, 114.

96. Email from Branch Rickey III, March 17, 2015.

97. Irvin, *Nice Guys Finish First*, 109; Joe King, "Campanella Not Antique but Modernizer," *The Sporting News*, July 18, 1951, 3.

98. Quoted in Golenbock, *Bums*, 114.

99. "Brown Dodgers Beat Crawfords," *Harrisburg Evening News*, April 23, 1945, 15.

100. Wilmer Harris is the source for the claim that Oscar occasionally pinch-hit for the Brown Dodgers. Telephone interview, July 1, 2003, JSP.

101. "Three-Team Twin Bill in U.S. League at Ebbets Today," *Brooklyn Daily Eagle*, July 22, 1945, 20; "Brown Dodgers at Ebbets Field on Aug. 5 in Twin Bill," *New York Amsterdam News*, August 4, 1945, B8.

102. Rickey, "Memorandum to Harry Walsh," in BRP.

103. "Rickey Sued for $15,000," *Sioux Falls Argus-Leader*, October 1, 1947, 1.

104. John L. Clark, "Wylie Avenue," *Pittsburgh Courier*, August 25, 1945, 14.

105. Quoted in Joe King, "Campanella Not Antique but Modernizer," *The Sporting News*, July 18, 1951, 3.

106. Campanella, *It's Good to Be Alive*, 108.

107. This account of the Rickey-Campanella meeting and its aftermath draws primarily from Campanella, *It's Good to Be Alive*, 105–15, and Lanctot, *Campy*, 115–24.

108. Campanella, *It's Good to Be Alive*, 108.

109. Campanella, *It's Good to Be Alive*, 109.

110. See Lanctot, *Campy*, 123–24. Lanctot points out that in fact Campanella soon cleared up his confusion with Rickey by signing a contract on October 25 to play "for the Brooklyn Brown Dodgers or any other club the Brooklyn organization might designate," meaning, of course, the Major League Dodgers.

111. Quoted in Golenbock, *Bums*, 114.

112. Quoted in *Newsday*, March 2, 1997.

113. Monte Irvin, telephone interview, undated, JSP.

114. Email from Branch Rickey III, March 17, 2015.

115. On Donaldson, see Sandoval and Nowlin, *Can He Play?*, 128.

116. Dusty Ballard, "Oscar Charleston Signed to Manage Stars for 1948 Season," *Philadelphia Tribune*, December 23, 1947, 11. On the umpires' uniforms, see Motley, *Ruling over Monarchs, Giants, and Stars*, 72–73.

117. "Cubans Nose Out Philadelphia, 7–6," *Harrisburg Telegraph*, May 23, 1947, 24.

118. "Black Barons Bow to Black Yankees, 7–2, *New York Amsterdam News*, August 2, 1947, 11.

119. Edward Robinson, "Abie's Corner," *Los Angeles Sentinel*, August 14, 1947, 22.

120. Dusty Ballard, "Stars May 'Shine' under Charleston," *Philadelphia Tribune*, January 24, 1948, 11.

121. Wilmer Harris, telephone interview, July 1, 2003, JSP.

9. Legend, 1948–

1. Tygiel, *Baseball's Great Experiment*, 302.

2. Tygiel, *Baseball's Great Experiment*, 248, 251.

3. Tygiel, *Baseball's Great Experiment*, 302.

4. Robinson, "What's Wrong with Negro Baseball," 16–24.

5. Luke, *The Baltimore Elite Giants*, 115.

6. Luke, *The Baltimore Elite Giants*, 128.

7. See Dusty Ballard, "Stars May 'Shine' under Charleston," *Philadelphia Tribune*, January 24, 1948, 11; Cash and Hunter, *Thou Shalt Not Steal*, 89–90.

8. Dusty Ballard, "Oscar Charleston Signed to Manage Stars for 1948 Season," *Philadelphia Tribune*, December 23, 1947, 11.

9. "Oscar Charleston's Death Closes Era of Great Negro Ball Players," *Chicago Defender*, October 23, 1954, 11.

10. On Partlow, see Tygiel, *Baseball's Great Experiment*, 176.

11. Malcolm Poindexter Jr., "Charleston to Pilot Stars Next Season," *Philadelphia Tribune*, September 8, 1951, 10.

12. Malcolm Poindexter Jr., "Sports-I-View," *Philadelphia Tribune*, May 31, 1952, 11.

13. Malcolm Poindexter Jr., "Sports-I-View," *Philadelphia Tribune*, May 31, 1952, 11.

14. Quoted in Wendell Smith, "Sports Beat," *Pittsburgh Courier*, August 21, 1954, 12.

15. See, for example, Tiny Parry, "Sportfolio," *Lebanon Daily News*, July 27, 1951, 18.

16. Earl Johnson, "Sports Whirl," *Pittsburgh Courier*, July 8, 1950, 31.

17. See, for example, "Philadelphia Stars Open Workouts in S.C. Camp," *Norfolk New Journal and Guide*, April 15, 1950, D20.

18. Alfred Duckett, "Henry Aaron Joins Bill Bruton as Favorite of Milwaukee Fans," *New York Age*, June 26, 1954, 22.

19. Izzy Katzman, "Bruton Springs from Millside Softball to Big-League Prospect," *Wilmington News Journal*, October 24, 1951, 32.

20. Klima, *Willie's Boys*, 218–19.

21. "Clowns Off to Fast Start, Take Seven of Ten Tilts," *Norfolk New Journal and Guide*, May 31, 1952, 21. Aaron hit two home runs in the Clowns' first ten games versus the Stars in 1952.

22. Al Moses, "Mays Shapes Up like Charleston," *Philadelphia Tribune*, July 17, 1951, 10.

23. Quoted in Dan Burley, "Confidentially Yours," *New York Amsterdam News*, August 14, 1948, 26. Burley writes that Oscar was prevented from joining the USO show because of an obligation to play ball in Cuba, but I do not think this is correct.

24. Wilmer Harris, telephone interview, July 1, 2003, JSP.

25. Joe Bostic, "The Scoreboard," *New York Amsterdam News*, June 3, 1950, 27.

26. Al Sweeney, "Bolden's Daughter Can Inspire Philly Stars," *Baltimore Afro-American*, March 31, 1951, 18. Hilda told the press that Oscar had been her favorite player as a child.

27. Quoted in "Lopsided Tilts Won by Clowns, American Giants," *Indianapolis Recorder*, September 1, 1951, 11.

28. Dan Burley, "Dan Burley's Sports," *New York Age*, April 30, 1949, 16.

29. "Speaking of Sports," *New York Amsterdam News*, September 8, 1951, 18.

30. Rogosin, *Invisible Men*, 128–29; Rogosin gets the story from a player named Jack Marshall, who never played for the Stars but may have gotten it from someone who did. Of course, the tale could be apocryphal.

31. Harold Hair, telephone interview, July 16, 2016.

32. Motley, *Ruling over Monarchs, Giants, and Stars*, 139.

33. Cliff Layton, telephone interview, August 21, 2015.

34. Jim Robinson, telephone interview, December 28, 2015.

35. Leonard with Riley, *Buck Leonard*, 127.

36. Kelley, *The Negro Leagues Revisited*, 67.

37. Jim Robinson, telephone interview, December 28, 2015.

38. O'Neil, *I Was Right on Time*, 51.

39. Trouppe, *Twenty Years Too Soon*, 35.

40. Quoted in Kelley, *The Negro Leagues Revisited*, 67.

41. Stanley Glenn, telephone interview, July 1, 2003, JSP.

42. Malcolm Poindexter Jr.: "Charleston to Pilot Stars Next Season; Team Play Improved," *Philadelphia Tribune*, September 8, 1951, 10, and "Sports-I-View," *Philadelphia Tribune*, May 31, 1952, 11.

43. Stanley Glenn, telephone interview, July 1, 2003, JSP.

44. Motley, *Ruling over Monarchs, Giants, and Stars*, 138, 112.

45. See Leonard with Riley, *Buck Leonard*, 70, and Motley, *Ruling over Monarchs, Giants, and Stars*, 139–40.

46. Motley, *Ruling over Monarchs, Giants, and Stars*, 140.

47. Leonard with Riley, *Buck Leonard*, 66–67.

48. Mahlon Duckett, telephone interview, July 1, 2003, JSP.

49. Jim Robinson, telephone interview, December 28, 2015; Motley, *Ruling over Monarchs, Giants, and Stars*, 141.

50. Related by Wilmer Harris, telephone interview, July 1, 2003, JSP.

51. Related by Wilmer Harris, telephone interview, July 1, 2003, JSP.

52. Stanley Glenn, telephone interview, July 1, 2003, JSP.

53. Mahlon Duckett, telephone interview, July 1, 2003, JSP. Chet Brewer said that he liked playing with Oscar for this reason. He'd throw the ball to Oscar on first, and "he could just take his hands and open up the seam on it" (quoted in Rogosin, *Invisible Men*, 72).

54. Harold Hair said that in his presence Oscar once took a baseball in his hands, twisted it, and tore the cover right off. I told Hair that I had always thought that was a legend, but he insisted that it had happened: "That was no legend." Harold Hair, telephone interview, July 16, 2016.

55. Trouppe, *Twenty Years Too Soon*, 117; Harold Hair, telephone interview, July 16, 2016; James Robinson, telephone interview, December 28, 2015.

56. Motley, *Ruling over Monarchs, Giants, and Stars*, 109–10.

57. Motley concludes: "How the three of us scaled that wall is still a mystery to me, but we did." Motley, *Ruling over Monarchs, Giants, and Stars*, 153. This anecdote may be a tall tale, but it nevertheless reveals something about how Charleston and O'Neil were perceived.

58. Herb Walker, telephone interview, July 2, 2015.

59. See Bill Cash, Andrew Porter, and Stanley Glenn, telephone interviews, June 30, July 3, July 1, 2003, JSP.

60. Stanley Glenn, telephone interview, July 1, 2003, JSP. Oscar's waist size is given in a letter from Pollock to Charleston, January 16, 1954; letter in author's possession.

61. Mahlon Duckett, telephone interview, July 1, 2003, JSP.

62. Aaron with Wheeler, *I Had a Hammer*, 20.

63. Leonard with Riley, *Buck Leonard*, 104.

64. Luke, *The Baltimore Elite Giants*, 4

65. Cliff Layton, telephone interview, August 21, 2015.

66. Dusty Ballard, "Stars May 'Shine' under Charleston," *Philadelphia Tribune*, January 24, 1948, 11.

67. Harold Gould, telephone interview, undated, JSP.

68. Stanley Glenn, telephone interview, July 1, 2003, JSP.

69. Decades later Bell suggested to interviewer Jim Bankes that Oscar had become morose and self-pitying in his later years. Bell said that Oscar asked him to tell everyone what a great ballplayer he had been, that the younger players didn't believe him and would laugh at him. Oscar, he implied, had become a figure of ridicule (Bankes, *The Pittsburgh Crawfords*, 113).

It's not impossible that Oscar had moments, after his playing career had ended, when he doubted whether his achievements would be long remembered. That would have been only human, and Oscar could not have been oblivious to the fact that among younger blacks there was little appetite for revisiting the old days. But there is no hint, in anyone else's recollections, of a mopey Oscar concerned about his legacy. Dozens of other men have testified to his personality in the 1940s and 1950s, and none of those testimonies corroborate Bell's. All remember him as cheerful and confident. If anything, Oscar evinced a *lack* of interest in burnishing his reputation. He never spoke, for example, about his work with Branch Rickey. As noted below in this chapter, he brushed off one suggestion that he was the greatest center fielder in Negro Leagues history, and he did not select himself for his all-time Negro Leagues all-star team in 1949. Nor is there any evidence that Oscar was an object of ridicule among younger players. Buck O'Neil and Monte Irvin recalled his name with reverence in their memoirs, and even Buck Leonard, who did not particularly like Oscar, spoke of him with the utmost respect. A few ex-Crawfords, including Judy Johnson and Ted Page, were not big personal fans. (Johnson said in 1987 that Oscar had been "a mean, miserable man to play for. And with a foul mouth" (see Bill Conlin, "Johnson's Memories in a League of Their Own," *Philadelphia Daily News*, July 30, 1987, 91). But the idea of Oscar as a pathetic figure who had to ride Paige's coattails in order to gain a paycheck during the last years of his life (as Bell also maintained) would seem to be a complete fabrication.

70. Malcolm Poindexter Jr., "Sports-I-View," *Philadelphia Tribune*, March 1, 1952, 10.

71. Chuck Davis, "Pupil Spanks Old Master in All Star Game," *Chicago Defender*, August 26, 1950, 17.

72. Indeed, Oscar may have been the one supplying the quote from McGraw. Syd Pollock asks him for it in a letter dated January 29, 1954, SPL.

73. Chuck Davis, "Pupil Spanks Old Master in All Star Game," *Chicago Defender*, August 26, 1950, 17.

74. Quoted in Fred Wilson, "Sport Shots," *Delaware County Daily Times*, May 5, 1948, 24.

75. Quoted in Norvin Collins, "Still 'Plenty' of Negro Baseball Prospects," *Wilmington News Journal*, July 14, 1948, 28.

76. "Oscar Charleston Agrees with Cobb's Views but Blames Economy for Guilt-Edged [*sic*] Game," *Philadelphia Tribune*, March 25, 1952, 11.

77. Bankes, *The Pittsburgh Crawfords*, 58.

78. Quoted in Bankes, *The Pittsburgh Crawfords*, 74.

79. Quoted in Malcolm Poindexter Jr., "*Tribune* Charities Holds First Sports Debate," *Philadelphia Tribune*, January 22, 1952, 10.

80. Malcolm Poindexter Jr., "Sports-I-View," *Philadelphia Tribune*, January 27, 1953, 10.

81. Quoted in Malcolm Poindexter Jr., "Sports-I-View," *Philadelphia Tribune*, April 11, 1953, 10.

82. Oscar was living at 2725 Sedgley Avenue, in a row house that is now, like so many of his former homes, gone.

83. Pollock letters to Charleston, December 30, 1953, and January 23, 1954, SPL.

84. Aaron with Wheeler, *I Had a Hammer*, 33.

85. Pollock letter to Charleston, December 30, 1953, SPL.

86. Cliff Layton, telephone interview, August 21, 2015; Herb Walker, telephone interview, July 2, 2015.

87. One reference work's claim that Johnson "threw as hard as many male pitchers" is just a tad exaggerated (Riley, *The Biographical Encyclopedia of the Negro Baseball Leagues*, 440), as are some of the claims made for Johnson in her biography (Green, *A Strong Right Arm*, which, admittedly, is written for children).

James Robinson said of Toni Stone, generally thought to have been the best of the three women to play in the NAL, "I admired the fact that she was able to handle all of that, being the only woman. She was a pretty good player. She was OK" (telephone interview, December 28, 2015).

Bob Motley wrote that "neither Toni nor Connie had a fluid swing or much prowess at the plate. Peanut was a pitcher, so hitting for average wasn't expected of her. Connie in particular would 'chop' at the ball. She relied mostly on her bunting technique to get base hits. Of the three, Toni was by far the best hitter, although she lacked power. She was a contact hitter, capable of plopping the ball over the infield. Where Toni and Connie were of great value was in the field. Both played second, and they could scoop up ground balls as well as any man. Neither had strong throwing arms, which is probably why they were positioned at second, but they could throw accurately and were relatively quick at turning a double play." Johnson, he wrote, "had a decent fastball and a developing curveball. She was a fierce competitor and adapted well to the art of brushing guys back who had gotten a hit off of her in their previous at-bat. Her aggressiveness aided her in the league, and she held her own most games" (Motley, *Ruling over Monarchs, Giants, and Stars*, 123).

Buck O'Neil remembered that Stone "was a pretty fair player, having played on her high school baseball team in Minnesota. She ran well, and she knew what she was doing around the bag. But she wasn't of the same caliber as our other players, and the pitchers did take it easy on her when the game wasn't on the line. There wasn't much resentment that I can recall; I think teammates and opponents knew the league was fighting for survival" (O'Neil, *I Was Right on Time*, 195).

88. Pollock letter to Charleston, January 30, 1954, SPL.

89. Pollock letter to Poindexter, February 5, 1954, SPL.

90. Morgan and Johnson quoted in Pollock, *Barnstorming to Heaven*, 252.

91. Pollock, *Barnstorming to Heaven*, 254–55.

92. "Oscar Charleston's Death Closes Era of Great Negro Ball Players," *Chicago Defender*, October 23, 1954, 11.

93. "Oscar Charleston in Philly Hospital," *Baltimore Afro-American*, October 9, 1954, 15; "Oscar Charleston in Philly Hospital," *Pittsburgh Courier*, October 9, 1954, 12.

94. Related by Stanley Glenn, telephone interview, July 1, 2003, JSP.

95. W. Rollo Wilson, "Clowns Manager Succumbs at Fifty-Seven," *Pittsburgh Courier*, October 16, 1954, 12.

96. Stanley Glenn, telephone interview, July 1, 2003, JSP; W. Rollo Wilson, "Clowns Manager Succumbs at Fifty-Seven," *Pittsburgh Courier*, October 16, 1954, 12; "Oscar Charleston Dies at Fifty-Eight," *Indianapolis Recorder*, October 9, 1954, 1.

97. Quoted in Russ J. Cowans, "Russ' Corner," *Chicago Defender*, October 23, 1954, 10. Baird would repeat this opinion about Charleston three years later, when he was working as a scout for the Kansas City Athletics. See Russ J. Cowans, "Russ' Corner," *Chicago Defender*, March 19, 1957, 20. On Baird's membership in the Klan, see Rives, "Tom Baird."

98. Quoted in Motley, *Ruling over Monarchs, Giants, and Stars*, 170.

99. Quoted in Wendell Smith, "Sports Beat," *Pittsburgh Courier*, August 21, 1954, 12.

100. Peterson, *Only the Ball Was White*, 242; Manley and Hardwick, *Negro Baseball*, 26.

101. Related by Stanley Glenn, telephone interview, July 1, 2003, JSP.

102. See, for example, Gregory Clay, "Robinson Fit Correct Mold for Baseball's Integration," *Arizona Daily Star*, April 13, 1997, 39, and "Negro League Hall of Famers," *Baltimore Sun*, April 29, 1990, 37.

103. Al Monroe, "What Happened to Negro Baseball?" *Chicago Defender*, May 3, 1961, 9.

104. Bankes, *The Pittsburgh Crawfords*, 125.

105. Jack Hernon, "Roamin' Around," *Pittsburgh Post-Gazette*, June 4, 1959, 27.

106. Quoted in Kelley, *The Negro Leagues Revisited*, 120.

107. Only two more players, John Henry Lloyd and Martín Dihigo, were elected before the committee voted to disband—far too quickly in the eyes of many. Another twenty-four Negro Leaguers were later selected for induction by the Veterans Committee and a second Special Committee on the Negro Leagues, which, thanks to the work of researchers in the intervening several decades, was able to do a much more thorough job.

108. Rodney Redman, telephone interview, December 28, 2015.

109. Bob Collins, "This Trip Would Be Worth the Expense," *Indianapolis Star*, June 17, 1976, 57.

110. Transcript in HOF.

Epilogue

1. Dave Garlick, "Banks Predicts Season Will Not 'Strike-Out,'" *Indianapolis Star*, July 19, 1981, 71. Of course as soon as this piece was printed, Katherine came forward, and Oscar's plaque was presented to her at her Indianapolis home. Why no one thought to simply place an appeal in the paper is a mystery. "Hall of Fame Award," *Indianapolis Star*, July 23, 1981, 34.

2. See, for example, Gregg Doyel's appreciative piece, "Seeking a Legend but Finding a Monster First," *Indianapolis Star*, November 10, 2015, C1.

3. Thomas Boswell, "List of Diamond Greats Really Grates," *Pacific Stars and Stripes*, May 12, 1999, 32.

4. "Dismukes Was the Original 'Dizzy' of Baseball," *Pittsburgh Courier*, July 15, 1961, 56.

BIBLIOGRAPHY

Aaron, Hank, with Lonnie Wheeler. *I Had a Hammer: The Hank Aaron Story*. New York: HarperCollins, 1991.

Alexander, Charles C. *John McGraw*. New York: Viking, 1988.

Ardell, Jean Hastings, and Andy McCue, eds. *The National Pastime: Endless Seasons: Baseball in Southern California*. Cleveland: Society for American Baseball Research, 2011.

Baker, William J. *Jesse Owens: An American Life*. New York: Free Press, 1986.

Bankes, James. *The Pittsburgh Crawfords: The Lives and Times of Black Baseball's Most Exciting Team*. Dubuque IA: William C. Brown, 1991.

Barra, Allen. *Rickwood Field: A Century in America's Oldest Ballpark*. New York: W. W. Norton, 2010.

Bjarkman, Peter C. *A History of Cuban Baseball, 1864–2006*. Jefferson, NC: McFarland, 2014.

Bjarkman, Peter C., and Bill Nowlin, eds. *Cuban Baseball Legends*. Phoenix: Society for American Baseball Research, 2016.

Blessing, Less. *Cobb*. New York: Dramatists Play Service, 1998.

Bodenhamer, David J., and Robert G. Barrows, eds. *The Encyclopedia of Indianapolis*. Bloomington IN: Indiana University Press, 1994.

Bolden, C. Nickerson. *Indiana Avenue: Black Entertainment Boulevard*. Bloomington, IN: AuthorHouse, 2009.

Brashler, William. *Josh Gibson: A Life in the Negro Leagues*. New York: Harper and Row, 1978.

Bruccoli, Matthew J., and Richard Layman, eds. *Some Champions: Sketches and Fiction by Ring Lardner*. New York: Charles Scribner's Sons, 1976.

Bruce, Janet. *The Kansas City Monarchs: Champions of Black Baseball*. Lawrence: University Press of Kansas, 1985.

Burgos, Adrian, Jr. *Cuban Star: How One Negro-League Owner Changed the Face of Baseball*. New York: Hill and Wang, 2011.

Campanella, Roy. *It's Good to Be Alive*. Lincoln: University of Nebraska Press, 1995 [1959].

Cash, Bill, and Al Hunter Jr. *Thou Shalt Not Steal: The Baseball Life and Times of a Rifle-Armed Negro League Catcher*. Philadelphia: Love Eagle Books, 2012.

Clark, Dick, and Larry Lester, eds. *The Negro Leagues Book*. Cleveland: Society for American Baseball Research, 1994.

Cottrell, Robert Charles. *The Best Pitcher in Baseball: The Life of Rube Foster, Negro League Giant*. New York: New York University Press, 2001.

Creamer, Robert W. *Babe: The Legend Comes to Life*. New York: Simon and Schuster, 1974.

Dawidoff, Nicholas, ed. *Baseball: A Literary Anthology*. New York: Library of America, 2002.

Debono, Paul. *The Chicago American Giants*. Jefferson NC: McFarland, 2007.

———. *The Indianapolis ABCs: History of a Premier Team in the Negro Leagues*. Jefferson NC: McFarland, 1997.

Feller, Bob, with Bill Gilbert. *Now Pitching, Bob Feller: A Baseball Memoir*. New York: Carol Publishing Group, 1990.

Figueredo, Jorge S. *Cuban Baseball: A Statistical History, 1878–1961*. Jefferson NC: McFarland, 2011.

Fussman, Cal. *After Jackie: Pride, Prejudice, and Baseball's Forgotten Heroes: An Oral History*. New York: ESPN, 2007.

Gay, Timothy. *Satch, Dizzy, and Rapid Robert: The Wild Saga of Interracial Baseball before Jackie Robinson*. New York: Simon and Schuster, 2010.

Genovese, Eugene D. *Roll, Jordan, Roll: The World the Slaves Made*. New York: Pantheon, 1974.

Golenbock, Peter. *Bums: An Oral History of the Brooklyn Dodgers*. Mineola NY: Dover Publications, 2010 [1984].

González Echevarría, Roberto. *The Pride of Havana: A History of Cuban Baseball*. New York: Oxford University Press, 1999.

Green, Michelle Y. *A Strong Right Arm: The Story of Mamie "Peanut" Johnson*. New York: Puffin Books, 2002.

Greenberg, Hank. *The Story of My Life*. New York: Times Books, 1989.

Gregory, Robert. *Diz: The Story of Dizzy Dean and Baseball during the Great Depression*. New York: Viking, 1992.

Guridy, Frank Andre. *Forging Diaspora: Afro-Cubans and African Americans in a World of Empire and Jim Crow*. Chapel Hill: University of North Carolina Press, 2010.

Hauser, Christopher. *The Negro Leagues Chronology: Events in Organized Black Baseball, 1920–1948*. Jefferson, NC: McFarland, 2006.

Heaphy, Leslie A. *The Negro Leagues, 1869–1960*. Jefferson NC: McFarland, 2003.

Heward, Bill. *Some Are Called Clowns: A Season with the Last of the Great Barnstorming Teams*. New York: Thomas Crowell, 1974.

Hirsch, James S. *Willie Mays: The Life, the Legend*. New York: Scribner, 2010.

Hogan, Lawrence D. *Shades of Glory: The Negro Leagues and the Story of African-American Baseball*. Washington DC: National Geographic, 2006.

Holway, John B. *Blackball Stars: Negro League Pioneers*. Westport CT: Meckler Books, 1988.

———. *Black Diamonds: Life in the Negro Leagues from the Men Who Lived It.* Westport CT: Meckler Books, 1988.

———. *Black Giants.* Springfield VA: Lord Fairfax Press, 2010.

———. *The Complete Book of Baseball's Negro Leagues: The Other Half of Baseball's History.* Fern Park FL: Hastings House Publishers, 2001.

———. *Josh and Satch: The Life and Times of Josh Gibson and Satchel Paige.* Westport CT: Meckler Books, 1988.

———. *Voices from the Great Black Baseball Leagues.* Revised ed. Mineola NY: Dover Publications, 2010 [1975].

Irvin, Monte, with Phil Pepe. *Few and Chosen: Defining Negro Leagues Greatness.* Chicago: Triumph Books, 2007.

Irvin, Monte, with James A. Riley. *Nice Guys Finish First: The Autobiography of Monte Irvin.* New York: Carroll and Graf, 1996.

James, Bill. *The New Bill James Historical Baseball Abstract.* Revised ed. New York: Free Press, 2001 [1988].

———. *Popular Crime: Reflections on the Celebration of Violence.* New York: Simon and Schuster, 2011.

James, Bill, and Rachel McCarthy James. *The Man from the Train: The Solving of a Century-Old Serial Killer Mystery.* New York: Scribner, 2017.

Jefferson, Margo. *Negroland: A Memoir.* New York: Vintage, 2015.

Kaplan, Jim. *Lefty Grove: American Original.* Cleveland: Society for American Baseball Research, 2000.

Kashatus, William C. *Jackie and Campy: The Untold Story of Their Rocky Relationship and the Breaking of Baseball's Color Line.* Lincoln: University of Nebraska Press, 2014.

Kelley, Brent. *The Early All-Stars: Conversations with Standout Baseball Players of the 1930s and 1940s.* Jefferson NC: McFarland, 1997.

———. *The Negro Leagues Revisited: Conversations with 66 More Baseball Heroes.* Jefferson, NC: McFarland, 2000.

———. *Voices from the Negro Leagues: Conversations with 52 Baseball Standouts of the Period 1924–1960.* Jefferson NC: McFarland, 1998.

King, Joe. "Campanella Not Antique but Modernizer." *The Sporting News,* July 18, 1951.

Klima, John. *Willie's Boys: The 1948 Birmingham Black Barons, the Last Negro League World Series, and the Making of a Baseball Legend.* Hoboken NJ: John Wiley and Sons, 2009.

Lanctot, Neil. *Campy: The Two Lives of Roy Campanella.* New York: Simon and Schuster, 2011.

———. *Fair Dealing and Clean Playing: The Hilldale Club and the Development of Black Professional Baseball, 1910–1932.* Syracuse NY: Syracuse University Press, 2007.

———. *Negro League Baseball: The Rise and Ruin of a Black Institution.* Philadelphia: Penn Press, 2004.

Leerhsen, Charles. *Ty Cobb: A Terrible Beauty.* New York: Simon and Schuster, 2015.

Leonard, Buck, with James A. Riley. *Buck Leonard: The Black Lou Gehrig: An Auto-biography*. New York: Carroll and Graf, 1995.

Lester, Larry. *Baseball's First Colored World Series: The 1924 Meeting of the Hilldale Giants and Kansas City Monarchs*. Jefferson NC: McFarland, 2006.

———. *Rube Foster in His Time: On the Field and in the Papers with Black Baseball's Greatest Visionary*. Jefferson NC: McFarland, 2012.

Loverro, Thom. *The Encyclopedia of Negro League Baseball*. New York: Facts on File, 2003.

Lowenfish, Lee. *Branch Rickey: Baseball's Ferocious Gentleman*. Lincoln: University of Nebraska Press, 2009 [2007].

Luke, Bob. *The Baltimore Elite Giants: Sport and Society in the Age of Negro League Baseball*. Baltimore: Johns Hopkins University Press, 2009.

———. *Willie Wells: "El Diablo" of the Negro Leagues*. Austin: University of Texas Press, 2007.

Manley, Effa, and Leon Herbert Hardwick. *Negro Baseball . . . Before Integration*. Edited by Robert Cvornyek. Haworth NJ: St. Johann Press, 2006 [1976].

Mann, Arthur. *Branch Rickey: American in Action*. Boston: Houghton Mifflin, 1957.

———. *The Jackie Robinson Story*. New York: Grosset and Dunlap, 1951.

McGraw, John J. *My Thirty Years in Baseball*. New York: Arno Press, 1974 [1923].

McNeil, William F. *Black Baseball out of Season: Pay for Play outside of the Negro Leagues*. Jefferson NC: McFarland, 2007.

———. *The California Winter League: America's First Integrated Professional Baseball League*. Jefferson NC: McFarland, 2002.

———. *Cool Papas and Double Duties: The All-Time Greats of the Negro Leagues*. Jefferson NC: McFarland, 2001.

McWhorter, John. *Winning the Race: Beyond the Crisis in Black America*. New York: Gotham, 2005.

Motley, Bob, with Byron Motley. *Ruling over Monarchs, Giants, and Stars: True Tales of Breaking Barriers, Umpiring Baseball Legends, and Wild Adventures in the Negro Leagues*. New York: Sports Publishing, 2012.

Nieto, Severo. *Early U.S. Blackball Teams in Cuba: Box Scores, Rosters and Statistics from the Files of Cuba's Foremost Baseball Researcher*. Jefferson NC: McFarland, 2008.

O'Neil, Buck. *I Was Right on Time*. New York: Simon and Schuster, 1996.

Owens, Jesse, with Paul G. Neimark. *Blackthink: My Life as Black Man and White Man*. New York: William Morrow, 1970.

———. *I Have Changed*. New York: William Morrow, 1972.

Paige, Leroy (Satchel), as told to David Lipman. *Maybe I'll Pitch Forever*. Lincoln: University of Nebraska Press, 1993 [1962].

Peterson, Robert W. *Only the Ball Was White: A History of Legendary Black Players and All-Black Professional Teams*. New York: Gramercy Books, 1999 [1970].

Pierce, Richard B. *Polite Protest: The Political Economy of Race in Indianapolis, 1920–1970*. Bloomington IN: Indiana University Press, 2005.

Pollock, Alan J. *Barnstorming to Heaven: Syd Pollock and His Great Black Teams.* Edited by James A. Riley. Tuscaloosa AL: University of Alabama Press, 2006.

Rampersad, Arnold. *Jackie Robinson: A Biography.* New York: Alfred A. Knopf, 1997.

Ribowsky, Mark. *A Complete History of the Negro Leagues, 1884 to 1955.* New York: Birch Lane Press, 1995.

——. *The Power and the Darkness: The Life of Josh Gibson in the Shadows of the Game.* New York: Simon and Schuster, 1996.

Ridley, Thomas Howard, Jr. *From the Avenue: A Memoir.* Self-published, 2012.

Riley, James A. *The Biographical Encyclopedia of the Negro Baseball Leagues.* New York: Carroll and Graf, 1994.

——. *Of Monarchs and Black Barons: Essays on Baseball's Negro Leagues.* Jefferson NC: McFarland, 2012.

Rives, Tim. "Tom Baird: A Challenge to the Modern Memory of the Kansas City Monarchs." In *Satchel Paige and Company: Essays on the Kansas City Monarchs, Their Greatest Star, and the Negro Leagues,* ed. Leslie A. Heaphy. Jefferson NC: McFarland, 2007.

Robertson, Oscar. *The Big O: My Life, My Times, My Game.* Lincoln: University of Nebraska Press, 2010

Robinson, Frazier, with Paul Bauer. *Catching Dreams: My Life in the Negro Baseball Leagues.* Syracuse NY: Syracuse University Press, 1999.

Robinson, Jackie. *Baseball Has Done It.* New York: Lippincott, 1964.

——. "What's Wrong with Negro Baseball?" *Ebony,* June 1948, 16–24.

Robinson, Jackie, and Alfred Duckett. *I Never Had It Made.* New York: Putnam, 1972.

Robinson, Jackie, and Wendell Smith. *Jackie Robinson: My Own Story.* New York: Greenberg, 1948.

Rogosin, Donn. *Invisible Men: Life in Baseball's Negro Leagues.* New York: Atheneum, 1983.

Rowan, Carl T., with Jackie Robinson. *Wait Till Next Year: The Story of Jackie Robinson.* New York: Random House, 1960.

Ruck, Rob. *Sandlot Seasons: Sport in Black Pittsburgh.* Urbana: University of Illinois Press, 1987.

Rust, Art, Jr. *"Get That Nigger off the Field": The Oral History of the Negro Leagues.* Brooklyn: Book Mail Services, 1992.

Sandoval, Jim, and Bill Nowlin, eds. *Can He Play? A Look at Baseball Scouts and Their Profession,* vol. 1. Cleveland: Society for American Baseball Research, 2011.

Schaap, Jeremy. *The Untold Story of Jesse Owens and Hitler's Olympics.* Boston: Houghton Mifflin, 2007.

Schulian, John. *Sometimes They Even Shook Your Hand: Portraits of Champions Who Walked among Us.* Lincoln: University of Nebraska Press, 2011.

Scott, Emmett J. *Scott's Official History of the American Negro in the World War.* 1919. Chicago: Homewood Press.

Shane, Ted. "Chocolate Rube Waddell." *Saturday Evening Post,* July 27, 1940, 78–81.

Simkus, Scott. *Outsider Baseball: The Weird World of Hardball on the Fringe, 1876–1950*. Chicago: Chicago Review Press, 2014.

Skinner, David C. "Twice Champions: The 1923–24 Santa Clara Leopardos." In *From McGillicuddy to McGwire: Baseball in Florida and the Caribbean*, 35–42. Cleveland OH: Society for American Baseball Research, 2000.

Snyder, Brad. *Beyond the Shadow of the Senators: The Untold Story of the Homestead Grays and the Integration of Baseball*. Chicago: Contemporary Books, 2003.

Strecker, Geri. "Winter Baseball in California: Separate Opportunities, Equal Talent." In Ardell and McCue, *The National Pastime*. https://sabr.org/research/winter-baseball-california-separate-opportunities-equal-talent.

Tarkington, Booth. *America Moved: Booth Tarkington's Memoirs of Time and Place, 1869–1928*. Eugene OR: FPR Books, 2015.

———. *Growth*. Garden City NY: Doubleday, Page, 1927.

———. *The Turmoil*. In Tarkington, *Growth*.

Thornbrough, Emma Lou. *Indiana Blacks in the Twentieth Century*. Bloomington IN: Indiana University Press, 2000.

Trouppe, Quincy. *Twenty Years Too Soon: Prelude to Major-League Integrated Baseball*. Revised edition. St. Louis: Missouri Historical Society Press, 1995 [1977].

Tye, Larry. *Satchel: The Life and Times of an American Legend*. New York: Random House, 2009.

Tygiel, Jules. *Baseball's Great Experiment: Jackie Robinson and His Legacy*. Expanded edition. New York: Oxford University Press, 1997 [1983].

U.S. Bureau of Labor Statistics. *War and Postwar Wages, Prices, and Hours, 1914–23 and 1939–44*. Bulletin No. 852 of the U.S. Bureau of Labor Statistics. Washington DC: U.S. Department of Labor, 1945.

Veeck, Bill. *Veeck—As in Wreck: The Autobiography of Bill Veeck*. New York: G. P. Putnam's Sons, 1962.

Whitaker, Mark. *Smoketown: The Untold Story of the Other Great Black Renaissance*. New York: Simon and Schuster, 2018.

White, Sol. *Sol White's History of Colored Base Ball, with Other Documents on the Early Black Game, 1886–1936*. Lincoln: University of Nebraska Press, 1995.

Will, George F. *Men at Work: The Craft of Baseball*. New York: Macmillan, 1990.

Williams, David Leander. *Indianapolis Jazz: The Masters, Legends and Legacy of Indiana Avenue*. Charleston SC: History Press, 2014.

Wolfinger, James. "African American Migration." In *The Encyclopedia of Greater Philadelphia*. http://philadelphiaencyclopedia.org/archive/african-american-migration/.

Yardley, Jonathan. *Ring: A Biography of Ring Lardner*. New York: Random House, 1977.

Yoder, Robert. *In Performance: Walter Howard Loving and the Philippine Constabulary Band*. Manila: National Historic Commission of the Philippines, 2013.

INDEX

baseball (*continued*)
gifts from fans in, 54–55, 118, 161, 200; integration of, 1–2, 5–7, 18, 50–53, 176, 215, 290, 293–95, 297–98, 305, 307; military, 49–54, 103, 290; Minor League, 60, 64, 103, 128, 199, 208, 290, 293, 297, 307, 309; Negro Leagues style of, 59, 62, 113–14, 194; racism and, 131, 192, 260–64; rankings of best players in, 10–14, 17, 333–34; "scientific," 59, 62, 114, 194; semipro, 43, 58, 64, 78, 80, 96, 103, 109, 115, 151–52, 159–60, 174, 176–77, 197, 206, 211, 218, 220, 231, 244, 250–51, 258, 279, 285–86, 288, 290, 319; talent distribution in, 64, 176; violence in, 20, 69, 245–46

Baseball Writers' Association of America, 330
Basie, William James "Count," 226
basketball, 184
Bassett, Pepper, 265, 267, 270
Bassler, Johnny, 128
Batavia Pirates, 290
Baugh, "Slingin'" Sammy, 18, 258
Bauman, Pat, 67–68, 70
Bayside NJ, 174
Bear Mountain NY, 294–95
Bebop, Spec, 2, 323, 326
Beckwith, John, 160, 163, 173, 179–80, 184, 186, 188–92, 261
Beeler Avenue (Indianapolis IN), 32
Bell, James "Cool Papa," xi, 9, 11–12, 17, 30, 135, 143, 235, 239–41, 243, 245, 247–48, 252–53, 258, 263, 267–68, 270, 319, 321, 330–31, 333
Bell, William, 240
Bench, Johnny, 30
Bender, Charles "Chief," 30
Benson, Gene, 13, 270, 287–88, 291, 304, 309
Berra, Yogi, 5
Bethel AME Church (Indianapolis IN), 132
Bethlehem PA, 334
Biddle Field (Carlisle PA), 161
Bill James Historical Baseball Abstract (James), 10–15
Birmingham AL, 117, 237, 283, 296, 314
Birmingham Black Barons, 5, 222, 283, 311, 325
Bismarck ND, 250
Blackwell, Charles, 121, 125
Blades, Ray, 275

Blalock, Bettie, 138, 141, 274
Blalock, Jane. *See* Charleston, Jane
Blalock, Martin Luther, 137, 141
Blessing, Lee, 319
Bloomington (baseball team), 219
Bloomsburg PA, 181–82
Blue, Lu, 128
Blue Laws, 44, 170
blues, 32
Blues Stadium, 317
Boeckel, Tony, 128
Boehler, George, 67
Boggs, Wade, 334
Bolden, Ed, 148, 169–70, 172–73, 179–80, 195–96, 199–202, 227, 239, 286, 288, 291, 306, 309, 312, 320
Bolden, Hilda, 312
Bonds, Barry, 174
Borgmann, Bennie, 13
Bostic, Joe, 294–95, 312
Boston Black Sox, 177
Boston Braves, 2, 128, 310
Boston MA, 2
Boston Red Sox, 5, 50, 56, 296
Boswell, Thomas, 333–34
Bowen, J. Rex, 294
Bowser, Thomas, 58, 67, 70, 73–75
Bowser's ABCs, 75
boxing, xi, 12, 20, 38, 42, 76, 198, 258, 281, 292
Boys Club Orchestra of North Indianapolis, 83
Bradley, Anna Charleston, ix, 28
Brady, Diamond Jim, 63
Breakers Hotel (Palm Beach FL), 85, 87, 148
Brewer, Chet, 210, 212–13, 242, 256, 266, 287–88
Briggs, Otto, 198, 201
Brightside. *See* Julia E. Work Training School
Britt, George, 180, 201, 218
Bronx Giants, 174
Bronzeville (Chicago), 108
Brooklyn Brown Dodgers, 297–301, 304–5
Brooklyn Bushwicks, 188, 197, 202, 257, 270, 318
Brooklyn Dodgers, 1, 18, 234, 292–95, 297–99, 302–4, 309
Brooklyn Farmers, 177
Brooklyn Robins, 67

Hill District (Pittsburgh PA), 220, 223, 226, 273
Hodges, Gil, 334
Holland, Elvis William "Bill," 49, 123, 145, 157, 214, 275
Holland PA, 319
Holloway, Crush, 133–34, 150, 201
Holway, John, 14, 156, 180, 273
Homestead Board of Education, 205
Homestead Grays, 17, 160, 163, 168, 179–82, 184–87, 197–99, 201, 203–14, 216–23, 227, 229, 232, 235, 239, 249–51, 257, 265–66, 270, 308
Honey Drippers, 324
Honolulu HI, 53, 67, 75, 188
Hooper, Harry, 88, 202
Hoosier Sweat Collier Factory, 32
Horne, Lena, 226
Hornsby, Rogers, xi, 57, 119, 124–25, 128, 259–60
Hot Springs AR, 206–7, 230
House of David, 222, 242
Houston TX, 207, 230, 281; race riot of 1917 in, 92–93, 105
Howard, LeRoy Layton, 138–41
Howard University, 77, 100
Hoyte, Waite, 270
Hubbard, Cal, 330
Hubbard, "Mountain" Jesse, 231
Hughes, Sammy, 259
Hunter, Bertrum, 240, 250, 253

Indiana Avenue neighborhood (Indianapolis, IN), 32, 39–44, 76, 82, 89, 131–32, 149–50, 280
Indianapolis ABCS, 15, 17, 43–44, 49, 56–64, 75–79, 83, 88–101, 105–7, 110, 113, 116–20, 122, 126, 128, 132–35, 140, 148–51, 158, 160, 168, 201, 205, 232, 235, 242, 280, 284, 333; as champions of black baseball, 80–82; and contests versus white all-star teams, 65–74, 92
Indianapolis Clowns, 1–3, 18, 20–21, 305, 311, 322–26
Indianapolis Colored World, 32
Indianapolis Colts, 16
Indianapolis Crescents, 43
Indianapolis Freeman, 38, 43, 60–61, 63, 68, 71–72, 77, 82–83, 96, 116
Indianapolis Gas Works, 32

Indianapolis Herculeans, 43
Indianapolis Hoosiers, 43, 63, 81
Indianapolis IN, 1, 15, 27, 31–32, 75, 111, 217, 280, 300
Indianapolis Indians, 65–66, 89, 116, 285, 312
Indianapolis Journal, 38
Indianapolis Merits, 61, 63
Indianapolis Mohawks, 43
Indianapolis Motor Speedway, 96
Indianapolis News, 32, 35–36, 85
Indianapolis News Building, 33
Indianapolis Public School No. 23, 41–42
Indianapolis Public School No. 42, 83
Indianapolis Recorder, 84, 262, 273, 280
Indianapolis Reserves, 58, 75
Indianapolis Star, 6, 15, 63, 65–67, 69–70, 78, 81, 90–91, 94–95, 99–101, 330, 333
Indianapolis Stove Company, 33
Indianapolis Unions, 43
Indianapolis Vendomes, 43
Indiana Reform School for Boys, 37
Industrial League (Philadelphia PA), 290
integration: and Branch Rickey, 6, 18, 293–99, 301–5; in Cuba, 215; impact of on Negro Leagues, 1–2, 307–8; of Interstate League, 176; in Manila League, 50–53; of Major League Baseball, 5–7, 293–95, 297–98, 305, 307; of Quartermaster Depot team, 290
Internal Revenue Service, 277
International League, 166, 191
International League Park, 78
Interstate 65, 39
Interstate 70, 39
Interstate League, 176–77, 179
Irsay, Robert, 16
Irvin, Monte, 5, 10, 304, 329
Island Park, 161, 164, 177, 188–90, 299, 306

Jack Benny Program, 283
Jackson, Dick, 172
Jackson, Rufus "Sonnyman," 227
Jackson, Sheep, 328
Jackson, "Shoeless Joe," 56
Jacksonville FL, 296
Jacobs Funeral Home (Indianapolis IN), 327
James, Bill, 10–15, 17, 76

Lombardi, Vince, 21, 144
Londos, Jim "the Golden Greek," 264
Long Island NY, 324
Longview TX, 239
Loogootee IN, 285
Los Angeles CA, 127, 132
Los Angeles Times, 127–29
Louis, Joe, 9, 262, 282–83, 292
Louisville Colonels, 66
Louisville KY, 278
Loving, Walter Howard, 55
L. S. Ayres Department Store, 33
Lugo, Orlando, 323
Lundy, Dick, 121–22, 163, 165, 183, 243, 260
Luque, Adolfo, 143, 157, 165, 200
Luzader, William T. "Sticks," 339
Luzon, Island of (Philippines), 47
Lyons, Jimmie, 60, 67, 87, 94, 101, 148

Machado, Gerardo, 215
Mack, Connie, 179, 201–2
Mack, Earl, 179–80
Mackey, James Raleigh "Biz," 119, 127–28,
    130, 133, 148–50, 165, 180, 192, 196, 203,
    220, 244, 268, 302
The Magnificent Ambersons, 34
Majestic Building, 33
Malarcher, Dave, 9, 83, 88, 91–92, 94, 101,
    105–7, 216, 242
Malloy, Jerry, ix
Maloney, A. M., 266
Manila, Philippines, 75
Manila Cablenews-American, 53
Manila League, 48–53
Manila Times, 52–53, 56
Manley, Abe, 227, 255, 308
Manley, Effa, 255, 284, 308
Mantle, Mickey, 14
Manush, Heinie, 152, 179
Marcell, Oliver, 121, 145, 157, 163, 173, 175, 183
Marianao (Cuban baseball team), 146, 153,
    215–16
Marines (Manila League baseball team),
    48, 50
Marion County (IN), 37, 45
Marshall, Bud, 140, 241
Marshall TX, 230

Martin, James, 168
Martin, Margaret, 168, 194
Martindale Avenue neighborhood (India-
    napolis IN), 33
Maryland Baseball Park, 116, 199
Mason-Dixon Line, 31, 230
Matlock, Leroy, 238, 240, 251–53, 258, 267, 270
Matthews, Wid Curry, 294
Maxwell, Jocko, 275
Mays, Willie, 5, 9, 11, 13–14, 17, 165, 309, 311,
    327–28, 331
McDonald, Webster, 144–45, 156, 237, 295, 300
McDuffie, Terris, 294
McGavock, Martha, 27
McGraw, Blanche, 157
McGraw, John, 9, 121, 157–58, 282, 319, 331
McGraw, Stephen, 157
McHenry, Henry, 287–88, 309
McHenry Henry Greys, 79
McKeesport PA, 222
McKinley, William, 32
McMahon, Edward, 76
McMahon, Jess, 76
McMahon, Vince, 76
McNair, Hurley, 128
Memphis Red Sox, 209, 227, 238
Memphis TN, 239, 314
Méndez, José, 58, 80, 99. 128
Mendez, Luis, 266
Merchant, Henry "Speed," 323
Meridian MS, 270
Mesa, Pablo, 145, 152, 157, 216
Metz, Frank, 66
Meusel, Bob, xi, 128–30
Meusel, Irish, 128–30
Meusel All-Stars, 128–30
Mexico, 263–64, 321
Mexico City, Mexico, 321
Miami (ship), 122
Miami FL, 281
Miller, Dutch, 67–68
Mills, Charlie, 122–23, 126
Mills Brothers, 254
Milwaukee Brewers, 309
Minoso, Minnie, 5
Mitchell, Mother, 230
Mize, Johnny, 259

St. Louis Stars, 133, 135, 141, 143, 151, 192, 208, 221, 283

St. Paul AME Church (St. Louis MO), 136

Stargell, Willie, 30

State Department, U.S., 266

State Soldiers and Sailors Monument, 33–34

statistics: compiled by Oscar Charleston, 62, 89, 102–4, 109–10, 119, 124, 130, 151, 153–54, 161, 164–65, 167, 172, 174–75, 183, 189, 199–200, 203, 209, 221, 232–33, 235, 238, 241, 256–57, 268, 319; quality of for Negro Leagues, 6, 116, 189, 209

Stearnes, Norman "Turkey," 152, 235, 243, 261, 329

Stengel, Casey, 233–34

Stephens, Helen, 278

Stephens, Paul "Country Jake," 196, 201, 203, 205, 209

Stone, Toni, 2, 323

Strawberry Mansion neighborhood (Philadelphia PA), 322

Strecker, Geri, 14, 196

Streeter, Sam, 143, 180, 220, 229, 239–40

Strong, Joseph, 266

Strothers, Colonel William, 158–59, 168, 176–77, 184, 186, 188, 190, 194–95

Sukeforth, Clyde, 294, 299, 301–2, 304–5

Sullivan, Ted, 312

Susquehanna River, 161, 188, 200

Suttles, Mule, 235, 243, 261

Sykes, Franklin "Doc," 77

Taft, William Howard, 48

Talge Mahogany Company Veneer and Sawmill, 33

"Talk O' Town" column (*Pittsburgh Courier*), 265, 273

Tampa FL, 285, 296

Tarkington, Booth, 16, 34, 44

Tarrytown NY, 323

Taylor, Ben, 58–59, 62, 64, 67, 81–83, 89, 91, 94–95, 117–18, 131–35, 148–50, 162, 168–69, 177, 186, 191, 199

Taylor, Candy Jim, 58–59, 82–83, 94, 98, 131, 216, 232, 255–56, 275

Taylor, C. I., 56–58, 60, 63, 65, 67–68, 74–75, 78–80, 82–83, 88, 90, 94, 97–101, 105–6, 108, 110, 116, 122–23, 148, 205, 217; baseball philosophies of, 59, 62, 66, 114, 117, 162, 249; civic-mindedness of, 59, 70–71, 84, 96, 132; death of, 131–32; relationship with Oscar Charleston, 70–73, 119–20, 126, 132, 280, 286

Taylor, Johnny "Steel Arm," 59, 131, 263, 269

Taylor, Olivia, 131–32, 148–49, 151, 158

Taylor, Schoolboy Johnny, 142, 253–54, 270–71, 279

Terre Haute Champagne Velvets, 63

Terry, Bill, 262

Texas League, 20

Thomas, Clint, 189, 203

Thomas, Dave "Showboat," 294

Thomas, Jeff, 27

Thomas, Lefty, 129

Thompson, Hank, 5

Thorpe, Jim, 30, 50

Three Rivers QC, 305

Thurston, Hollis, 329

Tiant, Luis, Sr., 224

Toledo-Indianapolis Crawfords, 18, 276–83, 296

Toledo OH, 276, 280, 285, 297

Topeka KS, 123

Toronto ON, 311

Torriente, Cristóbal, 14, 57–58, 80, 104, 107–8, 110, 148, 175, 320

Treasury Department, U.S., 100

Treat 'Em Roughs, 109

Treaty of Versailles, 105

Trent, Ted, 242

Triangular League (Cuba), 183

Trouppe, Quincy, 10, 13, 115, 305, 316

Trout, Mike, 17

Troy NC, 140

Trujillo, Rafael, 265–66, 268

Trujillo All-Stars, 268, 270

Tuskegee Institute, 83, 168, 190

24th Infantry, 45, 48–50, 52–53, 92

Tyler, Charles, 239

Tyler TX, 239

umpires: in Negro Leagues, 58, 59, 81, 92, 113, 116, 169, 253, 313, 318; Oscar Charleston and, 18, 68–72, 113, 144–45, 163, 169–73,